Regional Defence Profile
No 1

LATIN AMERICA

MEXICO
Mexico City
Habana
CUBA
HAITI
DOMINICAN REP
PUERTO RICO
JAMAICA
BELIZE
HONDURAS
GUATEMALA
EL SALVADOR
NICARAGUA
Managua
COSTA RICA
PANAMA
Tobago
TRINIDAD
Caracas
VENEZUELA
Georgetown
Paramaribo
Cayenne
GUYANA
SURINAM
GUIANA
Bogota
COLOMBIA
ECUADOR
Quito
Belem
BRAZIL
PERU
Lima
La Paz
BOLIVIA
Iquique
PARAGUAY
São Paulo
Rio de Janeiro
Valpariso
Santiago
ARGENTINA
URUGUAY
Buenos
Aires
Montevideo
CHILE
0
1000
Miles
0
1500
Km

Regional Defence Profile
No 1

LATIN AMERICA

By Adrian J. English

JANE'S

First published in the United Kingdom in 1988 by
Jane's Publishing Company Limited
238 City Road, London EC1V 2PU

ISBN 0 7106 0541 2

Distributed in the Philippines and the USA and its
dependencies by
Jane's Information Group Inc.
1340 Braddock Place, Suite 300,
PO Box 1436, Alexandria, Virginia
22313–2036 USA

Typeset by
Lasertext Limited, Stretford, Manchester, England.

Printed in Great Britain by
Butler & Tanner Ltd, Frome and London

Contents

Acknowledgements

The factual material on which this book is based could not have been collected without the assistance of many people, a large number of whom, including those who were most helpful, wish to maintain their anonymity, mainly due to their positions on active military service or in the defence industry. Among those not so constrained I must single out Brigadier General José Teófilo Goyret and Lieutenant Colonel Francisco Figueroa de la Vega, Argentine Army (retired), Major General Juan Lechín Suárez, Bolivian Army (retired), Vice Admiral Jorge Sepúlveda Ortiz and Rear Admiral Sergio Cabezas Dufeu, of the Chilean Navy, Miss Olga Kliwadenko, Press Officer of the Chilean Embassy in London, Lieutenant Alvaro Duarte Méndez, Colombian Navy and Commander Charles B. Robbins, US Navy. Invaluable assistance was also obtained from Messers Julian Alemán Urquiza, Pedro del Fierro, David Isby, Emilio Meneses, Miguel Navarro, Daniel Prieto Vial and A.J.R. "Bram" Risseeuw.

The assembly of illustrations for a work covering most of a continent was also a formidable task and would have been an insuperable one without the generous help of both private individuals such as Dr Robert Scheina, Lieutenant Hugo Barras and Francisco Calzada Jaúregui and the many manufacturers of defence equipment acknowledged in the picture captions while Derrick Ballington of *Jane's Defence Weekly* allowed me to plunder his painfully built-up photo library for material.

Jürg Meister and Chris Foss provided unending stimulus and encouragement while the present project would probably never have come to fruition without the support of Brendan Gallagher of Jane's. Alex Vanags-Baginskis of Jane's also suffered, without protest, the strains imposed by the peculiar symbiotic relationship between author and publisher's editor while Alec Spark converted my rough sketches into the finished maps and diagrammes which complement the text. Finally, due tribute must be paid to Geoff Wadsley who designed the layout of the finished work.

To all these my profound thanks.

Adrian J. English

Introduction

Jane's has been involved in the publication of reference books since Fred T. Jane produced the first edition of *All the World's Fighting Ships* in 1897. This book is the first volume in a new series of reference works which sets out to deal in concise form with the strategic importance and military potential of the various regions of the world. As such it does not limit itself to a mere recitation of manpower statistics and equipment inventories but seeks also to provide the essential geo-strategic, economic, political and historic background to its subject.

Twenty-five years ago it would have been difficult to rationalise commencing such a series with a volume on Latin America, a relatively unknown area regarded almost universally as a strategic backwater. The Cuban Revolution of 1959 changed this dramatically, although it was not until the missile crisis of October 1962 that the full strategic importance of Latin America was abruptly brought home to a horrified world when the installation of Soviet ballistic missiles a mere 90 miles from the coast of the United States almost precipitated nuclear Armageddon between the superpowers.

Two decades later there was a further demonstration of Latin America's strategic importance which was almost as traumatic as the Cuban missile crisis. In the spring of 1982 the Argentinian invasion of the Falkland (Malvinas) Islands provoked an improbable but sanguinary conflict between one of the principal local military powers and a major European one. The United States and most of the countries of NATO and the European Economic Community backed Britain, while the Soviet Union offered largely unwanted support to Argentina. In addition, most of the countries of Latin America, including Cuba but with the notable exception of Chile, rallied round Argentina in a unprecedented display of regional solidarity. The South Atlantic War provided a valuable testing ground for modern military hardware, much of which was found to be disappointingly wanting in performance, and there was a further display of Latin American military significance when the Argentinian air forces inflicted a level of damage which stopped just short of crippling the British naval task force sent to repossess the archipelago.

While the Cuban episode spelled out the peculiar strategic importance of that Caribbean island in no uncertain terms, and the Anglo-Argentine War focused attention on the south-west Atlantic, it is frequently forgotten that Latin American states also control both major points of access between the Atlantic and Pacific oceans and that the region contains many of this planet's remaining major untapped resources of raw materials. Despite the current debt crisis Brazil is well on its way to becoming a major world power, and Cuba has exerted an influence on world affairs altogether out of proportion to its size and material resources for almost three decades. Others of the smaller Latin American republics, notably Chile, Colombia and Venezuela, are also of a similary disproportionate potential strategic importance. The most extreme example of this phenomenon is Panama, a pigmy among nations which is nevertheless destined to become immensely important when it assumes full responsibility for the administration and defence of the Panama Canal in 1999.

For over a century the United States has exercised a jealous hegemony over a region which it regards as its own "backyard", actively seeking to confine the armed forces of the various independent states to an internal security role although ready to use military bases in their territory when expedient and somewhat grudgingly accepting them as active allies. Examples of the latter were Brazil's naval participation in both world wars and military involvement in the second, and Colombia's military and naval contributions to the United Nations forces in the Korean War.

Growing national pride, together with their increasing military potential, has prompted many Latin American countries, particularly the larger ones, to look elsewhere for the advanced military equipment which the United States has refused to provide. In several cases this has led to the development of significant local defence industries, to the point where Brazil is now one of the world's major exporters of defence equipment. Argentina and Brazil, at least, could develop nuclear weapons and delivery vehicles relatively quickly, and the medium-term military implications of the current construction of Cuba's first nuclear reactor must already be causing headaches among the defence planners of its neighbours.

Surprisingly, the United States, the major power with indisputably the greatest interest in the region, seems slowest to recognise that if the Latin American states are not accepted as partners in hemispheric defence they could ultimately become dangerous enemies. Instead, the USA seeks still to impose its will on them by the traditionally heavy-handed methods which have built up a lasting legacy of resentment.

For most of the 1960s and 1970s Cuba continued to provide the main strategic interest in a region still largely dominated by traditional political alignments, and where the armed forces appeared generally more interested in the usurpation of political power than the problems of national defence. While to a degree instrumental in the failure of Cuban-sponsored insurgencies and the abandonment of overt attempts at the active subversion of Cuba's neighbours, the imposition of national security doctrines from the mid-1960s onwards also generated resentment as armed forces were largely orientated towards the gendarmerie role. This led in turn to over-investment in super-sophisticated military hardware, the acquisition of which remained unjustified by any existing requirement and at a cost which led to the near bankruptcy of many, with related increased political problems.

The continued existence of a highly militarised Communist Cuba, only 90 miles off the south-eastern coast of the USA and ever ready to lend its support to revolutionary movements in one of the world's most volatile regions, does not of itself constitute a major threat to American security as long as the United States enjoys the goodwill at least of the countries which control the approaches to the Caribbean basin from the east, south and west. Such a threat was however posed by the appearance of a Cuban-supported Marxist regime in Grenada and by the triumph of the Sandinista revolution in Nicaragua in 1979, followed by the escalation of hitherto low-level insurgency into full-scale civil war in El Salvador in 1980.

The US invasion of Grenada in 1983 was intended not only to remove a regime which was as unacceptable to most of the inhabitants as it was to the United States but also to demonstrate to Cuba, the Sandinista regime in Nicaragua and the Farabundo Martí revolutionaries in El Salvador that there were limits to the degree of leftwards drift which the USA was prepared to tolerate in its nominally independent neighbours. In this it was at least partially successful.

But the situation in Central America has been generally handled by the United States in such a maladroit and largely counter-productive manner as to cause serious concern to its friends and allies. The apparent obsession of the Reagan administration with Nicaragua as it repeatedly defied Congress in its support of terrorist activities against the Nicaraguan regime led to condemnation by the International Court of Justice, outraged international opinion and culminated in the Irangate scandal of 1986-87, which threatened to involve the Presidency itself. During the second half of 1987 the United States suffered a further humiliation when its Central American Peace Plan, effectively aimed at giving the Nicaraguan "Contras" a spurious legitimacy, was rejected in favour of a plan produced by the governments of the five Central American republics themselves. This appeared to give the first real hope of an end to the insurgencies in El Salvador and Nicaragua.

Elsewhere, guerrilla insurgencies such as the M19 movement in Colombia and the Sendero Luminoso in Peru, far from showing any signs of a possible diminution, appeared to be of increasing intensity, providing problems not only for the governments of the host states but also for those of neighbouring countries.

A dawning political maturity is a recent but encouraging phenomenon throughout most of the region, where apparently democratic government is now more common than at any time during the previous two decades. This is also perceptible in the reorganisation and re-equipment programmes currently under way in the armed forces of countries such as Brazil and Venezuela. Having successfully dealt with local insurgencies, these nations now appear to have largely turned away from the futile border squabbles which governed most of the region's defence policies over the previous 150 years and to be looking towards playing a constructive role in hemispheric defence. Events such as the ratification of the 1980 treaty between Honduras and El Salvador and of the Beagle Channel Treaty between Argentina and Chile in 1984 also point to a similar tendency in the case of traditionally antagonistic countries. Peru and Ecuador do however continue to regard each other with an atavistic loathing which is reflected in their defence policies.

Latin America is now rarely out of the news. It is hoped that this book will provide a convenient background reference to the military forces and defence structures of the countries which make up this awakening colossus, and that its projected companions will perform a similar service with regard to the other regions of the world.

Any work of this nature, and particularly one dealing with a region as volatile as Latin America, is unfortunately doomed to almost instant obsolescence, being overtaken in some cases even during the necessary interval between the completion of writing and publication. It is hoped to update this series at regular intervals, and individuals and official agencies who note errors or discrepancies or who have additional material to contribute, including and especially illustrations, are invited to write to me care of the publishers.

Adrian J. English,
Dublin,
August 1987

ARGENTINA

(República Argentina)

Area: 1,072,754 sq miles (2,681,885 sq km)
Population: 31,328,000 (1986)
Total armed forces: 104,000
Reserves: 500,000
Available manpower: 2,500,000
Paramilitary forces: 43,000
GNP: $68,293 million (1984)
Defence expenditure: $1,335 million (1986)

Introduction

Argentina, the second largest country in Latin America and the eighth largest in the world, is bounded by Chile to the west, Bolivia to the north-west, Paraguay to the north, Brazil and Uruguay to the north-east and the South Atlantic Ocean to the east. Extending from 22° to 55° South latitude, Argentina enjoys a wide range of climatic conditions, from the tropical to the sub-Antarctic. The 3000-mile-long Atlantic coastline extends from the mouth of the River Plate almost to Cape Horn, at the extreme southern tip of the South American continent. The population is of over 85% European – mainly Spanish and Italian – descent, the small indigenous Indian minority being concentrated almost entirely in the region adjoining the Bolivian frontier. Approximately 40% of the entire population is located in the Greater Buenos Aires area, demographic imbalance being a major and growing national problem.

Although Argentina is now largely self-sufficient in industrial production and has built up a respectable export trade in manufactured products, principally within South America, agricultural remains the main economic activity, the principal agricultural exports being frozen or otherwise processed meat products and grain. Almost all raw materials are found in varying quantities although iron still figures as an important import. The country is almost self-sufficient in petroleum production and aims for total self-sufficiency, by the development of still unexploited oil and natural gas resources, by the 1990s. Although Argentina is extremely rich in natural resources, political mismanagement of the economy has brought the country to the verge of bankruptcy.

Following the defeat of two British attempts at conquest, in 1806 and 1807, the Municipal Council of Buenos Aires deposed the Spanish viceroy in 1810 and declared full independence in 1816. The early years of independence were chaotic and marked by a struggle for supremacy between Buenos Aires and the provinces of the interior. A war with Brazil between 1826 and 1828 resulted in the creation of Uruguay as a buffer state between the two countries. The unity of the provinces of the interior was finally established in 1853, although Buenos Aires formed a separate state between 1852 and 1860 and made an attempt to overthrow the government of the confederation in 1859. From 1865-70 Argentina joined with Brazil and Uruguay in the War of the Triple Alliance against Paraguay.

The large-scale construction of railways, from 1857 onwards, followed by the development of refrigeration, revolutionised the economy by providing access to overseas markets for the agricultural products of the interior. Within two decades Argentina had changed from a poverty-stricken backwater to the richest and most developed country in South America and by 1930 was rated among the ten wealthiest countries in the world.

In 1930 the armed forces overthrew President Hipólito Yrigoyén and a succession of military coups resulted in the accession of Colonel Juan Domingo Perón to the presidency in 1946. Perón evolved his own political doctrine of *Justicialismo* and pushed the country towards economic disaster by his policy of wholesale expropriation and nationalisation of private industry and progressively more economically outrageous concessions to organised labour. Finally coming into conflict with the Catholic church, the regime provoked a revolt by the armed forces in 1955. Perón being driven into exile.

The armed forces continued to be the dominant force in Argentine politics, the civilian presidents dents Frondizi and Illía being deposed in 1962 and 1966 respectively. Elections held in 1973 resulted in the Peronist party winning a majority of seats in the National Congress and the election as President of Dr Héctor Cámpora, who resigned to leave the way open for the return of Perón, duly elected in October. His second wife, María Estela, was elected Vice-President. Perón died nine months later, his widow succeeding him under the constitution. Under "Isabelita" Perón the country rapidly slid into near-anarchy, with large-scale urban terrorism, rural guerrilla activity and a series of economically damaging strikes culminating in her overthrow by the military in March 1976.

The military government restored internal order but failed to revive the faltering economy. In an attempt to distract public attention from its domestic problems the Junta invaded the Falkland Islands and South Georgia in April 1982, provoking a brief but disastrous war with Britain. This so discredited the armed forces that a year later they were forced to hold elections which returned a civilian administration under the presidency of Raúl Alfonsín.

Argentina is a federal republic of 22 provinces, one federal district and three national territories. Executive power is in the hands of the President, who selects his own cabinet. There is a bicameral federal legislature. The President appoints the governors of the 22 provinces, each of which has a legislative and judicial system which parallels the national system.

Traditionally, Argentine foreign policy has been dominated by competition with Brazil for local predominance in South America and by a chronic frontier dispute with Chile. The continuing territorial claim to the Falkland (Malvinas) Islands tends to become periodically exacerbated as a counterpoint to internal political and economic problems.

Argentina and Brazil seem to have agreed their respective spheres of influence from the mid-1970s onwards, and relations between the two countries have been progressively more cordial during the past decade. Relations between Argentina and Chile have however been marred periodically by extreme friction, almost leading to war in 1902 and 1978. Most recently, tension has been high over the disputed ownership of three small islands in the Beagle Channel at the southern tip of Tierra del Fuego. The matter was finally settled, following papal mediation in 1984.

Argentina's internal politics have largely evolved into a chronic confrontation between the Peronista movement and the armed forces, complicated by the factionalisation of the Peronists since the 1960s. Internal violence, which reached acute proportions under the second Perón regime, particularly after the death of Juan Perón, was effectively suppressed by the recent military government but could well flare up again.

Structure of the armed forces

In addition to the three traditional armed forces, Army, Navy and Air Force, there are two other forces: the *Gendarmería Nacional*, a federal constabulary employed principally as a frontier guard, and the *Prefectura Naval*, a coastguard force responsible for marine lifesaving and the maintenance of navigational aids in addition to fishery protection and coastal patrol. The present administration has removed the *Gendarmería* and *Prefectura Naval* from the respective jurisdictions of the commanders-in-chief of the Army and Navy to that of the Minister of Defence.

The President is supreme commander of the armed forces. As such, he has very far-reaching powers which are largely independent of Congress. Prior to 1967, the Minister of National Defence was largely responsible for the administration of the armed forces, on behalf of the President and via the secretaries of War, Marine and Aviation. A reorganisation of the defence structure in 1967 abolished the three secretariats and downgraded the office of Minister of Defence to parity with those of the commanders-in-chief of the Army, Navy and Air Force, the functions of the Minister becoming purely administrative. The present administration has reasserted presidential control over the service chiefs and reintroduced the Minister of Defence into the chain of command. While the President has the ultimate authority in the direction of the armed forces, he is assisted by two major advisory bodies: the National Security Council, which consists of the cabinet and the three individual service commanders-in-chief, and the Committee of Commanders-in-Chief of the Armed Forces, which as its name indicates consists of the three commanders-in-chief. The first body has a largely consultative function: the second controls the day-to-day activities of the Combined General Staff (*Estado Mayor Conjunto*), which serves as the principal co-ordinating body for the entire defence establishment.

All fit male citizens between the ages of 20 and 45 are liable either for one year's full-time service in the Army and Air Force or two in the Navy. Conscripts are allowed some choice of the force in which they undergo their military service and may pre-empt it by volunteering for similar periods of service in the Gendarmerie, Naval Prefecture or Federal Police. In practice, compulsory military service, occurs between the ages of 20 and 22. Following their release from military training conscripts belong to the first line reserve until the age of 29 and thereafter until the age of 39 to the second and until 45 to the third line reserves, known respectively as the National and Territorial Guards. Economic considerations have resulted in a reduction of the annual conscript intake of the order of 70% and current policy emphasises the development of a more streamlined and professional, if less numerous, military establishment.

Each of the armed forces maintains a comprehensive system of training establishments and Argentina also trains military personnel from adjoining countries, most notably naval and air force personnel from Bolivia and Paraguay, under long-standing agreements with their respective governments.

The country is divided into five Military Regions.

The First Military Region covers the federal capital and most of the provinces of Buenos Aires and La Pampa; the Second the provinces of Entre Rios, Corrientes, Misiones, Santa Fé, Formosa and the Chaco territory; the Third the provinces of Córdoba, Mendoza, La Rioja, San Juan, San Luis and southern Catamarca; the Fourth the provinces of Salta, Jujuy, Tucumán, Santiago del Estero and northern Catamarca and the Fifth southern Buenos Aires and La Pampa provinces plus the provinces of Neuquén, Rio Negro, Chubut, Santa Cruz and the territories of Tierra del Fuego, the Argentine Antarctic and the claimed territory of the Malvinas (Falkland) Islands.

The Navy divides the coastline and navigable river systems into three Naval Regions and the Tierra del Fuego Naval Command. The First Naval Region extends from Punta Medanos to Punta Ninfas; the Second from Punta Ninfas to Cape Espiritu Santo, the Third comprises the river systems of the north-east while the Tierra del Fuego Naval Command covers Tierra del Fuego and the Beagle Channel. For its part, the Air Force divides the country into four Air Regions. The Central Air Region corresponds to the First and Third Military Regions, the North-Eastern Region coincides with the Second Military Region, the North-Western corresponds to the Fourth Military Region and the Southern covers the same territory as the Fifth Military Region.

The new Defence Law, adopted by the Argentinian Congress in 1986, will involve the creation of a North Eatern Defence Force covering the 1st and 2nd Military Regions and of a North Western Defence Force, which in turn will cover the 3rd and 4th Military Regions. The existing 5th Military Region will form the base of the Patagonian and South Atlantic Manoeuvre Force, a new Strategic Reserve Force being formed with elements of the Army, Navy and Air Force.

Army

Manpower: 65,000

Formations: 3 army corps, comprising:
2 armoured cavalry brigades
5 mechanised infantry brigades (two incomplete)
1 airborne brigade
3 mountain brigades
1 jungle brigade

Major units: 27 infantry regiments (of which 4 airborne, 9 mountain and 3 jungle)
8 cavalry regiments (7 armoured and 1 ceremonial)

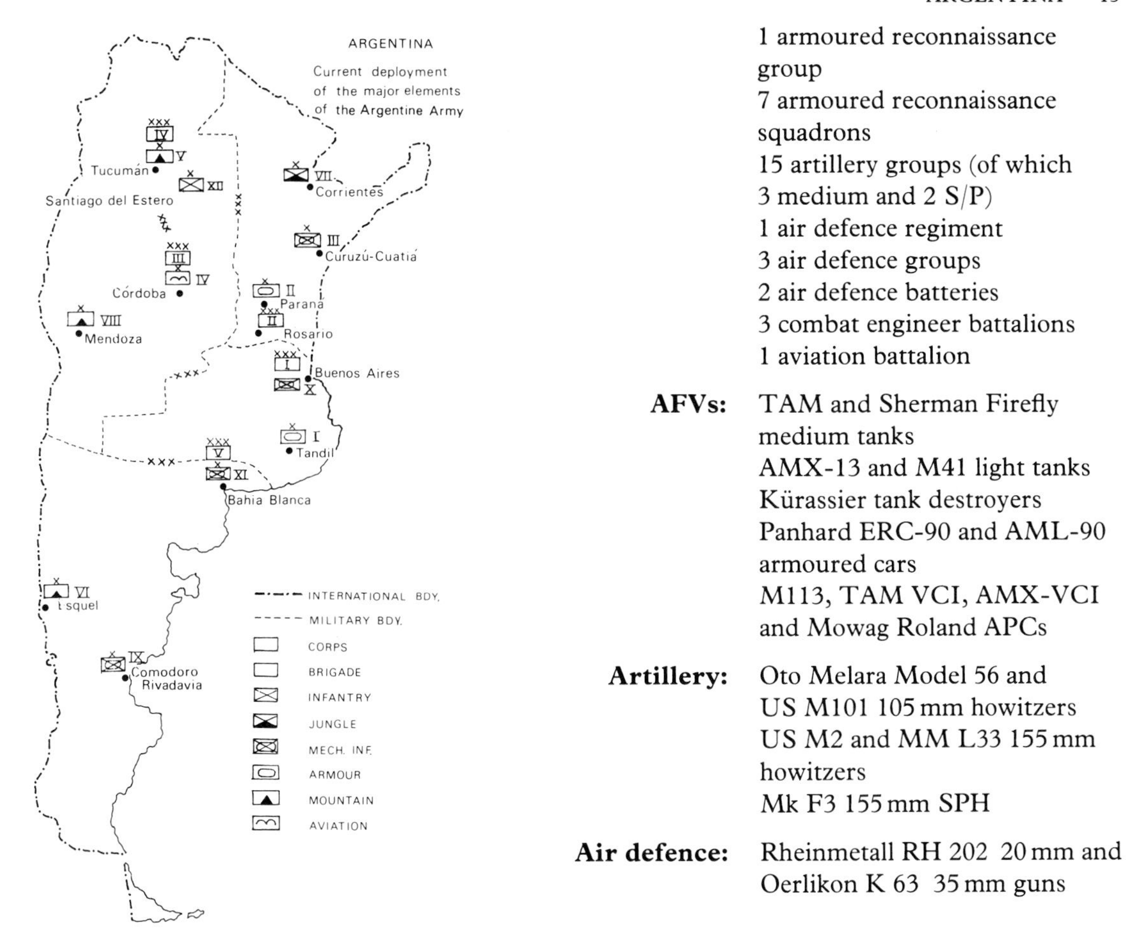

1 armoured reconnaissance group
7 armoured reconnaissance squadrons
15 artillery groups (of which 3 medium and 2 S/P)
1 air defence regiment
3 air defence groups
2 air defence batteries
3 combat engineer battalions
1 aviation battalion

AFVs: TAM and Sherman Firefly medium tanks
AMX-13 and M41 light tanks
Kürassier tank destroyers
Panhard ERC-90 and AML-90 armoured cars
M113, TAM VCI, AMX-VCI and Mowag Roland APCs

Artillery: Oto Melara Model 56 and US M101 105 mm howitzers
US M2 and MM L33 155 mm howitzers
Mk F3 155 mm SPH

Air defence: Rheinmetall RH 202 20 mm and Oerlikon K 63 35 mm guns

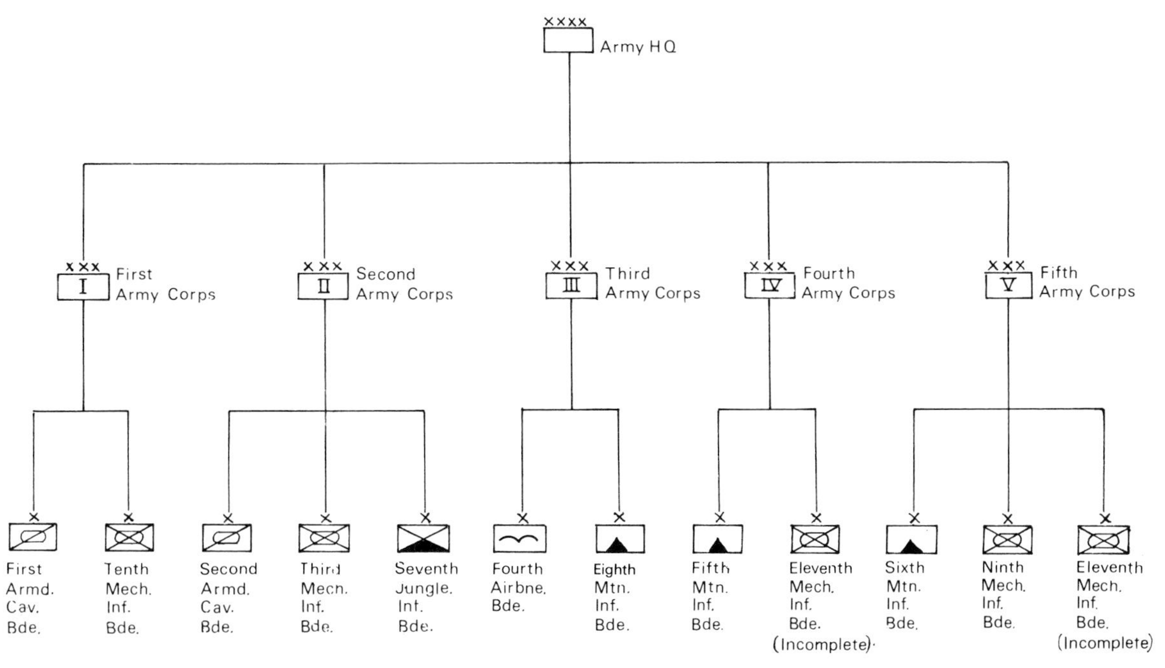

Missiles: SS-11 and 12, Bantam, Cobra and Mamba ATGWs
Mathogo, Blowpipe, Tigercat and Roland SAMs

Aircraft: Aeritalia G222, Beech King Air 100 and Queen Air B80, Cessna 180, 182J, U-17B, Citation and Skywagon
DHC-6, Piper Apache, Aztec, Navajo and Seneca, Rockwell Sabreliner and Swearingen Merlin light transports
Cessna T-41 trainers
Agusta A109A, Bell OH-13, UH-1H, 206A and 212, Fairchild-Hiller FH-1100, Aérospatiale Lama, Puma and Super Puma and Vertol Chinook helicopters

The Argentine Army came successively under strong French and German influences and was subject to a lesser degree than almost any other Latin American army to the otherwise all-pervasive influence of the United States following the Second World War, although internal subversion caused the adoption of US security doctrine from the 1960s onwards.

Until 1964 the Argentine Army consisted of nine infantry, three cavalry and one armoured divisions, comprising 31 infantry, 18 cavalry (of which four were armoured) and 13 artillery regiments, divided between five army corps, corresponding to the five Military Regions into which the country was divided and a cavalry corps, the elements of which were deployed throughout the national territory.

A radical reorganisation adopted in October 1964 suppressed both the IVth Army Corps and the Cavalry Corps and replaced the division by the brigade as the major tactical formation. Five infantry, eight cavalry and three artillery regiments were disbanded, the remaining infantry regiments being reduced to single battalions and the artillery units to groups. From the remaining units two armoured cavalry brigades and an airborne brigade were formed, together with three mechanised infantry, three mountain and one jungle brigades, each brigade consisting of three single-battalion regiments of the basic arm, a company-sized reconnaissance unit, a group of artillery, an engineer company, a signals company and a logistic battalion. The armoured division was split into two armoured cavalry brigades. Despite the suppression of the IVth Corps and its incorporation into the IIIrd Corps most of its allocated logistic and combat support units under the new table of organisation were formed thus facilitating its resurrection in the late 1970s in the face of increasing tension between Argentina and Chile over the Beagle Channel issue. The resurrection of the IVth Corps also involved the establishment of two additional mechanised infantry brigades. The latter however remained incomplete when Argentina invaded the Falkland Islands in April 1982.

The bulk of the IIIrd, IXth and Xth Mechanised Infantry Brigades, together with some army level units and units from the Ist Army Corps and the artillery group of the IVth Airborne Brigade fought in the Falklands debacle which

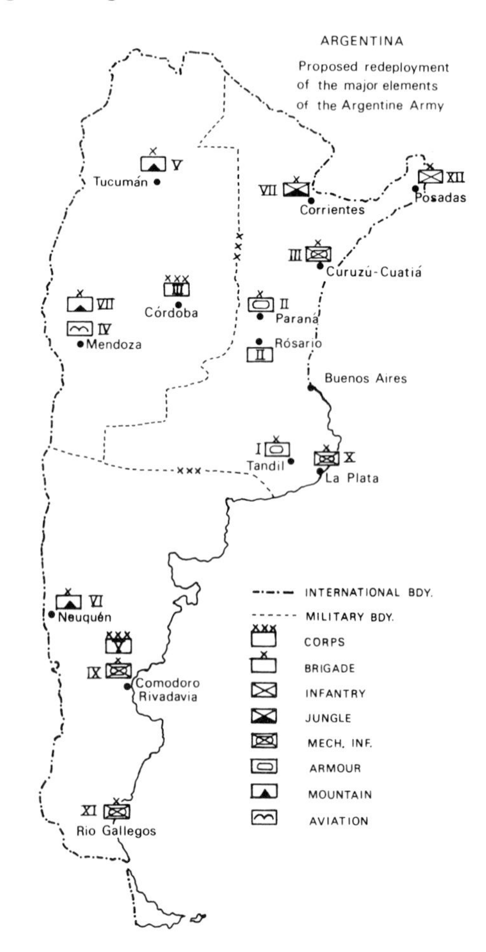

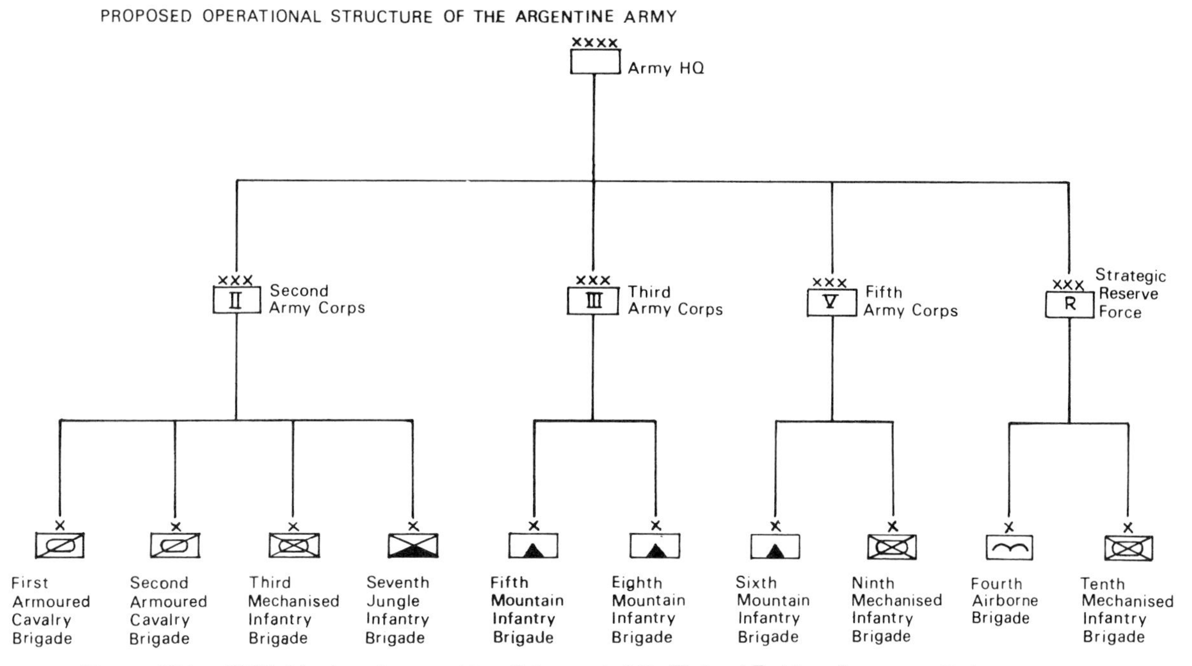

indirectly precipitated the return to civilian government in Argentina.

The new Defence Law of 1986 involves the incorporation of the Ist Army Corps into an enlarged IInd Corps to form a North Eastern Defence Force and the incorporation of the IVth Army Corps into the IIIrd to form a North Western Defence Force. The existing Vth Army Corps will form the basis of the Patagonian and South Atlantic Manoeuvre Force, the IVth Airborne and the Xth Mechanised Infantry Brigades being removed from the respective jurisidictions of the IIIrd and IInd Army Corps to form a Strategic Reserve Force.

The headquarters of the IVth Airborne and the Xth Mechanised Infantry Brigades will be transferred from Córdoba to Mendoza and Buenos Aires to La Plata, respectively.

The three new corps areas correspond to three hypothetical theatres of operations in the case of armed conflict between Argentina and any of its neighbours and it is also proposed ultimately to redeploy the majority of the tactical manoeuvre elements of the army to conform to the restructuring of the army into three corps commands. The training units at present largely situated at or in the immediate vicinity of the federal capital are also to be redeployed to various points in the interior and the headquarters of the Vth Brigade is to be transferred from Bahía Blanca to some as yet unspecified point south of the Colorado River, its most probable new location being Comodoro Rivadavia.

***Argentine infantry with FN MAG machine guns.* (G. von Rauch)**

The reorganisation proposals call for the reinforcement of the existing tactical manoeuvre elements to their full authorised peacetime establishments, using the personnel from the demobilised tactical and logistic support elements of the disbanded Ist and IVth Army Corps. It is also proposed to progressively re-equip and modernise the mechanised cavalry and artillery units, particularly with medium and self-propelled material. Other formations scheduled for reorganisation and re-equipment are the air defence artillery elements, with emphasis on their target acquisition capabilities; the restructuring and increased efficiency of the existing communications elements and preferential treatment as regards reorganisation and re-equipment for engineer construction units at the expense of the combat engineer elements.

The Argentine Army currently numbers approximately 65,000 all ranks, organised in three army corps and a Strategic Defence Force.

The Second Army Corps (HQ Rosario) comprises the Ist Armoured Cavalry Brigade (HQ Tandil, Buenos Aires) with the 2nd *Lanceros General Paz*, 8th *Cazadores General Necochea* and 10th *Húsares de Pueyrredón* armoured cavalry regiments, plus the 1st Armoured Reconnaissance Squadron, 1st SP Artillery Group, 1st Armoured Engineer Company, 1st Signals Company and 1st Logistics Battalion; the IInd Armoured Cavalry Brigade (HQ Paraná, Entre Rios) with the 1st *General Brandsen*, 7th *Coronel Estombo* and 6th *Blandengues* Armoured Cavalry Regiments – the 2nd Armoured Reconnaissance Squadron, 2nd SP Artillery Group, 2nd Armoured Engineer Company, 2nd Signals Company and 2nd Logistics Battalion; the IIIrd Mechanised Infantry Brigade (HQ Curuzú-Cuatiá, Corrientes) with the 4th, 5th and 12th Mechanised Infantry Regiments, 3rd Armoured Reconnaissance Squadron, 3rd Artillery Group, 3rd Engineer Company, 3rd Signals Company and 3rd Logistics Battalion; the VIIth Jungle Infantry Brigade (HQ Corrientes) with the 9th, 11th and 28th Jungle Infantry Regiments, plus the 7th Jungle Artillery Group, 7th Jungle Engineer Company, 7th Signals Company and 7th Logistics Battalion and the XIIth Mechanised Infantry Brigade which is still forming, with its HQ at Posadas.

The Third Army Corps (HQ Córdoba) is made up of the Vth Mountain Infantry Brigade (HQ Tucumán) with the 19th, 20th and 28th Mountain Infantry Regiments, plus the 5th Mountain Artillery Group, 5th Mountain Engineer Company, 5th Signals Company and 5th Logistics Battalion and the VIIIth Mountain Infantry Brigade (HQ Mendoza) with the 11th, 16th and 22nd Mountain Infantry Regiments, the 8th Mountain Artillery Group, 8th Mountain Engineer Company, 8th Signals Company and 8th Logistics Battalion.

The Fifth Army Corps (HQ Bahía Blanca) consists of the VIth Mountain Infantry Brigade (HQ Neuquén) with the 10th, 21st and 26th Mountain Infantry Regiments, the 6th Mountain Artillery Group, 6th Mountain Engineer Com-

***Ski troops of the Argentine Army's VIIIth Mountain Infantry Brigade.* (G. von Rauch)**

***Cobra ATGMs mounted on Unimog trucks.* (G. von Rauch)**

***AMX-13s of the 10th* Húsares de Pueyrredón *Armoured Cavalry Regiment.* (G. von Rauch)**

pany, 6th Signals Company and 6th Logistics Battalion; the IXth Mechanised Infantry Brigade (HQ Comodoro Rivadavia) with the 8th, 25th and 37th Mechanised Infantry Regiments, the 9th Armoured Reconnaissance Squadron, 9th Artillery Group, 9th Armoured Engineer Company, 9th Signals Company and 9th Logistics Battalion and the still incomplete XIth Mechanised Infantry Brigade (HQ Río Gallegos) comprising the 24th and 35th Mechanised Infantry and 11th Armoured Cavalry Regiments, the 11th Armoured Reconnaissance Squadron, 11th Artillery Group, 11th Engineer Company, 11th Signals Company and 11th Logistics Battalion.

The Strategic Reserve Force (HQ Campo de Mayo, B.A.) is made up of the IVth Airborne Brigade (HQ Mendosa) with the 2nd, 14th and 17th Airborne Infantry Regiments, the 4th Airborne Artillery Group, 4th Airborne Engineer Company, 4th Airborne Signals Company and 4th Airborne Logistics Battalion and the Xth Mechanised Infantry Brigade (HQ La Plata) with the 3rd *General Belgrano*, 6th *General Montes* and 7th *Coronel Conde* Mechanised Infantry Regiments, the 10th Armoured Reconnaissance Squadron, 10th Artillery Group, 10th Engineer Company, 10th Signals Company and 10th Logistics Battalion.

Each army corps has a variable number of combat and logistics support units, numbered in the sequence commencing with 121, in the case of the Second Army Corps and 141 and 181 respectively, in the case of the other two corps. These invariably include a medium artillery group, an anti-aircraft artillery battalion, an engineer construction battalion, a signals battalion, a military police battalion, an ordnance battalion and a logistics support battalion.

***M113 APC of the Argentine Army.* (G. von Rauch)**

Army level troops include the Buenos Aires Detachment (HQ Buenos Aires) with the *Granaderos a Caballo General San Martín* Mounted Escort Regiment and the 1st *Patricios* Mechanised Infantry Regiment, which both perform ceremonial duties at the federal capital. Further units, numbered in the sequence commencing with 601 are also to be found at Army level and include a special forces unit, a regimental-sized anti-aircraft unit, the 601st Combat Aviation Battalion, which is divided into two helicopter assault and one gunship companies, the 601st Aviation Support Company, which operates the fixed-wing aircraft of the Army Aviation Command, an amphibious engineers battalion, operating a number of transport vessels and landing craft on the river system adjoining the Brazilian frontier and signals, supply, transport, ordnance, medical and military police battalions.

The cavalry regiments are classified as either *Regimientos de Tanques* or *Regimientos de Tiradores Blindados*, the former being tank-heavy, the latter APC-heavy, both in the ratio of 3:1 among their four squadrons. The *Granaderos a Caballo*, in addition to their ceremonial function, for which they have a horsed squadron, are classified and equipped as a *Regimiento de Tiradores Blindados*. The mechanised infantry are APC mounted, the reconnaissance units containing a mix of armoured cars or tank destroyers and APCs.

Losses of all kinds of equipment were heavy in the Falklands War but have already been largely made good.

The basic infantry small arms are the 7.62 mm calibre Belgian FN FAL automatic rifle, manufactured under licence in Argentina and the locally developed 9 mm PAM-3 sub-machine gun. A new assault rifle is under development. The principal infantry support weapons are the 7.62 mm Belgian FN MAG general purpose machine gun, also manufactured under licence in Argentina and the 0.50-inch calibre US Browning M2 heavy machine gun. Mortars in both 81 mm and 120 mm calibres are manufactured locally and anti-armour weapons include RCLs in 75 mm, 90 mm and 105 mm calibres of both local and US manufacture while the French SS-11 and SS-12, the German Cobra and the locally produced Mathogo man-portable missile systems provide close-range anti-armour defence.

Armoured units are equipped with the 160 TAM and 100 Sherman Firefly medium tanks, 50 US M41 and 120 French AMX-13 light tanks, approximately 140 Austrian Kürassier tank destroyers, an indeterminate number of Panhard AML 90 and ERC 90 armoured cars and 160 examples of the TAM-VCI and 180 of the AMX-VCI infantry combat vehicles, plus 250 M113 tracked and 80 Mowag Roland wheeled APCs.

The standard light artillery weapon is the Italian Oto Melara Model 56 105 mm pack howitzer, manufactured under licence in Argentina, of which some 120 are available. Some old US M101 105 mm howitzers of Second World War vintage also remain on inventory. Heavier artillery support is provided by some 60 examples apiece of the US 155 mm M2 howitzer and of the locally developed MM L33 155 mm towed howitzer while 24 French F.3 155 mm SP howitzers are used in support of the armoured units. A 105 mm multiple rocket launcher, the SALM Pampera and a 127 mm weapon, the SAPBA-1, have been developed locally.

For anti-aircraft defence, the infantry has the British Blowpipe man-portable surface-to-air missile system, while heavier AA weapons include the German Rheinmetall 20 mm RH 202 and the Swiss Oerlikon 35 mm K 63 anti-aircraft guns and the British Tigercat and the French Roland surface-to-air missiles. Quantities of Bofors 40 mm L/60 AA guns also remain on inventory.

The Army Aviation Command operates a total of approximately 140 aircraft including three Aeritalia G.222s, five Aero Commanders, two Beech Queen Airs and a single King Air, three Cessna 180s, twelve 182s, two Citations, six Skywagons, five T-41Ds, a dozen U-17Bs, three DHC-6s, plus a single Rockwell Sabreliner and four Swearingen Merlins. Helicopters in service include nine Agusta A109s, two Bell 47s, about a dozen Bell UH-1Hs, seven Bell 206s, two Bell 212s, six Fairchild-Hiller FH-1100s, five Aérospatiale SA.315s, 16 SA.330Js and a Chinook. The most recent acquisitions are 24 Aérospatiale AS.332B Super Puma transport helicopters, delivered during 1986.

Recruits all receive their basic training in the units to which they are assigned, further specialist training being received at the *Escuelas de Aplicación* of the various arms and services of which the infantry, cavalry and artillery schools, as well as most of the supporting arms and services schools, are located at Campo de Mayo outside Buenos Aires. The Airborne Forces School is located at Córdoba while the mountain and jungle warfare schools are at Mendoza and Corrientes respectively. Regular NCOs are trained at the *Escuela de Suboficiales Sargento Cabral* at Campo de Mayo.

The *Colegio Militar de la Nación* at El Palomar, Buenos Aires, offers a basic five-year course to aspiring officers, who graduate with a university degree and the rank of *subteniente*. The course of the appropriate branch school must be completed for promotion to lieutenant and those of the *Escuela Superior de Guerra* for promotion to field rank and beyond or for staff appointments.

Each of the arms and services schools, the *Colegio Militar* and the NCO school has a demonstration unit approximating to the size of the basic unit of the respective arms and services in the case of the former and to a composite regiment in that of the latter.

Navy

Manpower: 24,000 (including about 5000 Marines and 3000 Naval Air Force)

Major units:
1 aircraft carrier
4 guided missile destroyers
(+ 2 on sale list)
7 guided missile frigates
(+ 2 under construction)
4 submarines
(+ 2 under construction and 4 projected)
6 fast attack craft
6 minesweepers
4 transports
1 landing ship
(+ 2 under construction)

Marines:
2 Fleet Marine forces:
1 brigade:
5 infantry battalions and
6 independent companies
1 amphibious vehicles battalion
1 reconnaissance group
1 field artillery battalion
1 air defence battalion
1 signals battalion

AFVs:
Panhard ERC 90 armoured cars
Panhard VCR/TT and Mowag Roland APCs
LVT-3/4, LVTP-7 and LARC-5 amphibious assault craft

Artillery: Oto Melara Model 56 105 mm howitzers

Air defence weapons:
Rheinmetall 20 mm and Oerlikon 30 mm and 35 mm AA guns
Blowpipe and Tigercat SAMs

Missiles: Bantam ATGW, Tigercat and Blowpipe SAMs

Naval aviation:
6 wings comprising:
2 fighter-bomber squadrons
2 light strike squadrons
1 maritime reconnaissance squadron
1 ASW squadron
2 transport squadrons
1 photographic squadron
2 helicopter squadrons
1 Antarctic squadron

***The Argentine aircraft carrier* Veinticinco de Mayo. (Dr R. Scheina)**

Fighter-bombers:	Dassault Super Etendard McDonnell Douglas A-4Q Skyhawk
Light strike aircraft:	Aermacchi MB.339 EMB-326 Xavante Beech T-34C
Maritime reconnaissance aircraft:	Lockheed L.188E Electra
ASW aircraft:	Grumman S-2A and E
Transports:	Douglas C-47 Lockheed L.188A Electra Fokker F.28 Beech King and Queen Air Pilatus PC-6
Helicopters:	Aérospatiale Alouette III and Sikorsky S-61
Training aircraft:	Aermacchi MB.326 Beech T-34C

Although Argentine privateers had ranged the oceans of the world during the War of Independence, the Navy declined during the turbulent early years of independent existence and even after reunification remained a limited coast defence and river force until the naval race with Chile at the turn of the century. From that it emerged as the most powerful fleet in Latin America, a position which it retained until massive US aid tipped the scales in favour of Brazil during the 1960s and 1970s.

The military junta which seized power in March 1976 found itself with a largely decrepit fleet of Second World War relics. The only exceptions were two Type 209 submarines, completed in sections in Germany in 1974 and subsequently assembled in Argentina, two modern fast attack craft, also German-built, and two Type 42 missile destroyers, which were under construction, one in Britain and another locally with British technical assistance. The strong position of the Navy in the military government was reflected in the undertaking of an extensive building programme, two enlarged Type 209 submarines being ordered in Germany in 1977 with an agreement for German technical assistance for the construction of four similar vessels in Argentina. The construction of six MEKO Type 360 missile destroyers was also authorised, the order being subsequently modified to four vessels of this type, to be built in Germany. In addition, six Type 140 frigates were to be built in Argentina with German technical assistance.

The Navy was heavily involved in the brief Anglo-Argentine War of 1982, losing the cruiser *General Belgrano*, the submarine *Santa Fé* and several minor vessels although generally aquitting itself well, naval aircraft being responsible for the sinking of two British destroyers, two frigates and a container ship and the Marines being considered the best Argentine ground troops.

The almost universal embargo on the supply of military equipment to Argentina following its invasion of the Falkland archipelago delayed the progress of the new construction programme to a certain extent. Nevertheless, the first two MEKO 360s, *Almirante Brown* and *La Argentina*, were finally delivered during 1983, to be followed by their sister ships *Heroína* and *Sarandí* a year later. *Santa Cruz*, the first of the new submarines, was also delivered at the end of 1984, followed by the second boat, *San Juan*, at the end of 1985.

The Type 42 DDGs had acquired a bad reputation during the Anglo-Argentine war, two of five British vessels of this type employed in the conflict being sunk with relative ease by Argentine aircraft and one badly damaged. Although the two Argentine vessels had been fitted with extensive electronic equipment to permit them to form a homogeneous battle group with the carrier *Veinticinco de Mayo* the difficulty in acquiring spares in the context of the continuing state of cold war between Britain and Argentina further diminished the potential usefulness of these two vessels. Both were laid up at the end of 1982, and a definite decision to dispose of them was taken during the first half of 1983.

The civilian administration which took office at the end of 1983 attempted to persuade the Navy to sell off some of its new constructions, hoping to use the proceeds to offset some of its financial liabilities. The Navy however successfully resisted all pressures in this respect, its position being strengthened by the fact that the necessary financial appropriations for the new construction programme had been voted before the return to civilian government and were already in hand. Using the funds appropriated during the military regime, the Navy also acquired additional aircraft, including the remaining nine Super Etendards of the original order of 14 to re-equip the carrier air group, plus 11 EMBRAER EMB.326 Xavante light strike aircraft and six Lockheed L.118E Electras converted for the maritime reconnaissance role.

The Marine Corps also received new equipment, including 12 Panhard ERC-90 Lynx armoured cars and 24 VCR/TT armoured personnel carriers. The only apparent victory of the Alfonsín administration in its on-going efforts to wrest some of its new equipment from the Navy was the announcement during the second part of 1986 that Thyssen Nordseewerke, the designers of the new submarines and builders of the only pair so far to enter service, had agreed to the sale by Argentina of two of the four boats of this type still to be completed.

The Argentine Navy currently numbers approximately 24,000 all ranks, including Marines and Naval aviation, its principal unit still being the 41-year old 15,900-ton aircraft carrier *Veinticinco de Mayo*. The new 2900-ton MEKO 360 type destroyers, *Almirante Brown*, *La Argentina*,

***The MEKO 360 DDG* Almirante Brown. (Blohm & Voss)**

Heroína and *Sarandí* are already in service, as are *Espora* and *Rosales*, the first two 1500-ton MEKO 140 frigates. Their sisterships *Gómez Roca*, *Parker*, *Robinson* and *Seaver* are in an advanced stage of construction. The 1000-ton French-built A-69 missile frigates *Drummond*, *Guerrico* and *Granville* complete a well-balanced and modern surface fleet. The submarine arm consists of the Type 209 "1200" class *Salta* and *San Luís*, together with the Type 209 "1700" class *Santa Cruz* and *San Juan*. A third Type 209 "1700" boat, *Santiago del Estero*, is building at a leisurely rate although there is no sign of the materialisation of the remainder of the submarine building programme.

The obsolete 40-year old, 900-ton locally-built frigates *King* and *Murature* remain in service for training but are of no military value in modern conditions. Minor surface combatants include the 260-ton German-built torpedo attack craft *Intrépida* and *Indómita* and four Israeli-built "Dabur" class vessels, plus six 30-year old British-built "Ton" class minesweepers and hunters and four armed tugs. There are also two surveying vessels, two surveying launches, the 3000-ton sail training ship *Libertad*, the 4200-ton landing ship *Cabo San Antonio* (plus two smaller vessels under construction in South Korea), the three 5800-ton transports *Canal Beagle*, *Bahía San Blas* and *Cabo de Hornos*, the 9600-ton polar transport *Bahía Paraíso*, the 11,800-ton icebreaker *Almirante Irizar*, a small oiler, nine tugs and some miscellaneous minor craft.

The major naval base is at Puerto Belgrano, with two dry docks and a floating dock. Next in importance is Dársena Norte, Buenos Aires, with two dry docks, several floating docks and a synchrolift. The Río Santiago naval base includes the naval shipyard and there is a minor base at Ushuaia, the submarine force being based at Mar del Plata. The naval stations at Puerto Deseado and Puerto Santa Cruz are scheduled for upgrading under the 1986 Defence Law.

The Marine Corps, which numbers 5000 all ranks, is organised into the 1st Marine Force (HQ

***DDGs* Almirante Brown *and* La Argentina. (Dr R. Scheina)**

Buenos Aires), a largely administrative entity which comprises the 4th Marine Infantry Battalion at Zárate and the 3rd and 5th Marine Infantry Battalions at Ushuaia and Rio Grande, respectively; the 2nd Marine Force (HQ Baterías) comprising the 1st Marine Brigade at Baterías, with the 1st and 2nd Marine Infantry Battalions at Puerto Belgrano and Baterías, the Amphibious Reconnaissance Group at Mar del Plata, the 1st Marine Field Artillery Battalion and Heavy Mortar Company, both at Puerto Belgrano and the Marine anti-tank and engineer companies at Baterías. There are also the 1st Amphibious Vehicles Battalion at Baterías, the 1st Marine AA Battalion and the 1st Marine Communications Battalion, both at Puerto Belgrano and the 1st Marine Security Company at Buenos Aires, the 4th at Río Santiago, the 5th at Punta del Indio Naval Air Base, the 6th at Azul, the 7th at Mar del Plata and the 8th at Comandante Espora Naval Air Base.

These are equipped with the FN FAL rifle in 7.62 mm calibre, the PAM-2 sub-machine gun in 9 mm, the FN MAG 7.62 mm and the Browning M2 0.50 calibre machine guns, together with 81 mm and 120 mm mortars and 75 mm, 90 mm and 106 mm recoilless rifles and Bantam anti-tank guided weapons. Mechanised units have 12 Panhard ERC-90 armoured cars, 24 VCR/TT and six Mowag Roland armoured personnel carriers in addition to 19 LVTP-7 and 15 LARC-5 amphibious landing vehicles. A total of 15 older LVT-3s and LVT-4s have been reactivated from reserve status after the Falklands campaign. Artillery units have 18 Oto Melara Model 56 105 mm howitzers and the anti-aircraft units are equipped with Rheinmetall RH 202 Mk 20 20 mm, Oerlikon 30 mm GCI and K 63 35 mm AA guns and numbers of Tigercat and Blowpipe surface-to-air missiles.

The 3000-man *Aviación Naval* is organised into three naval air forces, comprising six wings and 15 squadrons and operating a total of approximately 100 aircraft.

***The Type A69 frigate* Drummond.**
(Dr R. Scheina)

Fast attack craft Indómita and Intrépida.
(Dr R. Scheina)

The 1st Naval Air Force comprises the 1st Naval Air Wing (Punta del Indio Naval Air Base) with the 4th Naval Attack Squadron equipped with 11 Beech T-34Cs and the 4th Naval Air Wing (Punta del Indio Naval Air Base) with the 1st Naval Attack Squadron with six Aermacchi MB.326s, five 339s and 11 EMB-326 Xavantes, and the Naval Aerophotographic Squadron with five Beech Queen Air B80s.

The 2nd Naval Air Force consists of the 2nd Naval Air Wing (Comandante Espora Naval Air Base) with the Naval Anti-Submarine Squadron equipped with six Grumman S-2Es, the 2nd Naval Helicopter Squadron with five Sikorsky S-61D Sea Kings and the 3rd Naval Air Wing (Comandante Espora Naval Air Base) with the 2nd Naval Fighter/Attack Squadron, equipped

The Argentine Navy's sail training ship **Libertad.**

with 14 Super Etendards, the 3rd Naval Fighter/Attack Squadron with six Douglas A-4Q Skyhawks and the 1st Naval Helicopter Squadron with nine Aérospatiale Alouette IIIs.

The 3rd Naval Air Force is made up of the 5th Naval Air Wing (Ezeiza Airport, Buenos Aires) with the 1st Naval Logistic Support Squadron equipped with three Fokker F.28s and one Hawker-Siddeley 125, the 2nd Naval Logistic Support Squadron with three Lockheed L.188A Electras and the 6th Naval Air Wing (Almirante Zar Naval Air Base, Trelew) with the Naval General Purpose Squadron with four Grumman S-2As and five Queen Airs, the Naval Patrol Squadron with six Lockheed Electra L.188Es and the Naval Antarctic Air Squadron, with three Pilatus PC-6s.

Elements of the 2nd Naval Fighter/Attack, the 2nd Helicopter and the anti-submarine squadrons are normally deployed aboard the carrier *Veinticinco de Mayo*. Likewise, Alouettes of the 1st Helicopter Squadron are deployed aboard the Type A-69 frigates and the polar transport *Bahía Paraíso*. Twelve Agusta-Bell 212s are being acquired to equip the MEKO 360 and 140 type vessels.

***Argentine Marine in summer dress uniform.* (G. von Rauch)**

***BAe 125 communications aircraft of Argentina's Aviación Naval.* (British Aerospace)**

The 1st and 4th Naval Attack Squadrons provide the flying elements of the *Escuela de Aviación Naval*, in addition to their operational role. The *Aviación Naval* maintains two additional bases: *Base Aéronaval Contralmirante Quijada* at Río Grande and *Base Aéronaval Contralmirante Berisso* at Ushuaia, neither of which has any permanently assigned units although both housed combat units during the Falklands War.

The Navy includes 6000 conscripts, selection being however more rigorous than in the case of the Army or Air Force. The longer period of conscription to the Navy also permits more thorough training than in the other two services. This is carried out at the Navy's comprehensive system of schools, commencing with the Seamen's School at Puerto Belgrano and including the Fleet Mechanics School and the schools of communications, gunnery and anti-submarine warfare, most of which are located at either Puerto Belgrano or Río Santiago. The Submarine School is at Mar del Plata and the Marines and Naval aviation maintain their own complexes of training establishments at Baterías and Punta del Indio, respectively. In 1985 it was announced that the Navy was to enlist 5000 volunteers as the first move towards becoming a fully professional force.

The Naval Academy at Río Santiago offers a basic four-year course, followed either by a year at the *Escuela Politécnica Naval*, in the case of naval line and Marine officers, or 18 months at the Naval Aviation School at Comandante Espora, for aspiring officers of that branch. The *Escuela de Aplicación* offers a number of mid-career courses while successful completion of the courses of the Naval War College at Mar del Plata is a prerequisite for promotion to senior rank or for naval staff appointments. The Marines maintain a separate war college at Buenos Aires.

The main seminal foreign influence in the Argentine Navy has been that of the British Royal Navy, upon which it is consciously modelled. The naval air arm and Marines have however come under strong United States influences from the late 1930s onwards.

Under the proposals incorporated in the 1986 Defence Law the Strategic Manoeuvre Force will include the fleet, with one aircraft carrier and four MEKO 360 type destroyers, plus (ultimately) six MEKO 140 type and three A 69 type frigates, the submarine force, with two Type 209 "1200" and (ultimately) four Type 209 "1700" boats, the 1st Marine Brigade, which incorporates the Navy's principal amphibious warfare elements and the 5th Naval Air Wing.

The North-Eastern Defence Force will include the Navy's mine warfare squadron and river units, the 1st Marine Infantry Battalion, the 3rd Marine Infantry Battalion and the 1st, 2nd, 3rd and 4th Naval Air Wings.

The Patagonian and South Atlantic Manoeuvre Force will include the Navy's minor combat units based at Ushuaia, the 5th Marine Battalion at Rio Grande and the 6th Naval Air Wing.

Air Force

Manpower:	15,000
Major units:	10 air brigades comprising: 5 fighter squadrons 4 fighter-bomber squadrons 1 bomber squadron 2 ground attack squadrons 1 armed helicopter squadron 1 photographic squadron 1 ASR squadron 1 Antarctic squadron 6 transport squadrons 1 communications squadron
Fighters:	Dassault Mirage III and 5 IAI Nesher
Bombers:	Canberra B.62 and T.64
Fighter-bombers:	Douglas A-4P Skyhawk North American F-86F
Ground attack aircraft:	IA-58 Pucará
Photo-reconnaissance aircraft:	IA-50 and Learjet
Helicopters:	Aérospatiale Lama Bell 47 and UH-1H Hughes 500M Sikorsky S-58 and S-61 Boeing-Vertol CH-47
Transports:	Aero Commander 500 Boeing 707 DHC-6 Douglas C-47 and LC-47 Fokker F.27 and 28 IA-35 and 50 Lockheed C-130 and L.100-30 Sabreliner 75A
Tankers:	KC-130
Trainers:	Beech T-34 IA-35 MS.760A
Ground forces:	1 special forces group 1 anti-aircraft artillery group

Argentine military aviation dates from 1912 when a military aviation school was established at El Palomar, Buenos Aires. The *Aviación Militar* grew rapidly and in 1945 changed its title to *Fuerza Aérea Argentina* as an independent force of equal status to the Army and Navy. With the end of the Second World War, an ambitious expansion programme was embarked upon and during the early 1950s the Argentine Air Force was the largest in Latin America. It was the first Latin American military air arm to operate jet aircraft, with the acquisition of 100 Meteors in Great Britain and the only one to have a force of strategic bombers, composed of 45 British-built Lancasters and Lincolns. Following the overthrow of the Perón dictatorship in 1955 the Air Force contracted but contrived to maintain a nucleus of modern operational types until the late 1970s when growing tensions with Chile led to considerable expansion. The Air Force performed extremely well in the Falklands War but at the loss of some 44% of its operational strength. Despite the embargo on arms supplies to Argentina in the wake of the Falklands War these losses have been largely made good, mainly by purchases from Israel.

The Argentine Air Force currently numbers about 15,000 all ranks, with approximately 400 aircraft organised into six functional commands.

Air Operations Command controls the Ist Air Brigade (El Palomar, Buenos Aires) made up of the 1st Air Transport Group, comprising the Ist Transport Squadron equipped with six C-130E and Hs, a single Lockheed L.100-30 and two KC-130s, the IInd Transport Squadron, with five

Mirage III aircraft of the Argentine Air Force's 1st Fighter Squadron **(G. von Rauch)**

Fokker F.28s, the IIIrd Transport Squadron, with ten IA-50s, the IVth Transport Squadron, with six Fokker F.27s, the Vth Transport Squadron, with six Boeing 707s and the *Departamento de Aviones Presidenciales*, with two Fokker F.28s, one Sabreliner 75A and two Sikorsky S-57Ts; the IInd Air Brigade (*Base Aéreo Militar General Urquiza*, Paraná) which consists of the 2nd Bomber Group comprising only the Ist Bomber Squadron equipped with four Canberra B.62s and two T.64s and the 1st Aerophotographic Group, also with only a single squadron, the Ist Photographic Squadron equipped with six IA-50s and two Learjet 35As; the IIIrd Air Brigade (Reconquista) consisting of only the 3rd Attack Group with the IInd Attack and Reconnaissance Squadron and the IIIrd Attack and Reconnaissance Squadron, each equipped with 20 IA-58 Pucarás; the IVth Air Brigade (*Base Aéreo Militar El Plumerillo*, Mendoza) which consists of the 4th Fighter Group with the Ist Fighter-Bomber Squadron equipped with 11 F-86F Sabres and the IVth Fighter-Bomber Squadron with 14 Mirage IIIs; the Vth Air Brigade (*Base Aéreo Militar General Pringles*, Villa Reynolds, San Luís) comprising the 5th Fighter Group, with the IVth Fighter-Bomber Squadron and the Vth Fighter-Bomber Squadron, each equipped with 16 A-4P Skyhawks; the VIIth Air Brigade (*Base Aéreo Militar Dr Mariano Moreno*, Morón, Buenos Aires) consisting of the 7th COIN Group, comprising the Ist Attack and Reconnaissance Squadron equipped with eight Hughes 500Ms and seven Bell UH-1Hs, the IInd Helicopter Squadron, with two CH-47 Chinooks and the Medical Squad-

Argentine McDonnell Douglas A-4P Skyhawk fighter-bomber **(G. von Rauch)**

Fokker F.28 transport aircraft of the Argentine military airline LADE **(Fokker)**

ron with two Merlin IVAs; and the IXth Air Brigade (Comodoro Rivadavia) of which the sole unit is the 9th Transport Group, which effectively consists of the military airline *Lineas Aéreas del Estado*, organised as the VIth Transport Squadron, with a nucleus of seven Fokker F.27s and six DHC-6s and supplemented by aircraft borrowed from the other five transport squadrons as required.

It is expected that the 2nd Bomber Group will shortly be deactivated owing to the impossibility of obtaining spares from Britain for its Canberra aircraft. The IVth Brigade, which functions primarily as an operational conversion unit, also includes the aircraft of the *Curso de Entrenamiento y Formación de Pilotos*, which comprises seven Mirage IIIB and Ds and three Neshers. The Sabres had been scheduled for disposal at the time of the outbreak of the Falklands War but were retained in the face of the crippling losses of equipment suffered by the FAA in that conflict. The VIIth Brigade also includes the Air Force Special Forces, the *Group de Operaciones Especiales*.

There are also the Ist Search and Rescue Squadron (El Palomar) equipped with ten Aérospatiale SA.315B Lamas, the Ist Antarctic Squadron (Rio Gallegos) equipped with six DHC-6s, one Douglas LC-47 and two Sikorsky S-61Rs, the *Servicios Aéreos Nacionales del Estado* (Rio Gallegos) equipped with 12 Aero Commanders flown in support of various civilian agencies, and the Ist Calibration Squadron (Morón) equipped with three IA-50s and three Learjet 35As, all of which are outside the brigade structure.

Air Operations Command also controls the CELPA I and CELPA II rocket test centres, located respectively at El Chamical, La Rioja and Mar Chiquita, Buenos Aires.

Air Defence Command controls the VIth Air Brigade (Tandil, Buenos Aires) which consists of the 6th Fighter Group, with the IInd Fighter Squadron and the IIIrd Fighter Squadron, each equipped with 12 IAI Neshers, the VIIIth Air Brigade (*Base Aéreo Militar Dr Mariano Moreno*, Morón, Buenos Aires) consisting of the 8th Fighter Group with only a single squadron, the Ist Fighter Squadron, equipped with 12 Mirage IIIs, and the Xth Air Brigade (Río Gallegos) comprising the 10th Fighter Group, made up of Squadron I with eight Mirage IIIs and Squadron II with nine Mirage 5Ps.

This Command also controls the air early-warning system, consisting of *Grupos 1° and 2° De Vigilancia Aérea*, both based at Merlo, Buenos Aires and the *Grupo 1° de Artillería Antiaérea de la FAA*, based at Mar del Plata and organised as two squadrons equipped with a mixture of 20 mm Rheinmetall RH 202 and Oerlikon GDF-002 twin 35 mm AA guns.

Air Training Command controls all training

establishments and the Air Training Group (Córdoba) which comprises the flying elements of the *Escuela de Aviación Militar*, with 20 examples apiece of the Beech T-34 and MS.760A, and the Ist Communications Training Squadron with four each of the T-34, MS.760 and IA-35.

The T-34s and MS.760s are scheduled to be replaced respectively by the EMB-312 Tucano and the IA-63 Pampa of which 30 and 67 examples are on order. Deliveries of the IA-63 will also permit the reactivation of the IInd and IIIrd Fighter-Bomber Squadrons, which formerly formed part of the IVth Air Brigade.

In addition to its flying units each brigade includes a Base Group and a Technical Group of identical numerical designation and also controls a number of largely obsolescent communications and general purpose aircraft including some C-47s, IA-35s, Cessna 182s and Bell 47 helicopters.

Air Regions, Air Material and Air Personnel Commands have no flying components.

Under the global reorganisation of the Argentine armed forces embodied in the 1986 Defence Law the North-Eastern Defence Force will include the Air Force's IIIrd, VIth and VIIth Brigades, the North-Western Defence Force will include the IVth and Vth Air Brigades and the Patagonian and South Atlantic Manoeuvre Force will include the IXth and Xth Brigades. The Strategic Reserve Force will include the Ist and IInd Air Brigades.

The proportion of conscripts in the Air Force has been reduced to approximately 30%. Formerly some 50% of its enlisted personnel consisted of 12-month conscripts who received only rudimentary basic training, all skilled technical tasks being undertaken by long-service regulars. These are principally trained at the *Escuela de Especialidades* at Córdoba and the *Centro de Instrucción Profesional* at Ezeiza International Airport, Buenos Aires. The Air Force NCO School at Córdoba conducts both technical and non-technical courses.

Boeing-Vertol CH-47 Chinook helicopter of the 1st Antarctic Squadron of the Argentine Air Force **(Boeing Vertol)**

All aircrew are commissioned officers who have completed the four-year course at the *Escuela de Aviación Militar* at Córdoba. Post-graduate training is conducted at the Air Force Command and Staff School which conducts two basic courses, aimed respectively at captains and majors and at lieutenant-colonels and colonels. The successful completion of each is a pre-requisite for promotion to the next highest rank.

Although it has largely replaced the material lost in the Falklands War, the FAA is still experiencing difficulties in the acquisition of equipment above and beyond those to be expected in the prevailing economic conditions.

The United States has successfully blocked the acquisition of 32 Kfirs and 24 Skyhawks from Israel which has however given technical assistance with the upgrading of the existing fleet of Mirages in addition to that of the ten Mirage 5Ps purchased from Peru in 1983 and the 22 Mirage IIIs and ten Neshers which it sold to Argentina at the end of 1982. Argentina has expressed an interest in the Italo-Brazilian AM-X fighter and the success of the experimental modification of the IA-58 Pucará to single-seat configuration, permitting the carrying of an increased ordnance load, has prompted a programme for the conversion of the entire existing Pucará fleet to this standard. The IA-63 Pampa, which has full light strike capability, will also supplement the capabilities of the FAA in this area.

Paramilitary forces

Manpower:	12,000 (Gendarmerie) 9000 (*Prefectura Naval*) 22,000 (Federal Police)
Armoured vehicles:	Shorland armoured cars and Mowag Roland APC (Gendarmerie and Federal Police) M113 APC (Gendarmerie)
Patrol vessels:	5 coastguard cutters 25 large and 23 small patrol craft (*Prefectura Naval*) Small river patrol craft (Gendarmerie)
Aircraft:	Cessna 172, 182, 185, U206, 210, 310, 337 and 402 light aircraft Pilatus Turbo-Porter, Piper Aztec and Navajo light transports Bell 47 and Hiller FH-1100 helicopters (Gendarmerie) Bo 105 and Alouette II helicopters (*Policia Federal*) DHC-2, Douglas C-47 and Short Skyvan transports Bell 47, Hughes 500M and Aérospatiale Puma helicopters

There are three major paramilitary forces: the *Gendarmería Nacional*, the *Prefectura Naval Argentina* and the *Policía Federal*. There are also separate provincial and municipal police forces maintained by the 22 provinces and the larger urban centres.

The *Gendarmería Nacional* was established in 1917 under the control of the Ministry of War. In 1938, its jurisdiction was extended to the entire national territory, which it divided into North, Centre and South zones and its functions were extended to frontier patrol, the enforcement of federal law and disaster relief. The *Gendarmería*, which currently numbers 12,000 all ranks, is still primarily a frontier guard force and functions from three regional headquarters at Córdoba, Rosario and Bahía Blanca. Its main organic unit is the *Agrupación*, a level of command between that of a battalion and a regiment, each *Agrupación* being in turn subdivided into squadrons, groups and sections. The *Gendarmería* is equipped with an unspecified number of Shorland armoured cars (to be replaced by Israeli-built RAM V-2s) and Mowag Roland APCs, plus some 40 M113s, in addition to infantry personal and support weapons. The Air Division of the *Gendarmería* operates five Cessna 172s, four 182Hs, two examples each of the Cessna U206, 310 and 337 and single examples of the Cessna 185A, 210 and 402, in addition to a Piper Aztec, two Navajos and three Pilatus PC-6B Super-Porters. It also operates two Bell 473, one Hiller FH-1100 and seven other helicopters of various types. Enlisted personnel of the *Gendararmería* are all volunteers and receive their training in the force's own comprehensive system of training institutions. Officers graduate

OPV Halcón of Argentina's Prefectura Naval **(Bazán)**

after a three-year course at the National Gendarmerie Academy and both officers and enlisted personnel have access to the specialist training establishments of the Army, of which the force remains essentially an adjunct.

The *Prefectura Naval* derives its origins from the Port Captaincy Service, which was in existence before national independence and which in the early 1900s was brought under the control of the commander-in-chief of the Navy, its title being changed to *Prefectura Nacional Marítima.* In 1970 it acquired its present title. Following the Falklands War it was removed from naval jurisdiction and subordinated directly to the Ministry of Defence. The 9000-man *Prefectura Naval* is closely analagous to the United States Coast Guard and is concerned primarily with the prevention of smuggling, fishery protection, lifesaving, the maintenance of navigational aids and the regulation of the national ports. Its major units are the five 900-ton helicopter-carrying offshore patrol vessels *Mantilla, Azopardo, Thompson, Prefecto Piques* and *Prefecto Derbes,* which were launched in Spain in 1981/82. There are also the 1000-ton former whalecatcher *Delfín* and the 200-ton patrol vessels *Tonina, Dorado, Mandubí* and *Robalo,* plus the *Lynch, Toll* and *Erezcano* of the 95-foot US Coast Guard cutter type. The most numerous class in service is the 80-ton German-built Z-28 type, originally numbering 20 units, of which one was sunk and another captured intact by the Royal Navy during the Falklands War. It also operates almost 300 lifeboats, lightships and very small inshore patrol craft. The *Division de Aviación* of the *Prefectura Naval* operates five Short Skyvan transports, plus two Bell 47, six Hughes 500M (to be replaced by Helibras HS.350F Ecureuils) and three Puma helicopters. In emergencies the *Prefectura* can equip small landing forces and shore units with light infantry weapons. Enlisted personnel are all volunteers and receive their training in the various training establishments operated by the force. Officers graduate, after three years of study, from the *General Matías de Irigoyén* Cadet School at Tigre, near Buenos Aires and petty officers pursue a two-year course at the Escuela *Martín Jacobo Thompson* at Zárate. There is also the *Prefectura Naval* Staff College at Olivos, which imparts post-graduate training to officers at various stages of their careers.

The *Policía Federal* is descended from the Buenos Aires Municipal Police, established in 1821. Directly subordinate to the Ministry of the Interior and with a current strength of 22,000, this force is primarily concerned with conventional police and internal security functions in the federal capital for which it has available a number of light armoured vehicles and aircraft in addition to light infantry weapons. These include Shorland armoured cars and Mowag Roland wheeled APCs, four MBB Bo 105 and two Alouette II helicopters. It maintains small delegations in the provincial capitals and is also available to reinforce provincial police forces in cases of emergency. The *Policía Federal* is divided between the Public Order Division and the Corps Division, the latter including the Traffic Police, Mounted Police and the Canine Corps. There is also a Feminine Division and the Federal Police also controls the Buenos Aires Fire Department, which has a secondary function of riot control. Operationally, the force is divided into six *Circunscripciones* which are in turn subdivided into 50 *Comisarías*. Enlisted personnel consist largely of one-year volunteers, as compulsory military service can be pre-empted by volunteering for service in the force. On enlistment, recruits receive an intensive three-month course of instruction before being assigned to units for on-the-job training. Officers must complete the two-year course of the *Coronel Ramón L. Falcón* Police Academy located in the Buenos Aires suburb of Caballito. There is also a Superior Police School, which provides post-graduate training at various points during the officer's career.

In addition to the above three forces, operated by the federal government, each province and most of the major cities maintain their own police forces. These generally conform to the structure and organisation of the Federal Police but vary in strength, equipment and standard of training with the economic situations of the provinces and cities which maintain them.

***The locally-developed FM 81 mm mortar* (Drn. Gral. de Fábricas Militares)**

Sources of defence material supply and current requirements

The traditional suppliers of Argentine ground defence material include Germany, France, Denmark, Sweden and Britain while the Navy traditionally favoured vessels of British construction, although US, German and Italian yards also received orders. The Air Force was initially equipped largely with French and Italian material, later supplemented by British equipment, to which aircraft of German and US origins were added in the years immediately preceding the Second World War. Large quantities of surplus British, Italian and US aircraft were acquired in the years immediately following the Second World War, together with much Allied war surplus ground defence equipment and a large number of naval vessels, the United States, France and Canada becoming the main suppliers of defence equipment from the 1960s onwards. From the 1970s onwards Israel began to supply significant quantities of second-hand combat aircraft and some small naval vessels to Argentina, continuing to do so following the Falklands War when Brazil also attracted orders for second-line aircraft.

Although still dependent on external suppliers

to an unacceptable degree, in some areas Argentina is now the most self-sufficient country in Latin America in defence production.

Argentina had manufactured its own small arms and ammunition since the early years of the present century and the outbreak of the Second World War gave the ideal of self-sufficiency a new immediacy. In 1941, the Argentine defence industry was grouped together under the umbrella title of *Fabricaciones Militares Argentinas* which included the small arms plant at Rosario, a small arms ammunition factory at Puerto Borghi, Santa Fé, the artillery ammunition plant at Río Tercero, Córdoba, the powder and explosives complex of Villa Marín, Córdoba, the AFNE shipyards at Río Santiago and the *Fábrica Militar de Aviones* at Córdoba, plus ten other factories producing such items as fuzes, chemicals and transport and communications equipment. Two types of sub-machine gun, a medium tank and an infantry gun of original design were developed during the 1940s, although only the former item entered quantity production. During the late 1950s and throughout the 1960s defence production, although continuing to diversify, consisted largely of the manufacture of foreign equipment under licence.

FM 120 mm mortar
(Drn. Gral. de Fábricas Militares)

Following the refusal of the United States to supply up-to-date material of the types required by Argentina in the late 1960s, the so-called "Plan Europa" was adopted whereby the focus shifted to France, Germany and Italy as the main overseas sources of equipment supply. As a result, AMX-13 light tanks and AMX-VCI APCs were first acquired from France and later assembled under licence in Argentina as were numerous examples of the Italian Oto Melara Model 56 105 mm pack howitzer and the Swiss Mowag Roland wheeled APC. In 1973 a new tank, the TAM (*Tanque Mediano Argentino*) was developed on the chassis of the Marder APC in collaboration with Thyssen-Henschel of Germany, an infantry combat vehicle, the VCI, also being developed, both types entering production in Argentina during the late 1970s. A command post variant, a mortar carrier, an armoured recovery vehicle and an SP howitzer, all based on the TAM VCI, have subsequently been developed, a 155 mm towed howitzer of local design has also been successfully developed and placed in production.

Although nine minesweepers of original design had been built locally during the late 1930s, followed by four minelayers, which were modified to serve as escort vessels before completion, the shipbuilding industry had not developed as quickly as might have been expected. The Type 42 missile destroyer *Santísima Trinidad* was however built for the Navy during the 1970s. The Argentine shipyards now have the capacity to build naval vessels up to and including the size and complexity of guided missile destroyers, frigates and submarines, having recently completed two MEKO 140 type corvettes for the Navy with four more vessels of this type and a Type 209 submarine completing.

Aircraft had also been produced locally from the 1930s onwards and a number of interesting combat types of original conception were in series production during the 1940s and 1950s. Although during the 1960s the *Fábrica Militar de Aviones* largely concentrated on the licence production of foreign-designed types, the locally developed

***The TAM VCI infantry combat vehicle* (Thyssen Henschel)**

IA-35 Huanguero light transport/crew trainer and the IA-50 Guaraní general purpose aircraft both entered limited production and the IA-58 Pucará ground attack aircraft was also developed during the late 1970s. The Pucará was highly effective in the Falklands War and has attracted widespread foreign interest and a small export order from Uruguay. Although the negotiations for the production of the A-4 Skyhawk in Argentina, reported during 1986, seem fated to be frustrated by the US government, there is no reason why the development and construction of first-line types could not be recommenced. Production of the IA-63 Pampa trainer/light strike aircraft, developed in collaboration with German industry, is already in hand for the FAA.

Argentina's atomic energy programme is under naval control and following the debacle of the Falklands War of 1982, despite repeated denials, the acceleration of a nuclear weapons programme seems highly likely, especially since the announcement of the mastery of the techniques of the enrichment of uranium in 1985. With existing technology, Argentina could probably produce a nuclear-powered submarine within two years and it has been reckoned that nuclear weapons could be developed, without outside assistance, within three. There are also two establishments engaged in rocket research: CELPA I (*Centro Experimental de Lanzamiento de Proyectiles Auto propulsados* I) at El Chamical and CELPA II at Mar Chiquita. Delivery vehicles already in existence could deliver nuclear warheads over medium ranges.

Argentina is now largely self-sufficient as regards the supply of small arms, infantry support weapons, ammunition, transport and communications equipment, and increasingly so regarding the production of armoured fighting vehicles and artillery pieces, in addition to being able to supply many of its own needs in the field of naval vessels and military aircraft.

While the goal of complete self-sufficiency in defence production remains unfulfilled and such interesting types as the TAM and VCI armoured vehicles and the Pucará aircraft have not yet attracted the same degree of foreign interest and commercial success as the more modest products of the Brazilian defence industry, Argentina's defeat in the 1982 war against the United Kingdom and the effects of the arms embargo enforced by most developed countries during that conflict cannot but reinforce the national resolve to minimize dependence on external suppliers and self-sufficiency in defence production is one of the objectives of the 1986 Defence Law.

Currently, local industry provides for most of the needs of the Argentine Army and is expected to supply all of its requirements by 1990. Current or pending requirements of the Argentine Navy include an aircraft carrier to replace the *Veinticinco de Mayo*, fast attack craft and amphibious assault vessels. The Argentine Air Force also requires fighters, long-range bomber/strike aircraft, troop transports, tanker aircraft and helicopters.

Summary and prospects

Prior to the Falklands War, the Argentine armed forces were considered among the best organised, trained and equipped in Latin America. The training and organisation and above all the leadership of the Army proved defective during the brief conflict with Britain although the minor surface units of the Navy and the Marines acquitted themselves respectably and the Naval aviation and Air Force performed quite superbly.

The failure of the Falklands adventure, embarked upon with staggering lack of foresight and preparation by the Argentine military government, did not, as was predicted, lead to the immediate overthrow of the military by the civilian population. However, the personalities most intimately associated with the debacle rapidly departed from the national stage and the disappointing performance of the military in the Falklands War precipitated the return of civilian rule within 18 months of its termination.

The civilian administrations of the Raúl Alfonsín, inheriting an almost bankrupt treasury and a crippling burden of foreign debt, was forced to take unpopular austerity measures and met with total obduracy in its attempts to restore negotiations with the British government regarding the ultimate fate of the Falklands. An early triumph however was the negotiation of a peace treaty with Chile which appeared to resolve the Beagle Channel dispute, although many relatively moderate nationalists considered that the Treaty made excessive concessions to the latter country.

The Alfonsín administration also embarked upon what appeared to be the systematic demoralisation of the armed forces by the implementation of a pay freeze, a series of show trials of military personnel involved both in the ill-starred adventure which led to war with and defeat by Britain and the so-called "dirty war" which accomplished the defeat of left-wing terrorism during the 1970s.

The annual conscript intake was drastically reduced and the acquisition of new and replacement equipment severely curtailed. Although the latter had a particularly serious effect on the Army, the Navy and Air Force both managed not only to replace their losses of material during the Anglo-Argentine War but largely completed the re-equipment programmes already under way in 1982 and which had been financed before the return to civilian government.

Having successfully weathered several small and rather half-hearted military revolts and apparently reduced the bulk of the military to an acceptable state of political docility and

IA-58 Pucará ground attack aircraft

***IA-63 Pampa trainer/light-strike aircraft* (Author)**

despite the continuing economic crisis, with which it continued to endeavour to grapple with indifferent success, in the late 1980s the Alfonsín administration seemed to be embarking on a reconstruction of the Argentine military establishment with an emphasis on leaner, largely professional armed forces, with a high degree of self-sufficiency in equipment supply. Despite the fact that the annual conscript intake remained restricted, massive pay increases during 1987 seemed reasonably certain to attract a larger proportion of long-service professional personnel.

Although the foreign policy of the Alfonsín administration has been characterised by attempts to resolve Argentina's existing international disputes by diplomatic means and had been crowned with success as regards the successful negotiation of the Beagle Channel Treaty with Chile, its efforts to resolve the Falklands/Malvinas dispute on a diplomatic level continued to be singularly ill-starred. President Alfonsín himself, the most moderate Argentine leader whom any British government is likely to face on the issue, stated in 1984 that Argentine patience in this regard was not inexhaustible and alluded to a possible ultimate resort to more violent means if Britain remained intractible.

Despite the recent accord between Argentina and Chile it is also obvious that the establishment of both the proposed North Western Defence Force and the Patagonian and South Atlantic Manoeuvre Forces are intended to deter a real or imagined threat from the Chilean neighbour. The inclusion of the term "South Atlantic" in the designation of the latter element owes more to the continuing unrealized national aspiration towards the repossession of the Falklands than to any immediate operational capability orientated in that direction. The concentration of four of the existing ten fully formed brigades in the IInd Army Corps area would also seem to indicate that the entente between Buenos Aires and Brasilia is rather more fragile than has been imagined.

While the performance of the Argentine Army in its first foreign war in over 100 years was disappointing, a combination of the experience gained during its blooding in the Anglo-Argentine War and the organisational and other reforms currently in progress should render it a much more formidable institution in the medium term. The Argentine Navy has now also regained the position of regional primacy which it has held throughout most of the present century and is once more the most formidably equipped in Latin America and the Air Force is second only to that of Cuba as regards equipment and the undisputed leader in the region as regards combat experience.

BELIZE

(Belice)

Area: 8870 sq miles (22,973 sq km)
Population: 163,400 (1985)
Total armed forces: 600 (3000 planned)
Reserves: 500
Available manpower: 13,000
Paramilitary forces: nil
GNP: $192.5 million (1985)
Defence expenditure: $3.6 million (1984)

Introduction

Known as British Honduras until 1973, Belize is bordered on the west and south by Guatemala, which claims its entire territory, on the north by Mexico, which claims a third of it and on the east by the Caribbean. Over 51% of the population is Negro, primarily of British West Indian origins, 22% are of mixed European and Amerindian origins, 19% are pure Amerindian and the remainder are a mixture of European, Chinese and Indian.

The most important products are hardwoods and sugar. All manufactured products and most food must be imported.

Belize attracted little attention from the Spaniards and the first European colonists were English log-wood cutters from Jamaica, who settled on the coast with their black slaves from 1638 onwards. Although subjected to sporadic harrassment from the Spaniards, the English settlers prospered. England however made no attempt to annexe the territory on a formal basis. After independence, in 1821, both Guatemala and Mexico claimed Belize as successors in title to the Spanish Crown. Little attempt was however made to enforce this claim and in 1859 Guatemala signed a treaty recognising British sovereignty and the existing frontiers between Belize and Guatemala provided that Britain should build a road linking Guatemala City with the Caribbean. Britain declared Belize a colony in 1862 and a Crown colony nine years later. In 1884 Belize became an independent British colony and in 1964 full self-government was attained. Finally, in 1981, Belize became an independent member of the British Commonwealth.

The treaty of 1859 between Britain and Guatemala, although signed by the President of the latter country, was never formally ratified and Britain did not comply with its obligation to build the road linking Guatemala City and the sea. The treaty was therefore rejected by subsequent Guatemalan governments, almost all of which have revived the territorial claim at one time or another. Although the Mexican government had signed a treaty renouncing its claims to Belize in 1893, the subsequent revival of Guatemala claims also caused Mexico to renew its claims to the northern portion of the territory. Diplomatic

relations between Britain and Guatemala were broken off in 1963 and Guatemalan claims have remained unaffected by the offer of Mexico to waive its own territorial claims if Guatemala will do likewise. Most Latin American governments have however recognised the independence of Belize.

Belize is an independent state within the British Commonwealth. The Crown, as Head of State is represented by a governor and commander-in-chief. There is a bicameral legislature. Executive power is in the hands of the Premier and cabinet who are elected from the legislature.

Belize appears to be internally stable, the major threat to its security coming from the annexation claims by Guatemala. The independence of Belize is currently guaranteed by Britain and the value of this guarantee has been greatly reinforced by Britain's victory over Argentina in the Falklands War of 1982.

Armed forces

Manpower:	600 (3000 planned)
Units:	1 infantry battalion
Heavy equipment:	2 patrol boats 2 aircraft

A tri-service Belizean Defence Force, with a target strength of 3000 men and women, is in process of formation, with British training assistance. This force is based on the company-sized rapid intervention unit formerly maintained by the Belize Police, which is otherwise an unarmed civilian force. The Belizean Defence Force consists primarily of a ground element, which to date is made up of a single infantry battalion with three regular and three reserve rifle companies, plus an administrative and a support company, both composed of regulars. It is equipped with light infantry weapons of British origins, including the L1A1 SLR rifle in 7.62 mm calibre, the Sterling L2A3 sub-machine gun in 9 mm calibre, the Bren L4A1 and GPMG L7 machine guns, both in 7.62 mm and six L16 81 mm mortars. There is

RAF Harrier aircraft in Belize
(Jane's Defence Weekly)

also a maritime element with two 20-metre patrol boats and an air wing equipped with two Pilatus/Britten-Norman Defender general-purpose aircraft.

The main military base is at Price Barracks, 10 km from Belize City, where all training is carried out. There is also a ground forces base at Belizario Camp near San Ignacio on the frontier with Guatemala, which is currently garrisoned by the 2nd Rifle Company of the Belizean Defence Force. Both the marine and the air elements are based at Belize City and there is an air strip at Punta Gorda.

Of the three reserve companies, one is based at Corizal in the north of the country, with a platoon at Orange Walk; another is located at Belize city, with a platoon at Cayo and the bulk of the third is stationed at Stann Creek in the south of the country, with a platoon at Punta Gorda.

Although other ranks receive their basic training in the country, officers, senior NCOs and specialists are trained either in the United Kingdom, Canada or the United States. There are also small British and US service missions engaged in on-the-spot training of the Belizean Defence Force.

RAF Rapier SAM and Puma helicopter at Belmopan

The small British garrison which has been present in the country since 1975 numbers approximately 1500 and consists essentially of a single infantry battalion supported by a troop of Scorpion tanks, a field battery, an air defence battery with four Rapier missile launchers, an engineer squadron, a flight of four Harrier fighters, four Puma helicopters of the RAF and four Army Gazelles. A British frigate, stationed in the Caribbean, is also on call.

Sources of equipment supply and current requirements

All current equipment of the Belize Defence Force is of British origins. Equipment in use is confined to infantry personal weapons and light support arms. As the Defence Force develops, it will require additional mortars, anti-armour and air-defence weapons and possibly some light armoured vehicles and artillery pieces, plus additional aircraft, particularly helicopters. One or two additional patrol craft may also be acquired for the maritime element. The force is unlikely to reach a stage of development at which even such equipment will be required for several years and equipment requirements seem likely to be met from Britain for the foreseeable future.

Summary and prospects

Belize is a very small and poor country, of doubtful viability as an independent entity. Although Belize is geographically part of Guatemala, the Belizeans have nothing in common with their neighbours either historically, ethnically or politically. However, any Guatemalan attempt to enforce that country's territorial claim to Belize on a military level remains highly unlikely while Britain continues to guarantee Belizean independence and backs up this guarantee with a military presence. Although it was announced in the latter part of 1983 that British troops would be withdrawn from Belize within the next 12 months, the British garrison remained at the time of writing. Problems may occur when eventually the British garrison is withdrawn, but any Guatemalan armed aggression against Belize would receive widespread international censure. In this respect also it is significant that Guatemalan aspirations receive singularly little support from other Latin American countries.

Although politically stable, a certain internal threat exists by virtue of the extensive activities of narcotics smugglers. Belize is a major illicit producer of marijuana and clashes have occurred between elements of the Belize Defence Force and the smugglers. A further possibility is that Guatemalan guerrillas may infiltrate across the frontier between the two countries and create foci of left-wing subversion within Belize. The main threat to the survival of Belize, in the long term, is its problematic ability to sustain an independently viable economy once the British economic aid, made available in the immediate post-indpendence period, is withdrawn.

BOLIVIA

(República de Bolivia)

Area: 424,160 sq miles (1,098,580 sq km)
Population: 6,524,000 (1986)
Total armed forces: 28,000
Reserves: 150,000
Available manpower: 500,000
Paramilitary forces: 14,000
GNP: $8,221 million (1984)
Defence expenditure: $216,076,000 (1984)

Introduction

Despite successive losses of territory to almost all of its neighbours, Bolivia remains the fifth largest country in South America. Entirely landlocked, it is bordered by Peru to the west, Chile to the south-west, Argentina to the south, Paraguay to the south-east and Brazil to the north and east. The population, of which over 60% is pure Indian, 30% of mixed blood and less than 10% of European origins, is largely concentrated in the Andean plateau or Altiplano, at altitudes ranging from 10,000 to 17,000 ft, the remainder of the national territory being singularly sparsely populated.

In spite of extensive and largely unexploited mineral resources, the economy is largely dependent on the export of a single product: tin. Although 70% of the population is engaged in agriculture, food figures highly among imports. Industry is undeveloped and most manufactured products must also be imported. The country is however self-sufficient in petroleum production and exports a small surplus of petroleum products. Attempts to expand and diversify the economy are hindered by defective communications. An important, if illicit, export is cocaine, together with cocaine-based narcotics.

Advanced pre-Columbian civilisations flourished on the eastern shores of Lake Titicaca, itself the legendary origin of the Incas who conquered what is now Bolivia about AD 1200 and incorporated it into their empire. Although Spanish conquistadores from Peru established control of the country from 1538 onwards, revolts against Spanish colonial rule began in Bolivia earlier than elsewhere with an unsuccessful rising in La Paz in 1661. Ironically, Bolivia was to be the last South American country to establish its independence with the final surrender of the royalist forces in 1825.

From 1835 to 1839 Bolivia formed part of a confederation with Peru which successfully resisted invasions from Argentina and Chile but succumbed finally to internal dissensions. The disastrous Pacific War of 1879-83, fought by an alliance of Bolivia and Peru against Chile, resulted in the victory of the latter and the loss of Bolivia's Pacific coastal province of Antofagasta. Further territorial losses occurred as a result of the brief Acre War with Brazil in 1904. Deprived of their access to the sea via the Pacific, the Bolivians sought to gain somewhat indirect access to the Atlantic by the establishment of a port on the navigable Paraguay river. The territory in question was however claimed, apparently with equal right, by Paraguay which had enforced its claims by occupation. Following the failure of protracted diplomatic negotiations and a series of frontier incidents, relations between the two countries degenerated into full-scale warfare. The Chaco War of 1932-35, which ensued, resulted in defeat and further territorial losses for Bolivia.

This succession of military defeats created a period of extreme political instability, culminating in the revolution of 1952 which largely overthrew the existing politico-social institutions of the country. Political instability has continued with an average of more than one violent change of government for each year of the country's independence.

Bolivia is a unitary republic of nine departments. Executive power is in the hands of the President, who chooses his own cabinet. There is a bicameral legislature.

Bolivian foreign policy is centred on the regaining of access to the sea and the prevention of further territorial losses. The first and major aspiration depends on a satisfactory accord with Chile, such accord having been apparently near realization in the mid-1970s although ultimately the negotiations came to nothing. Having lost almost half of its original area to its neighbours, a certain national paranoia in this respect is understandable, the most recent perceived threat coming from Brazil with regard to the iron-rich area of El Mutún, although Bolivian fears in this respect would appear to be unfounded. Despite the fact that the Paraguayans have not provided Bolivia with the port facilities on the Upper Paraguay river required under the Treaty of Buenos Aires of 1938, which brought the Chaco War to an end, relations with that country are relatively cordial. Having an informal alliance with both Peru and Argentina, Bolivia offered military assistances, in the form of the loan of transport aircraft, to the latter country in the South Atlantic War of 1982.

Although an attempt at Marxist revolution by Cuban agitators, led by Ernesto "Ché" Guevara in the mid-1960s received scant popular support and resulted in the death of their leader, chronic internal instability remains a major problem. The major internal political forces are the armed forces and the highly organised tin miners. A more recent problem is the threat of a over-spill of *Sendero Luminoso* guerrilla activity from Peru.

Structure of the armed forces

The President is supreme commander of the armed forces, with the title of Captain General. As such, his authority is normally exercised through the Supreme Council of National Defence and the Minister of National Defence. The President nominates the commanding generals and chiefs of staff of the three armed forces. The functions of the Minister of National Defence are purely administrative, operational command being exercised jointly by the Committee of Chiefs of Staff, composed of the chiefs of staff of the three armed forces. A peculiar provision of the Bolivian constitution allows the President to assume active command of the armed forces in time of war, provided that he delegates his civilian executive powers to the Vice-President.

The country is divided into six military regions of which the 1st (HQ La Paz) covers the southern portion of La Paz department; the 2nd (HQ Sucre) the departments of Chuquisaca and Cochabamba; the 3rd (HQ Tarija) covers the departments of Tarija, eastern Chuquisaca and Santa Cruz; the 4th (HQ Potosí) the departments of Oruro and Potosí; the 5th (HQ Trinidad) covers most of Santa Cruz and Beni departments and the 6th (HQ Cobija) the department of Pando and parts of La Paz and Beni.

The military regions are administrative in character and do not correspond exactly to the tactical deployment of the armed forces. Military service has been compulsory for all fit males between the ages of 18 and 49 since 1904 but in practice is enforced on a rather haphazardly selective basis, most of the conscripts being Indians. Non-commissioned and warrant officers, all of whom are volunteers, tend to be drawn from

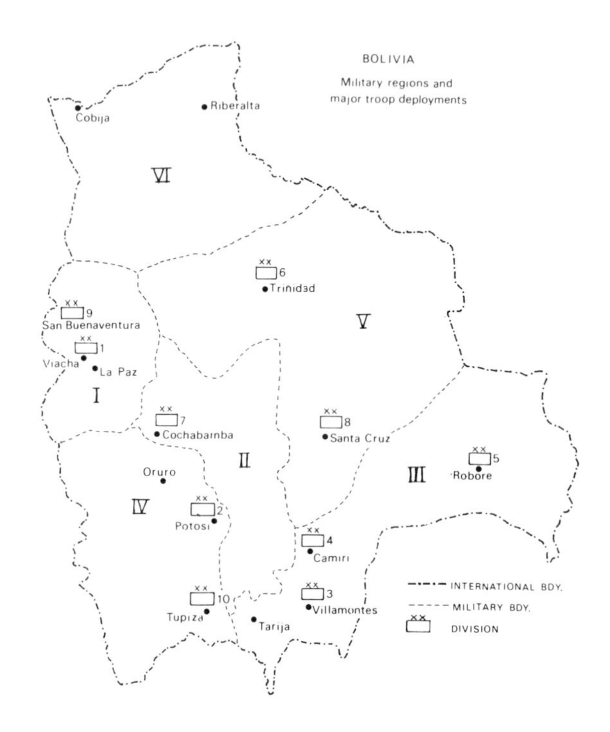

the mixed blooded "Cholos". Officers of the three armed forces receive their basic training at the *Colegio Militar Coronel Gualberto Villaroel* at La Paz, the course being of five years duration, on completion of which graduates are commissioned as second lieutenants and ensigns and proceed to the specialist schools of their respective arms and services.

Army

Manpower:	20,000
Formations:	10 divisions
Major units:	19 infantry regiments (including 2 motorised, 3 Andean and 2 ranger) 1 paratroop battalion 2 armoured battalions 6 cavalry regiments (1 mechanised and 5 horsed) 3 artillery regiments 1 engineer regiment and 4 independent battalions
Armour:	Kürassier tank destroyers EE-9 Cascavel and V-150 armoured cars EE-11 Urutú, M113 and Mowag Roland APCs
Artillery:	Bofors Model 1935 75 mm L/40 field guns US M116 75 mm pack howitzer US M101 105 mm howitzer Vickers EE 75 mm field guns Vickers CC 105 mm howitzers
Aircraft:	Beech Super King Air Cessna 421 Piper Cheyenne

The Bolivian Army was all but exterminated in the disastrous Pacific War against Chile, following the end of which it had to be laboriously rebuilt almost from scratch. Its reorganisation and equipment was still far from complete when the seccessionist movement in the Acre territory broke out in 1900. A French military mission functioned in the country from 1905 until 1909, being followed by a German mission from 1911 until 1914. German mercenaries where again contracted to train the army during the 1920s as Bolivia and Paraguay each prepared for a military confrontation which became daily more inevitable. Incidents in the disputed region occurred with increasing frequency, finally escalating to full-scale hostilities in July 1935. The three-year long Chaco War which ensued cost Bolivia 57,000 dead out of some 250,000 mobilised and over US$200 million. In the closing stages of the war, the Bolivian government successively contracted a Spanish and a Czech military mission, the effects of both of which were minimal. An Italian military mission, active from 1937 until the outbreak of the Second World War, also left little mark, apart from the reorganisation of the staff college in 1938 and the dissemination of Fascist propaganda. From 1942 onwards US military and aviation missions were active in the country, limited Lend-Lease military aid being also received. With the end of the Second World War and particularly following Bolivia's signature of the Rio Treaty of 1947, additional quantities of US equipment were obtained.

***Member of the 1st* Colorados *Infantry Regiment of the Bolivian Army, which performs ceremonial duties at La Paz* (Author)**

Following the 1952 revolution, the Army ceased to exist for a short period, being replaced by Peoples' Militias. After the Cuban revolution, Bolivia became a prime target for Communist-inspired subversion and a Special Forces Instruction Centre was established at Cochabamba. Subsequently, a Ranger School was established at Santa Cruz, with US instructors, three battalions of Rangers being formed. These troops played an important part in the interception of Ernesto "Ché" Guevara's guerrilla group in October 1967. US military aid also increased greatly during this period.

During the 1960s the Bolivian Army expanded from six to eight nominal divisions and in the late 1970s a further expansion to ten divisions, to be subordinate to four army corps, was projected. Only the Ist and IInd Army Corps were in fact established and the organisation of the two additional divisions remained incomplete. In 1984 it was decided to abandon the corps structure and the units of the partially-formed 9th Division were absorbed into the 6th Division. During 1987 it was announced that a new 9th Division was to be established, with its headquarters at San Buenaventura in the northern part of La Paz department.

The Bolivian Army currently numbers approximately 20,000 all ranks.

The 1st Division (HQ Viachi) consists of the 5th *Lanza* Andean and 23rd *Max Toledo* Motorised Infantry Regiments, the 1st *Tarapacá* Armoured Battalion and the 2nd *Bolivar* Artillery Regiment;

The 2nd Division (HQ Oruro) comprises the 3rd *Pérez* Infantry, 17th *Illimani* Andean and 24th *Méndez Arcos* Ranger Infantry Regiments, the 2nd *Topater* Amoured Battalion and the 1st *Camacho* Artillery Regiment;

The 3rd Division (HQ Villamontes) is made up of the 20th *Padilla*, 27th *Campero* and 33rd *Chorolque* Infantry Regiments;

The 4th Division (HQ Camiri) comprises the 6th *Campos* and 11th *Boquerón* Infantry, the 2nd *Avaroa* Cavalry and the 3rd *Bullaín* Artillery Regiments;

The 5th Division (HQ Roboré) consists of the 9th *Warnes* and 12th *Florida* Infantry and the 6th *Castrillo* Cavalry regiments;

The 6th Division (HQ Trinidad) comprises the 11th *Bagé* and 20th *Jordán* Infantry and the 2nd *Ballivián* Cavalry Regiments;

Bolivian infantry with Kürassier tank destroyer of the 1st* Tarapacá *Armoured Battalion
(A. J. Risseeuw)

The 7th Division (HQ Cochabamba) is made up of the 2nd *Sucre* Infantry, the 19th *Capitan Victor Ustares* Andean and the 26th *René Barrientos* Motorised Infantry Regiments;

The 8th Division (HQ Santa Cruz) consists of the 7th *Azurduy* and 27th *Manchego* Ranger Infantry and the 8th *Braun* Cavalry Regiments;

The new 9th Division (HQ San Buenaventura) is still in process of formation.

The 10th Division (HQ Tupiza) has the 4th *Loa* Infantry and the 7th *Chichas* Cavalry Regiments as its only embodied units.

Although each division has an establishment of three infantry regiments, a cavalry or armoured unit, an artillery regiment and an engineer unit, it will be noted that only two of the ten formations now in existence approach their full authorised allocation of units and several are virtually skeletonised.

Army level troops include the 1st *Colorados* Infantry and the 4th *Ingavi* Mechanised Cavalry Regiments, which together perform ceremonial functions at La Paz, the Parachute Battalion of the *Centro de Instrucción de Tropas Especiales* at Cochabamba and an Engineer Command made up of the 1st *Pando* Engineer Regiment, with battalions at La Paz and Santa Cruz, the 2nd *General Román* Engineer Battalion at La Paz, the 4th *Alto de la Alianza* Egineer Battalion at Riberalta, the 5th *Ovando* Engineer Battalion at Sucre and the 6th *Riosinho* Engineer Battalion at Cobija.

The Army is equipped with the Swiss SiG 510 rifle, the Belgian FN FAL (manufactured in Argentina) and the German G3, all in 7.62 mm calibre and the Israeli Galil rifles, in 5.56 mm. The US M3A1 sub-machine gun in 0.45-inch calibre and the Israeli Uzi sub-machine guns in 9 mm are both in use. Infantry support weapons include the US Browning M2 machine gun in 0.50-inch calibre and the M1917 and M1919, both in 0.30-inch, in addition to numbers of Argentine assembled FN MAGs and Swiss SiG 710s, both in 7.62 mm, the US M40A1 106 mm RCL; the French Brandt mortar in both 60 mm and 81 mm and the US M2 4.2-inch mortar. Armoured fighting vehicles in service include 36 examples of the Austrian Kürassier tank destroyer, plus 24 of the Brazilian EE-9 Cascavel and 15 of the US Cadillac Gage V-150 Commando armoured cars. There are also 24 Brazilian EE-11 Urutú 24 Swiss Mowag Roland and 60 US M113 APCs. Artillery consists of six examples apiece of the US M101 105 mm and M116 75 mm howitzers, 12 of the Swedish Bofors 75 mm L/40 field gun (obtained second-hand from Argentina) and approximately 50 Vickers 75 mm guns and a dozen 105 mm howitzers of Chaco War vintage.

Bolivian infantry with Mowag Rowland APC (A. J. Risseeuw)

The Army also operates single examples of the Beech Super King Air 200, the Cessna 421 and the Piper Cheyenne although there is no army air corps as such.

Aspiring officers must complete the five-year course of the *Colegio Militar Coronel Gualberto Villaroel* at La Paz before commissioning in the rank of second-lieutenant. Following a period of practical experience with units, company grade officers undergo specialized training at the *Escuela de Especialización de Armas General José Ballivián* at Cochabamba, engineer officers undergoing a professional course at the *Escuela de Ingeniería General José Manuel Pando* at La Paz. For promotion to field grade or staff appointments, the appropriate courses of the *Escuela de Comando y Estado Mayor Mariscal Andrés Santa Cruz* at Cochabamba must be successfully completed. Most officers receive part of their training abroad, either in the United States or in neighbouring countries, principally Argentina and Peru.

NCOs are all volunteers, recruited on completion of their period of compulsory military service. These receive their training at the *Escuela de Clases Sargento Maximiliano Paredes* at Cochabamba, with specialist training at the *Escuela de Especialización de Armas.*

Conscripts receive their training mainly in the units to which they are assigned. At Cochabamba there is the *Centro de Instrucción de Tropas Especiales*, which has an attached paratroop battalion. The *Centro de Instrucción de Operaciones en la Selva* at Riberalta trains troops in jungle warfare. There is a special forces school, with US instructors, at Santa Cruz.

Navy

Manpower:	4000 (including Marines)
Major units:	19 small lake and river patrol craft

	1 oceangoing freighter
	2 transport/training launches
	2 hospital launches
	1 surveying launch
Marines:	1 battalion and 5 independent companies
Aircraft:	North American AT-6 Cessna U206

Before the loss of its sea coast, Bolivia maintained a small naval force. However, following Bolivia's defeat in the Pacific War and the consequent loss of its litoral its Navy ceased to exist. Although Bolivia had lost its sea coast to Chile, the recovery of an outlet to the sea became the cornerstone of Bolivian foreign policy. To underline this, the *Fuerza Fluvial y Lacustre* (River and Lake Force) was created in 1963 under the jurisdiction of the Ministry of Defence to patrol inland waterways and Lake Titicaca. Later in the same year, the *Dirección General de Capitanías de Puerto* (General Directorate of Port Captaincies) was also created as a subordinate element of the *Fuerza Naval y Lacustre* (as it was then known). In 1966 the title of the force was changed to *Fuerza Naval Boliviana* (Bolivian Naval Force), personnel being sent to Argentina for training. In 1982 a further change of title established this force as the *Armada Boliviana* (Bolivian Navy).

The Bolivian Navy currently numbers approximately 4000 all ranks and is deployed between five naval districts.

The 1st Naval District (HQ Riberalta) covers the Beni river with the 1st Flotilla, consisting of eight patrol launches and a floating medical clinic.

The 2nd Naval District (HQ Tiquina) covers the northern portion of Lake Titicaca with the 2nd Flotilla, comprising three patrol launches, the floating medical clinic *Julián Apaza* and a hydrographic research vessel.

The 3rd Naval District (HQ Guayaramerín) patrols the Madre de Dios river with the 3rd Flotilla, made up of four launches.

The 4th Naval District (HQ Guaqui) covers the southern portion of Lake Titicaca with the 4th Flotilla, which consists of only two launches.

The 5th Naval District (HQ Puerto Suárez) patrols the Upper Paraguay river with the 5th Flotilla, which also comprises only two launches.

In addition to the various river and lake craft, mostly falling in the 50 to 100-ton displacement range, which make up the five flotillas, there are two 50-ton transport launches with a secondary training function: *Almirante Grau* and *Mariscal Santa Cruz*, plus some very small launches used for subsidiary duties, and also the 6400-ton oceangoing freighter *Libertador Bolívar*, received as a gift from Venezuela in 1977 and used for commercial purposes with a naval crew, operating either from Rosario in Argentina or Nueva Palmira in Uruguay, where Bolivia enjoys customs-free zones, by arrangement with the respective governments.

The principal naval installation is at Tiquina, where there are repair facilities for the small craft of the Lake Titicaca Flotilla. There are also naval stations at Guaqui, Guyaramerín, Puerto Busch, Puerto Horquilla, Puerto Suárez, Puerto Villaroel, Riberalta and Trinidad.

The Bolivian Navy also includes a Marine Corps of which the principal unit is the *Almirante Grau* Marine Infantry Battalion based at Tinquina. Each of the five Naval Districts also has a Marine Security Detachment and there is a miniscule Naval Air Service, equipped with two ex-Argentine North American AT-6s and a single Cessna 206G.

Although naval personnel continue to receive part of their training in Argentina, there are now both a Naval School (*Escuela Naval Militar*) and a Naval Staff College (*Escuela de Guerra Naval*), both located at Tiquina and established with the assistance of an Argentine naval mission.

Air Force

Manpower:	4000
Major units:	3 air brigades, comprising: 2 fighter groups 2 tactical support groups 1 helicopter group 1 special operations group 1 transport group
Fighters:	North American F-86F Canadair AT-33A
Tactical support aircraft:	North American AT-6G
Helicopters:	Aérospatiale Lama and Helibras Gavião

	Bell 212
	Hughes 500M
Photographic:	Cessna 402
	Learjet 25B
Transports:	Lockheed C-130
	Fokker F.27
	Beech King Air 200
	Cessna 414
	Convair 440 and 580
	Douglas C-47 and C-54
	IAI Arava
	Pilatus PC-6B
	Sabreliner
	Lockheed Electra
Training:	Aerotec Uirapurú
	Cessna T-41
	North American T-6
	Pilatus PC-7
	Cessna 152
Ground forces:	1 base defence regiment
	1 paratroop battalion
AA Artillery:	Oerlikon twin 20 mm guns

A military aviation school was established in 1915, although the first aircraft were not acquired until four years later, various additional aircraft being obtained during the next five years. In 1925, with hostilities between Bolivia and Paraguay looming, the *Escuela de Aviación* was put on a less precarious footing and during the same year orders were placed for sufficient aircraft to form a combat group, plus additional material for the training group. During the Chaco War the Bolivian Air Corps established aerial superiority from the outset, being opposed by a numerically inferior and less well equipped Paraguayan air arm. No additional aircraft were acquired during the immediate post-war period although an Italian aviation mission operated in the country between 1937 and 1941. A US aviation mission replaced the Italian one in 1941 and reorganised the *Cuerpo de Aviación* as the *Fuerza Aérea Boliviana*, although the force remained subordinate to the Army. Following the Japanese attack on Pearl Harbor, the Bolivian tin mines were considered a strategic target and a number of aircraft were received from the United States under Lend Lease. With the end of the Second World War and in particular following Bolivia's signature of the Rio Treaty of 1947, considerable quantities of additional equipment were acquired from the United States.

Cadets of the Bolivian Air Force's German Busch Flying School

Following the 1952 revolution the regular armed forces ceased to exist, at least officially, for several weeks and for several years afterwards the Air Force remained little more than a token force, most of its flying personnel having been the victims of political purges. However, in 1957, the *Fuerza Aérea* finally became completely independent with coequal status with the Army. While

F-86 Sabre fighter aircraft of the Bolivian Air Force

the 1960s were a fairly lean period for the FAB, the 1970s saw some considerable, if unspectacular expansion.

The Bolivian Air Force currently numbers some 4000 all ranks, manning a total of approximately 200 largely obsolete aircraft and is organised in three brigades comprising a total of nine groups.

The Ist Air Brigade (HQ Walter Arce Air Base, El Alto, La Paz) combines the 31st Fighter Air Group equipped with 18 Lockheed T-33As, with the 71st Air Transport Group, incorporating the military airline TAM (*Transporte Aéreo Militar*) and operating two Lockheed C-130s, six Fokker F.27s, four Convair 440s, seven Douglas C-47s, a single C-54, four IAI Aravas and 17 Pilatus PC-6Bs. El Alto also accommodates the National Photogrammetric Service equipped with two examples apiece of the Cessna 402 and the Learjet 25B and the VIP Transport Squadron equipped with a single Lockheed Electra, two Sabreliners, two Beech King Air 220s and single examples of the Cessna 404 and 421B, together with two Bell 212 helicopters.

Bolivian T-33A and F-86 aircraft

The IInd Air Brigade (HQ Colcapirúa Air Base, Cochabamba) combines the 41st Tactical Air Group (Capitán Arturo Valle Air Base, El Tejar, Tarija) equipped with six armed North American AT-6 trainers and the similarly equipped 52nd Tactical Air Group (Trinidad) with the 91st Air Cover Group (Colcapirúa), a general purpose helicopter unit, operating eight SA.315B Lamas and eight similar HB.315 Gaviãos.

The IIIrd Air Brigade (HQ El Trompillo Air Base, Santa Cruz) consists of the 32nd Fighter Air Group (El Trompillo) operating four elderly F-86F Sabre fighters and 14 armed AT-33N trainers, the 61st Special Operations Air Group (Roboré) equipped with ten Hughes 500M helicopter gunships and the flying elements of the Military Aviation College based at El Trompillo

***Fokker F.27 transport aircraft of the Bolivian military airline TAM* (A. J. Risseeuw)**

***Bolivian Lockheed C-130 Hercules transport aircraft* (Lockheed Aircraft)**

and comprising the 11th and 21st Air Training Groups equipped with 12 examples apiece of the Cessna A-152 and the Aerotec T-23 Uirapurú, six SIAI SF.260Cs, nine Cessna T-41s and 22 Pilatus PC-7s.

A few miscellaneous light aircraft perform liaison and general purpose functions in support of the operational elements.

The Air Force also includes an infantry regiment for air base defence and a paratroop battalion and controls all air defence artillery units which are equipped with approximately 50 twin 20 mm Oerlikon AA guns dating from the mid-1930s.

All enlisted personnel of the Air Force are volunteers.

Officers complete the five-year course of the Military College at La Paz before commissioning into the Air Force with the rank of second-lieutenants. Flying officers then transfer to the Flying School at Santa Cruz for specialist training. Officers receive additional mid-career post-graduate training at the Command and Staff School at Cochabamba and many also pursue additional courses of study abroad.

The Bolivian Air Force is currently in critical need of new combat equipment, a reported order for 12 Mirage 50s, in 1985, having failed to materialise. Bolivia has been reported to be interested in the acquisition of a small number of Argentinian IA-58 Pucará ground-attack aircraft and IA-63 Pampa trainer/light strike aircraft.

Paramilitary forces

Manpower: 14,000

The Bolivian National Police or *Carabineros* has been in existence, under various names, since 1886. In 1930, a General Directorate of Police was established at La Paz to serve as a national police headquarters and in 1937 the force acquired its present title. Until the revolution of 1952 the *Carabineros* were subordinate to the Ministry of National Defence, effectively forming an adjunct of the Army. Although still preserving a paramilitary organisation and available as a reserve for the Army in case of war, the *Carabineros* now come under the jurisdiction of the Ministry of the Interior. The force is the sole law enforcement agency having nation-wide jurisdiction and includes the Customs Police, which also performs frontier guard duties.

The current strength of the *Carabineros*, which has more than doubled during the past ten years, is approximately 14,000. Approximately 80% of this number are uniformed, the remainder carrying out crime detection, forensic science, administrative or logistic functions. The force is heavily involved in civic action in the more remote and less populous regions of the country. Approximately 50% of the total uniformed strength of the force is stationed at La Paz, where over 60% of its non-uniformed elements are located. The basic unit is the brigade, one of which is stationed in each of the country's nine departments. Each brigade is divided into an urban and provincial (rural) command. In addition to the brigade stationed at La Paz, there are also two separate regiments of *Carabineros* which form a rapid intervention force. There are also special detachments located in the departments of Santa Cruz and Potosí. In addition to their internal security and law enforcement functions, the *Carabineros* also man a total of 27 frontier posts. The force is armed basically with side arms and obsolete infantry weapons including a small quantity of heavy and light machine guns and 60 mm mortars. Recruitment is entirely voluntary. Enlisted personnel receive most of their training on the job during the first four months after enlistment. There is a Police Academy, offering a four-year course for officers but many of the officer personnel have been seconded from the Army. A US police mission has been active since 1956 and has raised standards considerably. Chosen personnel are sent on training courses either to the United States or to the larger neighbouring countries.

A Traffic Police force was established in 1939 under the jurisdiction of the Ministry of the Interior and consists of a Highway Patrol and traffic direction police in the major population centres. Its functions are confined to the administration of traffic law. Only officers of this force are normally armed although some obsolete small arms and infantry support weapons of the type used by the *Carabineros* are available at its headquarters. A peculiarity of this force, which numbers about 600 all ranks, is that all motorcycle patrol men are commissioned officers.

All municipalities are entitled to raise local police forces for the enforcement of local ordinances. Only La Paz has so far established such a force. The La Paz Municipal Police numbers approximately 400 uniformed and 100 non-uniformed members, none of whom are armed and whose functions are in effect limited to the enforcement of parking regulations and local bye-laws.

The Revolutionary Militias, which were of considerable importance during the 1950s and for a brief period replaced the national armed forces, have declined in importance and now function largely as the strong-arm adjunct of the trade union movement.

Sources of defence material supply and current requirements

France and Germany were the major suppliers of defence material to Bolivia during the first quarter of the 20th century. In the mid-1920s, an impressive contract for the supply of war material was signed with Vickers of Great Britain and during the Chaco War, equipment was obtained from whatever sources were available, small arms being purchased in Czechoslovakia, Denmark, France and the United States. During the late 1930s, armoured vehicles were purchased from Italy and anti-aircraft and anti-tank guns from Switzerland. From 1941 onwards almost all equipment obtained came from the United States which remained the main source of supply until the mid-1970s although quantities of second-hand equipment, including artillery pieces, were acquired as gifts from Argentina, from which country quantities of small arms ammunition were also purchased. Brazil also provided some second-hand equipment, including aircraft, during the 1970s. During the past ten years, Bolivia has purchased quantities of weapons and equipment from Switzerland, France, Germany, Spain, Israel and more recently Brazil, Taiwan and Austria.

During the Chaco War Bolivia manufactured hand grenades but current military production is confined to explosives. It is hoped to expand this to include the manufacture of small arms ammunition.

Although the equipment of the Army has been largely brought up to date by recent purchases, Bolivia still lacks an adequate armoured force and the existing artillery equipment is largely obsolete. The Air Force also requires modern combat equipment and tactical support aircraft. Anti-aircraft artillery, which is operated by the Air

Force, is also totally obsolete and in urgent need of replacement. The country's poor economic position is however likely to remain an obstacle to any major equipment acquisitions in the foreseeable future.

Summary and prospects

With the exception of their early successes in repelling Argentine and Peruvian invasions during the first half of the 19th century, the Bolivian armed forces have a dismal history of almost unbroken defeat in each foreign war in which they have engaged, almost all of which have also resulted in major losses of territory. Successive territorial losses, not only to their more powerful neighbours, but even to Paraguay, a grindingly poor country with only 30% of Bolivia's population, have engendered an almost pathological fear of further expansionist ambitions on the part of the country's neighbours. Bolivia's present frontiers are however relatively secure and few if any of the neighbouring countries would appear to have designs on Bolivia's remaining territory. Although actually poor, the country is potentially extremely wealthy if its enormous undeveloped natural resources can be exploited. Still extremely thinly populated, demographic pressures are also unlikely to be a problem in the foreseeable future.

The interception and capture of Ernesto "Ché" Guevara's guerrilla band in 1967 was an important morale booster for the Bolivian Army as was the lack of success which Guevara's attempts to plant Cuban-style Communism received among the peasants of Bolivia's north-eastern lowlands. Internal instability however remains a major problem, although following the major upheaval of the 1952 revolution, this once more tends to be largely limited to the expression of the conflicting ambitions of factions within the armed forces. The major and most powerful disaffected civilian social group continues to be the highly trade-unionised tin miners.

Bolivia has recently earned considerable international opprobrium by the apparent indifference of successive governments to the export of cocaine, the García Meza administration (1980-82) in particular almost openly conniving at the traffic in this drug. The administration of Dr Paz Estensorro has made considerable efforts to control the narcotics traffic and successfully sought United States assistance in this respect in 1986. Whatever the morality of the situation, the large-scale exploitations of the cocaine trade has revolutionised the Bolivian economy, which as a result has retained some buoyancy during a period which saw the contraction of the economies of many Latin American States, much of the new-found wealth being channelled into a long-overdue re-equipment of the armed forces. In part due to the difficulty in finding suppliers, this has resulted in a heterogeneous selection of ill-assorted material, rivalled only by that of the Peruvian armed forces and from a logistic point of view possessed of a similarly inherent potential for chaos. The Bolivian Army of the late 1980s is nevertheless better equipped than at any time since the Chaco War and from being the most derided in continental South America must now be treated with a certain respect. The Air Force is however in urgent need of re-equipment and the Navy remains essentially a token force for the policing of inland waterways.

BRAZIL

(República Federativa do Brasil)

Area: 3,290,000 sq miles (8,521,100 sq km)
Population: 140,000,000
Total armed forces: 285,900
Reserves: 850,000
Available manpower: 12,000,000
Paramilitary forces: 240,000
GNP: $214,705 million (1985)
Defence Expenditure: $1,055 million (1984)

Introduction

Measuring over 2700 miles from north to south and as much from east to west at its broadest point, Brazil is the largest country of South America and the fifth largest in the world. Sharing frontiers with every country of South America except Chile and Ecuador, it is bounded by Colombia to the north-west, Venezuela and the Guianas to the north, Argentina and Uruguay to the south, Paraguay and Bolivia to the south-west and Peru to the west. Brazil is also the most populous country of Latin America, approximately half of its people being of European extraction, 33% mixed Negro and European, 10% pure Negro and the remainder mostly aboriginal Indians with small Asian – mainly Japanese and Korean – minorities, located mainly in the south and south-east.

Proverbially the world's largest coffee producer, Brazil also exports other tropical products, including sugar, cotton and cocoa. Industrialisation is well advanced, industrial production now satisfying most of domestic demand and providing a healthy surplus for export. A major economic and strategic weakness in the past has been the lack of significant deposits of petroleum, the country's dependence on imported oil being somewhat reduced by the development of vegetable-based fuel substitutes and additives. The recent discovery of significant off-shore oil deposits to the east of the continental bulge promises to remedy even this deficiency.

Brazil was first visited by Portuguese explorers in 1500 and although a viceroy was appointed in 1572, throughout the colonial period Portuguese rule remained considerably less organised and rigid than that of the Spaniards in the parts of Latin America which they dominated. Independence occurred in 1821 when Prince Pedro of Portugal, whom the Portuguese king had left as regent on his return to Portugal from which he had been forced to flee by Napoleon, was crowned as Emperor of Brazil without effective opposition from the mother country.

A war with Argentina between 1826 and 1828 resulted in the secession of Uruguay and its establishment as an independent Republic and following a military revolt Pedro abdicated in 1831 in favour of his five-year-old son, a regent ruling on behalf of the infant Emperor until his 15th birthday. A period of semi-anarchy, characterised by separatist revolts, came to an end shortly after the assumption of the throne by the new Emperor Pedro II who proved an enlightened monarch, his reign seeing much progress and large-scale European immigration. During this period Brazil fought a brief war against the Argentine tyrant Rosas in 1852 and between 1865 and 1870 joined with Argentina and Uruguay in the bloody war of the Triple Alliance against Paraguay. Pedro eventually came into conflict with the land-owning aristocracy when he attempted to emancipate the Negro slaves and was forced to abdicate in 1889 when a republic was declared. For the first five years of its existence, the Brazilian republic was under military government, a civilian administration being finally installed in 1894.

Brazil joined with the Allies in both World Wars despite being ruled by the neo-fascist dictator Getulio Vargas between 1930 and 1945. In 1964 the armed forces assumed power following what was perceived as an excessively leftward trend in the government of President Goulart. A new constitution which drastically curtailed civil rights was adopted in 1967 and the armed forces remained in power until 1984 when Tancredo Neves became the country's first democratically-elected President in over two decades. Senhor Neves died before he could be installed as President and his Vice-President José Sarney assumed the Presidency in March 1985.

Brazil is a federal republic of 22 states, four federal territories and one federal district. Executive power is vested in the President, who selects his own cabinet. There is a bicameral federal legislature, each state having its own elected governor and legislature.

The left-wing threat which provided the pretext for the seizure of power by the military in 1964 has been effectively defused. Although low-level rural and urban guerrilla activity has been replaced by a growing national crime wave of epidemic proportions, the country appears more politically stable than many of its neighbours.

As the only Portuguese-speaking country in a predominantly Spanish-speaking continent Brazil is regarded with some suspicion by all neighbouring countries. The threat of Brazilian expansionism, which is a popular myth in Spanish-speaking South America, would however appear to be more apparent than real.

Traditionally rivalry with Argentina for dominance within the continent appears to have lapsed, with the tacit agreement of the respective spheres of influence of the two countries. Mutual co-operation in the military field has been improving since the mid-1970s and until the South Atlantic War upset the delicate strategic balance in the area, the development of a South Atlantic Treaty Organisation under the joint leadership of Argentina and Brazil and with the active encouragement of the United States, appeared to be well under way. Brazil offered limited vocal and some material support to Argentina during the Anglo-Argentine War.

Structure of the armed forces

The President is supreme commander of the armed forces but his authority in this respect is less absolute than in the case of most Latin American countries, being highly circumscribed by the powers of the legislature. The only exception is in conditions of extreme national emergency, which are explicitly defined.

There are separate Army, Navy and Air Force Ministries, reflecting extreme inter-service rivalry which has militated against the creation of an over-all Ministry of National Defence. Although there is a combined General Staff, its functions are restricted to planning and it has neither executive, administrative nor operational command functions. Each of the armed forces also maintains its own general staff.

The President is assisted in his functions as supreme commander by the National Security Council, the combined General Staff and the individual general staffs of the three armed forces. The National Security Council is a large and unwieldy body, made up of the President, Vice-President, the entire cabinet, the combined General Staff, the three service chiefs of staff and senior personnel of the three armed forces.

Each of the armed forces divides the country geographically for administrative and operational purposes on a largely non-coincident basis.

The Army divides the country into 11 Military Regions of which the 1st (HQ Rio de Janeiro) covers the states of Espiritu Santo, Guanabara and Rio de Janeiro; the 2nd (HQ São Paulo) the state of São Paulo; the 3rd (HQ Porto Alegre) the state of Rio Grande do Sul; the 4th (HQ Juiz de Fora) the state of Minas Gerais; the 5th (HQ Curitiba) the states of Paraná and Santa Catarina; the 6th (HQ Sao Salvador) the states of Bahía and Sergipe; the 7th (HQ Recife) the states of Rio Grande do Norte, Paraíba, Pernambuco and Alagoas; the 8th (HQ Manáus) the states of Acre, Amapá, Amazonas, Pará, Rondônia and Roraima; the 9th (HQ Corumbá) the state of Mato Grosso; the 10th (HQ Fortaleza) the states of Ceará, Maranhão and Piauí; and the 11th (HQ Brasília) the Federal District of Brasília and the state of Goiás.

The Navy observes its own territorial organisation with seven Naval Districts of which the 1st (HQ Rio de Janeiro) covers the northern third of the south-east coast, the 2nd (HQ São Salvador) the southern half of the east coast, the 3rd (HQ Recife) the northern half of the east coast and the continental "bulge", the 4th (HQ Belêm) the north-east coast and the Amazon, the 5th (HQ Florianópolis) the southern third of the south-east coast and the 6th (HQ São Paulo) the central third of the south-east coast. The 7th Naval District (HQ Brasília) consists of Naval Headquarters and apart from a Marine security group contains no operational elements.

The Air Force, for its part, has seven Regional Air Commands of which the Ist (HQ Belêm) covers the states of Pará and Maranhão and the Federal Territory of Amapá; the IInd (HQ Recife) the states of Pernambuco, Paraíba, Rio Grande do Norte, Piauí, Alagoas, Sergipe, Bahía and the Federal Territory of Fernando de Noronha; the IIIrd (HQ Rio de Janeiro) the states of Rio de Janeiro, Espirito Santo, Minas Gerais and the islands of Trinidade and Martín Vaz; the IVth (HQ Sao Paulo) the states of São Paulo and southern Mato Grosso; the Vth (HQ Canoas) the states of Rio Grande do Sul, Paraná and Santa Catarina; the VIth (HQ Brasília) the federal capital and the states of Goiás and western Mato Grosso; and the VIIth (HQ Manáus) the states of Amazonas, Acre and Rondônia and the Federal Territory of Roraima.

Since 1908 military service has been nominally compulsory for all fit males between the ages of 21 and 45. In practice, service is highly selective, only slightly more than 11% of those nominally liable serving for nine to 12 months, after which they pass to the First Line reserve for eight and subsequently to the Second Line reserve for 14 years. First Line reservists are nominally liable to an additional two to four weeks annual full-time training but this provision does not seem to be enforced. Almost all conscripts are assigned to the Army and even in this service more than 60% of the other ranks are long-service volunteer professionals.

Each of the armed forces maintains its own comprehensive system of training establishments, besides which there is a tri-service staff college, the *Escola Superior de Guerra*, located at Rio de Janeiro.

Army

Manpower: 182,900

Formations: 7 geographical commands comprising 8 divisions, further divided into:
1 armoured cavalry brigade
4 mechanised cavalry brigades
3 armoured infantry brigades
10 motorised infantry brigades
3 infantry brigades
1 mountain brigade
1 paratroop brigade
2 jungle brigades
1 mixed brigade

Major units: 1 Presidential Guard battalion
65 infantry battalions (incl 7 armoured, 26 motorised, 3 mountain and 7 jungle)
3 paratroop battalions
3 local defence battalions
1 special forces battalion
6 frontier battalions
4 tank regiments
15 cavalry regiments (2 Guard, 3 armoured and 10 mechanised)
20 artillery groups (incl 1 airborne, 1 mountain, 4 S/P and 5 medium)
2 air defence groups
7 coast defence groups
7 combat engineer battalions
4 combat engineer companies
2 railway battalions
9 construction engineer battalions

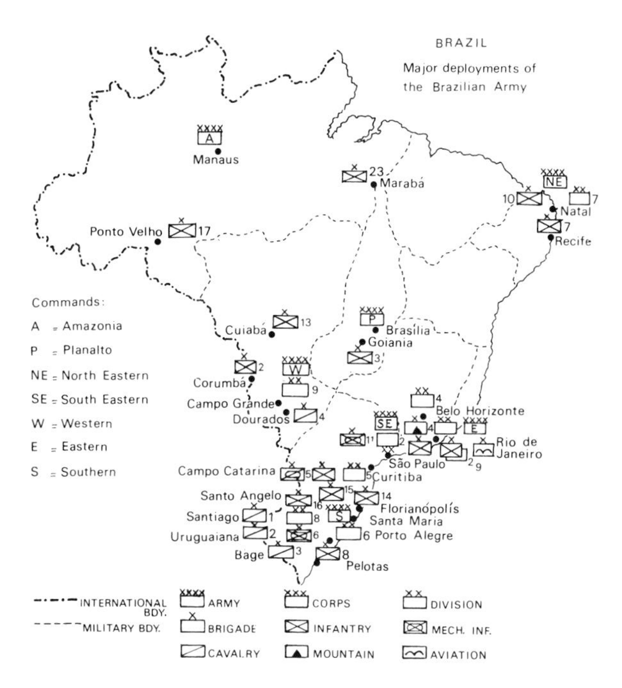

AFVs: M4 Sherman medium tanks (stored)
X-1A, X-1A2, M3A1, M41 and M41B light tanks
EE-9 Cascavel and M8 armoured cars
M113 and EE-11 Urutú APCs

Artillery: M2A1 and M101 105 mm howitzers
M7 and M108 105 mm SPH
M114 155 mm howitzers

Air defence weapons: Oerlikon 35 mm
Bofors L/60, L/70 and M1 40 mm
M118 90 mm guns (stored)

Missiles: Cobra ATGWs
Roland and Hawk SAMs

Due to the peculiar circumstances of Brazil's independence from Portugal, the Portuguese forces in the country became overnight the Army of the New Empire of Brazil. The Brazilian armed forces were involved in wars against Argentina in 1825-28 and again in 1851-52 and in 1865 joined in alliance the Argentina and Uruguay against the Paraguayan tyrant Francisco Solano López. Brazil emerged victorious from the five-year long war of the Triple Alliance but at the cost of 40,000 dead and $300 million in cash.

In 1905 Marshal Hermes de Fonseca, as Minister of War, embarked on the serious reorganisation of the Brazilian Army but when Brazil declared war on the Central Powers in October 1917, the Army had still not reached a stage of development which would have permitted the dispatch of an expeditionary force to Europe and active Brazilian participation in the First World War was confined to the naval level. The lessons of the First World War reinforced the growing French influence which had been noted in the Brazilian Army for over 30 years and in 1920 a French military mission was contracted to complete the modernisation of the Army. This continued to function until shortly before the outbreak of the Second World War in 1939.

Brazil declared war on Germany and Italy (though not on Japan, in deference to the large Japanese minority resident in southern Brazil) in August 1942 and quantities of Lend-Lease material began to pour into the country. A Brazilian Expeditionary Division was formed and this sailed for Europe in July 1944, entering service on the Italian front in September. A United States military mission was active in Brazil between 1948 and 1960, its influence largely supplanting all residual French influences.

In 1967 the Army underwent a major reorganisation, the existing armoured division, four mechanised divisions and seven infantry divisions being disbanded and replaced by eight "army divisions", each to consist of two to three brigades, each in turn to comprise three battalions of infantry or regiments of cavalry, a mechanised cavalry reconnaissance squadron, a group of artillery, an anti-aircraft battery, a battalion or company apiece of engineers and signals and a logistic battalion. The four existing army corps now became "armies", the 1st Army (HQ Rio de Janeiro) covering the 1st and 4th Military Regions with two divisions, the 2nd Army (HQ São Paulo) covering the 2nd and 9th Military Regions with a single division; the 3rd Army (HQ Porto Alegre) covering the 3rd and 5th Military Regions with three divisions and the 4th Army (HQ Recife) covering the 6th and 7th Military Regions with only one division. There were also the Amazon and Planalto commands, which were not subordinate to any of the army or divisional commands,

Brazilian armoured infantry disembarking from M113 APC

plus an independent armoured cavalry brigade and a paratroop brigade at Rio de Janeiro. In 1985 a further reorganisation under the PLAN FT90 replaced the "armies" with Military Commands and involved some minor redeployments of units.

The Brazilian Army currently consists of approximately 182,900 all ranks and is organised into both garrison and manoeuvre elements.

Eastern Military Command (HQ Rio) embraces the 1st and 4th Military Regions and is garrisoned by the 1st Local Defence Battalion and 3rd Local Defence Company, the 2nd Guards Cavalry Regiment, the 1st, 2nd, 3rd, 8th and 10th Motorised Coast Artillery and 1st Anti-Aircraft Groups and the 1st Army Signals, 19th Logistic and 1st Military Police Battalions. Its tactical manoeuvre elements are the 1st and 4th Divisions, the 9th Motorised Infantry Training Brigade and the unnumbered Paratroop Brigade.

The 1st Division (HQ Rio) consists of the 1st Motorised Infantry Brigade (HQ Petrópolis) with the 21st, 22nd and 32nd Motorised Infantry Battalions, 1st Mechanised Cavalry Squadron, 21st Field Artillery Group, 21st AA Battery and 21st Logistic Battalion and the 2nd Infantry Brigade (HQ Niterói) comprising the 3rd, 38th and 56th Infantry Battalions and the 30th Field Artillery Group, plus the 15th Mechanised Cavalry Regiment, 11th Medium Artillery Group, 1st Combat Engineer and 1st Logistic Battalions at divisional level.

The 4th Division (HQ Belo Horizonte) consists only of the 4th Mountain Infantry Brigade (HQ Belo Horizonte) with the 10th, 11th, 12th and 55th Mountain Infantry Battalions, the 4th Mechanised Cavalry Squadron and 4th Mountain Artillery Group, plus the 4th Combat Engineer Battalions, 4th Signals Company and 17th Logistic Battalion at divisional level.

The 9th Motorised Infantry Training Brigade (HQ Rio) consists of the 1st, 2nd and 57th Motorised Infantry Training Battalions, the 9th Cavalry Training Squadron, 31st Field Artillery Training Group, 9th AA Training Battery, 9th

Combat Engineer and 9th Signals Training Companies and the 25th Logistic Battalion while the Paratroop Brigade (HQ Rio) comprises the 25th, 26th and 27th Paratroop and 1st Special Forces Battalions, the 1st Airborne Cavalry Squadron, 8th Airborne Field Artillery Group, 1st Airborne Combat Engineer and 20th Airborne Signals Companies and the 20th Airborne Logistic Battalion.

South Eastern Military Command (HQ São Paulo) coincides with the 2nd Military Region and is garrisoned by the 37th and 39th Motorised Infantry Battalions, the 2nd Local Defence Battalion, the 2nd Frontier Company, the 6th Motorised Coast Artillery and 2nd Anti-Aircraft Groups and the 2nd Military Police Battalion. Its sole manoeuvre element is the 2nd Division (HQ São Paulo) which is made up of the 11th Armoured Infantry Brigade (HQ Campinas) with the 4th and 28th Armoured Infantry Battalions, the 2nd Tank Regiment, 11th Mechanised Cavalry Squadron, 2nd SP Field Artillery Group, 11th AA Battery and 2nd Logistic Battalion, and the 12th Infantry Brigade (HQ Caçapava) with the 2nd Rifle and the 5th and 6th Infantry Battalions, the 20th Field Artillery Group and the 12th AA Battery, plus the 12th Medium Artillery Group, 2nd Combat Engineer Battalion, 2nd Signals Company and 22nd Logistic Battalion at divisional level.

Western Military Command (HQ Campo Grande) coincides with the 9th Military Region and is garrisoned by the 9th Local Defence and 2nd Frontier Companies, the 6th Motorised Coast Artillery Group and the 9th Construction Engineer Battalion. Its manoeuvre element is the 9th Division (HQ Campo Grande) comprising the 13th Motorised Infantry Brigade (HQ Cuiabá) with the 44th, 58th and 66th Motorised Infantry Battalions, the 1st Company of the 4th Mechanised Reconnaissance Regiment and the 18th Field Artillery Group, and the 4th Mechanised Cavalry Brigade (HQ Dourados) with the 10th, 11th and 17th Mechanised Cavalry Regiments, the 1st Squadron of the 4th Mechanised Cavalry Regiment and the 9th Field Artillery Group, plus the 9th Combat Engineer Battalion, 14th Signals Company and 18th Logistic Battalion at divisional level. This Command also houses the 2nd Mixed Brigade (HQ Corumbá) which is made up of the 47th Infantry and 17th Rifle Battalions.

Southern Military Command (HQ Porto Alegre) embraces the 3rd and 5th Military Regions and is garrisoned by the 3rd Local Defence and 1st Frontier Battalions, the 1st Local Defence, 5th Frontier and 2nd and 3rd Infantry Companies, the 2nd Independent Cavalry Squadron, 14th Medium and 2nd Anti-Aircraft Artillery Groups and the 12th Combat and 5th Construction Engineer, 1st Railway, 1st and 3rd Signals and 3rd Military Police Battalions and the 5th Military Police Company. This Command contains the most important concentration of troops in the entire country, its manoeuvre elements consisting of the 3rd, 5th and 6th Divisions, plus the 1st, 2nd and 3rd Mechanised and the 5th Armoured Cavalry Brigades.

The 3rd Division (HQ Santa Maria) consists of the 6th Armoured Infantry Brigade (HQ Santa Maria) with the 7th and 29th Armoured Infantry Battalions, the 4th Tank Regiment, 3rd SP Field Artillery Group and 6th AA Battery and the 16th Motorised Infantry Brigade (HQ Santo Angelo) with the 17th and 61st Motorised Infantry Battalions, the 19th Mechanised Cavalry Regiment, the 3rd Squadron of the 5th Mechanised Cavalry Regiment and the 27th Field Artillery Group, plus the 29th Field and 13th Medium Artillery Groups, 3rd Combat Engineer Battalion, 3rd Signals Company and 4th Logistic Battalion at divisional level.

The 5th Division (HQ Curitiba) comprises the 5th Armoured Infantry Brigade (HQ Ponta Grossa) with the 13th and 20th Armoured Infantry Battalions, the 5th Tank Regiment, 5th Mechanised Cavalry Squadron, 5th SP Field Artillery Group, 5th Signals Company and 5th Logistic Battalion, the 14th Motorised Infantry Brigade (HQ Florianópolis) with the 23rd, 62nd and 63rd Motorised Infantry Battalions and the 28th Field Artillery Group, and the 15th Motorised Infantry Brigade (HQ Cascavel) with the 30th, 33rd and 34th Motorised Infantry Battalions, the 1st Squadron of the 21st Mechanised Cavalry Regiment, the 26th Field Artillery Group and the 15th Combat Engineer Company, plus the 15th Medium Artillery Group and 27th Logistic Battalion at divisional level.

The 6th Division (HQ Porto Alegre) consists of only the 8th Motorised Infantry Brigade (HQ Pelotas) with the 8th, 9th, 18th and 19th Motorised Infantry Battalions and the 6th Field

Artillery Group, plus the 16th Medium Artillery Group, the 6th Combat Engineer, 6th Signals and 8th Logistic Battalions at divisional level.

The 1st Mechanised Cavalry Brigade (HQ Santiago) comprises the 1st and 2nd Mechanised and 4th Armoured Cavalry Regiments, the 19th Field Artillery Group, 11th Signals Company and 9th Logistic Battalion; the 2nd Mechanised Cavalry Brigade (HQ Uruguaiana) consists of the 8th and 14th Mechanised and the 6th Armoured Cavalry Regiments, the 22nd Field Artillery Group, 3rd AA Battery, 12th Signals Company and 10th Logistic Battalion; the 3rd Mechanised Cavalry Brigade (HQ Bagé) is made up of the 3rd and 7th Mechanised and the 9th Armoured Cavalry Regiments, the 25th Field Artillery Group, 2nd AA Battery, 13th Signals Company and 3rd Logistic Battalion, while the 5th Armoured Cavalry Brigade (Santa Catarina) consists of the 24th Armoured Infantry Battalion, the 1st and 3rd Tank Regiments, the 1st SP Field Artillery Group, 5th AA Battery, 1st Signals Company and 1st Logistic Battalion.

North Eastern Military Command (HQ Recife) embraces the 6th, 7th and 10th Military Regions and is garrisoned by the 14th, 35th and 40th Infantry Battalions, the 19th, 23rd, 24th, 25th and 28th Rifle Battalions, the 1st Infantry and the 2nd, 4th and 10th Local Defence Companies, the 16th Mechanised Cavalry Regiment, 10th Field Artillery Group, 14th AA Battery, 4th Signals and 4th Military Police Battalions and the 6th Military Police Company. The manoeuvre element of this Command is the 7th Division (HQ Recife) made up of the 7th Motorised Infantry Brigade (HQ Natal) with the 15th, 16th and 31st Motorised Infantry Battalions and the 17th Field Artillery Group and the 10th Motorised Infantry Brigade (HQ Recife) with the 59th, 71st and 72nd Motorised Infantry Battalions, the 10th Mechanised Cavalry Squadron and the 7th Field Artillery Group, plus the 7th Combat Engineer Battalion, 7th Signals Company and 14th Logistic Battalion at divisional level. This Command also houses the 1st Construction Engineer Group (HQ João Pessoa) which is made up of the 1st, 2nd, 3rd and 4th Construction Engineer Battalions.

The M41 tank still forms the main equipment of the armoured units of the Brazilian Army

Planalto Military Command (HQ Brasília) coincides with the 11th Military Region and is garrisoned by the Presidential Guard Battalion, the 1st Guards Cavalry Regiment, the 2nd Railway Battalion and the Brasília Military Police Battalion. Its manoeuvre element is the 3rd Motorised Infantry Brigade (HQ Goiania) with the 36th, 41st, 42nd and 43rd Motorised Infantry Battalions, the 3rd Mechanised Cavalry Squadron, 32nd Field Artillery Group, 1st AA Battery, 23rd Combat Engineer and 6th Signals Companies and the 16th Logistic Battalion.

Amazonia Military Command (HQ Manáus) embraces the 8th and 12th Military Regions and is garrisoned by the 2nd and 4th Special Frontier Battalions, the 6th Jungle Infantry Battalion, the 5th Local Defence, 1st Signals and 12th Military Police Companies. Its manoeuvre elements consist of the 17th Infantry Brigade (HQ Porto Velho) with the 1st and 54th Infantry Battalions and the 23rd Jungle Infantry Brigade (HQ Marabá) with the 50th, 51st, 52nd and 53rd Jungle Infantry Battalions. Also subordinate to this Command are the Amapa Frontier Command (HQ Macapá), the sole unit of which is the 3rd Special Frontier Battalion; the Southern Frontier Command (HQ Tabatinga) which comprises the 1st Special Frontier Battalion and the 4th and 7th Frontier Platoons; and the Roraima Frontier Command (HQ Boa Vista) made up of the 2nd Special Frontier Battalion and the 12th Mechanised Cavalry Squadron. The Command also houses the 2nd Construction Engineer Group (HQ Manáus) which consists of the 5th, 6th and 7th Construction Engineer Battalions and the 1st Construction Engineer Company.

***Locally-developed EE-9 Cascavel armoured cars equip Brazil's mechanised cavalry* (Engesa)**

As will be noted the composition of the divisions and brigades varies considerably. An objective of the Plan FT90 is the standardisation of divisional and brigade structures and of their equipment, using primarily Brazilian produced material.

The infantry are primarily equipped with the 7.62 mm calibre Imbel M964 and M969 rifles, which are versions of the FN FAL, produced locally under licence. The main sub-machine gun in service is the locally-developed Uru in 9 mm calibre, supplemented by the Beretta M972, which is produced locally under licence; the Madsen M46, M50 and M53 types also being encountered. Infantry support weapons include the 7.62 mm FN FAP and MAG machine guns, the former manufactured locally by Imbel, the US Browning M1919A1 in 0.30-inch calibre and the M2 in 0.50-inch calibre, together with Imbel 60 mm, 81 mm and 120 mm and US M1 and M29 81 mm and M2 4.2-inch mortars. The main anti-armour weapons in use are locally-produced versions of the US 106 mm RCL and the Cobra ATGW, which is manufactured in Brazil under licence. Some TOW ATGWs are being obtained.

Armour consists mainly of 386 examples of the US M41A3 light tank, modified locally as the M41B, 80 and 30 examples respectively of the X1A and X1A2 modifications of the US M3 light tank, together with 140 examples of the unmodified M3A1. There are also 140 examples of the locally-designed EE-9 Cascavel and 30 of the US M8 armoured cars, plus 150 EE-11 Urutú wheeled APCs and some 300 US M113 tracked APCs. Approximately 60 examples of the US M4 Sherman medium tank are in storage.

The artillery is now largely equipped with locally-modified US M101A1 105 mm howitzers, in addition to examples of the original weapon and the similar M2A1, the total number of pieces of this calibre being approximately 420, plus 60 M108 and 10 M7 105 mm SPHs. There are also some 150 US M114A1 155 mm towed howitzers and locally-developed 108 mm and 114 mm rocket launchers.

The major air defence weapons are some 240 examples of the Bofors 40 mm L/70 and L/60 and of the US 40 mm M1, the former produced locally under licence, together with some 30 GDF-002 twin 35 mm pieces and an indeterminate number of locally-modified versions of the US M55 quadruple 0.50-inch calibre machine gun. There are also four tracked SP versions of the French Roland. Approximately 100 US M1A1 90 mm AA guns remain in storage.

While the Brazilian Air Force has jealously guarded its monopoly of Brazilian military aviation since its formation, it was announced in 1985 that the Army was establishing its own air service which was to be equipped solely with helicopters and in 1987 the first course of army pilots graduated from the flying school of the Brazilian Navy.

Although military service has been theoretically compulsory since 1908, some 50% of the Army's enlisted personnel still consists of long-service volunteers. Approximately 82,000 conscripts are however trained each year, the obligatory one-year period of training being reduced in practice to 43 weeks and divided into a basic period of orientation, known as "adaptation", followed by a period of training in a unit, referred to as "formation" and finally a test of assimilated information in operational training, known as "application". Although no external distinction is made between conscripts and volunteers, the former are regarded as transients who are not quite the equal of regular enlisted personnel. Conscripts generally tend to be drawn from the more deprived sections of society and receive training in basic skills, including literacy, if necessary, during their comparatively brief period of military service. Regular enlisted personnel follow basically the same pattern of initial training to that of the conscripts but continue their training in the specialist school of the arm or service to which they are assigned. There is a comprehensive selection of such specialist schools, most of them located in the vicinity of Rio de Janeiro, although the Jungle Warfare School is located at Manáus. There are also separate schools for the various ranks of NCO. Senior NCOs may also complete a course qualifying them for admission to the Military Academy and ultimate commissioning as officers.

Aspiring officers may commence their military education at the age of 11 or 12 in one of the nine *Colegios Militares*, originally founded for the education of the orphans of serving officers but

The M101 105 mm howitzer remains the principal weapon of the Brazilian field artillery

***The Avibras LM-07/36 70 mm MLR which supplements the M101 howitzer in the direct fire role* (Jane's Defence Weekly)**

now open to all on a competitive basis. These impart a high quality secondary education with a distinctly military flavour and are to some degree analogous to the US private military academies. On completion of their general education in the above establishments, students pass automatically to the *Escola Preparatoria de Cadetes do Exército* at Campinas, 100 km west of Rio de Janeiro, where they complete a three-year course of pre-military education. From there they pass directly to the Military Academy of Agulhas Negras, also at Campinas, which has a student body of about 3000. The basic course of the Military Academy is of four years duration, the first two of which are devoted to general subjects at university level, the second two years being devoted to purely military subjects.

On attaining the rank of captain, all officers must complete a command and staff course at the *Escola de Aperfeicoamento de Ofiçais*, which qualifies them for further promotion up to the rank of colonel. This completes the officer's compulsory professional education but those aspiring ultimately to the highest ranks may voluntarily undergo the course of the Command and Staff School, founded in 1905 and developed by the French military mission which functioned throughout the 1920s. This establishment also trains students from other countries, including Argentina, Bolivia, Colombia, Paraguay, Peru, Uruguay, Venezuela, Portugal and even the United States. Another training institution is the *Centro de Estudios do Pessoal*, to which selected officers may be sent for courses aimed basically at the development of above-average intellectual capacity. Of the many specialist schools, the Institute of Military Engineering offers a two-year technical course to officers, NCOs and civilians and a three-year professional course which is considered one of the best in the country. Only medical officers are recruited by direct entry and are commissioned without completing the full course of the Military Academy.

The summit of Brazil's very comprehensive military educational system is the joint service Superior War College, founded at Rio de Janeiro in 1949 under the advice of the US military mission and moved to Brasília in 1975.

Under the Plan FT90 the strength of the Brazilian Army is scheduled to increase to 296,000 by 1993. An assault rifle, based on the FNC, is

***The Avibras Astros II area-saturation MLR system in action* (Jane's Defence Weekly)**

under development and a new general-purpose machine gun, the Uirapurú, is entering service. The locally-developed EET-1 Osorio and MB-3 Tamoyo MBTs are scheduled to re-equip the tank and armoured cavalry units respectively during the 1990s, the XMP-1 Charrúa APC being designated as the ultimate replacement of the M113. The locally-developed Astros II MRL is also beginning to supplement the existing tube field artillery and both a towed and an SP 155 mm howitzer, based on the Austrian GH N-45, are under development.

Navy

Manpower: 50,300 (including Naval aviation and Marines)

Major units:
1 aircraft carrier
10 obsolete destroyers
6 missile frigates
1 training frigate

7 submarines
6 minesweepers
9 large patrol vessels
6 patrol craft
6 river patrol vessels
2 LSTs
4 attack transports

Marines: 1 amphibious division:
3 infantry battalions
1 artillery battalion
1 engineer battalion
1 service battalion
1 special operations battalion
10 regional groups

Naval aviation: 4 helicopter squadrons

Equipment: Sikorsky SH-34Ds and Js
Westland Wasp, Whirlwind and Lynx
Bell 206B Jet Rangers
AS.332 Super Puma and AS.350 Ecureuil

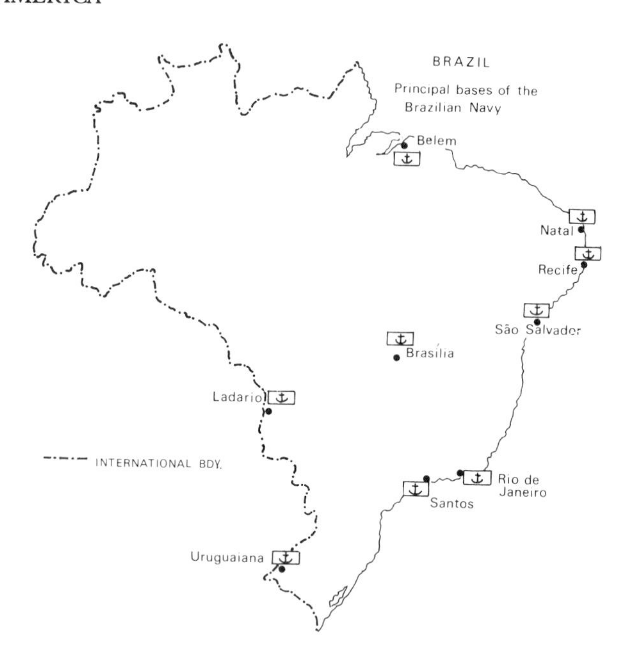

Three years after Brazil became independent the Uruguayan war between Brazil and the United Provinces of Rio de la Plata broke out, the Brazilian fleet blockading Buenos Aires and scoring several victories over the Argentinian fleet. Sporadic hostilities between Brazil and Argentina continued after the Uruguayan war ended in 1828, with occasional actions between vessels of the opposing navies, culminating finally in another Argentino-Brazilian war in 1852. Although allied with Argentina and Uruguay, the Brazilian Navy bore the brunt of the fighting in the Triple Alliance War against Paraguay of 1865-70 and Brazil entered the 1870s with the most powerful fleet in Latin America. Construction during the 1870s was however limited although the mid-1880s saw an increase in the number of major sea-going warships and the Brazilian Navy yielded its premier position to that of Chile. Frontier tensions between Argentina and Chile provoked a naval arms race between these two countries during the 1890s and the Brazilians, who felt themselves at an increasing relative disadvantage, embarked on an ambitious naval construction programme. Two "Dreadnought" type battleships were laid down in Great Britain in 1907 and when completed in 1910 were the most powerful warships afloat.

After entering the First World War on the side of the Allies in October 1917, a Brazilian naval squadron joined British and French forces in patrolling the north-west African coast in August 1918 and the two Brazilian dreadnoughts were preparing for service with the Grand Fleet when the Armistice put an end to hostilities. In 1922 a US naval mission arrived in Brazil and United States influence became predominant in the Brazilian Navy. Further construction programmes during the interwar years were largely frustrated by lack of funds and on the eve of the Second World War the Brazilian Navy was a notably less impressive force than it had been in 1914.

Considerable Lend-Lease aid was received from the United States almost immediately after Brazil became an active belligerent in August 1942. The efforts of the Brazilian Navy during the Second World War consisted principally of anti-submarine patrol and convoy escort duty in the South Atlantic. After the war the remaining antiquated material was largely replaced by US war-surplus equipment although six locally-built destroyers were completed in the early 1950s, three other destroyers having been built locally during the mid-1940s. In 1956, the Brazilian Navy acquired its first aircraft carrier with the purchase of HMS *Vengeance*, which was renamed *Minas Gerais*. During the mid-1960s the older existing material began to be replaced by a mixture of new construction and the continued transfer of modernised but essentially obsolescent US vessels. From the mid-

1960s the Brazilian Navy replaced that of Argentina as the most powerful naval force in Latin America although with the completion of its current construction programme the Argentinian Navy recovered its position of primacy in the late 1980s.

The Brazilian Navy currently consists of over 50,000 officers and ratings, manning a fleet devoted principally to anti-submarine training and built around the 15,900-ton light ASW carrier *Minas Gerais*. Reflecting the lessons of the Falklands War, it was announced in 1983 that this vessel would be refitted as an attack aircraft carrier, but at the time of writing she remained equipped only for anti-submarine warfare.

The other major surface units of the Brazilian fleet are the 3200-ton missile frigates *Niterói*, *Defensora*, *Constitução*, *Liberal*, *Independencia* and *União* and the similar 2400-ton frigate-type training ship *Brasil*. The first four of 16 projected 1600-ton missile corvettes *Inhauma*, *Jaceguary*, *Frontín* and *Julio de Noronha*, are also completing and due to enter service in 1988. The obsolete 2400-ton US "Gearing" class destroyers *Marcilio Dias* and *Mariz e Barros*, together with the 2200-ton "Allen M. Sumner" class *Mato Grosso*, *Sergipe*, *Alagoas*, *Rio Grande do Norte* and *Espirito Santo* and the 2000-ton "Fletcher" class *Piauí*, *Santa Catarina* and *Maranhão* also remain in service.

The Brazilian submarine fleet consists of the "Oberon" class *Humaitá*, *Tonelero* and *Riachuelo* in addition to the obsolescent 1900-ton US "Guppy" type *Goiáz*, *Amazonas*, *Bahia* and *Ceará*. The first two of a projected 12 Type 209 "1400" class diesel-electric submarines, the 1260-ton *Tupy* and *Timbira*, are also completing and due to enter service in 1988/89.

The only mine warfare craft are the six 230-ton German-built "Aratú" class coastal minesweepers and the surface fleet is completed by the nine 900-ton "Angostura" and the six 100-ton "Piratini" class patrol vessels. Sea-lift and a limited amphibious assault capability is provided by the 4800-ton

***The Brazilian Navy's aircraft carrier* Minas Gerais (Jane's Defence Weekly)**

***Locally-built missile frigate* Indepencia *of the Brazilian Navy's escort force* (Author)**

transports *Barroso Pereira*, *Custodio de Mello*, *Ary Parreiras* and *Soares Dutra*, the 4160-ton LST *Duque de Caxias*, the 1650-ton *Garcia d'Avila* and some small landing craft. Major auxiliary units include the surveying vessels *Almirante Saldanha*, *Almirante Camara*, *Sirius*, *Canopus*, *Argus*, *Orión* and *Taurus* and the fleet replenishment tanker *Marajó*. There are also the Antarctic research vessel *Barão de Teffe* and the submarine rescue ship *Gastão Moutinho*, plus numerous minor auxiliary and service craft.

In addition to the sea-going fleet, the elements of which are subordinate to the commanders of the naval districts in which they are deployed, there are separate Amazon and Mato Grosso flotillas. The Brazilian Navy's river forces include the 690-ton river gunboats *Pedro Texeira* and *Raposo Tavares*, the 550-ton *Porto Esperança*, the 340-ton *Roraima*, *Rondônia* and *Amapá* and the 500-ton floating medical clinics *Oswaldo Cruz* and *Carlos Chagas*, which together form the Amazon Flotilla, the Mato Grosso Flotilla consisting of the 620-ton monitor *Parnaiba*, the 285-ton river transport *Paragussú*, and the 70-ton *Piraim* and the 600-ton oiler *Potengí*, plus some very small patrol and service craft.

The major naval bases are Rio de Janeiro, which is the main fleet base, with three dry docks and a floating dock, and Aratú, which houses the mine-

***Ex-US Second World War destroyers still form the backbone of the Brazilian Navy's escort force* (Author)**

warfare school and has a dry dock and a floating dock. There are also bases at Belêm, which has one dry dock and Natal, which has a floating dock. There is a submarine base at Niterói. The Amazon Flotilla is based at Manaus and the Mato Grosso Flotilla at Ladario.

The Brazilian Marines, who currently number approximately 14,500 all ranks, are organised as a Fleet Marine Force (HQ Fort Sao Jose, Rio de Janeiro) comprising the nucleus of an amphibious division with the *Riachuelo*, *Humaitá* and *Paissandú* Marine Infantry Battalions, a Marine artillery group and the 1st Marine Engineer and Service Battalions, plus a Reinforcement Command comprising the *Toneleros* Special Operations Battalion and engineer, transport, medical and logistic units. There are also eight regional groups, employed in the defence of naval installations and stationed at Rio de Janeiro, São Salvador, Recife, Belêm, Santos, Uruguaiana, Ladario and Brasília, plus two Security groups, which are located at Ilha Trinidade and São Pedro da Aldeia, respectively.

These are equipped with the Imbel M964 and M969 rifles in 7.62 mm calibre, together with the Uru, the Beretta M972 and the US M3 submachine guns in 9 mm and 0.45-inch calibres respectively. The main infantry support weapons are the FN FAP and MAG in 7.62 mm and the Browning M1919 0.30-inch and M2 0.50-inch calibre machine guns, in addition to US M29 81 mm mortars. US M20 3.5-inch and Jeep-mounted M40 106 mm recoilless rifles are the principal anti-armour weapons. The Marines operate six examples of the EE-9 Cascavel armoured car, together with a similar number of EE-11 Urutú wheeled APCs and 40 examples of the M113 tracked APC, 16 LVTP-7s and some obsolete DUKW amphibious vehicles. Artillery units are equipped with eight examples each of the US M102 105 mm and M114 155 mm howitzers and of the M1 40 mm AA gun, plus some SS-06 108 mm rocket launchers.

Brazilian Naval aviation operates about 60 helicopters and consists of ASW Helicopter Squadron HS-1 with ten Sikorsky SH-3D and H Sea Kings, operated in the anti-submarine role from aboard the carrier; Reconnaissance and Attack Helicopter Squadron HA-1 with nine Lynxes operated from the six "Niterói" class frigates and the training ship *Brasil*; General Purpose Helicopter Squadron HU-1, with 11 AS.350B Ecureuils and six Wasps deployed aboard the ex-US destroyers and some fleet auxiliaries; General Purpose Helicopter Squadron HU-2 with three AS.332F Super Pumas and three Westland Whirlwinds, which are intended mainly for co-operation with the Marines; and Helicopter Training Squadron HI-1, with 16 Bell 206Cs. The main land base is at São Pedro da Aldeia.

The Naval School at Ilha Villegaignon, in Guanabara Bay, offers a five-year course for officer cadets, the final year of which is spent at sea. The nine-month advanced course of the Naval War College at Ilha de Exadas leads to promotion to senior rank or staff appointments and there are a number of specialist schools, including the Naval

***Ex-US "Fletcher" class destroyer* Santa Catarine *alongside the LST* Garcie D'Avila *and fleet oiler* Marajó at Niteroi (Author)**

"Oberon" class submarine **Tonelero (Author)**

Research Institute, which is concerned with scientific and technological training and research. There is also a Naval College at Angra Dos Reis and Apprentice Schools for enlisted personnel at Ceará, Pernambuco, Espirito Santo and Santa Catarina, a General Training Centre at Belêm and a Riverine Warfare School at Pirapora, Mato Grosso. The Navy also administers the Merchant Marine Academy at Rio and a school for fishermen in Rio Grande do Sul.

***Marine guard at the Brazilian Naval War College, Rio* (Author)**

The Fifteen Year Naval Modernisation Programme, adopted in 1985, which if fully implemented will give Brazil undisputed regional primacy as a naval power, proposes the construction of an attack aircraft carrier of approximately 25,000 tons, plus one light anti-submarine carrier displacing about 15,000 tons, to replace *Minas Gerais*. A total of 16 "Inhauma" class corvettes will be built, the first eight of which will be armed with four Exocet SSMs, one 4.5-inch Vickers Mk II, two Breda/Bofors 40 mm L/70s and two triple Mk 32 anti-submarine torpedo tubes. The later vessels will substitute Barracuda for Exocet SSMs and will also carry eight Avibras SSAI-N anti-submarine rocket launchers, substituting an Avibras FILA 20 mm anti-aircraft/anti-missile gun system for the two 40 mm. The two Type 209 submarines currently completing will be followed by four Type NAC 1s and six Type NAC 2s (locally developed improvements of the basic Type 209). These will be followed, in turn, by Brazil's first SSN, the hull of which will be a stretched version of the Type 209 displacing 2700 tons submerged. Propulsion will be by a 12 MW reactor, with electric drive, to give a submerged speed of 25 to 30 knots. The armament will be six tubes for either conventional or wire-guided torpedos, with 12 reloads.

The "Oberon" class submarines will be modernised and retained into the 21st century although the "Guppies" will be scrapped. The "Fletcher" class DDs will also be disposed of but most of the "Sumners" and "Gearings" will be re-engined and will have their AA armaments replaced by

FILA 20 mm gun systems. The "Niterói" class frigates will be rearmed with Brazilian Barracuda SSMs in place of Exocets and FILA 20 mm gun systems in plate of Seacat SAMs.

The "Piratini" class patrol vessels will be replaced by six more modern vessels of local construction and eight larger patrol vessels, each of 450 tonnes, will be acquired and armed with 5-inch guns removed from the "Fletcher" class DDs, plus two 40 mm L/70s. An indeterminate number of additional minesweepers, with composite timber and fibre-glass hulls, is also to be built, as are one LSD of the French "Ouragan" class and one LST of unspecified characteristics.

The Marines are to receive 35 M41C light tanks and the Whirlwinds of the *Aviação Naval* are in the process of replacement by six Aérospatiale AS.332F Super Pumas and its Wasps by a total of 20 AS.350B Ecureuils. At least 16 Super Lynxes are also expected to be acquired in the medium term to equip the "Inhauma" class corvettes.

Avibras SBAT-70 air-to-surface rocket system, mounted on naval Wasp helicopter **(Avibras)**

Air Force

Manpower:	50,700
Major units:	19 groups: 2 interceptor squadrons 3 fighter-bomber squadrons 3 light strike squadrons 2 reconnaissance squadrons 4 maritime recce/SAR squadrons 1 embarked ASW squadron 13 transport squadrons 6 observation/liaison squadrons 7 helicopter squadrons
Interceptors:	Dassault Mirage III
Fighter-bombers:	Northrop F-5 AM-X
Light strike aircraft:	EMBRAER AT-26 Xavante
Reconnaissance aircraft:	EMBRAER RC-95 Bandeirante and RT-26 Xavante
Maritime recce aircraft:	Lockheed RC-130 EMBRAER P-95 Bandeirante
ASW aircraft:	Grumman S-2A and E
Transports:	Lockheed C-130 and KC-130 DHC-5 Boeing 707 and 737 Vickers Viscount HS.748 and 125 EMBRAER C-95 Bandeirante EMB-120 Brasília EMB-121 Xingu EMB-810 Séneca
Helicopters:	Aérospatiale SA.330L Puma AS.332M Super Puma Helibras HB.350 and 355 Esquilo Bell 47, UH-1 and 206 Hughes OH-6
Trainers:	EMBRAER AT-26 Xavante and T-27 Tucano Aerotec T-23 Uirapurú Neiva T-25 Universal

The Brazilian Army set up a flying school in February 1914 but this was forced to close down in July of the same year due to lack of funds. The Brazilian Navy formed an air arm in 1916 and the

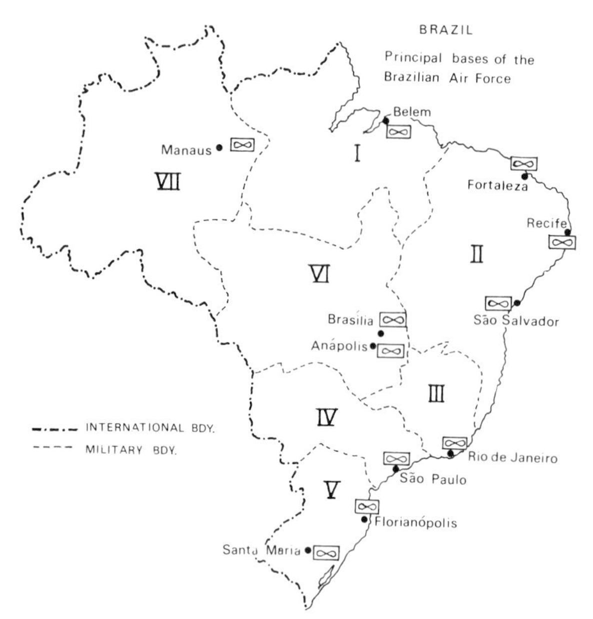

army air service was re-established on a permanent basis in November 1918. In 1920 a French military mission, which included an aviation component, arrived in the country. Growing US influence during the 1930s was reflected in the increasing number of US aircraft types purchased and in January 1941 the Army and Naval air services were amalgamated into the new Brazilian Air Force. Aircraft of the Air Force carried out neutrality patrols of Brazilian territorial waters from the outbreak of the Second World War. After Brazil declared war on Germany and Italy in August 1942, it made base facilities available to the United States and received extensive Lend-Lease aid. A fighter group and a liaison and observation squadron served in Italy in support of the Brazilian Expeditionary Division from October 1944 onwards.

Although by the end of the war the Brazilian Air Force had a total of over 1100 aircraft its operational efficiency declined rapidly in the post-war years, most of its surviving aircraft being grounded due to lack of spares when Brazil signed the Rio Treaty of Mutual Defence in 1947. Although the early 1950s were characterised by considerable political instability, the period was also one of renewed development for the Brazilian Air Force, the first jet aircraft, in the form of 72 Gloster Meteors, being purchased in 1953. With the purchase of the aircraft carrier *Minas Gerais* in 1956 the Navy had hoped to re-establish its own air arm. The Air Force however successfully defended its position as the sole operator of fixed-

Brazilian Northrop F-5 fighter with SBAT-70 rocket system **(Jane's Defence Weekly)**

wing aircraft and after eight years of wrangling, a Presidential Decree of January 1965 limited the Navy to the operation of helicopters.

Although quantities of additional material had begun to be received in the late 1950s, by the early 1970s the existing operational equipment was nearing the end of its useful life. A large-scale re-equipment programme during the 1970s, in which the products of the rapidly-developing local aerospace industry figured prominantly, however remedied many of the deficiencies.

The Brazilian Air Force currently numbers approximately 50,000 all ranks operating over 1000 aircraft and is organised in five Commands.

Air Defence Command consists of the 1st Air Defence Group (Anápolis) with two squadrons, equipped with a total of 15 Mirage IIIs.

Tactical Air Command comprises the 1st Fighter Group (Santa Cruz) with two squadrons equipped with a total of 20 Northrop F-5B and Es; the 4th Fighter Group (Fortaleza) with three squadrons equipped with a total of 75 AT-26 Xavantes; the 8th Air Group comprising the 1st Squadron (Manáus) with ten examples of the EMBRAER EMB-810 Séneca and the Bell UH-1H, the similarly equipped 2nd Squadron (Recife) and 5th Squadron (Santa Maria) and the 3rd Squadron, at Campo dos Afonsos, with six SA.330 Pumas; the 10th Air Group, comprising the 1st Squadron (Santa Maria) with eight RC-95 Bandeirantes and the 2nd Squadron (Campo Grande) with 12 RT-26 Xavantes; the 11th Air Group (São Paulo) comprising only a single squadron with ten UH-1Hs; the 13th Air Group (Santa

EMB-326 Xavante trainer/light strike aircraft of the Brazilian Air Force

Cruz) also comprising only one squadron with ten EMB-810s; the 14th Fighter Group (Canoas) again comprising only one squadron, with ten F-5s and the 5th Air Group (Campo Grande) also with only one squadron with ten EMBRAER C-95s.

Coastal Command consists of the 6th Air Group (Recife) comprising only a single squadron with three RC-130s and ten P-95 Bandeirantes; the 7th Air Group (Salvador) made up of two squadrons, each with ten P-95s; the 10th Search and Rescue Group comprising the 2nd Squadron (Campo Grande) with ten P-95s and the 3rd Squadron (Florianópolis) with ten UH-1Hs. The Embarked Air Group comprising the 1st Squadron (Santa Cruz) with eight Grumman S-2As and the 2nd Squadron, aboard the aircraft carrier *Minas Gerais*, with six S-2Es, is also subordinate to this Command.

Air Transport Command consists of the 1st Transport Group (Campo dos Afonsos) comprising the 1st Squadron with six C-130s and the 2nd Squadron with two KC-130s and four Boeing 707-320Cs; the 2nd Transport Group (Galeão) comprising the 1st Squadron with eight C-95 Bandeirantes and 12 HS.748s and the 2nd Squadron with 20 C-95s; the 1st Troop Transport Group (Campo dos Afonsos) with two Squadrons, each of six DHC-5s; the 9th Air Group (Manáus) with a single squadron of eight DHC-5s; and the

***Brazilian Lockheed C-130 transport aircraft* (Lockheed Aircraft Corpn)**

DHC-5 transport aircraft of the Brazilian Air Force

Special Air Transport Group (Brasília) comprising the 1st Squadron with two Boeing 737s, a Vickers Viscount and three Bell 206s, and the 2nd Squadron with 11 BAe 125s and 12 EMBRAER EMB-121 Xingus.

Outside the group organisation but still subordinate to Air Transport Command are the 1st Air Transport Squadron (Belêm), the 2nd Air Transport Squadron (Recife), the 3rd Air Transport Squadron (Galeão), the 4th Air Transport Squadron (Cumbica), the 5th Air Transport Squadron (Brasília) and the 6th Air Transport Squadron (Porto Alegre), each equipped with six Bandeirantes and four Sénecas.

Air Training Command operates a total of 60 AT-26 Xavantes, 100 T-27 Tucanos, 80 T-23 Uirapurús and 80 T-25 Universals plus a few Bandeirantes and comprises the Air Force Academy at Pirassununga, equipped mainly with Tucanos, plus some Xavantes and Bandeirantes; the Tactical Application and Crew Training Centre at Natal, comprising the 1st and 2nd Air Training Squadrons equipped respectively with Xavantes and Universals and the 3rd Air Training Squadron with Bandeirantes; the Military Pilot Formation Centre at Natal, with Xavantes, Uirapurús and Universals; the Helicopter Training Centre at Santos, with 16 Bell 47s, eight UH-1s and two 206s, plus four Hughes OH-6s; the Air Technical Centre at São João dos Campos, with Bandeirantes, Xavantes and Universals; the Air Cadets Preparatory School at Barbacena, with Bandeirantes and Uirapurús and the Inspection and Vigilance Group at Rio de Janeiro, with six Bandeirantes.

This Command also includes the Air Force Command and Staff School at Canoas, which trains officers for promotion to superior rank or for staff appointments; the Air Force Officers Advanced Training School at São Paulo, which imparts post-graduate training, qualifying for promotion to field rank; and the Air Force Specialists School at Guaratingueta, São Paulo, all of which are non-flying.

The Air Cadets Preparatory School usually has approximately 600 pupils undergoing preparation for automatic entry to the Air Force Academy at Pirassununga which offers a five-year course for officer cadets. The Air Force Specialists School trains officers and enlisted men for non-flying duties, including base security, for which there is a corps of Air Infantry. The Air Force Technical Centre runs a five-year course for aeronautical, electrical and electronic engineers.

Current expansion programmes envisage the acquisition of six Mirages and 26 F-5s to offset attrition, together with 79 AM-X fighter/ground-attack-aircraft, two EMBRAER Brasília executive transports, eight Aérospatiale AS.332M Super Puma and 40 Helibras HB.350 and 355 Esquilo helicopters, plus an additional 50 Tucano trainers.

UH-1 helicopter airlifting a 70 mm MLR **(Avibras)**

Paramilitary forces

Manpower:	190,000 military police 50,000 civil police
Equipment:	Infantry personal and support weapons

The Brazilian police system is complex but consists basically of three tiers: Federal Police, State Military Police and State Civil Police, all of which are paramilitary in character.

The Federal Police, which numbers approximately 15,000 all ranks, is subordinate to the Department of Federal Police and is primarily engaged in the control of entry and exit via the country's land, sea and air frontiers, national security and liaison with international police organisations. To this end, the force polices air, sea and river ports and land frontier crossing points and guards the President, members of the government and foreign diplomats at the federal capital, also protecting major federal government installations throughout the country. In addition, it provides a central data processing and intelligence collecting and disseminating service for the various state police forces and in many respects parallels the activities of the Federal Bureau of Investigation in the United States. The Federal Police operates the National Police Academy, which graduates approximately 2400 police officers per year. It does not however carry out ordinary police functions in either the federal capital or the four federal territories, each of which has its own police force, directly analagous to the various state police forces. Of these, the Federal District Police Force at Brasília, numbers approximately 6000 and may be taken as a typical example.

Two other federal law enforcement agencies are the Federal Highway Police and Federal Railway Police, both of which are subordinate to the Ministry of Transportation and Public Works and which, as their names imply, police the national highways and major railway stations. There is also the Dock Police Force which guards warehouses, etc, at the national ports. Currently, the establishment of a coast guard force is also being studied by the federal government.

Each state and federal territory maintains both a military and a civil police force. The Military

***Member of the military police of Rio de Janeiro state* (Author)**

Police forces, which have been subordinate to the Ministry of the Army since 1969, are commanded by active service army officers and are organised on military lines, being divided into battalions and companies and equipped with infantry pesonal and support weapons up to and including mortars and anti-tank rocket projectors. Although specifically intended as a reserve for the Army, the Military Police forces are the principal internal security, law enforcement and crime prevention agencies in the country and are divided between the state capitals and urban and rural areas throughout the respective states. The São Paulo Military Police, the largest in the country, numbers approximately 55,000 all ranks. Fire-fighting comes within the scope of the Military Police, fire-fighting equipment doubling as water cannon for riot control. The State Civil Police forces are subordinate to the respective Secretaries of Public Safety of the various States. The civil police forces are principally engaged in crime detection and the apprehension of criminals, crime prevention falling within the jurisdiction of the Military Police. The state police forces also include Highway Patrol sections, while the São Paulo State Police also includes a Railroad Police force. Several state police forces also include a Forest Police force, subordinate to the State Secretary of Agriculture. All police forces are armed.

Sources of defence material supply and current requirements

Traditionally, Brazil bought most of its army equipment in Germany and shopped mainly in Britain for naval vessels, although from colonial times onwards, Brazil's own shipyards provided a significant proportion of the requirements of the Navy. From the 1920s onwards, French material followed French influence in the Army and military aviation although growing US influence on equipment procurements was also noted, especially from the mid-1930s onwards. From the early 1940s, the United States became the major supplier of defence material although the Brazilian shipbuilding and aeronautical industries were already making moves towards autonomy. Currently almost 50% of the country's requirements in defence material ar met from its own resources.

From the early 1960s, local industry began to supply the needs of the armed forces as regards small arms and ammunition, followed by infantry support weapons. In the late 1960s, tentative moves were made towards the modernisation of some of the Army's obsolete armoured fighting vehicles, using locally developed technology, Brazil rapidly becoming a world leader in this field. This was followed by the development of original wheeled armoured vehicles, with notable success, the products of Brazilian industry being extensively exported, particularly to the Arabic-speaking counties of North Africa and the Middle East. Brazil is currently developing two main battle tanks and a tracked APC of original conception. Other tracked vehicles may be expected to follow.

The Brazilian shipbuilding industry had supplied a proportion of the requirements of the Navy from colonial times. The construction of the "Carioca" class minelayers, in the 1930s, followed by the "Marcilio Dias" and "Acre"

Above: ***The locally-developed EET-1 Osorio MBT which together with the MB-3 Tamoio will re-equip the armoured units of the Brazilian Army*** **(Engesa)**

Below: ***The EE-3 Jararacá scout car, which although not used by Brazil is in service with several Latin American armies*** **(Engesa)**

Right: ***The EE-11 Urutú APC which together with the EE-9 Cascavel has enjoyed considerable export success*** **(Engesa)**

classes of destroyers in the 1940s and 1950s, heralded a more serious and consistent attempt to produce a significant proportion of the Navy's requirements in major surface combatants. These have been followed by a steady progression of patrol craft and auxiliary vessels, culminating in the local construction of two of the six British-designed "Niterói" class guided-missile frigates in the early 1970s. More recently a training frigate of modified "Niterói" class design has been built in Brazil and the first four of a projected series of 16 slightly smaller modern escort vessels are nearing completion. The first conventionally powered submarine of a proposed series of 12 is at an advanced stage of construction and the intention to commence the construction of a nuclear-powered submarine during the 1990s has been announced.

Brazil already has a functioning nuclear reactor with two more under construction and others projected and it has been estimated that nuclear weapons could be developed, without outside assistance, within six years of a decision to do so.

The Brazilian aircraft industry has also been active since the 1930s, aircraft of indigenous design having been successfully developed in the early years of this century. Aircraft of local conception first became market successes in the mid-1970s and Brazil currently has a flourishing aerospace industry, the greatest success of which to date has been the adoption of the EMBRAER

Close support version of the Urutú with 90 mm gun **(Engesa)**

The Astros II MLR system mounted on a Tectran 4 × 6 truck **(Avibras)**

Tectran ammunition truck reloading a similar vehicle equipped with the Astros II saturation bombardment system **(Avibras)**

Contraves Fieldguard Fire control system for the Astros II MLR mounted on Tectran truck **(Avibras)**

T-27 Tucano as the basic trainer of the British Royal Air Force. Brazil is also the only major producer of helicopters in Latin America (in cooperation with Aérospatiale of France) and has developed a fighter/ground-attack aircraft in cooperation with Aermacchi of Italy. Brazilian industry has also developed a series of highly successful ballistic rockets.

Summary and prospects

Having largely avoided both the incessant internal turbulence of its neighbours and the equally futile succession of sterile frontier disputes indulged in by many of them, Brazil has developed more rapidly than most countries of the region, overtaking Argentina as the natural leader of Latin America. Brazil has also developed the nearest thing to a completely successful multi-racial society in existence and has cunningly exploited its heterogeneous racial origins to commercial advantage in its dealings with as diverse commercial clients as the emergent states of black Africa, the militantly white-supremacist Republic of South Africa and the Arabic-speaking countries of the southern and eastern Mediterranean and the Middle East.

On the basis of its sheer physical bulk alone, Brazil must achieve major power status by the end of the present century. Hitherto lacking only petroleum among its natural assets and having already developed sensible alternative energy sources with readily available vegetable materials, Brazil is also a world leader in energy conservation and alternative technology. Recent offshore oil exploration has also yielded encouraging results as regards the country's future independence in the area of fossil fuels. Its growing industrial power has already made Brazil the major industrial country in Latin America and a natural leader in the "Third World". With immense and still largely untapped natural resources, its current problems in servicing foreign debts may be expected to be of only transient importance.

The Brazilian armed forces, which traditionally have been structured to counter any military threat which might be posed by Argentina, either alone or in alliance with Uruguay and Paraguay and for the past 25 years have accepted an essentially internal security role in the case of the Army and Air Force and the role of an anti-submarine training force in that of the Navy, are now consciously looking outward towards the consolidation of the country's existing frontiers and the defence of the international status quo in the South American continent, aspiring to act as a positive equilibrant in one of the World's most volatile regions. Already largely self-sufficient as regards their equipment needs, they propose to be entirely so by the turn of the century and with rapidly developing rocket technology and the potential to develop their own nuclear weapons promise to make Brazil a power to be reckoned with by the year 2000.

Brazil may also be expected to have become a major exporter of defence material before the end of the century, being already the largest exporter of military equipment in the "Third World". Sensibly avoiding innovation for its own sake and concentrating on designs lending themselves readily to large-scale production with existing industrial and technical resources, the products of the Brazilian defence industry have enjoyed a degree of market success in sharp contrast to that of the failure on the export market, to date, of the frequently more spectacular products of the longer-established defence industry of neighbouring Argentina. Among notable successes in this respect are that of the Gurgel company in soft-skinned vehicle production, that of Engesa and Bernardini in the field of armoured fighting vehicles and of EMBRAER, Neiva and more recently Helibras in the field of aircraft development and production.

CHILE

(República de Chile)

Area: 286,000 sq miles (740,740 sq km) excluding island territories
Population: 12,307,000 (1986)
Total armed forces: 99,000
Reserves: 300,000
Available manpower: 1,000,000
Paramilitary forces: 27,000
GNP: $15,996 million (1985)
Defence expenditure: $1,242 million (1985)

Introduction

The seventh largest country in South America, Chile extends from the tropics almost to Antarctica, with an overall length of some 2600 miles but a median width of only 100. The 4000-mile Pacific coast forms the western boundary of the country which is otherwise bordered by Peru to the north, by Bolivia to the north-east and Argentina to the east. The population is homogeneous, consisting of about 95% mixed Amerindian and European and less than 3% pure Indian stock but is extremely unevenly distributed, some 77% inhabiting the central region and large portions, particularly of the southern regions, being almost unhabited.

Chile's major exports are copper, nitrates and iron ore. Although primarily an agricultural country, over 60% of all food is imported. Industrial production is largely related to the processing of the country's major mineral products, together with industries related to the forest products of the south. Fishing is of considerable importance and Chile is second only to Japan as a major seafood producer.

Chile was visited by the Spaniards in 1535 and colonised from 1541 onwards. The War of Independence lasted for almost eight years and was successfully concluded only in 1818. Having gone on to assist in the liberation of Peru, the first President of the Chilean Republic, Bernardo O'Higgins, was overthrown in 1823 and a period of anarchy followed being terminated by the triumph of the Conservatives, led by Diego Portales, in 1830. Between 1836 and 1839 a war against the confederation of Bolivia and Peru resulted in victory for Chile and although in 1865–66 Chile joined Peru in a naval war against Spain, she was again ranged against an alliance of Peru and Bolivia in the Pacific War of 1879–83 from which she emerged victorious once more, gaining territory at the expense of both of her adversaries.

Unlike most countries of Latin America, Chile largely escaped the internal instability which characterised the early history of most other independent states in the region. This tradition was broken in 1891 by a brief civil war between the supporters of the President Balmaceda and those of the Congress which resulted in the victory of the latter group. Stability returned until 1924 when, following conflict between the Liberal President Alessandri and the Conservative-dominated Congress, the armed forces intervened. Colonel Carlos Ibáñez del Campo took over as President and ruled as a benevolent dictator from 1927 to 1931 when the effects of the Depression reduced the country to near anarchy, ten governments holding office in a single year. Elections in 1932 restored stability with a succession of moderate democratically-elected administrations, including one led once more by Ibáñez, now a General, in the mid-1950s, culminating in the formation of a minority Marxist administration in 1970 by Salvador Allende, following an inconclusive election in which he secured only 36% of the votes cast.

Allende's attempts at the conversion of Chile to a Marxist state resulted in economic disaster and social chaos, being condemned as unconstitutional by both Congress and the Supreme Court. Finally, the armed forces seized control of the government in 1973 by a bloody coup d'etat during which Allende committed suicide. Although ostracized not only by countries of a Marxist-Socialist orientation but also by many of the democratic countries of the West, the new military regime of General Augusto Pinochet restored social and economic stability and apparently gained the support of almost 68% of the electorate in the referendum for the adoption of a new constitution, held in 1980.

Chile is a unitary, centralised republic divided into 25 provinces, which have recently been grouped into 13 economic and administrative regions. Each administrative region is presided over by a *Gobernador* and each province by an *Intendente,* both officials being appointed by the central government. The new Constitution, approved by the 1980 referendum, provides for a strong executive and a bicameral legislature. Its provisions however are not to be fully adopted before 1988 and General Pinochet remains President in the interim, having announced his intention to present himself as presidential candidate when elections are finally held.

Chilean foreign policy has been largely dominated by rivalry with Argentina which almost led to war between the two countries in the early 1900s, until the mediation of King Edward VII of Great Britain. Under the resulting General Arbitration Treaty of 1902 both parties agreed to submit all future boundary disputes to the arbitration of the British Crown. Recourse to this Treaty over the disputed ownership of the islands of Lennox, Picton and Nueva, at the southern tip of Tierra del Fuego, resulted in an arbitral award in favour of Chile in 1977, which Argentina refused to recognise. Considerable tension was generated between the two countries and only the South Atlantic War between Argentina and Britain defused the threat of hostilities. Further mediation by the Pope, in the context of a less uncompromisingly nationalistic attitude by the new civilian government in Argentina, finally culminating in the acceptance of the Beagle Channel Treaty which was ratified by both countries in 1984. As a direct result of the Argentino-Chilean dispute, Chile was the only Latin American country to withhold its support for Argentina in the Anglo-Argentine War of 1982, observing a neutrality which was notably benevolent towards Britain. Tension also exists perennially with both Bolivia and Peru. Both countries aspire to repossess the territories lost in the Pacific War although, in the case of Peru, these were ceded in perpetuity to Chile by the Treaty of Tacna-Arica of 1929 and in that of Bolivia by the Treaty of 1904 which finally terminated the state of hostilities between the two countries. Diplomatic relations with Bolivia were broken in 1962, resumed in 1975 and broken again in 1978 following the failure of negotiations aimed at the re-establishment of direct Bolivian access to the sea.

A strong current of left-wing political opinion had its aspirations realised in the formation of the Allende administration, the excesses of which would appear to have greatly diminished left-wing support in Chile, many of Allende's supporters having also fled the country following the coup which resulted in his overthrow and death. The military regime would seem to retain at least the tacit support of the great majority of the population who perceive it as a lesser evil than a return to the conditions prevailing under Allende. From the middle of 1983 onwards however high unemployment and an overall deterioration in the economic situation have lent added credibility to left-wing agitation, supported to a degree even by politicians of the centre frustrated by their prolonged exclusion from the democratic process and by radicalised elements in the majority Roman Catholic Church. Anti-government demonstrations led to considerable bloodshed, culminating in an unsuccessful assasination attempt against General Pinochet in September 1986.

Structure of the armed forces

The Chilean Army, Navy and Air Force, although by no means the strongest or best equipped, are among the best trained and most efficient in Latin America and through training missions have had a formative influence upon many others of the armed forces of the region.

Under the currently suspended constitution, the President is responsible for the internal security of the republic and its defence against external aggression. His powers as commander-in-chief of the armed forces are however subject to the sanction of Congress. In time of war, the President may designate a senior military officer as commander of the armed forces, although he himself remains com-

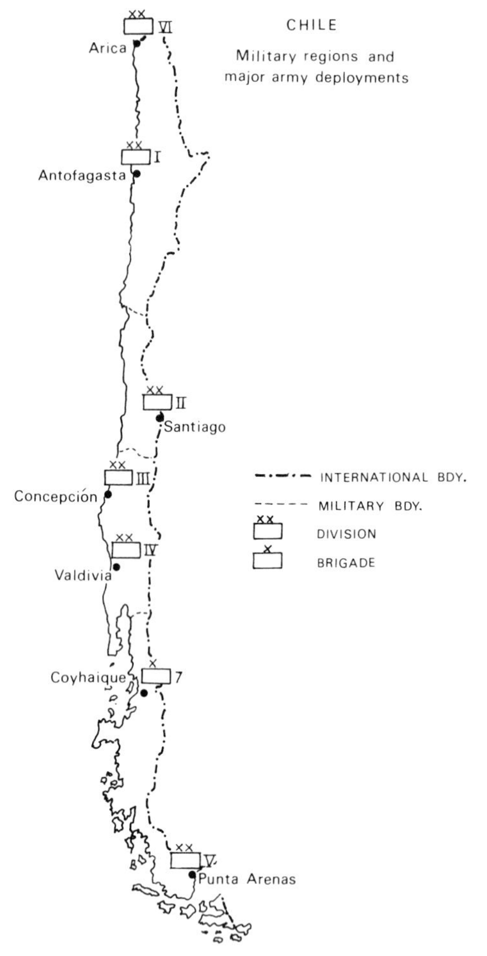

mander-in-chief. In peacetime, the Minister of National Defence is effectively responsible for the administrative control of the armed forces, assisted by the sub-secretaries of National Defence for the Army, Navy and Air Force, each of whom both advises the minister and discharges similar functions with regard to his own service to those of the minister with regard to the overall national defence establishment. The President is advised by the Supreme Council of National Security which consists of the Ministers of National Defence, Foreign Relations, Finance, Development, Economy and Reconstruction; the Chief of the National Defence General Staff and the Commanders-in-Chief of the Army, Navy and Air Force. The minister is advised by the Superior Council of National Defence, the National Defence General Staff, the Council for the Health of the Armed Forces, the Office of the Controller General and the three service sub-secretaries. There is a combined National Defence General Staff, in addition to which each of the three armed forces maintains its own general staff.

Since 1900, military service has been compulsory for all fit male citizens between the ages of 18 and 45. In practice, a selective draft system is employed and only a small proportion of those liable for service undergo one year of training in the Army or Air Force or two years in the Navy. The number selected annually is approximately 30,000, the overwhelming majority of whom serve in the Army. On the completion of their period of training conscripts are required to serve in the Active reserve for a period of 12 years and then in the Second reserve until the age of 45.

For defensive purposes, the country is divided into six Military Areas of which Area No 1 (HQ Antofagasta) covers the provinces of Antofagasta and Atacama, Area No 2 (HQ Santiago) the capital and the provinces of Coquimbo, Aconcagua, Valparaíso, Santiago, O'Higgins and Colchagua, Area No 3 (HQ Concepción) the provinces of Curicó, Talca, Maule, Linares, Ñuble, Concepción, Bío-Bío and Malleco, Area No 4 (HQ Valdivia) the provinces of Cautín, Valdivia and Llanquihue, Area No 5 (HQ Punta Arenas) the provvinces of Chiloé, Aysén and Magallanes and Area No 6 (HQ Iquique) the province of Tarapacá. Army and Air Force units are deployed within this framework. The Navy however divides the coastal regions of the country into three Naval Zones, corresponding respectively to the coastal proportions of the 1st, 2nd and 6th, the 3rd and 4th, and the 5th Military Areas.

Each of the armed forces maintains its own complex of training establishments which are of uniformly high quality. There is also the National Defence Academy, a tri-service educational establishment maintained by the Ministry of National Defence and the courses of which must be successfully completed before promotion to senior rank in any of the armed forces.

Army

Manpower:	57,000
Formations:	6 divisions 1 brigade
Major units:	24 infantry regiments (of which 8 motorised and 7 mountain)

1 special forces regiment
6 special forces battalions
2 armoured regiments
8 cavalry regiments (of which 2 armoured, 3 motorised and 3 horsed)
7 artillery regiments
5 engineer regiments
3 engineer battalions

AFVs: AMX-30, M4 and M51 Sherman medium tanks
AMX-13, M24, M-41 and M3A1 light tanks
EE-9 Cascavel armoured cars
M113, Mowag Piranha and EE-11 Urutú APCs

Artillery: Oto Melara Model 56 and US M101 105 mm howitzers
Mk F.3 155 mm SPH

Air defence weapons: RH202 twin 20 mm and Oerlikon K 63 twin 35 mm

Missiles: Milan ATGWs
Blowpipe SAMs

After ejecting the Spaniards from their own country, Chilean soldiers, together with those of Argentina and Colombia, were largely instrumental in winning the independence of Peru, few surviving the lengthy struggle. In 1830 Diego Portales, as Minister of War, reorganised the Chilean Army and established it on a firm basis, making it the redoubtable force which vanquished the Confederation of Bolivia and Peru in the war of 1836–39 and once more defeated the same two countries in the Pacific War of 1879–83. From 1886 onwards Prussian influence replaced that of France and although it engaged in no foreign wars after 1883 the Chilean Army achieved such prestige throughout Latin America that many of the other states of the region sent selected officers for post-graduate training in Chilean military schools, the governments of Ecuador, Colombia and El Salvador contracting full-scale Chilean military missions to train their respective armies while Chilean officers were engaged as instructors in the military schools of several of the other countries of the region.

Chilean infantry in parade uniform
(Chilean Army)

German influence remained strong throughout the first three decades of the 20th century. From 1944 onwards however significant quantities of lend-lease equipment began to arrive in exchange for the availability of Chilean bases to the United States and with them US training assistance and influence. Following the conclusion of the Second World War and with the signature of the Rio Treaty of 1947 further US equipment was also acquired, Chile becoming the major Latin American recipient of US military assistance during

Chilean infantry with MG 42 machine gun in desert country adjoining the Bolivian frontier
(Chilean Army)

Chilean infantry with Jeep-mounted M40A1 106 mm RCLs **(Chilean Army)**

the 1960s although some equipment continued to be purchased in Europe.

Following the 1973 coup the Chilean armed forces experienced considerable difficulty in acquiring additional material. In the late 1970s international attitudes towards the Chilean military regime began to ease and the equipment situation improved somewhat despite the rejection of further US military assistance by the military government, following US criticism of the regime's human rights record.

The Chilean Army currently numbers approximately 57,000 all ranks and is divided into six divisions (one for each military area) each of which consists, in theory, of three infantry regiments, one reinforced mountain regiment, a cavalry brigade of two regiments, a field artillery regiment, an engineer battalion, a signals battalion and supporting logistic services. Recent tensions with both Argentina and Peru have however occasioned some redeployments so that the composition of the divisions is no longer standard.

The Ist Army Division (HQ Antofagasta) is made up of the 7th *Esmeralda*, 15th *Calama* and 23rd *Copiapó* Motorised Infantry Regiments, the 1st Commando Battalion, the 8th *Exploradores* Motorised Cavalry Regiment, the 5th *Antofagasta* Artillery Regiment, the 1st *General Herrera* Engineer and 1st *El Loa* Signals Regiments and the 1st *Tocopilla* Logistic Battalion.

The IInd Army Division (HQ Santiago) comprises the 1st *Buín*, 2nd *Maipo*, 3rd *Yungay* and 19th *Colchagua* Motorised Infantry Regiments, plus the 21st *Arica* Reinforced Motorised Infantry and 18th *Guardia Vieja* Reinforced Mountain Regiments, the 2nd Commando Battalion, the 2nd *Libertadores* Armoured, the 1st *Tacna* Artillery Regiment and the 2nd Engineer, 2nd Signals and 2nd *Bellavista* Logistic Battalions.

The IIIrd Army Division (HQ Concepción) consists of the 6th *Chacabuco*, 10th *Lautaro* and 13th *Andallén* Infantry Regiments, plus the 9th *Chillán* Mountain Regiment and the 16th *Talca* and 17th *Los Angeles* Reinforced Mountain Regiments, the 3rd Commando Battalion, the 3rd *Húsares* and 6th *Dragones* horsed and 7th *Guías* Motorised Cavalry Regiments, the 3rd *General Silva Renard* Artillery Regiment the 3rd Engineer and 3rd Signals Regiments and the 3rd *General Novoa* Logistic Battalion.

The IVth Army Division (HQ Valdiva) is made up of the 8th *Tucapel* and 12th *Sangra* Infantry Regiments, plus the 20th *La Concepción* Reinforced Mountain Regiment, the 4th Commando Battalion, the 2nd *Cazadores* horsed Cavalry Regiment, plus the 4th *Coraceros* Armoured Cavalry Regiment, the 2nd *General Maturana* Artillery Regiment, the 4th *Arauco* Engineer and 4th *Membrillar* Signals Regiments and the 4th Logistic Battalion.

The Vth Army Division (HQ Punta Arenas) is the only division to include a subordinate major formation – the 7th Brigade (HQ Coyhaique), made up of the 14th *Aysén* Reinforced Mountain, the 22nd *O'Higgins* Infantry and the 4th *Miraflores* Artillery Regiments – comprising also the 11th *Caupolicán* Infantry Regiment, the 5th Commando Battalion, the 5th *Lanceros* Motorised Cavalry Regiment, the 7th *Chorrillos* Artillery Regiment and the 5th Engineer, 5th Signals and 5th Logistic Battalions.

The VIth Army Division (HQ Arica) consists of the 4th *Rancagua* and 5th *Carampangué* Infantry Regiments, plus the 24th *Huamachuco* Reinforced Mountain Regiment, the 6th Commando Battalion, the 1st *Vencedores* Armoured and 1st *Granaderos* horsed Cavalry Regiments, the 6th *Dolores* Artillery Regiment, the 6th *Azapa* Engineer Regiment and the 6th *Tarapacá* Signals and 6th *Pisagua* Logistic Battalions.

Army troops, which are nominally part of the 2nd Army Division, include the Army Headquarters Battalion at Santiago, the *Boinas Negras* Special Forces Regiment at Peldehue, the 1st *Independencia* Aviation Regiment at Rancagua, the 7th *General Vega* Engineer Regiment at Puente Alto, the 7th *Aconcagua* Engineer Battalion at Quillota, the 7th Signals Regiment at Santiago and the 1st *Huelén* Transport Battalion, also at Santiago.

As will be noted, the divisions of the Chilean Army have become essentially administrative rather than tactical formations, the IInd and IIIrd Divisions being approximately twice the size of the remaining four divisions and the regiment being the effective tactical level of command. The

Chilean M41 tank **(G. von Rauch)**

Mowag Piranha APCs of the Chilean Army **(Chilean Army)**

infantry regiments consist of from one to four battalions, those referred to as 'reinforced' being effectively brigades with integral reconnaissance, engineer, signals and logistic elements and each including a battery of heavy mortars. Current doctrine envisages the formation of three Israeli-type Ugdot, based respectively on the Ist and VIth, the IInd, and the IIIrd, IVth and Vth divisions in time of war.

The main rifles in service are the SiG 510, which is used by the infantry; the FN FAL, which equips the mountain troops and the HK-33, which is used by the special forces. Old US M1 rifles and carbines in 0.30-inch calibre are also to be found in use by second-line troops. Sub-machine guns in use include the Madsen Model 1953 and the Uzi, both in 9 mm calibre and the US MAC M10, in 0.45-inch. The 7.62 mm FN FALO is used as a squad weapon and machine guns in service include the German MG 42 in 7.62 mm and the Browning M2HB 0.50-calibre. Mortars in service are the US M19 60 mm, M1 and M29 81 mm and the French Hotchkiss-Brandt 120 mm, recently supplemented by locally produced mortars in the latter two calibres. Anti-armour weapons comprise the Milan ATGW and the US M40 106 mm RCL.

The principal tanks in service are about 150

Close support version of the Piranha APC with 90 mm gun **(Industrias Cardoen)**

M4 and M51 Shermans, 21 AMX-30s, 47 AMX-13s and about 50 examples of the US M24 and 60 of the M41. A few US M3A1 light tanks are still in use for training. There are also 30 EE-9 Cascavel armoured cars, plus 30 examples of the EE-11 Urutú APC, 100 M113 tracked APCs and 150 examples of the Mowag Piranha in its APC configuration, plus 50 mortar carrier and 20 close-support versions armed with the French F1 90 mm gun, all of the latter being locally assembled.

Artillery units are equipped with 72 examples of the US M101 and 36 of the Oto Melara Model 56 105 mm towed howitzers and a dozen French Mk F.3 155 mm SP howitzers. Air defence is

Chilean M101 105 mm howitzer above the snow line in the Andes **(Chilean Army)**

Chilean special forces disembark from Puma helicopter **(Chilean Army)**

primarily the responsibility of the Air Force but the Army has some Swiss HSS-639 single and Oerlikon K 63 twin 20 mm AA guns. Fifty Blowpipe missile launchers are a recent acquisition.

The Aviation Regiment operates a total of about 60 aircraft, including six CASA 212 and four Piper Navajo light transports, 16 Cessna R172 and three 337 observation aircraft, which are also used for training, two examples apiece of the Bell 206 and UH-1H, plus about a dozen Aérospatiale SA.315B Lamas, a similar number of SA.330 Pumas and two AS.332 Super Puma helicopters.

The *Escuela Militar General Bernardo O'Higgins*, the Staff College and the NCO School are all located at Santiago. Aspiring officers must successfully complete the five-year course of the former before commissioning in the rank of second lieutenant and must complete an additional course at the Staff College to qualify for promotion to field rank or appointment to the General Staff. The Army has a comprehensive range of specialist schools, providing courses for both officers, NCOs and conscripts. The Infantry School is at San Bernardo, the Mountain Warfare School at Rio Blanco and the Special Forces School at La Colina Air Base, Santiago. The Cavalry School is at Quillota and the Armoured Forces School at Antofagasta while the Artillery School is at Linares, the Engineers' School at Tejas Verdes and the Signals School at Santiago. Each school has a demonstration regiment or battalion which together potentially form a seventh division.

Navy

Personnel:	27,000 (including Marines and naval aviation)
Major units:	1 obsolete cruiser 6 missile destroyers 2 obsolete destroyers 2 missile frigates 4 submarines 1 APD 1 submarine chaser 2 missile attack craft 4 torpedo attack craft 2 LSTs
Marines:	4 detachments (each with one reinforced battalion, a commando company, a field battery and an AA unit) 1 amphibious assault battalion 1 support battalion
Naval special forces:	1 group of frogmen commandos
Heavy equipment:	LVTP-5 amphibious APCs Mowag Roland APCs M-101 105 mm howitzers Crotale SAMs
Naval aviation:	1 maritime recce/ASW squadron 1 general purpose squadron 1 helicopter squadron 1 training squadron
Aircraft:	EMB-111 maritime reconnaissance CASA 212, EMB-110, Piper Navajo and IAI Westwind transports PC-7 trainers SA.316 Alouette III and Bell 206 helicopters

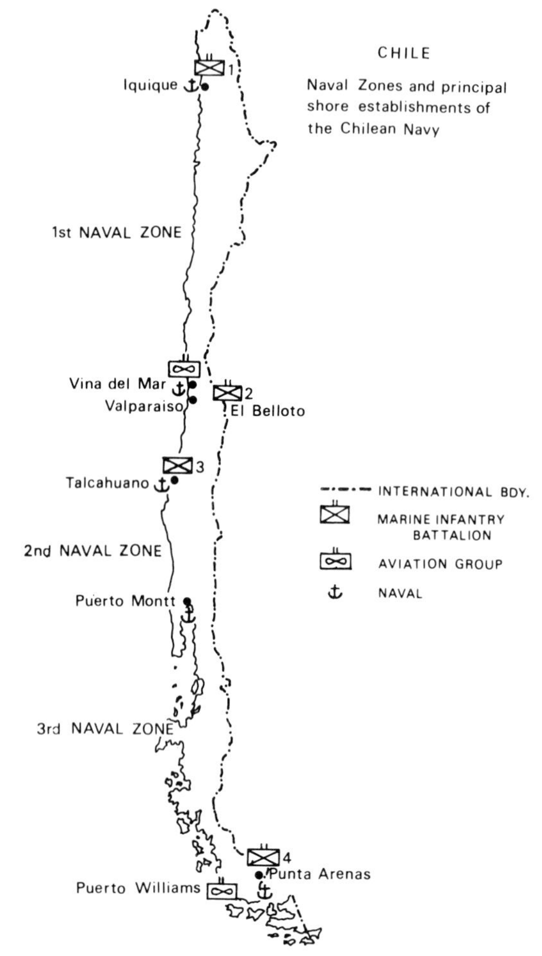

Chile formed a Navy during the early stages of the War of Independence. In 1818 a Naval Academy was established and by November of that year, when the famous British admiral, Thomas Cochrane (Lord Dundonald) assumed command of the revolutionary fleet, it was already a significant force which went on to support the Argentino-Chilean army in expelling the Spaniards from Peru. Following the achievement of independence the Chilean armed forces were gradually run down but the Navy nevertheless established control of the sea during the war of 1836–39 against Peru and Bolivia. Although by then further depleted, the Chilean Navy was nevertheless largely influential in bringing the 1865–66 war with Spain to a successful conclusion. Following this war a slow but significant naval build-up was embarked upon which left Chile with the third most powerful fleet in Latin America by the outbreak of the Pacific War in 1879. After some initial setbacks Chile established control of the sea and by January 1881 had effectively annihilated the remnants of the Peruvian fleet, emerging as the major naval power in Latin America.

Naval expansion continued under the impetus of an increasingly bitter boundary dispute with

Top: ***The veteran Chilean cruiser*** **O'Higgins (Lt H. Barras)**

Above: ***DLG*** **Prat** ***(ex-HMS*** **Norfolk*)*** **(Author)**

Argentina. The General Arbitration Treaty of 1902, which defused the tension between Chile and Argentina, however involved the cancellation of part of the naval building programmes of both countries, working effectively to the benefit of Argentina which now attained naval parity with Chile. The outbreak of the First World War occasioned the confiscation by the Royal Navy of two battleships and four destroyers building in Britain for Chile while the delayed entry of the United States into the conflict permitted the completion of two battleships building in that country for the Argentine Navy, which thus established a margin of material superiority over that of Chile which it has maintained to the present day.

A British naval mission which functioned from 1923 until 1932 reinforced the already very strong anglophile orientation of the Chilean Navy. Although one of the two confiscated battleships and the three surviving destroyers were now returned to Chile by Britain and a naval construction programme added six additional destroyers and three submarines, plus several auxiliary vessels, to the fleet during the late 1920s, economic stringency determined that no further major acquisitions were made and the Chilean Navy continued to function with a diminishing amount of progressively obsolescent equipment.

With the end of the Second World War Chile took advantage of the availability of large quantities of relatively modern naval vessels at bargain prices to replace its more antiquated equipment.

***DDG* Alimirante Riveros**

War surplus material continued to form the backbone of the Chilean Navy into the 1960s, during which additional second-hand equipment was acquired from the United States to supplement a very limited programme of new construction. The Chilean Navy remained in third place in the Latin American naval league until the 1970s when the Peruvian Navy usurped Chile's traditional position as a regional navy power. This situation was mitigated but not reversed by a modest new construction programme and the acquisition of four 'County' class missile destroyers by Chile from the Royal Navy between 1984 and 1987.

The Chilean Navy currently has a total strength of 27,000 all ranks, including Marines and Naval aviation

The major operational command is the Fleet of which the obsolete 10,000-ton US 'Brooklyn' class cruiser *O'Higgins* is the largest unit. Potentially more useful are the four 5400-ton ex-British 'County' class missile destroyers *Blanco Encalada, Prat, Cochrane* and *Latorre,* together with the much-modernised 2700-ton purpose-built *Almirante Riveros* and *Almirante Williams,* which are however almost 30 years old. There are also the two 2500-ton 'Leander' class missile frigates *Lynch* and *Condell* and the obsolete ex-US 'Sum-

***Ex-US "Sumner" FRAM II destroyer* Ministro Zentend (Author)**

"Batral" class LSTs **Maipo** *and* **Rancagua (Asmar)**

ner' FRAM II class destroyers *Ministro Zenteno* and *Ministro Portales,* plus logistic support elements, the most important of which are the 27,000-ton fleet oiler *Almirante Montt* and the 17,000-ton *Araucano.*

The submarine service forms a separate operational command with the 1300-ton 'Type 209' *Thomson* and *Simpson* and the 1600-ton 'Oberon' class *O'Brien* and *Hyatt,* the 4600-ton depot ship *Angamos* and a subordinate group of frogmen commandos.

Also forming an operational command, the transport force consists of the 2600-ton transport *Aquiles,* the 750-ton 'Batral' class LSTs *Maipo, Rancagua* and *Chacabuco* and the 300-ton landing craft *Elicura* and *Orompello.* The remaining vessels, including the 1400-ton APD *Uribe,* the 400-ton 'Reshef' class missile attack craft *Casma* and *Chipana* and the 130-ton torpedo boats *Guacolda, Fresia, Quidora* and *Tegualda,* the 300-ton 'PC' type patrol vessel *Papudo,* the armed tugs *Aldea* and *Lautaro,* plus some minor patrol vessels, auxiliaries and service craft, are distributed among the naval zones and districts. There are also the 3400-ton four-masted sail training ship *Esmeralda,* the 2000-ton Antarctic transport and research vessel *Piloto Pardo* and the 1300-ton 'Cherokee' class salvage tug *Yelcho,* used as a surveying vessel.

The current construction programme provides for the replacement of the existing transport *Aquiles* by a new vessel of 2800 tons which will bear the same name while the projected construction of up to six more 'Reshef' class missile attack craft at Talcahuano has been shelved due to economic stringency. In the medium term it is proposed to acquire a light aircraft carrier and it is also hoped to acquire up to four additional 'Leander' class frigates.

The 1st Naval Zone (HQ at Valparaíso naval base) has one floating dock and contains most of the training establishments including the Arturo Prat Naval Academy and the Naval War Academy, both located, together with the Supply School, at Valparaíso. The School of Operations, the Armaments School, the School of Marine Engineering and the Marine Corps School, are located at Viña del Mar. Also subordinate to this Zone is the Northern Naval District, with its HQ at Iquique.

The 2nd Naval Zone, with its HQ at the main naval base at Talcahuano, has two dry and three floating docks, and contains the Submarine School, the Seamen's School and the Naval Artisans' School and the Chiloé Naval District (HQ Puerto Montt).

***EMB-111 maritime reconaissance aircraft of Chile's* Aviación (Author)**

The 3rd Naval Zone has its HQ at the naval base at Punta Arenas. The Beagle Channel Naval District, with its HQ at Puerto Williams, is also subordinated to this zone. A new naval dockyard is under construction at Bahía Catalina, near Punta Arenas.

The 5200 Marines are organised into the 1st *Patricio Lynch* Detachment (Iquique), the 2nd *Miller* Detachment (Viña del Mar), the 3rd *Sargento Aldea* Detachment (Talcahuano) and the 4th *Cochrane* Detachment (Punta Arenas), each comprising a reinforced battalion, a commando company, a field battery, an anti-aircraft battery and logistic support units. There are also embarked detachments, an amphibious assault battalion and a logistic battalion. Equipment is largely the same as that of the infantry units of the Army, the US M-16 rifle in 5.56 mm calibre being substituted for the SiG 510. The Marines have some 30 LVTP-5 amphibious landing vehicles, about 40 Mowag Roland APCs, 16 US M101 105 mm howitzers and about 20 Roland APC mounted Crotale SAMs.

Naval Aviation numbers about 600 all ranks, manning a total of approximately 40 aircraft, organised operationally into two groups, based at El Belloto and Puerto Williams respectively and comprising General Purpose Squadron VC-1 with three CASA 212 Aviocars, three EMBRAER EMB-110 Bandeirantes and a Piper Navajo, Helicopter Squadron VS-1 with ten Aérospatiale Alouette IIIs and four Bell 206As, Maritime

***Fleet oiler* Almirante Montt *(Ex-HMS* Tidepool*)* (Author)**

Reconnaissance Squadron VP-1 with six EMBRAER 111As and Training Squadron VT-1 with ten Pilatus PC-7s, all operating principally from El Belloto Naval Air Base, Valparaíso, with minor bases at Punta Arenas and Puerto Williams. A recent acquisition is a single IAI Westwind 2 for photographic reconnaissance and use as a VIP transport. The acquisition of half a dozen or so ENAER T-35B Aucán basic trainers is projected and the Navy would like to establish a combat element equipped with the navalised version of the ENAER/CASA A-36 Halcón which can carry two British Aerospace Sea Eagle air-to-surface missiles. A new naval air base at Torquemada, 20 km to the north of Viña del Mar, which will permit the operation of higher performance aircraft than those at present in service, is also under construction and is scheduled to replace El Belloto as the main base of the *Aviación Naval* on completion.

The Chilean Coast Guard or the 'General Directorate of the Maritime Territory and the Merchant Navy', to give it its official title, is an integral part of the Navy and has an establishment of approximately 1600 all ranks, being treated for training purposes as a semi-autonomous specialisation analogous to that of the Marines or Naval aviation. The Chilean coastline is currently divided into 13 '*Gobernaciones Marítimas*', comprising, a total of 46 port Captaincies. The sea-going elements of the service comprise the two 215-ton converted fishing vessels *Cabo Ódger* and *Marinero Fuentealba,* employed primarily as buoy tenders, the 80-ton coastal patrol craft *Castor,* the ten Brazilian-built 43-ton high-speed cutters of the 'Pillán' class, the 25-ton *Ona* and *Yagán,* 11 inshore patrol craft, two pilot cutters and some very small harbour patrol craft, in addition to numerous small surface skimmers and Zodiac craft used for inshore patrol and rescue. The service also operates the 140-ton floating medico-dental clinic *Cirujano Videla,* which operates mainly in the coastal waters of the island of Chiloe

***Chilean naval CASA-212 Aviocar light transport* (Author)**

***Alouette III helicopter aboard DLG* Prat (Author)**

and the 14-ton air-sea rescue launch *Kimitahi,* based at Easter Island.

Chile accepts responsibility for maritime search and rescue up to 120 degrees west longitude, or effectively to within approximately 2000 miles to the west of its coastline, maintaining search and rescue co-ordination centres at Iquique, Valparaíso, Talcahuano, Puerto Montt and Punta Arenas. As none of the vessels operated by the Coast Guard are suitable for deep-sea patrol or rescue work the service can call on the ships and aircraft of the Navy proper and in particular its helicopters, for support, when necessary. The various port Captains continue to maintain and man lifeboats for inshore rescue.

The Arturo Prat Naval Academy provides a five-year course for naval officer cadets. Officers must complete post-graduate courses at the Naval War Academy for promotion to flag rank or appointment to the Naval General Staff. Selected petty officers may qualify for commissioned rank by completing a two-year course at the Naval Academy but are ineligible for promotion beyond the rank of Captain. Non-commissioned personnel, who are predominantly volunteers, receive their training at the service's comprehensive range of specialist schools.

Air Force

Personnel: 15,000

Major flying units: 5 wings comprising:-
1 interceptor squadron
3 fighter-bomber squadrons
2 light strike squadrons
2 transport squadrons
1 search and rescue squadron
1 navigational training squadron
1 photographic reconnaissance squadron

Mirage 50 fighter of the 4th Fighter Group of the Chilean Air Force (Jane's Defence Weekly)

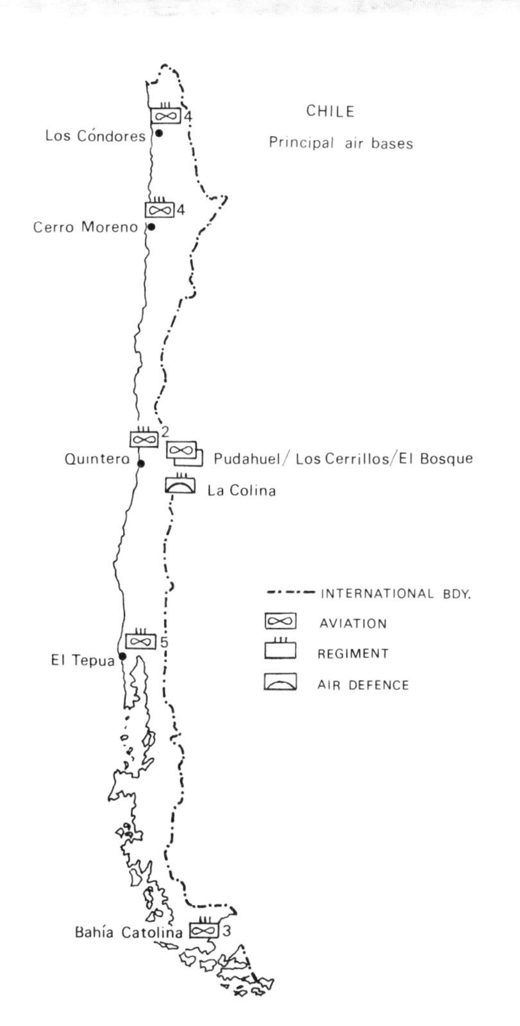

Air defence units:	1 air defence regiment 5 air defence groups
Fighters:	Northrop F-5, Dassault Mirage 50 and Hawker Hunter F.71 and T.72
Strike aircraft:	ENAER/CASA A-36 Halcón Cessna A-37B
Reconnaissance aircraft:	Canberra PR.9 Learjet 35A
Transports:	Boeing 707, Lockheed C-130, Douglas C-47 and DC-6, DHC-6, Beech King Air and Super King Air
Helicopters:	Aérospatiale Puma and Lama, Bell UH-1H and Sikorsky S-55
Trainers:	ENAER/CASA T-36, ENAER T-35A Pillán, ENAER T-35B Aucán, Beech T-34, Cessna T-41 and T-37

The Chilean Air Force is the world's fourth oldest independent military air arm. A School of

Northrop F-5 fighter of the Chilean Air Force's 7th Fighter Group **(Author)**

Military Aeronautics was formed in 1913 and although the First World War severely impeded the development of Chilean military aviation its end permitted the expansion of the Army's air service and the formation of a Naval aviation service. Both services continued to grow and the military and naval air arms were merged as the *Fuerza Aérea de Chile* in March 1930. Unfortunately, the formation of the Air Force coincided with a growing economic crisis, reflected in cutbacks in the armed forces, with a lack of new procurements and a steady attrition of the existing material. Following the entry of the United States into the Second World War, a US air mission was established in Chile and the country began to benefit from military aid under Lend-Lease.

With the signature of the Rio Treaty of Mutual Defence in 1947, Chile began to receive more modern combat equipment and the Air Force grew slowly during the succeeding years although during the late 1950s the deletion of its obsolete combat equipment, without adequate replacement, reduced it primarily to a transport and training force. Limited amounts of modern equipment were acquired from the mid-1960s onwards but during the years immediately following the coup which overthrew the Allende regime, the Chilean Air Force, like the Army and Navy, experienced great difficulties in acquiring new material or spares for existing equipment. Following Chilean co-operation with Britain during the 1982 Anglo-Argentine War however, some replacements were forthcoming for the losses by attrition of the Hawker Hunter fighter-bombers which still formed the backbone of the Chilean Air Force.

The Air Force is currently organised into three commands – Combat, Personnel, and Logistics – with a total strength of approximately 15,000 all ranks and some 280 aircraft in 1986.

Combat Command controls five wings which operate most of the flying equipment of the FACH.

The 1st Wing (Cerro Moreno, Antofagasta) comprises the 7th Group with 16 Northrop F-5Es and Fs, plus the 8th Group and the 9th Group, each with 16 Hawker Hunter F.71s and T.72s; the 2nd Wing (Quintero, Valparaíso) consists only of the 11th Group equipped with 11 Beech 99As and functions as an instrument flying and navigational training unit; the 3rd Wing (HQ Bahía Catalina, Punta Arenas) is made up of the 12th Group (Punta Arenas) with 14 Cessna A-

***The Hawker Hunter fighter-bomber, still in service with the 8th and 9th Fighter-Bomber Groups of the Chilean Air Force* (Author)**

37Bs and the 6th Group (Bahía Catalina) with ten DHC 6s; the 4th Wing (HQ Los Cóndores, Iquique) combining the 1st Group (Los Cóndores) with 14 Cessna A-37Bs and the 4th Group (Pudahuel) with 16 Dessault Mirage 50s while the 5th Wing (El Tepual, Puerto Montt) is essentially a search and rescue unit and consists only of Group No 5, equipped with five DHC-6s and six Sikorsky S-55 helicopters.

Each wing includes a liaison flight equipped with assorted light aircraft and helicopters, including a total of three Beech Twin Bon: nzas, ten Cessna 180s and nine SA.315 Lamas, plus an anti-aircraft artillery group, equipped with Oerlikon K 63 twin 35 mm AA guns. There is also the *Regimiento de Artillería Anti-Aérea* at La Colina which adds Crotale SAMs to the foregoing tube artillery equipment. The 1st and 4th Wings each include an Electronic Communications Group. Air Force ground defence units are equipped with the Israeli Galil rifle in 5.56 mm calibre, light automatic weapons and the locally-produced Carancho airfield defence vehicle.

Personnel Command controls the Air Force Staff and Technical Colleges, neither of which operates any aircraft, in addition to the *Escuela de Aviación Capitán Ávalos* equipped with 17 ENAER/CASA T-36 Halcóns, 20 Cessna T-37s, 26 ENAER T-35 Pillans and 30 Beech T-34s. All three schools are located at El Bosque, Santiago. This command also controls the Specialists' School, equipped with eight Cessna T-41s and ten Piper 236 Dakotas, the *Academia de Guerra Aérea* (Air Force Staff College) and the *Academia Politécnica Aérea* (Air Force Technical College) neither of which operates any aircraft. The *Escuela de Aviación* offers a basic three-year course to officer cadets, followed by two years of specialised training before commissioning. As with the Army and Navy, the completion of the course of the *Academia de Guerra Aérea* is a prerequisite for appointments to the Air General Staff or for promotion to senior rank.

Logistics Command controls two non-flying wings, the Supply Wing and the Maintenance Wing both with their headquarters at El Bosque.

In addition to the above units there is the 10th Group, a transport unit with two Lockheed C-130s, eight Douglas C-47s, eight Bell UH-1Hs and three 212s, plus a single Aérospatiale SA.330 Puma and the Photographic Survey Squadron

***Cessna A-37B light strike aircraft* (Author)**

with two Canberra PR.9s, two Learjets, two Beech King Air 90s and a Beech Super King Air 200, both based at Los Cerrillos, Santiago and directly subordinate to Air Force Headquarters.

The former 3rd Group, which operated the majority of the helicopter assets of the FACH from Temuco, has been deactivated and its equipment dispersed among the various wings, most of it going to the 10th Group.

The Mirage 50s are in process of a general upgrading to Kfir standards, with the assistance of Israel Aircraft Industries. The Cessna A-37s are also in the process of replacement by the ENAER/CASA A-36 Hacón, the similar T-36 being the designated replacement of the Cessna T-37 in the advanced training role, a total of 37 aircraft of both types being on order. The T-35A Pillán and T-35B Aucán, of which a total of 60

***The ENAER/CASA T-36 Halcón strike trainer which is scheduled to replace the A-37 in the ground-attack role* (Jane's Defence Weekly)**

examples are on order, will also ultimately replace the Beech T-34 as the standard basic and intermediate trainer. The older light helicopter types will also be gradually replaced by an ultimate total of 30 examples of the Messerschmitt-Bölkow MBB Bo 105 which is being manufactured under licence by ENAER. Two EMBRAER EMB-120 transports and three Aérospatiale AS.322 Super Pumas are also on order.

Paramilitary Forces

Manpower:	27,000
Heavy equipment:	Mowag Roland APC
Patrol craft:	Small launches
Aircraft:	Swearingen Metro FH-1100 MBB Bo 105

In 1927 all existing law enforcement agencies were incorporated into a single national force, the *Carabineros de Chile,* which has a paramilitary organisation and is a potential reserve for the armed forces. The force was normally under the jurisdiction of the Ministry of the Interior but has been transferred to that of the Ministry of Defence during the national emergency following the overthrow of the Allende regime. The *Carabineros* are commanded by a director-general and are organised into six zones corresponding to the army's six divisional areas, each of which is in turn sub-divided into *prefecturas, sub-prefecturas, comisarías, sub-comisarías, tenencias, retenes* and *puestos avanzados.* There are a number of specialised sections including Traffic Control, Highway Patrol, Riot Control, Forest Rangers and Frontier Guards. The *Carabineros* are also responsible for customs control and provide the Presidential guard. The standard of recruitment is high, the *Carabineros* enjoying a prestige and universal respect which is almost unique among Latin American police forces and the force has its own Police School and Staff Officers School. In addition to normal police equipment, the *Carabineros,* which currently number approximately 27,000, have a range of light infantry weapons and 20 Mowag Roland APCs at their disposal and operate 10 small patrol craft, three service craft and 13 rescue craft. In addition, they have a mixture of fixed and rotary-winged aircraft, including four Swearingen Metros, a single Hiller FH-1100, a Bell 206 and ten Messerschmitt-Bölkow MBB Bo 105s.

Sources of defence material supply and current requirements

Traditional Chilean military procurement policies faithfully mirrored the influences at work on the individual armed forces. Thus the Army showed a distinct preference for weapons of German design if not necessarily German manufacture, although somewhat surprisingly the French Hotchkiss machine gun was standard in the 1930s. For similar reasons, the Navy has largely confined its patronage for new construction to British yards. The Air Force, again mirroring its formative influences, was initially equipped largely with British material although large quantities of US-built aircraft, together with the products of the renascent German aircraft industry, appeared in the mid-1930s. Quantities of US material began to reach the Army and Air Force, though strangely not the Navy, as military aid during the Second World War and for almost two decades US war surplus material came to dominate the inventories of the Chilean armed forces, as in the case of most others in the region. In the 1960s more diverse markets were explored, Belgian, Swiss and German small arms being adopted, together with quantities of French and Swiss AFVs, Italian artiller pieces, Israeli and Spanish naval vessels and French combat aircraft.

With the widespread boycott of the military regime following the downfall of Allende, Chile found many traditional sources of equipment closed and procurement was pursued on an ad hoc basis, material being acquired from whatever sources were available. This inevitably resulted in an increasingly heterogeneous and unbalanced equipment inventory. During this period, the Navy and Air Force encountered particular difficulties in the acquisition of replacements and spares and much ingenuity was employed in prolonging the life of otherwise obsolete or worn-out material. While most suppliers are now adopting a more reasonable attitude towards the present

Locally-developed Famae 81 mm mortar **(Author)**

Famae 120 mm mortar **(Author)**

Chilean regime, certain actions in the recent past, such as the British Labour government's refusal to deliver naval vessels and aircraft already paid for during the period 1974/79, cannot but have shaken Chilean faith in the reliability of many of its traditional suppliers. France, Israel and more recently Brazil, have made heavy inroads into the Chilean defence equipment market and despite the Chilean Navy's recent purchase of second-hand British naval vessels, future procurements will probably continue to be based more broadly than was traditionally the case.

Although a highly industrialised state by South American standards, with one sixth of the work force employed in manufacturing, Chile did not, until recently, have an arms industry worthy of the name although several small naval vessels had in the past been built in local yards and the construction of light aircraft had also taken place sporadically. The international boycott of the military regime by most of the world's manufacturers of defence material however threw the Chileans back upon their own resources and local industrial potential was accordingly expanded with dramatic speed. Starting almost from scratch in the mid-1970s, Chile now manufactures its own small arms, including the SiG 542 rifle, which is scheduled to replace the SiG 510, infantry support weapons, including mortars of up to 120 mm calibre and ammunition of all calibres up to and including 105 mm. The production of light armoured vehicles (both under licence, by agreement with the Swiss Mowag corporation and of such interesting locally-developed types as the Alacrán half-track and the Orca general-purpose load-carrier) is now well established. In addition, mines, aircraft bombs and anti-aircraft weapons of local development, aircraft (in collaboration with the Spanish, German, Israeli and US aerospace industries) and naval vessels up to the size of landing ships, small patrol craft and naval auxiliaries are now also produced locally. Although still far from attaining the ultimate ideal of complete self-sufficiency in defence production, Chile not only now supplies many of its own needs but also has a growing export trade in the products of its defence industries.

Cardoen-Mowag Piranha AFVs – from left to right anti-aircraft vehicle with twin 20 mm guns, radar surveillance vehicle, light support vehicle with 30 mm guns, heavy support vehicle with 90 mm gun (Industrias Cardoen)

The Alacrán armoured half-track with MLR (Industrias Cardoen)

***The Orca armoured load-carrier* (Industrias Cardoen)**

***Mirage 50, modified to Kfir standards by ENAER with Israeli technical assistance* (Author)**

***A-36 Halcón aircraft with British Aerospace Sea Eagle air-to-surface missiles* (Author)**

ENAER T-35B Aucán trainer (Author)

MBB Bo 105 helicopter, assembled in Chile (Jane's Defence Weekly)

Summary and prospects

Chile was the first Latin American country to organise its armed forces on a formal professional basis and from an early date earned a well justified reputation for the efficiency of its Army and Navy. As the only Latin American country with a truly maritime tradition, the Chilean Navy has also, almost inevitably, emerged as a unique institution. With an unbroken history of victory in the few foreign wars in which they have engaged, the Chilean armed forces have also gained a reputation for near invincibility and are regarded with a healthy respect throughout Latin America.

Until the recent accord with Argentina, war between the two countries seemed possible and a degree of tension continues between Chile and its northern neighbours Peru and Bolivia.

As the only country in the Americas to expel a Marxist government, Chile also remains a prime target for left-wing political subversion although the military regime devotes 64% of its revenues to education, health and social welfare. Despite the recent escalation of attempts by the militant left to destabilise the military government and the disproportionate coverage which they have received in the international news media, the armed forces and the paramilitary *Carabineros* appear wholly adequate to protect the country against any threat of external aggression or internal subversion.

COLOMBIA

(República de Colombia)

Area: 455,335 sq miles (1,139,600 sq km)
Population: 27,540,000
Total armed forces: 69,000
Reserves: 200,000
Available manpower: 2,300,000
Paramilitary forces: 51,500
GNP: $32,686 million (1985)
Defence expenditure: $274,050,000 (1985)

Introduction

Bounded by Panama to the north-west, by Venezuela to the east, by Brazil to the south-east and by Ecuador and Peru to the south-west, Colombia is the fourth largest country of South America in terms of area and the third in terms of population and occupies a pivotal strategic position, with coastlines on both the Pacific and the Caribbean. The population is heteregeneous, 58% being of mixed European and Amerindian blood, 14% of more or less pure European origins and of the remainder 4% are Negros, 14% Mulattos, 7% aboriginal Indians and 3% 'Zambos' – a mixture of Indian and Negro.

The economy is primarily based on agriculture, Colombia being the world's second largest coffee producer. Exports consist mainly of tropical products, including fruit, tobacco, sugar and cotton. The extensive mineral wealth is largely unexploited although the mining and cutting of emeralds is economically important and Colombia is self-sufficient in petroleum production, with a surplus for export. Industry is underdeveloped and manufactured goods figure highly among imports.

The country was first visited by Spaniards in 1500 but permanent settlement dates only from 1525. Successive insurrections from 1794 onwards failed until 1810 when an independent junta was set up at Bogotá. Nine years of bloody warfare, culminating in the battle of Boyacá on 7 August 1819 effectively secured the independence of Colombia, Ecuador and Venezuela as the Republic of Gran Colombia. This however lasted for less than ten years, the first five of which were occupied in continued warfare against Spain. In 1828 there was also a brief war with Peru. Venezuela seceded in 1829, to be followed by Ecuador the following year. From 1858 to 1885 Colombia was a federal republic. Following a revolution in 1885, a new constitution established the country as a unitary centralised republic. The remainder of the 19th century was characterised by almost incessant warfare between the Conservatives and the Liberals, a full-scale civil war between 1899 and 1902 costing over 100,000 lives. As a result, Colombia was unable to offer effective opposition when the province of Panama, supported by United States commercial interests, seceded and set itself up as an independent republic in 1903.

In 1932, Peruvian aggression against the small Colombian colony of Leticia in the Amazonian region of the country provoked a brief frontier war in which the Colombians were victorious. Colombia escaped significant involvement in both World Wars, making a token declaration of war against the Axis powers in the latter stages of the Second World War, but actively supported the United Nations in the Korean War, even though the country itself was racked by civil war throughout that conflict.

Rivalry between the Conservatives and Liberals had continued to dominate the history of Colombia throughout the 20th century, an undeclared civil war, known locally as *'La Violencia'*, claiming the lives of over 200,000 people between 1946 and 1958. A precarious equilibrium has been preserved between the Conservatives and Liberals over the last three decades and Colombia remains one of the few Latin American countries to have continually enjoyed more or less democratic government over such a period.

Colombia is a unitary republic of 23 departments, five *intendencias* and four *comisarias*. Executive power is vested in the President and there is a bicameral legislature.

Polarisation between the two major political factions continues to be the predominant influence in national political life and has to a certain extent buffered Colombia against the major international 'isms', although Conservative sympathies tended towards the Axis in the Second World War while the Liberals supported the Allies. Recently and especially from 1962 onwards, the importance of the political left, in the international sense, has increased. Nevertheless the Colombian Communist movement is fragmented between Stalinist, Leninist, Trotskyite and Maoist factions as well as exponents of Cuban-style Marxism. Guerrilla activity, previously confined to rural areas, has recently moved into the cities. Violent crime of a non-political character is of epidemic proportions and Colombia has become a centre of the illicit narcotics trade. Recently Colombia has joined with Mexico, Panama and Venezuela in the Contadora Group to oppose United States policies in Central America.

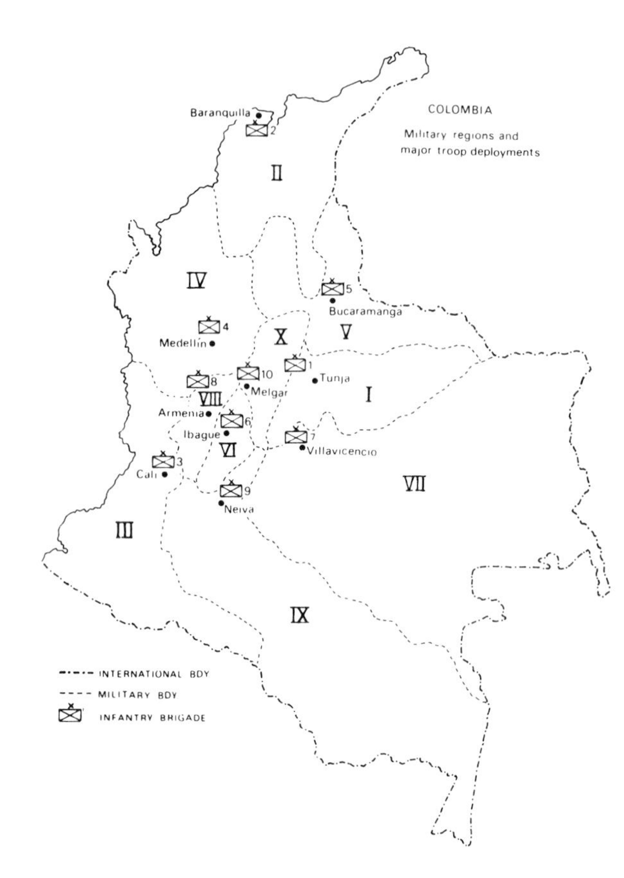

Structure of the armed forces

The President is commander-in-chief of the armed forces. The Minister of Defence who is the highest ranking general of the Army, in practice exercises both operational and administrative control over the three armed forces and the National Police. There is also the office of General Commanding the armed forces, who is invariably an Army officer and a Combined General Staff which co-ordinates the activities of the three armed forces and of the National Police. Each of the individual armed forces also has its own commander-in-chief and general staff. The Supreme Council of National Defence, composed of the Ministers of the Interior, Foreign Affairs and Finance, together with the General Commanding the armed forces, acts in an advisory capacity to both the President and the Minister of Defence. The Chief of the Combined General Staff acts as secretary to this council. Another consultative organ is the High Military Council, which consists of the General Commanding the armed forces, the Chief of the Combined General Staff, the commanders-in-chief of the Army, Navy and Air Force and of the important Military Institutes Brigade, the Director of the Staff College and the Director of the Division of Military Industries.

The country is divided into ten Military Regions, of which the 1st (HQ Boyacá) covers the national capital and most of Boyacá department; the 2nd (HQ Barranquilla) covers the departments of Guajira, Magdalena, Bolívar, César and parts of Córdoba; the 3rd (HQ Cali) covers the departments of Valle del Cauca, Cauca, Nariño, part of Choco and the *Intendencia* of Putumayo; the 4th (HQ Medellín) covers the department of Antioquia, most of Choco and parts of Córdoba; the 5th (HQ Bucaramanga) covers the department of Norte de Santander and the *Intendencia* of Arauca; the 6th (HQ Ibagué) covers only part of Tolima department; the 7th (HQ Villavicencio) covers the department of Meta and part of Boyacá plus the *Intendencias* of Vichada and Vaupés; the 8th (HQ Armenia) covers the departments of

Quindio and Risaralda; the 9th (HQ Neiva) covers the departments of Huila and the *Intendencia* of Caquetá and the 10th (HQ Melgar) covers parts of the departments of Cundinamarca and Tolima.

Military service is nominally obligatory for all fit males between the ages of 18 and 50. In practice, this is implemented as a form of selective service, approximately 12% of the numbers liable in fact serving a two-year period of military training. On completion of their active service conscripts pass to the reserve, the useful pool of trained reserve manpower being estimated at about 200,000. No effective reserve mobilisation system appears to exist.

Army

Manpower: 53,000

Formations: 10 mixed brigades
1 training brigade

Major units: 1 Presidential Guard battalion
26 infantry battalions
1 ranger battalion
1 paratroop battalion
1 armoured group
6 mechanised cavalry groups
6 artillery battalions
1 AA artillery battalion
6 engineer battalions

AFVs: M4A3 medium tank
M3A1 light tank
EE-9 Cascavel and M8 armoured cars
EE-11 Urutú, M20 and M3A2 APCs

Artillery: M101 105 mm and M116 75 mm howitzers

Air defence weapons: M1A1 40 mm

The formidable revolutionary army which had won the independence of half a continent was replaced by an entirely inferior institution, composed of ill-equipped and largely untrained troops, for the most part forcibly recruited and commanded by officers who lacked all but the most rudimentary grounding in the profession of arms. Unable to prevent the secession of Venezuela and Ecuador, the Army declined in importance throughout the 19th century, finding itself frequently both outnumbered and outclassed by the private armies of the almost incessantly warring political factions. In 1907 the first attempts at the professionalisation of the armed forces were initiated and between 1909 and 1911 the Colombian government contracted a Chilean military mission to train and reorganise the Army. The Leticia incident of 1932–33 occasioned a further reassessment of the importance of the Colombian armed forces and the considerable expansion of both the Army and Navy was not reversed with the return of peace.

Given the immense importance of its strategic position relative to the Panama Canal, the United States made great efforts to ensure that the attitude of Colombia during the Second World War, even if falling short of active billigerence, should remain as benevolent as possible to the Allied cause, persuading the Colombian government to accept both military and naval training missions in 1942, and also supplied limited quantities of defence equipment to Colombia.

Following the end of the Second World War and in particular after its ratification of the Rio Treaty in 1947, Colombia received additional quantities of war surplus material from the United States and with Colombian participation in the Korean War US military assistance increased dramatically. From the early stages of the Korean conflict, Colombia maintained a 1000-strong reinforced infantry battalion in Korea where it performed with distinction. It was relieved three times, thus giving useful combat experience in modern conventional military operations to some 4000 members of an army which had not participated in such operations since the War of Independence over a century earlier. The undeclared civil war which erupted in 1946 and occupied the attentions of the Colombian Army for the next 12 years, however gave a definite counter-insurgency emphasis to the role of the Colombian armed forces.

The Colombian Army currently numbers approximately 53,000 all ranks of whom some 24,000 are conscripts.

Each of the ten Military Regions is garrisoned by a mixed brigade and variable complement of independent units.

The Ist Brigade (HQ Tunja) garrisons the 1st

Military Region with the 1st *Bolívar*, 2nd *Sucre* and 3rd *Barbula* Infantry Battalions, the 1st *Páez* Mechanised Cavalry Group and the 1st *Tarquí* Artillery, 1st *Baraya* Engineer, 1st Military Police, and 1st Service Battalions.

The IInd Brigade (HQ Barranquilla) garrisons the 2nd Military Region with the 4th *Nariño,* 5th *Santander* and 6th *Santa Marta* Infantry Battalions, the 2nd Mechanised Cavalry Group and the 2nd Artillery, 2nd *Albán* Engineer, 2nd Military Police and 2nd Service Battalions.

The IIIrd Brigade (HQ Cali) garrisos the 3rd Military Region with the 7th *Junín,* 8th *Pichincha* and 9th *Boyacá* Infantry Battalions, the 3rd Mechanised Cavalry Group and the 3rd Artillery, 3rd Engineer and 3rd Service Battalions.

The IVth Brigade (HQ Medellín) garrisons the 4th Military Region with the 10th, 11th and 12th Infantry Battalions, the 4th Mechanised Cavalry Group and the 4th Artillery, 4th Engineer and 4th Service Battalions.

Colombian infantry disembark from UH-1H helicopter

***The cavalry units of the Colombian Army use the Brazilian EE-9 Cascavel armoured car* (Jane's Defence Weekly)**

The Vth Brigade (HQ Bucaramanga) garrisons the 5th Military Region with the 13th *Rooke,* 14th *Ricaurte* and 15th *García Rovira* Infantry Battalions, the 5th *Maza* Mechanised Cavalry Group and the 5th *Galán* Artillery, 5th *Caldas* Engineer and 5th Service Battalions.

The VIth Brigade (HQ Ibagué) garrisons the 6th Military Region with the 16th, 17th and 18th Infantry Battalions, the 6th Mechanised Cavalry Group, and the 6th Artillery, 6th Engineer and 6th Service Battalions.

The VIIth Brigade (HQ Villavicencio) garrisons the 7th Military Region with the 19th and 20th Infantry and the 7th Service Battalions.

The VIIIth Brigade (HQ Armenia) garrisons the 8th Military Region with the 21st *Cisneros* and 22nd *Ayacucho* Infantry and the 8th Service Battalions.

The IXth Brigade (HQ Neiva) garrisons the 9th Military Region with the 23rd *Vencedores Santana* and 24th *Tenerife* Infantry and the 9th Service Battalions.

The Xth Brigade (HQ Melgar) garrisons the 10th Military Region with the 25th *Juanambu* and 26th *Patriotas* Infantry and the 10th Service Battalions.

While these deployments represent the normal stations of the units which compose the ten regional brigades, individual units may occasionally be deployed outside their home region to reinforce adjoining brigades.

The Military Institutes Brigade comes under the direct control of Army Headquarters and consists of the Presidental Guard Battalion, the Military School Cadet Battalion, the Infantry School Battalion and the *Lanceros* Ranger School Battalion, plus the demonstration battalions of the cavalry, artillery and engineer schools and of the School of Combat Support Services.

Other Army level troops are the Paratroop Battalion based at Villavicencio, the *General Rincón Quiñónez* Mechanised Group at Bagotá and the *Nueva Granada* Anti-Aircraft Artillery Battalion at Barrancabermeja. There are also a supply battalion, a maintenance battalion and the 11th Military Police Battalion, all based at Bogotá.

The principal infantry weapon is the G3 assault rifle. Some units however still use the FN FAL. The Madsen M46, M50 and M53 sub-machine guns are all in use, together with some Walther MP-Ks and MAC-10s. Machine guns in use are still predominantly US models of the Second World War vintage, including the Browning

Colombian M2A1 105 mm howitzer firing

Automatic Rifle, the Browning M1917 and M1919, in 0.30-inch calibre and the 0.50-inch calibre M2HB, now supplemented by some HK21 light machine guns in 7.62 mm calibre. Mortars in service are principally the US M19 60 mm and M1 81 mm although some M2 107 mm models are also reportedly in service. Principal anti-armour weapons are the US M20 75 mm and M40 106 mm RCLs although some old M18 57 mm weapons may also remain on inventory. Experiments involving the mounting of TOW ATGWs on the turrets of obsolete M8 armoured cars have been carried out.

Armoured vehicles nominally on inventory include about 30 M4A3 Sherman medium and a similar number of M3A1 Stuart light tanks, plus some 50 M8 Greyhound armoured cars, M20 armoured utility vehicles and 60 M3A2 half-track APCs, most of which are no longer serviceable. The alleged existence of some 50 M113 APCs has not been confirmed. During the early 1980s the mechanised units were largely re-equipped with approximately 120 examples of the Brazilian EE-9 Cascavel armoured car and about 80 of the EE-11 Urutú wheeled APC. Reports of the existence of some EE-3 Jararacá scout cars remain unconfirmed.

The artillery is equipped with 48 US M2A1 105 mm and 20 M116 75 mm howitzers, the only air defence weapon observed in service being the US 40 mm M1A1, of which some 30 examples are believed to be on hand.

The two-year period of compulsory military service permits a reasonable level of training and as conscripts receive most of their training in the schools of application of their respective arms and services, the level of potential efficiency of the line units is higher than in the case of armies where these also fulfill a subsidiary training function. Officers receive their professional education at the *Escuela Militar,* located like the majority of the Army's training institutions at Bogotá, which offers a five-year course leading to a commission in the rank of second lieutenant. Specialist training is received in the schools of application of the various arms and services and higher level professional training for officers, essential for promotion to field rank and above, is received at the Staff College. Many officers have also undergone supplementary specialist courses in the United States or in the Panama Canal Zone and a US military mission has been continuously active in Colombia since 1942.

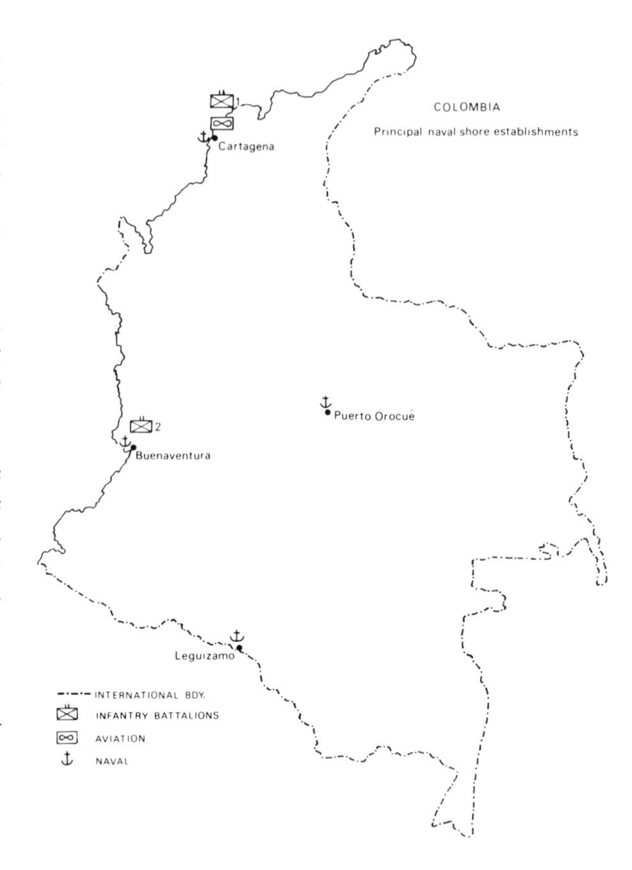

Navy

Manpower:	9700 (including 2500 Marines)
Major units:	1 obsolete destroyer 4 missile frigates 2 submarines 4 large patrol vessels 2 fast attack craft 4 river gunboats
Marines:	2 Marine infantry battalions + 3 independent companies
Aircraft:	Piper Cherokees and Aero Commanders MBB Bo 105 helicopters

During the Wars of Independence, the Revolutionary Navy scored several victories over the forces of the Spanish Crown. The political chaos which characterised most of the 19th century however stifled the growth of the Navy and culminated in the formal abolition of the naval forces during the economic crisis of 1845. While the Colombian Navy was not to re-emerge officially until 1907, a small naval force appears to have continued to exist unofficially throughout most of this period. The Leticia conflict saw a spectacular increase in the size of the Navy and a number of retired Royal Naval officers were contracted to train the personnel of the greatly expanded fleet. In 1942 the United States, with an eye to the defence of the Panama Canal, established a naval mission in Colombia although Lend-Lease aid was confined to a few small patrol craft.

Somewhat surprisingly, Colombia did not avail of the opportunity presented by the appearance of large quantities of modern naval vessels on the market at bargain prices, following the end of the Second World War, to expand its naval fleet and replace obsolete material, only a single frigate and a small oiler being acquired from US surplus stocks. In 1947, however, the construction of small naval vessels commenced at the naval dockyard at Cartagena. Colombian participation in the Korean War occasioned the transfer of two more frigates from the United States, all three frigates of the Colombian Navy serving in turn in Korean waters and some new construction was also initiated as an indirect result of these operations. During the 1960s and 1970s limited transfers of obsolescent US naval vessels and some new construction continued to take place.

The Colombian Navy, which currently numbers approximately 9700 all ranks, is organised into the Caribbean Coast Command, with its headquarters at Cartagena and the Pacific Coast

Top: *Colombian missile frigate* Almirante Padilla (Dr R. Scheina)

Above: *Submarines* Pijayo *and* Tayrona *of the Colombian Navy* (Dr R. Scheina)

Command, based at Buenaventura. There are also the Western River Forces Command, covering the Putumayo river and its navigable tributaries and based on Puerto Leguizamo and the Eastern River Forces Command, covering the Meta river and with its headquarters at Puerto Orocué.

The largest combat unit of the Colombian fleet is the 30-year old 2650 - ton Swedish-built destroyer *Siete de Agosto,* although this vessel is now of very limited military potential. The most modern and important units of the Colombian Navy are however the four 1500 - ton type FS 1500 missile frigates *Almirante Padilla, Caldas, Antioquia* and *Independiente,* completed in Germany during 1983–84. There are also the two 1200 - ton Type 209 '1200' submarines, *Pijayo* and *Tayrona,* together with the two 60 - ton Italian-built midget submarines, *Intrépido* and *Indomable.* The rest of the fleet consists of four 1235 - ton former US 'Cherokee' class armed tugs employed as patrol vessels, the two 225 - ton US 'Asheville' class fast attack craft *Quitasueño* and

***Patrol vessel* Pedro de Heredia (Dr R. Scheina)**

Albuquerque and two smaller patrol craft. Auxiliary vessels include the 1150 - ton sail training ship *Gloria,* the 830 - ton surveying vessels *Malpelo* and *Providencia,* the 670 - ton *San Andrés* and the 380 - ton *Quindio,* the 630 - ton transport *Ciudad de Quibdo,* the 534 - ton sea-going tug *Bahía Utria* and eight smaller tugs.

The river patrol force consists of the 180 - ton river gunboats *Riohacha, Leticia* and *Arauca* and the 140 - ton *Cartagena,* eight smaller river patrol craft, the 70 - ton river transports *Mario Serpa, Hernando Gutiérrez* and *Socorro,* all of which double as floating medical clinics, and two tugs.

The principal naval base is Cartagena on the Caribbean coast, which has three floating docks of from 700 to 6700 tons, a slipway and a synchrolift and there are lesser naval stations at Barranquilla and Santa Marta. Other bases are located at Buenaventura on the Pacific coast, which is being expanded; Palanquero, on the Magdalena river; Leguizamo, on the Putumayo; and Orocué and Puerto Carreño, both on the river Meta which forms the frontier with Venezuela. In this region, the Marines also maintain outposts at Puerto Ospina and Puerto Asís. All training establishments are located at Cartagena where all important repairs are also carried out.

The Marines form a separate command with

***River gunboat* Leticia**

***River patrol boat* Carlos Galindo**

two battalions – the 1st at Cartagena and the 2nd at Buenaventura – with independent companies at Barranquilla, Leguizamo and Orocué and use the same infantry personnel and support weapons as the Army but have no heavy equipment.

The Colombian Navy re-established an air arm on 18 January 1984. Three twin-engined Aero Commander fixed-wing aircraft are used for communications and maritime reconnaissance, three single-engined Piper PA-28-140 Cherokees for training and general purpose duties and two MBB Bo 105 helicopters serve in the air-sea rescue role. Aircraft of the latter type are scheduled to operate from the frigates of the 'Almirante Padilla' class and four navalised Bo 105s are on order, together with two additional aircraft of this type for training purposes.

Officer cadets pursue a five-year course at the *Almirante Padilla* Naval School at Cartagena before commissioning in the rank of ensign. The course of the Command and Staff School, also located at Cartagena, must be successfully completed to qualify for promotion to flag rank or for staff appointments. Ratings receive their training at the Recruit Training Centre and the Naval Technical School, which are also located at Cartagena. The Marines also maintain a training school at Cartagena.

Expansion plans centre on the construction of four missle corvettes to replace the armed tugs currently used for sea-going patrol, the acquisition of additional coastal patrol craft and the expansion of the naval air arm. The completion of the new naval base at Buenaventura will also greatly expand the operational potential of the Colombian Navy on the Pacific coast.

Air Force

Manpower:	6300
Major units:	2 combat groups 1 attack and recce group 1 tactical support group 1 transport group 1 helicopter group
Fighters:	Mirage Vs
Tactical support aircraft:	A-37Bs and AT-33As
Transports:	C-130s, C-54s, C-47s, DC-6s, Fokker F.28s, HS.748s, CASA 212s, IAI Aravas and DHC-2s
Helicopters:	Bell 47s, UH-1s, 206s & 212s Hughes 300 and 500s Hiller UH-12s
Trainers:	AT-33s, T-34As, T-37Cs and T-41Ds

A Military Aviation School was established in 1922 and closed two years later, due to financial difficulties. Colombia's second military flying school was finally established in 1925, the Navy having by now also formed a small air arm. When hostilities between Colombia and Peru developed in August 1932 neither the Colombian Army or Navy had any aircraft stationed in the theatre of operations nor any facilities for operating them in that region. Almost 60 aircraft were acquired

***Floating medical clinic* Socorro**

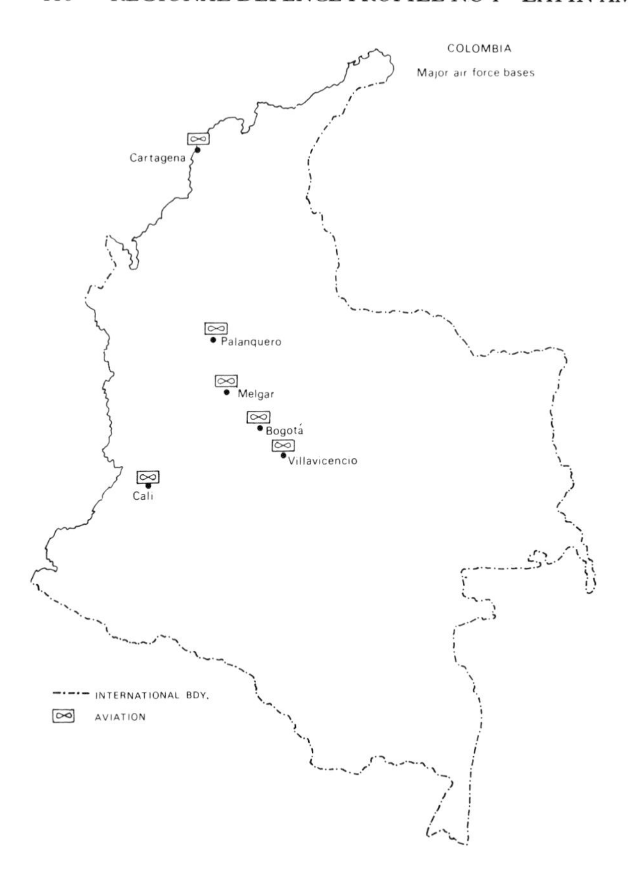

within a matter of weeks and were flown largely by German and US mercenary pilots. During the period of tension following the Leticia conflict additional quantities of aviation equipment continued to be acquired. Colombia began to receive quantities of mainly second-line aircraft under Lend-Lease from 1942 onwards and although the United States itself still lacked an independent air force, the US Service Missions recommended the amalgamation of Colombia's military and naval aviation as a single unified force and the Colombian Air Force was established in 1943. Following Colombia's ratification of the Rio Treaty in 1947, additional quantities of equipment, including the first modern combat aircraft were received.

The Colombian Air Force units took no active part in the Korean War, but the country's military and naval participation qualified it for increased US military aid. This consisted principally of additional light communications and training types but in 1954 Colombia became the first Latin American country to acquire US-built jet aircraft with the delivery of six Lockheed T-33A armed trainers. The Colombian Air Force's remaining obsolete material, including much of the equipment obtained during 1942–45 now rapidly vanished and the 1960s were a period of modest expansion. Following the refusal of the United States to supply modern jet fighters, the Colombian government turned to France as a supplier and 18 Mirages were purchased in 1970, only small quantities of non-combat types being acquired during the remainder of the decade.

Currently the Colombian Air Force is organised into three major operational commands – Combat, Transport and Training – with a total of over 300 aircraft and a personnel strength of about 6300.

Combat Command consists of the 1st Combat Group (at Germán Olano Military Air Base, Palanquero) with two squadrons equipped with 15 Mirage Vs; the 2nd Combat Group (at Apiay) with a single squadron equipped with ten AT-33As and the Attack and Reconnaissance Group (at Luís Gómez Niño Military Air Base, Barranquilla) with one squadron equipped with ten Cessna A-37s, another with 18 Hughes 500Es and Ms and a reconnaissance unit with four RT-33As.

Military Air Transport Command consists of the Military Air Transport Group (at El Dorado International Airport, Bogotá) with no squadron organisation, equipped with three Lockheed C-130s, four DC-6s, six C-54s and 14 C-47s, plus two IAI Aravas and nine DHC-2s; the Presidential Flight (also at Bogotá) with single examples of the Boeing 707, Fokker F.28, HS.748 and Bell 212; and the Helicopter Group (HQ Luís F. Pinto Military Air Base, Melgar) which is equipped with 18 Bell UH-1Bs and Hs, ten Bell 206s, ten Hughes 500Ms and 13 300Cs. The military airline SATENA is also subordinate to this command and is equipped with two C-54s, eight C-47s, eight CASA 212s, 12 Pilatus PC-6Bs, three HS.748s and a single Fokker F.28.

The helicopters of the Helicopter Group are deployed throughout the country as operational requirements dictate. There are also a number of light aircraft used for communications duties outside the group structure which include a Beech Queen Air, two King Air 90s, two Piper Navajos, a single Seminole and a Cherokee, a Cessna 185, a 340, a 401, two 310s and three 404s.

Training and Tactical Support Command controls the Military Aviation School (at Marco Fidel Suárez Military Air Base, Cali) which is equipped with 21 Beech T-34As, 30 Cessna T-41Ds, eight T-37Cs and ten Lockheed T-33As; the Tactical Support Group (also at Cali) with one squadron

C-130 transport aircraft of the Colombian Air Force **(Lockheed Aircraft Corpn.)**

equipped with ten Cessna A-37Bs and another with nine Bell UH-1Hs; and the Helicopter School (at Luís F. Pinto Military Air Base, Melgar) which is equipped with 11 Bell OH-13s, four Hiller UH-12s and nine Hughes OH-6As.

The Naval Support Group, previously based at Cartagena and recently equipped with only four DHC-6Cs, appears to have been disbanded since the revival of naval aviation.

Officer cadets must successfully complete the five-year course of the Air Force Academy at Cali before commissioning in the rank of second lieutenant, the successful completion of other courses at various stages of their careers being necessary for promotion to higher rank or appointment to the Air General Staff. The Air Force NCO School is at Madrid, Cundinamarca, all other training estabalishments being located at Cali.

The Colombian Air Force has become primarily an air transport and training force, with a large helicopter component intended principally for co-operation with the Army and Navy and with official civil agencies. The small combat component, completely inconsistent with Colombia's strategically important position, seems unlikely to increase dramatically in the forseeable future. An order for 12 IAI Kfir fighters, announced in 1981 and a project to upgrade the existing Mirage Vs to Kfir standards, with Israeli technical assistance, announced the following year, have both fallen through for economic reasons. The most interesting pending acquisition, announced in June 1986, is that of six Sikorsky UH-60A Blackhawk helicopters.

Paramilitary forces

Manpower:	50,000 National Police 1500 Coast Guard
Heavy equipment:	10 patrol vessels (Coast Guard) 36 helicopters (National Police)

Colombia maintains two paramilitary forces: the National Police and the Coast Guard.

The National Police was established in 1891 and until 1962 the activities of this force were confined to the national capital and its numbers were correspondingly small. In 1962 however, the various departmental police forces of the republic, which had hitherto existed as independent entities nominally subordinate to the Minister of National Defence (and hence institutionally endowed with a paramilitary character) were combined to form a homogeneous national police force with the responsibility for maintaining public order in the entire national territory. Nevertheless, some of the larger cities continued to maintain independent police forces whose functions were effectively limited to the direction of traffic and the enforcement of parking regulations.

In the prevailing state of chronic internal instability at the time of its foundation, it was inevitable that the functions of the National Police should be extended to embrace a paramilitary internal security role in addition to their normal policing commitments. As a direct result, special units trained in counter-insurgency techniques and armed with light infantry weapons were formed within the National Police and given the title of *Carabineros*. The *Carabineros*, who are largely mounted in the rural areas in which they principally function, are separately organised and wear distinctive uniforms from those of the main body of the National Police of which they nevertheless form an integral part.

With total effectives of 50,000, of whom some 5000 are *Carabineros*, the Colombian National Police is organised in 24 sections – one for each of the administrative departments of the republic and one for the national capital, these sections being divided in turn into districts, stations, substations and posts. The National Police operates a total of 36 light helicopters of various types and a large number of motor vehicles. Arms include light infantry weapons up to and including machine guns and generally of types retired from service with the Army on grounds of obsolescence. In recent years, a nationwide epidemic of violent non-political crime has re-emphasized the traditional police functions of this force.

Founded in 1979 as an auxiliary service to the Navy, the Coast Guard which is mainly involved in the prevention of smuggling, particularly of narcotics, has a strength of about 1500 and currently operates about ten small patrol vessels including the 130-ton *Carlos Albán* and *Nito Restrepo*, the 100-ton *Olaya Herrera* and *Rafael del Castillo y Rada* and the 85-ton *Carlos E. Restrepo*.

Sources of defence material supply and current requirements

Most of the material actually in service with the Army is of US origins and almost all of it is either obsolete or obsolescent. Of the small amount of material supplied during the past decade, the most impressive in quantity has been the G3 rifle acquired from the Federal German Republic. Shortly beforehand, quantities of rifles were also acquired from France and Belgium and the Danish Madsen sub-machine gun remains the standard light automatic, even though it is no longer manufactured in its country of origin. Before the Second World War Colombia purchased most of its automatic weapons and artillery from Czechoslovakia. However, given that country's political orientation, any future custom by Colombia seems remote. Colombia recently decided to replace its existing obsolete wheeled AFV inventory with 200 vehicles of Brazilian origin and further orders may follow. Colombia has patronised more diverse sources for the supply of naval equipment, destroyers having been acquired from Portugal and Sweden and miniature submarines from Italy, while more recently the Federal German Republic has benefitted from Colombian orders for submarines and frigates. The refusal of the United States to sell modern combat aircraft to Colombia, as in the case of other Latin American countries, has led to the loss of a market in which US industry had held a virtual monopoly for almost half a century. Having already turned to France, Spain and Israel for combat and transport aircraft, Colombia may be expected to satisfy its future requirements from the keenest bidder.

Although Colombia is consciously developing its industrial base, its capacity for the manufacture of defence material remains extremely limited. Small arms ammunition has been manufactured in the country continuously since the early 1930s and the production of small arms, including the FN FAL rifle, the Madsen sub-machine gun and a copy of the Browning M1919 air-cooled light machine-gun, has been undertaken in the country. The poor quality of the end products however occasioned the abandonment of these projects. Colombia has however developed a greater degree of self-sufficiency in the construction of light naval craft than in any other area of defence production. Since 1950, the majority of the minor vessels of the Colombian Navy have been both designed and built in the country, the most ambitious shipbuilding operation undertaken to date having been the assembly of the two miniature submarines purchased from Italy in 1972 and exported in pre-fabricated sections to the Cartagena naval dockyard. Colombia also has a nascent aerospace industry which so far has limited its efforts to the assembly of light aircraft for agricultural purposes.

Summary and prospects

Any examination of the Colombian armed forces must take into account the peculiar situation created by a chronic problem of internal instability, liable to become acute with minimal provocation, in juxtaposition with the lack of any obvious immediate external threat, despite the country's pivotal strategic position. In this context, it is understandable that the country's fairly modest resources have been concentrated in the perfection of the internal security and counter-insurgency capabilities of its armed forces.

The organisational structure of the Army would appear to be well suited to both its actual and potential roles. With the Brazilian AFV purchase the Colombian government has shown a belated realisation of the most critical shortcoming in its current equipment inventory, although it still lacks modern tracked armour, artillery and both anti-armour and air defence weapons. The pending US withdrawal from the Panama Canal Zone is also beginning to cast its shadow and there is evidence that official thinking is reverting towards the re-equipment of the armed forces for a more conventional military role. Modern battle tanks are reported to be on Colombia's current shopping list and the acquisition of both modern tube artillery and anti-tank and anti-aircraft missiles must also be engaging the attention of Colombian military planners.

Given the primarily internal security orientation of the Colombian armed forces over the past 35 years, the Navy's concentration on the construction of large numbers of small craft of limited military potential, at the expense of the acquisition of major surface combatants, is understandable. The recent acquisition of submarines and of missile frigates appears to hint at a reversion to a more conventional role although two submarines alone would be of little use to a country with extensive coastlines on both the Pacific and the Caribbean. As with most Latin American navies, that of Colombia seems to have almost totally ignored any provision for mine warfare although some defensive minelaying would also seem to make considerable sense in the approaches to the Caribbean coast ports and the estuary of the Magdalena river. The excellently trained and efficient Marine Corps also notable lacks any significant amphibious warfare capacity.

The Air Force, with only two squadrons of modern fighters, would certainly need several more fighter squadrons for the effective defence of the country's major population centres. Given the continuing internal security problem and the constant possibility of its escalation, the limited light strike capability of the Air Force is also surprising. A major defect in the equipment of the Air Force is the lack of maritime reconnaissance/ASW capability. The recent re-establishment of a naval air arm may eventually remedy this defect.

The Colombian armed forces, on the few occasions when they have been proven in battle, have shown themselves to be of high quality. Due perhaps largely to its consistent internal problems, Colombia has declined to respond to the periodic arms races which have preoccupied its neighbours and dissipated their resources and by so doing has also failed to achieve the influential status to which its size and key geographical position entitle it. There is some evidence however that recent Colombian governments, consistently with their adoption of a more independent role in international affairs, are beginning to take their growing responsibilities in hemispheric defence somewhat more seriously. As it is, they have been hindered in any major projects for the expansion or re-equipment of their Armed Forces by the current economic crisis which afflicts all countries of the region.

COSTA RICA

(República de Costa Rica)

Area: 19,700 sq miles (51,023 sq km)
Population: 2,600,000
Paramilitary forces: 6000
Reserves: 10,000
Available manpower: 200,000
GNP: $3,626 million (1985)
Defence expenditure: $20,210,000 (1984)

Introduction

Costa Rica, the second smallest country of Central America, with coasts on the Pacific and the Caribbean, is bordered by Nicaragua to the north-west and by Panama to the south-east. The population is unique in Central America, being of predominantly European origin. There are approximately 40,000 Negros and less than 1500 aboriginal Indians.

Agriculture is Costa Rica's main economic activity, although light industry, mainly concerned with the processing of agricultural products, has developed in recent years. Foreign commercial involvement, principally by US companies but to a considerably less marked extent than in the other countries of Central America, is mostly in the field of banana growing.

Following the expulsion of the Spaniards, Costa Rica, together with the remainder of Central America, was annexed by Mexico from 1821 until 1824. From 1824 to 1828 it formed part of the United Provinces of Central America and it was not until 1838, following a bloody war with Nicaragua, that it was established definitely as an independent republic. Between 1853 and 1857 Costa Rica was once again involved in hostilities, when the North American filibusterer William Walker attempted to carve out a private empire in Central America. Apart from these conflicts it was however remarkably free from the combination of internal political instability and external threat which characterised the formative years of most of its neighbours. Some frontier clashes with Panama occurred in 1921, leading to a seven-year-long breach in diplomatic relations between the two countries, the disputed frontier being finally settled by treaty in 1944. There had also been bloodless revolutions in 1917 and 1919 but the only serious internal disturbance this century was the civil war of 1948, which claimed almost 1600 lives. The major external threat has come traditionally from Nicaragua. An attempted invasion by followers of former President Rafael Calderón Guardia, supported by the Nicaraguan dictator General Anastasio Somoza, was repelled with limited material support from the USA in 1955 and recently there is again a perceived threat from Nicaragua arising from the activities of guerrillas opposed to the present Nicaraguan regime whose operations from Costa Rican territory have resulted in incursions by Nicaraguan troops.

The country is a democratic republic of seven provinces. Executive power is in the hands of the

President and there is a single chamber legislative assembly.

In the past Costa Rica has pursued a relatively independent foreign policy, as exemplified by the reopening of diplomatic relations with Cuba in 1976. It gave active support to the Sandinista revolution in Nicaragua and until recently also gave moral support to the left-wing guerrillas in El Salvador. A catastrophic decline in an economy based on the export of relatively luxurious commodities, together with the activities of Nicaraguan counter-revolutionaries based in its territory, have led Costa Rica to align itself more closely with the US in exchange for considerable economic and some military assistance. A combination of the current economic crisis and the generally explosive situation in Central America has led to the expansion of the security forces and the dispatch of key personnel for counter-insurgency training to Chile, South Korea and Taiwan.

Paramilitary forces

Manpower:	6000
Major civil guard units:	Presidential Guard 1 counter insurgency battalion 9 security companies Coast Guard Air section
Heavy equipment:	M113 APCs M3A1 scout cars 20 mm AA guns
Patrol vessels:	9 patrol craft 1 tug
Aircraft:	DHC-3, Cessna U206 Piper Apache, Aztec, Seneca and Cherokee Sikorsky S-58, FH-1100 and Hughes 500

Following the 1948 civil war, the armed forces were formally abolished and replaced by a paramilitary Civil Guard which combined internal security and defence functions.

The command structure of the Civil Guard is diffuse and designed to frustrate any attempts to use them for political purposes. Although the President is commander-in-chief of all public security forces, the Civil Guard comes under the administrative jurisdiction of the Minister of Public Security but receives its budgetary allocation of funds from the Minister of Finance, via estimates prepared by the Minister of the Interior, while its training establishments come under the jurisdiction of the Minister of the Presidency. There is a civilian Director General of Public Forces, who controls operations on a day-to-day basis while the senior officer of the Civil Guard holds the title of Director, with the rank of colonel.

***Members of the recently-formed* Relámpago *Immediate Reaction Battalion of Costa Rica's* Guardia Civil (Jane's Defence Weekly)**

Recruitment is entirely voluntary.

The Civil Guard combines the functions of Army, Navy, Air Force and National Police and was originally intended to have very limited military capacity and a primarily internal security function. Since the mid-1970s there has been an increasing reversion towards a conventional military role. Although the Guard remains the main national police force, it is supplemented in rural areas by a separate force, the Town and Village Police, which has purely police functions.

The Guard is organised on military lines and basically deploys a company in each of the seven provinces of the republic. About 40% of its total effectives are located at San José, the capital. These include the Presidential Guard, which is an elite unit of approximately battalion strength, and another battalion strength unit, combining the 1st and 2nd Companies. The so-called '3rd Company', which functions both as a strategic reserve, a depot and a training unit, also approaches battalion strength. There is also the Traffic Force, which as its name indicates, functions as a highway patrol, plus a plain-clothes detective element. Problems on the frontier with Nicaragua have led to the recent formation of a counter insurgency battalion, trained by US special forces.

Equipment in use includes US M16A1 rifles in 5.56 mm calibre and M1 Garand rifles in 0.30-inch, Beretta M38/49 and Thompson sub-machine guns in 9 mm and 0.45-inch calibres respectively, Browning Automatic Rifles and Browning M1919 machine guns, all in 0.30-inch calibre, and M60 machine guns. Support weapons include US M1 81 mm mortars, M67 90 mm RCLs and M203 genade launchers. A few M113 APCs were acquired in the late 1970s and some M3A1 White scout cars may remain in service. No artillery is known to exist although the recent purchase of quantities of 20 mm ammunition, together with no identified purchases of weapons of this calibre for many years, would appear to indicate that some old 20 mm Breda AA guns, dating from the 1930s, may still be in use. The more modern equipment is operated by the new counter-insurgency battalion.

A coast guard force was established as an integral part of the Civil Guard shortly after its foundation. This has recently been expanded and currently maintains one large and five smaller patrol craft, plus a rescue tug, on the Caribbean coast and three small patrol launches on the Pacific coast. Three additional small patrol craft were to be transferred by the United States during 1986.

An air section was also established, on a de facto basis, during the 1955 invasion but most of its aircraft were written off shortly after the termination of hostilities. No further combat aircraft were acquired although some small transport and liaison types were maintained. This force has recently been expanded and consists of three DHC-3s, four Cessna U206Gs, two Piper Cherokees and single examples of the Piper Apache, Aztec and Seneca, plus four Hughes 500Es and single examples of the Sikorsky S-58 and Fairchild-Hiller FH-1100 helicopters. A CASA C-212 light transport and two Cessna T-41 trainers are on order.

All personnel are trained at the National Police School founded in 1963, and a high proportion of the Guard's personnel have undergone additional training in the United States or in the Panama Canal Zone. The Civil Guard Volunteer Reserve duplicates the strength of the active force. Equipment is available for a total force of 10,000.

The police functions of the Civil Guard are basically confined to the national and provincial capitals, the policing of rural areas and lesser urban centres being the responsibility of the Town and Village Police. This force is commanded at national level by an Inspector General, responsible to the Minister of the Interior. The provincial detachments, at canton and district level, come under the jurisdiction of the provincial governor but the force has no authority within the provincial capitals.

There is also the Fiscal Guard, which comprises the Treasury Police and the Customs Police. The Treasury Police is primarily concerned with national security and the investigation of serious crime. The functions of the Customs Police are self-explanatory.

Of the above forces, only the Civil Guard has any military functions or capability.

Sources of equipment supply and current requirements

Most equipment on hand is either obsolete or obsolescent and is mostly of US origins although increasing tensions in the region have occasioned the recent acquisition of heavier and more modern equipment, again mainly from the United States. There is no domestic arms industry and Costa Rica does not manufacture military equipment of any kind. Future requirements, which include small arms, armoured vehicles, infantry support and anti-armour weapons, plus patrol craft and helicopters, seem likely to continue to be largely met by the United States, the current order for a single Spanish-built light transport aircraft notwithstanding.

Summary and prospects

Recent operations of the Costa Rican security forces have been confined to repelling border incursions during the Nicaraguan civil war of 1978/79 and attempts to curtail the activities of ex-patriate Nicaraguan counter-revolutionaries operating in the northern frontier region. The latter have reached such a level that the Costa Rican government has accepted training assistance from the United States in the improvement of the counter-insurgency capabilities of the Civil Guard from 1985 onwards although it declined an offer to station an engineer construction battalion of the US Army in the northern frontier zone.

Increasing instability in Central America and fear of political contamination from Nicaragua, concommitent with Costa Rica's increased economic dependence on the United States and the country's added strategic importance as the scheduled date for US withdrawal from the Panama Canal Zone draws closer, seem destined to force the Civil Guard to revert increasingly to a conventional military role. Increased acquisitions of heavier and more modern equipment, almost certainly from the United States, also seem likely.

Although Costa Rica's altruistic experiment in the abolition of its armed forces in a geographical region where militarism is a firmly established tradition, may seem to be progressively more of a pious fraud, the Civil Guard has established an enviable reputation for efficiency and respect for democratic government during its four decades of existence.

CUBA

(República de Cuba)

Area: 44,200 sq miles (114,478 sq km)
Population: 10,200,000
Total armed forces: 162,000
Reserves: 640,000
Available manpower: 850,000
Paramilitary forces: 620,000+
GNP: $17,150 million (1984)
Defence expenditure: $1,612 million (1985)

Introduction

Cuba, the largest and most westerly of the Greater Antilles, is separated from Florida, which lies 90 miles to the north, by the Florida Strait and from Haiti, 50 miles to the east, by the Windward Passage. Jamaica lies 90 miles to the south and the nearest point of Mexico, Cape Catoche, lies slightly more than 100 miles to the west, being separated from Cuba by the Yucatan Channel. Of the total population some 51% are of mixed European and Negro blood. 37% are white, 11% Negro and 1% Chinese. Although approximately 20% of the population is concentrated in the Havana area, population density throughout the country is evenly distributed.

Sugar is the mainstay of the Cuban economy, tobacco, coffee and other tropical products being next in importance as exports and the re-export of refined Soviet crude oil, purchased at a discount in its raw form, has become an important earner of foreign currency. Nickel mining is also important and there are large reserves of this mineral. Imports consist principally of fuel, chemicals and manufactured goods although the country is not entirely self-sufficient in food production. Industries are principally related to the main agricultural products, including the manufacture of cigars, but also include oil refining and the processing of wood products and the government has a deliberate programme of industrial development.

Cuba was discovered by Columbus on 27 October 1492 and first colonised in 1511. By the mid-16th century the aboriginal inhabitants had largely succumbed to overwork, ill-treatment and imported diseases, African slaves being introduced to work the sugar plantations in 1526. The buoyancy of the economy largely buffered the island against the revolutionary unrest which resulted in the independence of most of the Spanish American colonies during the first quarter of the 19th century although unsuccessful revolts occurred in 1837, 1848, 1850 and 1851 and a more serious uprising lasted from 1868 until 1878. Yet another unsuccessful revolt occurred in 1879 and the final stage of Cuba's struggle for independence began in 1895.

The United States used the pretext of the destruction of the battleship *Maine* in mysterious circumstances in Havana harbour to declare war on Spain in February 1898 and the Spaniards capitulated in August, following a series of defeats on land and sea. Cuba was occupied by US troops until 1902 when Tomas Estrada Palma was elected as first President of the Cuban republic. After its military withdrawal, the US retained a naval base at Guantánamo and forced the Cubans to accept the Platt Amendment to their constitution whereby the United States retained their right to intervene in Cuban domestic affairs, another US occupation, following a revolt in 1906 lasting until 1909. Gerardo Machado was virtual dictator from 1925 until 1933 when he was forced out of office by a general strike, being replaced by Carlos Manuel de Céspedes who was in turn overthrown by an army revolt in September 1933, led by Sergeant Fulgencio Batista. Although the Platt Amendment was abrogated in 1934 Cuba continued to be a virtual dependency of the United States. Batista now became the major figure in Cuban politics, ruling generally through a series of figurehead presidents although he assumed the Presidency himself in 1940–44 and again in 1952.

An abortive attack on an army barracks in Santiago de Cuba in 1953 gave the first prominence to a young lawyer named Fidel Castro. Released from prison in a general amnesty two years later, Castro fled to Mexico where he organised a small group of Cuban expatriates for an 'invasion' of their homeland which was eventually mounted in December 1956. During the next two years Castro's guerrillas expanded in numbers, wearing down Batista's poorly motivated Army in a progressive war of attrition. Combined with isolated acts of urban terrorism and several small and unsuccessful revolts in the Army and Navy this precipitated Batista's flight from Cuba on New Year's Eve 1958.

Castro emerged from the beginning as the effective leader of post-Batista Cuba although he did not immediately assume the Presidency. A clean-up of the deep-rooted institutionalised corruption coincided with the expropriation of foreign (predominantly US) owned business interests, inevitably provoking the enmity of the United States government, which responded with trade sanctions and the persuasion of all members of the Organization of American States, except Mexico, to break off diplomatic relations with Cuba in 1960. In 1961 the CIA–backed Bay of Pigs invasion finally polarised relations between Cuba and the United States, although Castro did not declare himself to be a Marxist-Leninist until eight months later. The United States having virtually declared war on the Cuban regime, it was inevitable that Cuba should turn to the other superpower, the Soviet Union, for economic and military assistance. The latter reached its peak in the Cuban missile crisis of 1962 which almost precipitated the third World War.

Following the failure of 'Che' Guevara's revolutionary mission to Bolivia in the late 1960s and the suppression of similar efforts at the export of the Cuban revolution to most other Latin American countries, Cuban efforts in this direction largely turned eastwards towards Africa and the Middle East. This lessened friction with its Latin American neighbours to the extent that seven countries had already resumed relations with Cuba before the Organization of American States voted to lift economic and diplomatic sanctions against it in 1975. A decline even in the overt hostility between Cuba and the United States also became perceptible during the 1970s, diplomatic relations being resumed in 1977. The election of Ronald Reagan to the US Presidency in 1981 however resulted in a resumption of the 'cold war' with Cuba.

Cuba is a highly centralised Socialist republic of 14 provinces which are in turn subdivided into 169 municipalities. Representation is based on the principle of "Popular Power" at municipal, provincial and national levels, with elections at five-year intervals. Legislative power is nominally vested in the Council of Ministers, from which the Executive Committee or cabinet is elected. Real executive power is in the hands of the President of the National Assembly and Council of State and of the Council of Ministers and First Secretary of the Cuban Communist Party, Dr Fidel Castro. Only one political party is tolerated, the structure of the Cuban Communist party being closely interwoven with that of government.

The viability of the Cuban economy progressively declined during the first years following the country's rejection of the capitalist system and Cuba survived economically only by virtue of massive subsidies from the Soviet Union. Recent improvements in economic performances, resulting in a budget surplus in 1982–83, may lessen the country's economic dependence on Soviet assistance, estimated at US $2.5m per day at its peak although the economy has suffered as a result of a poor sugar harvest in 1986 and the drop in the world price of oil.

Cuba gave active support to the Sandinista revolution in Nicaragua, both morally and on a material level by the provision of quantities of small arms and equipment. Since the success of the revolution in that country, an increasing level of Cuban assitance has continued, including the provision of advisers and instructors in the handling of the heavy military equipment subsequently transferred, but principally in the form of technical assistance in the rebuilding of the country's civilian infra-structure. Cuba has also supported the left-wing guerrillas in El Salvador, mainly morally but also with the supply of very limited quantities of military equipment. Cuban military and civilian advisers are also widely active in Third

World countries with a left-of-centre political orientation.

Structure of the Armed Forces

Fidel Castro is commander-in-chief of the Revolutionary Armed Forces. His brother, Raúl Castro, as Minister of the Armed Forces, directs the Joint General Staff and is responsible for the day-to-day running of Cuba's formidable military machine. The Revolutionary Army, Navy and Air Force each has its own staff, under the control of the Joint General Staff.

The country is divided into three major geographical commands of which the Western Command (HQ Havana) covers the capital and the provinces of Havana and Pinar del Río, Central Command (HQ Matanzas) covering the provinces of Matanzas, Villa Clara, Cienfuegos and Sancti Spiritus and Eastern Command (HQ Santiago de Cuba) the provinces of Santiago de Cuba, Guantánamo, Granma, Holguín, Las Tunas, Camagüey and Ciego de Ávila. The Isle of Youth (formerly the Isle of Pines) has the status of an autonomous military region.

All male citizens between the ages of 16 and 45 are liable for military service, the initial period of military training lasting three years between the ages of 17 and 20. Women who are enlisted on a voluntary basis, also perform many subsidiary functions in the Revolutionary Armed Forces and man some air defence units. Military training also involves constant and comprehensive indoctrination in Marxist dogma and the structures of the Cuban Communist party and those of the Revolutionary Armed Forces are closely interwoven.

Over 75% of all officers are graduates of the six *Camilo Cienfuegos* Military Schools which give pre-military training to children between the ages of 11 and 17. Officers may also be appointed directly or may be promoted from the ranks. Preference in the allocation of military cadetships is given to members of the Young Communist Union and a majority of the members of the officer corps of the Revolutionary Armed Forces are active members of the Communist Party. Each of the armed forces maintains its own comprehensive system of training establishments. The *General Máximo Gómez* Military Academy imparts advanced post-graduate military education to officers of the Revolutionary Army, Navy and Air Force. Many commissioned and enlisted personnel also receive part of their training in the Soviet Union.

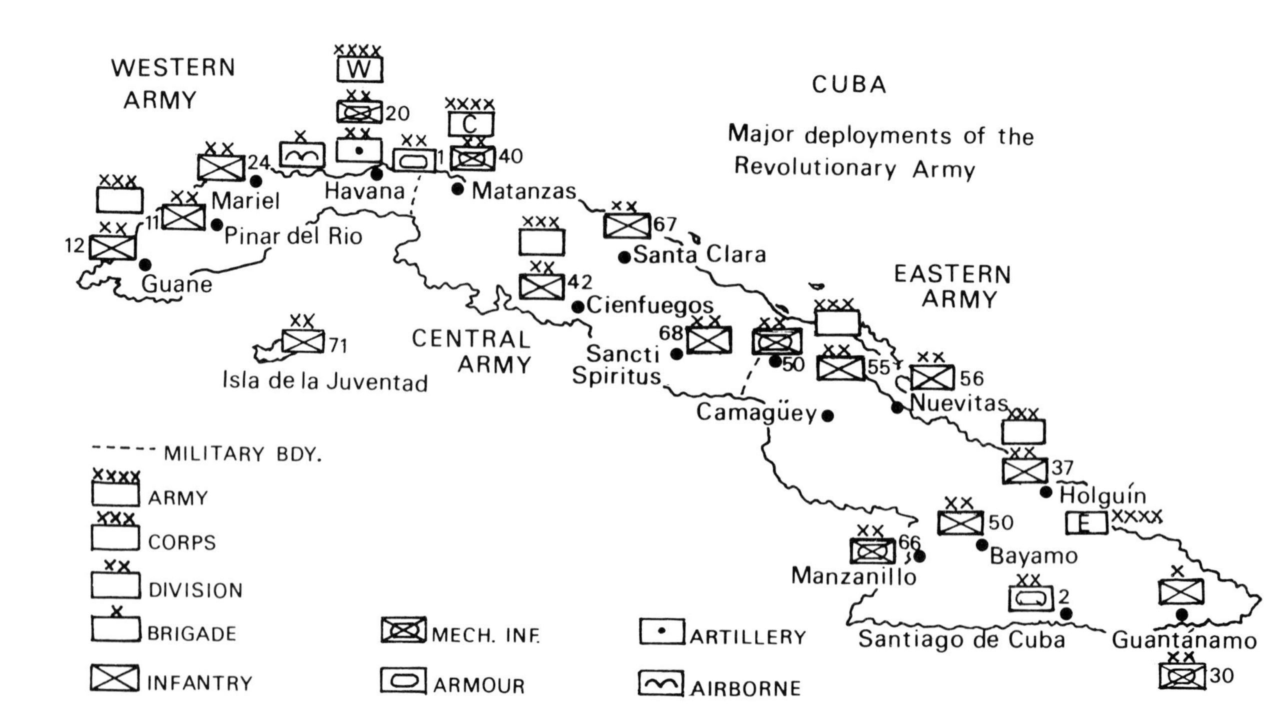

Army

Manpower: 130,000

Tactical formations: 3 Armies comprising 4 army corps:
2 armoured divisions
(1 understrength)
4 mechanised divisions
11 infantry divisions (6 cadres)
1 artillery divison
1 airborne brigade
1 frontier brigade

Major units: 47 infantry regiments (18 cadres)
8 local security regiments
1 security battalion
2 paratroop battalions
3 frontier battalions
11 armoured regiments
(3 understrength)
13 armoured reconnaissance battalions
11 motorised reconnaissance battalions
27 artillery regiments (13 cadres)
1 missile regiment
25 air defence regiments
(17 cadres)
13 engineer battalions

AFVs: T-62, T-54 and T-55 battle tanks
PT-76 light tanks
BRDM-1 scout cars
BMP ICVs
BTR-40, BTR-60 and BTR-152 APCs

Artillery: M-30, A-19 and D-74 122 mm guns
M-46 130 mm guns
D-1, D-20 and ML-20 152 mm guns
SU-100 100 mm SPG
M-1943 160 mm mortars
BM-21 122 mm, M-51 130 mm, BM-13 132 mm, BM-14 140 mm, BMD-20 200 mm and BM-24 240 mm MRLs
Frog-5 rocket launchers
SSC-2A SSMs

Anti-armour: ZIS-2 57 mm guns
ZIS-3 76.2 mm guns
D-44 and D-48 85 mm guns
Sagger and Snapper ATGWs

Air defence: ZPU-1, ZPU-2 and ZPU-4, 14.5 mm guns
TR-152AZPU twin SP 14.5 mm guns
ZU-23 23 mm guns
M53/59 twin SP 30 mm guns
M1939 37 mm guns
S-60 57 mm guns
ZSU-57-2 twin SP 57 mm guns
KS-12 and 12A 85 mm guns
KS-19 100 mm guns
SA-2, SA-3 and SA-7 SAMs

A militia was established in 1906 but a standing Army as such was not organised until 1908, a military college being established at Havana in 1911. In 1915 an organic law organised the general staff and combined the permanent army and the *Guardia Rural* constabulary into the *Ejército Nacional*. After the accession to power of Fulgencio Batista in 1933 the title of the Army was changed to *Ejército Constitucional De Cuba*. Following the Japanese attack on Pearl Harbor in December 1941, Cuba declared war on the Axis powers and Lend–Lease military aid began to arrive from the United States from 1942 onwards. In 1942 an obligatory service law was enacted requiring all fit male citizens between the ages of 20 and 25 to undergo a four-month period of full-time military training. After the end of the Second World War, in which the Cuban Army escaped any active involvement and with Cuba's signature of the Rio Treaty of 1947, additional quantities of equipment were received from the United States.

With the success of Castro's revolution, the Constitutional Army ceased to exist, its place being taken initially by the Revolutionary Militia and a new Revolutionary Army existed by mid-1959. Enormous quantities of equipment began to pour into Cuba from the Eastern bloc following the abortive Bay of Pigs invasion in April 1961, Soviet military involvement in Cuba reaching its zenith during the Cuban missile crisis. Despite

***Cuban mechanised infantry with BMP tracked APC* (Verde Olivo)**

the removal of Soviet strategic weapons from Cuba following this confrontation with the United States, Soviet military aid continued on a massive level. By 1963 organised guerrilla resistance to the Castro regime had been eliminated and in the same year compulsory military service, which had been allowed to lapse after the end of the Second World War was reintroduced.

Cuban military involvement outside the western hemisphere was first noted in the early 1960s when active support was given to the Algerian Liberation front, a Cuban military mission functioning in Algeria until 1965. A military mission also served in Ghana between 1961 and 1966 and as early as 1969 Cuban 'volunteers' had been noted in Guinea Bissau and ultimately an estimated 12,000 Cuban troops served in the Angolan War of Independence. Following Angolan independence from Portugal, Cuban troops were also active in supporting the Soviet–backed Popular Movement for the Liberation of Angola (MPLA) in the civil war against the Western-supported National Front for the Liberation of Angola (FNLA), total Cuban strength in Angola reaching an estimated 30,000. Cuban resistance was largely instrumental in enabling the MPLA to resist South African intervention in support of the opposing faction. Cuban military assistance also proved decisive in the fighting between Ethiopia and Somalia in the Ogaden in 1978. Cuban forces have since been active in Mozambique, Somalia, Ethiopia, Yemen and Syria and have also been reported in the Congo, Afghanistan, Libya, Madagascar, São Tome, Tanzania and Zambia.

At its peak strength in the early 1970s the Revolutionary Army numbered about 200,000 and consisted of three regional armies, subdivided into six army corps, one for each of the traditional provinces into which the country was then divided. With the disappearance of these geographical divisions in 1976, which coincided with an improvement in relations with the United States, the Army was reorganised into four army corps, with a decrease in strength of about 35%. The Revolutionary Army has a current strength of approximately 130,000 all ranks.

Cuban security is both obsessive and all-pervasive, units being known even to their own members rather by four digit military unit numbers than by their true designations, e.g. the 1st Armoured Division being invariably referred to as Military Unit No 1011 and the 24th Infantry Division as Military Unit No 3234. Almost nothing is released regarding the composition or deployment of the Revolutionary Armed Forces, apart from occasional references to units by their MU numbers.

The Western Army (HQ Havana) is thought to consist of the *Pinar del Río* and *La Habana* Mixed Security Regiments, the 1st Armoured Division (HQ Managua), the 20th Mechanised Division (HQ Havana) and the *Pinar del Río* Army Corps (HQ Pinar del Río), which in turn is believed to be made up of the 11th Infantry Division (HQ Pinar del Río), the 12th Infantry Divison (HQ Guane) and the 24th Infantry Division (HQ Mariel).

The Central Army (HQ Matanzas) is believed to comprise the *Matanzas, Santa Clara* and *Cienfuegos* Mixed Security Regiments, the 40th Mechanised Division (HQ Matanzas) and the *Las Villas* Army Corps (HQ Santa Clara), which in its turn is thought to be made up of the 42nd Infantry Division (HQ Cienfuegos), the 67th Infantry Division (HQ Santa Clara) and the 68th Infantry Division (HQ Sancti Spiritus).

The Eastern Army (HQ Santiago de Cuba) is thought to comprise the *Santiago, Holguín* and *Camagüey* Mixed Security Regiments; the 2nd Armoured Division (HQ Santiago de Cuba), the 30th Mechanised Division (HQ Guantánamo) and the 50th Mechanised Division (HQ Bayamo), the *Guantánamo* Frontier Brigade, and the *Holguín* and *Camagüey* Army Corps, the former of which is believed to be made up of the 37th Infantry Division (HQ Holguín) and the 38th Infantry Division (HQ Las Tunas) and the latter of the 55th Infantry Division (HQ Camagüey) and the 56th Infantry Division (HQ Ciego de Avila).

The Isle of Youth Military Region (HQ Nueva Gerona) is believed to be garrisoned by the 71st Infantry Division (HQ Nueva Gerona).

At Army level there are known to be the Army HQ Security Battalion, the two-battalion Paratroop Brigade (HQ Havana), the Artillery Division (HQ La Cabaña Fortress, Havana) which is believed to be made up of three heavy artillery, one missile and one air defence regiments, and headquarters, supply, maintenance and medical units.

Each army and army corps includes a single armoured reconnaissance battalion, an artillery regiment, and air defence regiment and engineer, signals, logistic and medical battalions. Each division consists of three regiments of the main arm, a reconnaissance battalion, an artillery regiment and engineer, NBC warfare, signals, service, supply and medical units. Armoured and mechanised divisions add a mechanised infantry and an armoured regiment respectively, have armoured reconnaissance units, add a maintenance battalion and increase the size of their other support units from companies to battalions. Infantry divisions have only motorised reconnaissance units, mounted mainly on soft-skinned vehicles and have company-level support units. Each division of whatever type has a transport battalion and is also supposed to have an air defence regiment but the latter are mainly reserve units and in peace time exist only in the case of armoured and mechanised divisions. Each infantry division would also theoretically have an armoured regiment on mobilisation.

The overall strength of the Revolutionary Army is considerably lower than that indicated by its relative proliferation of units, their establishments being smaller than in normal western practice. The full peace-time establishment of a Cuban infantry division is 5900, that of a mechanised division 8200 and of an armoured division 6200. A Cuban infantry regiment, at full peace establishment, numbers only 1010 all ranks, each of its two battalions numbering only 349. Armoured regiments consist of only 720 all ranks and each of their three tank battalions musters a mere 110, with 21 tanks, while artillery regiments number 975. There are also three levels of combat readiness, ranging from units at full establishment, through those only partially embodied at about 60% strength to those containing only a cadre of regular personnel equivalent to approximately 30% of their authorised strength. The 1st Armoured Division, the four mechanised divisions and the infantry division on the Isle of Pines are thought to be at almost full strength, as are the paratroop and frontier brigades. The 2nd Armoured Division and one infantry division of each army corps are at 60% of establishment, the remaining divisions being effectively only cadres. The Cuban Expeditionary Forces in Angola and Ethiopia each has the status of an army, as jointly have the Foreign Military Assistance Forces deployed in smaller numbers in other countries, but do not appear to be organised above regimental level.

The Cuban infantry are armed principally with the Soviet AKM and AKMS assault rifles in 7.62 mm calibre, the older AK-47 having been passed on to the Militia. The Czech M23 9 mm sub-machine gun is the principal light automatic, the PK and RPK 7.62 mm machine guns being used in the light and the 12.7 mm DShKM in the heavy support roles. Quantities of DPM RP-46 and RPD 7.62 mm light machine guns also remain in service, particularly with second-line units. Following Soviet practice, mortars are extensively used, the principal types in service being the M-1937 82 mm, the M-1938 and M-1943 120 mm and the M-1943 160 mm. Anti-armour defence is mainly provided by Sagger and Snapper ATGWs although large quantities of obsolescent anti-tank guns, including the ZIS-2 57 mm, the ZIS-3 76.2 mm and both the D-44 and D-48 85 mm, are still in widespread use.

There is a total of over 1000 tanks in service or storage, including about 350 T-62s and some 650 T-54/55s, with approximately 60 PT-76s for

T-62 tanks of the Cuban Revolutionary Army on parade **(Verde Olivo)**

reconnaissance purposes. There are also about 100 BRDM-1 and BRDM-2 scout cars and approximately 500 APCs including BTR-40s, BTR-60s and BTR-152s, plus about 50 BMP infantry combat vehicles. Artillery equipment consists of a total of approximately 1400 pieces including M-30 122 mm howitzers, A-19 and D-74 122 mm guns, M-46 130 mm guns, D-1 152 mm howitzers and D-20 and ML-20 152 mm gun-howitzers. There are also at least 100 SU-100 assault guns. As in the Soviet Army, multiple rocket launchers, including the BM-21 122 mm, M-51 130 mm, BM-13 132 mm, BM-14 140 mm, BMD-20 200 mm and BM-24 240 mm, are extensively used. There are also a number of Frog-5 long-range rocket launchers and some SSC-2A SSMs. Air defence is primarily the responsibility of the Air Force but the Army has some SA-3 and SA-7 SAMs and uses a wide variety of mainly obsolescent anti-aircraft guns for close defence, including the ZPU-1, 2 and 4 14.5 mm heavy machine gun, the TR-152AZPU twin SP 14.5 mm, the ZU-23 23mm, the M53/59 twin SP 30mm, M1939 37mm, S-60 57mm, the ZSU-57-2 twin SP 57 mm, the KS-12 and 12A 85 mm and the KS-19 100 mm.

Officer cadets receive their professional training at either the *General Antonio Maceo* Interarms School at Ceiba del Agua, Havana, which trains armoured troops, mechanised infantry, engineering and logistic troops, the *General José Maceo* Interarms School at Santiago de Cuba, which trains armoured troops, motorised infantry, artillery and engineer troops, or the *General Carlos Roloff* Communications and Chemical troops School at San José de las Lajas, Havana. The *Camilo Cienfuegos* Artillery School at Havana provides advanced training for artillery officers. Courses are of four years duration (five in the case of engineers) and lead to the award of a degree in science or engineering. The tri-service *Máximo Gómez* Military Academy in western Havana province, provides post-graduate courses for company and field grade officers and trains potential staff officers. Many officers also receive post-graduate training in the Soviet Union. The training of enlisted personnel takes place largely in the units to which they are assigned.

While the old *Ejército Constitucional* was one of the most militarily unimpressive forces in Latin America, the *Ejército Revolucionario* is the most formidable army in the region, providing an effective deterrent to any temptation to armed intervention in Cuba even by the United States and with a proven combat record in the recent post-colonial wars in Africa and elsewhere.

***Cuban armoured vehicle crewmen beside their tank* (Verde Olivo)**

Navy

Manpower:	13,500 all ranks (incl Marines)
Major units:	2 frigates 4 submarines (1 training) 22 missile attack craft 12 torpedo boats (hydrofoils) 4 submarine chasers 26 fast patrol craft 14 minesweepers 2 LSMs
Marines:	1 amphibious assault battalion base security units
Heavy equipment:	BTR-60PB APCs SSC-2b SSMs

A Coast Guard was formed in 1901, a year before the end of the US occupation. The Cuban Navy was formally established in 1909, inheriting the equipment and personnel of the former Coast Guard. The new Navy expanded slowly, a Naval Academy being established at Mariel, to the west

The frigate* Mariel *of the Cuban Revolutionary Navy fires one of its SA-N-4 SAMs
(Verde Olivo)

of Havana, in 1916 although the 1920s and 1930s were largely a period of stagnation. During the Second World War, in which Cuba was a nominal belligerent from December 1941 onwards, the United States transferred a number of small patrol craft to the Cuban Navy. Following the end of the war, the Navy continued to expand with the acquisition of war surplus material and most of its older vessels were discarded.

The success of the revolution had little immediate impact on the Navy although towards the end of 1959 the growing radicalisation of the revolutionary regime and the increase in influence of the Cuban Communist party caused the defection of many military and naval officers, with an inevitable decline in efficiency. The Navy accordingly took little part in the resistance to the Bay of Pigs invasion. When Soviet military assistance to Cuba increased to a massive level the following year the Navy received numbers of submarine chasers, missile attack craft and torpedo boats and quantities of small craft continued to be received from the Soviet Union as the lack of spares progressively rendered the existing vessels of the pre-revolutionary fleet unserviceable.

During the late 1970s the Cienfuegos naval base was expanded and provided with facilities for the maintenance and support of submarines, an average of two Soviet submarines being based

CUBA

Principal naval and air bases

Havana
Varadero
Mariel
San Antonio de los Baños
San Julián
Santa Clara
Cienfuegos
Camgüey
Santiago de Cuba

MILITARY BDY.
AVIATION
NAVAL

"Osa" class missile attack craft – the backbone of the Cuban Navy's surface forces **(USN)**

there from 1979 onwards. In the latter year, the Cuban Navy also received its own first submarines, a Soviet 'Foxtrot' class boat being delivered in February 1979, followed by a more elderly 'Whiskey' class boat in May of the same year. A second 'Foxtrot' class boat followed in January 1980 and a third was delivered early in 1984.

The Cuban Revolutionary Navy currently numbers approximately 13,500 all ranks. Following the organisational pattern of the Army, it is divided into three territorial commands of which the Western Naval Flotilla covers the coasts of the provinces of Pinar del Río and Havana and the Isle of Youth and includes the Havana and Mariel naval bases, the Central Naval Flotilla covers the coasts of Matanzas, Villa Clara, Cienfuegos and Sancti Spiritus Provinces and includes the naval bases of Cienfuegos and Varadero, and the Eastern Naval Flotilla covers the coasts of the provinces of Ciego de Ávila, Camagüey, Las Tunas, Holguín, Granma, Santiago de Cuba and Guantánamo and includes the Punta Ballenatos naval base.

An "Osa" attack craft fires one of its SS-N-2 SSMs **(Verde Olivo)**

Operationally, the sea-going units of the fleet comprise a submarine division with three 2000–ton 'Foxtrot' class diesel-electric boats, a missile boat flotilla with 18 165–ton 'Osa' and four 75–ton 'Komar' class missile attack craft, a torpedo boat flotilla with nine 190–ton 'Turya' and three 170–ton 'Stenka' class attack hydrofoils, a submarine chaser flotilla with two 1700–ton 'Koni' class frigates, plus four 170–ton 'SO 1' class anti-

***One of the Cuban Navy's three "Foxtrot" class submarines* (Jane's Defence Weekly)**

submarine patrol vessels, and a minesweeper division with four 350–ton 'Sonya' and ten 70–ton 'Yevgenya' class coastal and inshore minesweepers. Apart from the submarines, which are permanently based at Cienfuegos, these vessels are deployed between the three territorial flotillas in response to operational requirements. Each of the territorial flotillas also incorporates a number of divisions of patrol craft, operating a total of 26 units of the 50–ton 'Zhuk' class.

In addition to the above vessels, there is a single 1000–ton 'Whiskey' class submarine used for training, the 5000–ton *Vigésimo Aniversario,* a converted passenger vessel apparently used for both naval and merchant marine training, the 530–ton trawler *Siboney,* used as a seagoing tender to the Naval Academy, the 1100–ton surveying vessel *Taino,* the 750–ton *Guama* and 11 hydrographic launches, the old 800–ton lighthouse tender *Enrique Collazo* and the smaller 100–ton *Bertha,* the 835–ton ocean-going tug *Caribe* and two 300–ton 'Yelva' class diving tenders, as well as about a dozen miscellaneous harbour craft and auxiliaries. Most of the combat vessels of the Revolutionary Navy appear to be unnamed and are known only by their pennant numbers. Numerals in the 100 series are reserved for submarines, although they are not normally carried, small attack craft being numbered in the 200 series and large in the 400 series, anti-submarine vessels carrying pennant numbers in the 300 series and mine-warfare craft being numbered in the 500 series.

The 1000–man Cuban Marine Corps is thought to consist of an amphibious assault battalion known as the *Flotilla de Guardia Desembarco del Granma* and a security unit of variable size at each naval base. A limited amphibious warfare capacity is provided by two 800–ton Soviet–built LSMs and about half-a-dozen smaller landing craft. The Marines have the full range of personal and support weapons available to the infantry units of the Revolutionary Army, plus about 30 BTR-60PB amphibious APCs. There are also a number of naval-manned shore-based missile batteries, equipped with about 50 SSC-2b Samlet SSMs.

The Naval Academy has been moved from Mariel to Punta Santa Ana to the west of Havana, having been given university status in 1977. It trains all naval and merchant marine officers, the length of the courses varying between four and five years with their degree of specialisation and graduates about 100 midshipmen annually. Senior naval officers receive post-graduate training either at the *General Máximo Gómez* Military Academy or in the Soviet Union. Enlisted personnel are trained at the Centre for the Training of Naval Specialists at Playa del Solado and there is a submarine school at Cienfuegos.

A Cuban Marine leaps from his BTR-60 APC **(Verde Olivo)**

Cuban Marines come ashore from "Polnochny B" class LSM during amphibious assault exercises **(Verde Olivo)**

The Cuban Navy is now a compact and efficient coast-defence force, the recent establishment of a submarine element indicating a possible orientation towards a more offensive role although the lack of any significant amphibious assault or sea-lift capacity probably reflects a conscious decision by Cuba's Soviet pay-masters to limit its capacity to provoke the United States to an unacceptable degree. Despite the recent scrapping, without replacement, of most of its older small surface combatants, as at present constituted, the Revolutionary Navy provides a formidable deterrent to any attempt at overt US military intervention in Cuba without providing sufficient threat to shipping in the Caribbean and Gulf of Mexico to cause any undue concern to the US Navy or the navies of any of the other regional naval powers such as those of Mexico, Colombia or Venezuela.

Above: *Marines come ashore, supported by BTR-60 amphibious APCs*

Below: *Crewmen of the Cuban Revolutionary Navy on the bridge of an "Osa" class missile attack craft* **(Verde Olivo)**

Right: *Cuban naval recruits studying the twin 25 mm AA gun* **(Verde Olivo)**

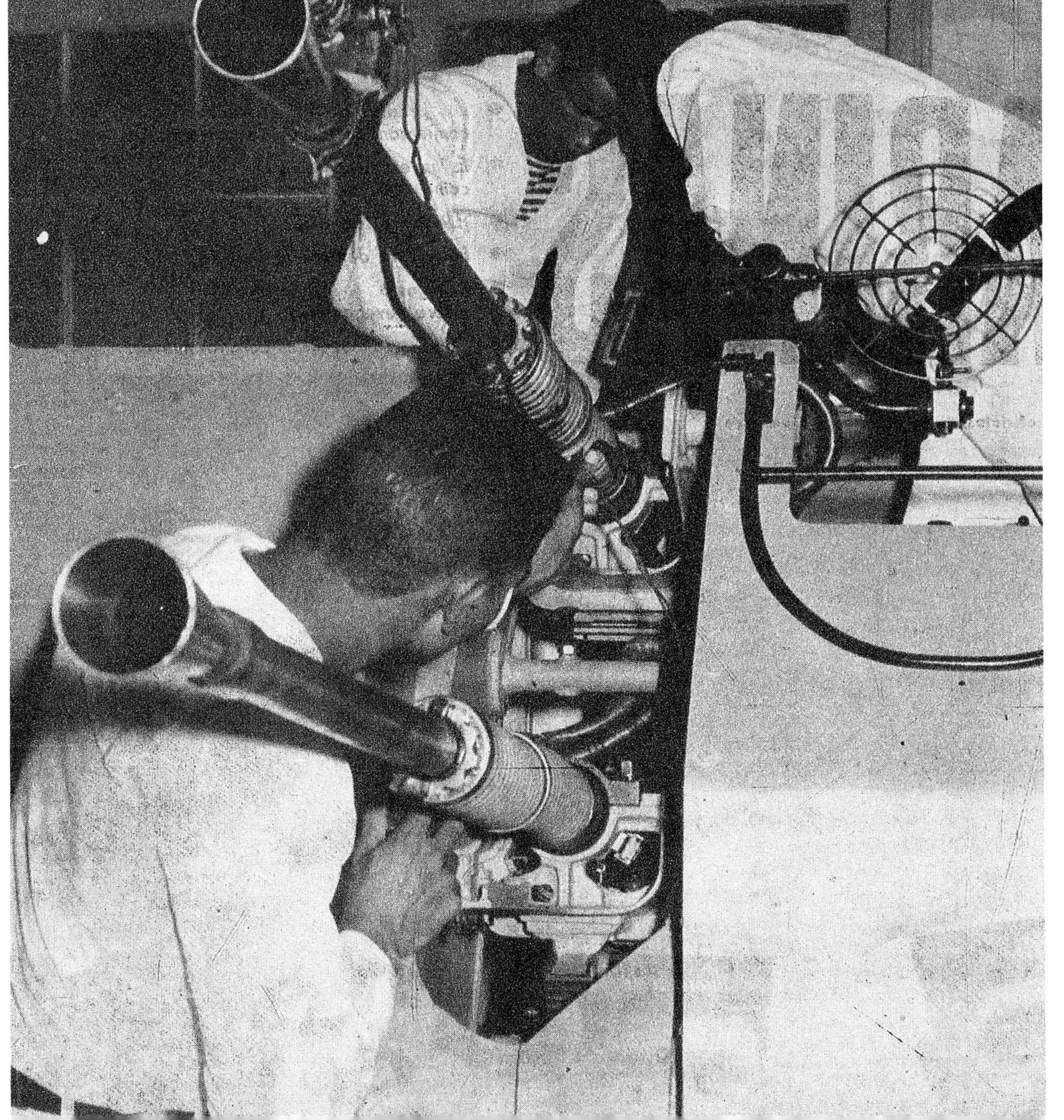

Air Force

Manpower: 18,500 (including air defence forces)

Units: 3 brigades comprising
5 fighter and 3 tactical support regiments:
16 interceptor squadrons
9 fighter/ground-attack squadrons
4 transport squadrons
1 attack helicopter squadron
1 helicopter ASW squadron
6 general-purpose helicopter squadrons

Interceptors: MiG-21 and MiG-23

Fighter/ground attack aircraft: MiG-17, MiG-19 and MiG-23

Transports: Il-14, An-2, An-24 and An-26

Helicopters: Mi-1, Mi-2, Mi-4, Mi-8, Mi-14 and Mi-24

***A MiG-21 fighter of the Cuban Revolutionary Air Force* (Verde Olivo)**

Trainers: MiG-23U, MiG-21U, An-2, Aero L-39 and Zlin-326

Ground forces: 4 air defence missile brigades

SAMs: SA-3 and SA-7

In 1915 proposals for the establishment of a military air arm were presented to the Cuban government and in May 1919 the first squadron of the *Cuerpo de Aviación* was activated. Following the revolution of 1933 Cuban military aviation was reorganised, being sub-divided into the *Aviación del Ejército* and *Aviación Naval*. Cuba's declaration of war on the Axis powers, within days of the Japanese attack on Pearl Harbor, was reflected in a flow of second-line aircraft from the United States under Lend Lease. Following Cuba's signature of the Rio Treaty of Mutual Defence of 1947, the first modern combat aircraft also began to be received. In 1955 another reorganisation combined both army and naval aviation elements in a semi-autonomous force with the title of *Fuerza Aérea Ejército de Cuba*.

Following the success of the Castro-led revolution the name of the force was changed again to *Fuerza Aérea Revolucionaria*. The Revolutionary government found itself with a motley collection of largely unserviceable aircraft and the *Fuerza Aérea Revolucionaria* was able to play only a

***Cuban infantry leap from an Mi-8 helicopter of the Revolutionary Air Force* (Verde Olivo)**

limited part in repelling the Bay of Pigs invasion. Some MiG-15 UTI conversion trainers had been presented to the *Fuerza Aérea Revolucionaria* by the Soviet Union in 1960 and after Castro's unequivocal espousal of Communism these aircraft were followed by large numbers of Soviet combat, transport and training aircraft. The Air Force, now known as the *Defensa Anti-Aérea y Fuerza Aérea Revolucionaria* (DAAFAR), remained a semi-autonomous adjunct of the Revolutionary Army until 1972 when it was raised to co-equal status with the Army and Navy.

The DAAFAR currently numbers approximately 18,500 all ranks, operating some 500 aircraft estimated to include 15 MiG-23S, 60 MiG-21F, 40 MiG-21PFMA and 80 MiG-21bis interceptors, 36 MiG-23F, 50 MiG-17 and 30 MiG-19 fighter-bombers, about 15 Il-14, 20 An-2 and a similar number of An-26 transport aircraft, plus 24 Mi-4, 24 Mi-8, 12 Mi-14 and 12 Mi-24 helicopters. Training is carried out in about 30 Zlin 326s, 20 Aero L-39s, 20 MiG-21Us and two MiG-23Us, plus a few Il-14s and An-2s and five Mi-1 and three Mi-2 helicopters.

Territorially the DAAFAR is organised into three Air Zones, on the same basis as the Revolutionary Army, each containing an air brigade of variable composition, units being deployed between the three Air Zones in accordance with operational requirements.

According to the most recent information available, the Western Air Brigade, designated the Bay of Pigs Guard Brigade, is thought to consist of two interceptor regiments (six squadrons of MiG-21s) based at San Antonio de los Baños and Baracoa, a tactical support regiment (three squadrons of MiG-23s) based at Guines, an independent fighter squadron (equipped with MiG-23s) based at San Julián, which also houses all of the training elements of the DAAFAR, and two transport squadrons, based at Havana and San Antonio de los Baños. The Central Air Brigade, which is designated Battle of Santa Clara Guard Brigade, is also believed to contain two interceptor regiments (six squadrons of MiG-21s) based at Santa Clara and Sancti Spiritus, a tactical support regiment (three squadrons of MiG-17s) based at Santa Clara, and an ASW helicopter squadron

***The crew of an SA-2 SAM of Cuba's Revolutionary Air Defence Force prepare for action* (Verde Olivo)**

(equipped with Mi-14s) based at Cienfuegos together with a single transport squadron. The Eastern Air Brigade has a single interceptor regiment (three squadrons of MiG-21s) based at a Camagüey, a tactical support regiment (three squadrons of MiG-19s) based at Holguín, and single attack helicopter and transport squadrons, both based at Santiago de Cuba. The six general purpose helicopter squadrons are thought to be evenly divided between the three Air Zones.

Each Air Zone also contains an anti-aircraft missile brigade, in addition to which there is an anti-aircraft missile brigade for the defence of the capital. The missile brigades each contain three battalions and comprise a total of about two dozen SAM batteries with V750VK Guideline missiles and about a dozen batteries with SA-3 Goas and SA-7 Grails. There is also a particularly comprehensive electronic early warning system.

Operationally, the interceptor squadrons are subordinate to Air Defence Command, which also controls the anti-aircraft missile brigades. The fighter-bomber squadrons are subordinate to Tactical Air Command which also controls the single

***Personnel of the Military Technical Institute, the main training establishment of the Cuban Revolutionary Air Force, on parade* (Verde Olivo)**

helicopter attack and helicopter ASW squadrons, while the transport units are subordinate to Logistic Support Command and training units to Air Training Command.

Most training is carried out at the Aviation Cadet School at San Julián, which offers courses in sophisticated aircraft and missile operation. With specialist technical and flying training schools, the former located in Havana province and the latter at San Julián, the period of training for officers varying between four and five years according to specialisation. The *Instituto Téchnico Militar* at Havana offers comprehensive specialist training in communications, avionics and aeronautical engineering and for anti-aircraft troops. All flying personnel receive part of their training in the Soviet Union where combat aircrew also receive additional advanced training. Officers receive post-graduate training at specific points in their careers at the *General Máximo Gómez* Academy, also supplemented by advanced courses in the Soviet Union.

The Cuban Revolutionary Air Force is currently the best equipped and one of the most efficient military air arms in Latin America.

Patrol boat of the Cuban Frontier Guard Troops **(Verde Olivo)**

Paramilitary forces

Manpower: 15,000 National Revolutionary Police
3500 border troops
1500 Ministry of the Interior Special Troops
100,000 Labour Youth Army
500,000 Territorial Troop Militia

A constabulary, the *Guardia Rural* and a coast guard were set up before the end of the United States military occupation. As its named indicates, the *Guardia Rural* was primarily a rural constabulary and there was also a National Police Force, responsible for law enforcement and security in the larger urban areas. Although the Coast Guard was absorbed into the Navy on the formation of the latter in 1909, a Maritime Police was formed, as an adjunct of the Navy, during the late 1940s. With the triumph of the revolution in 1959, the existing police forces ceased to exist, internal security initially being the responsibility of the Revolutionary Militia.

All internal security functions now fall within the ambit of the Ministry of the Interior. The main uniformed law enforcement agency is the National Revolutionary Police, with a strength of approximately 15,000. The Ministry also controls two battalions of special troops, with a combined total strength of about 1500. These are trained as a military rapid intervention unit, all members being parachute-qualified and elements of this force have participated in Cuba's overseas military operations. Also subordinate to the Ministry of the Interior are the 3500 Border troops, which are primarily concerned with the prevention of unauthorised entry to or exit from the country by sea or air. They operate a total of about 20 small patrol craft, including the launches *Guanabacoa, Camilo Cienfuegos, Escambray, Maceo, Cuartel Moncada, Finlay* and *Martí,* all built in Spain from 1971 onwards. This force should not be confused with the Army's Frontier Guard Brigade which is engaged exclusively in the security of the perimeter of the US base at Guantánamo. The Ministry of the Interior special forces are equipped with the latest available light infantry

Elderly militiaman at Havana **(Verde Olivo)**

Women play an important part in the Territorial Troop Militias **(Verde Olivo)**

weapons but the other internal security forces have to make do with obsolescent material no longer in service with the regular armed forces.

Backing both the Revolutionary Armed Forces and the internal security forces of the Ministry of the Interior are the 500,000 members of the Territorial Troop Militia and the 100,000-strong Youth Labour Army. These also are equipped with the useful cast-offs of the regular Revolutionary armed forces.

From 1973 onwards, the Revolutionary Militias were integrated into the reserve structure of the Revolutionary armed forces. The Territorial Troop Militia, which superseded the Revolutionary Militias in May 1980, consists of men over the age of 16 who have been exempted from compulsory military service and women who are not subject to it and is largely funded by popular subscription. There is no known upper age limit for membership, approximately 40% of its members being women. It is organised in about 200 regiments, further organised into approximately 1000 battalions and although primarily an infantry force includes mounted units and some artillery and anti-aircraft elements.

The Youth Labour Army is primary employed in civic action but undergoes some pre-military training and has light infantry weapons at its disposal.

Sources of defence material supply and current requirements

Although Cuba was probably historically more firmly within the US sphere of influence than any other country of Latin America and consequently military procurement policies laid heavy stress on the acquisition of US manufactured equipment, even during the early post-independence period artillery was acquired in France and some naval vessels were ordered in Great Britain and Germany. Although equipment of US origins continued to predominate, small quantities of material were purchased in Europe.

During the latter stages of the Batista dictatorship the US government embargo on the export of defence material to Cuba forced it to turn elsewhere for its armaments and small arms were procured in Belgium and the Dominican Republic, armoured vehicles and aircraft were purchased in Britain and artillery pieces were obtained in Italy. During the period immediately following the revolution this trend continued, despite the brief renewal of US sales to Cuba during 1959. Following the reintroduction of trade sanctions against the Revolutionary government in 1960 Cuba began to turn increasingly towards the eastern bloc for armaments.

Since the development of Cuba as a virtual Soviet satellite, almost all defence material has come from either the Soviet Union or other countries of the eastern bloc, small quantities of Chinese equipment also being acquired during the early 1970s. Although a few police launches were ordered in Spain during the early 1970s, the Soviet bloc seems likely to remain Cuba's almost exclusive supplier of defence material for the forseeable future.

The Revolutionary armed forces are adequately equipped for their main role which is the deterrence of US armed intervention in Cuba. Somewhat surprisingly, local industry does not appear to have developed any significant capacity for the manufacture of defence material, although some small arms ammunition and explosives are now reported to be produced.

Summary and prospects

Cuba occupies a unique position as the only Soviet satellite in the Western Hemisphere. It also contains both a US naval base at Guantánamo on its east coast and a submarine base used by the Soviet Navy at Cienfuegos, in the south. Paradoxically Cuba remains nominally allied to its greatest enemy, the United States, through the Rio Treaty of 1947, which has never been formally abrogated and has no formal military or political alignment with its closest friend, the Soviet Union, being ostensibly non-alligned as regards it foreign policy.

The Cuban revolution was at least partly the byproduct of myopic United States foreign policy in the country which more than all others in the region had been the subject of US political interference and economic exploitation. Despite his apparent betrayal of his middle-class supporters when he declared Cuba a Marxist state the charismatic personal appeal of Fidel Castro, who continues to enjoy an almost universal public respect verging in adulation, is certainly a major factor in the degree of success obtained by the Cuban revolution and its continued survival. At the same time, the continued hostility of the United States, with the concommitant threat of the reimposition of a neocolonial tyranny, provides a powerful focus of popular support for the revolutionary leadership which might diminish considerably if the threat of US intervention in the country's affairs were to be removed. Cuba is also fortunate inasmuch as geographical remoteness has permitted the replacement of the tutelage of the United States with that of the Soviet Union to the country's nett advantage and without a comparable degree of sacrifice of national independence to that enforced by the USSR upon its eastern European satellite states.

Early attempts at the export of Cuba's own form of Marxist revolution to other countries of Latin America were however singularly unsuccessful. While the Castro government continues to give active support to left-wing revolutionary movements, such as those in El Salvador and to left-wing administrations, as in Nicaragua and until recently in Grenada, the country now pays its debts to the Soviets principally by the provision of armed support for pro-Soviet elements in black Africa and to a lesser extent, the Middle East.

Total Cuban personnel deployed outside the country, by no means all of whom are military, are believed to number as follows:-

Afghanistan: 100 military advisers

Algeria: 170 military and civilian advisers

Angola: 27,000 military and 8000 civilian personnel

Congo: 300 military and 200 civilian personnel

Ethiopia: 3000 almost entirely military personnel who are being gradually withdrawn

Guinea-Bissau: 100 military and 50 civilian personnel

Iraq: 2200 mainly military personnel

Libya: 3000 military and civilian advisers

Malagasy: 50 military advisers

Mozambique: 750 military and 150 civilian personnel

Nicaragua: 500 military and 3000 civilian personnel

São Tome: 75 civilian medical personnel

South Yemen: 500 military personnel

Tanzania: 100 civilian personnel

Zambia: 25 military advisers

Cuba is probably the world's most completely militarised country, the degree of popular involvement in defence and internal security exceeding even that of Israel. The Cuban armed forces are the second most numerous in Latin America (after those of Brazil, which has 14 times Cuba's population) and are certainly the best equipped of any in the region. Granting that, the Army has not been provided with strategic weapons, the Navy remains essentially still confined to a coastal defence role and the Air Force remains predominantly a fighter and tactical support force.

Although now regarded with some justification as one of the hemisphere's elder statesmen, Fidel Castro has frequently shown signs of impatience with the militarily passive role imposed on him by the Soviet Union, upon which Cuba remains almost totally dependent for the logistic support of its armed forces. While this situation would appear destined to remain unchanged for the forseeable future, Cuba's neighbours must view the military implications of such developments as the establishment of a Cuban submarine force and the current construction of Cuba's first nuclear reactor with some anxiety.

The existence of a heavily armed Communist Cuba also continues to exacerbate the latent instability of much of Latin America and paradoxically provides a continuing rationalisation for support by successive US governments for precisely the same type of political regime in other Latin American countries, as that which originally provoked the Cuban revolution.

DOMINICAN REPUBLIC
(República Dominica)

Area: 18,800 sq miles (48,692 sq kms)
Population: 6,275,000
Total armed forces: 22,500
Reserves: 6000
Available manpower: 500,000
Paramilitary forces: 10,000
GNP: $4,656 million (1985)
Defence Expenditure: 68,890,000 (1986)

Introduction

The Dominican Republic occupies the eastern two-thirds of the island of Hispaniola and is therefore bounded by Haiti to the west, the Atlantic Ocean to the north and the Caribbean Sea to the south. No less than 73% of the population consists of persons of variable admixtures of European and Negro blood, 16% are pure whites and 11% pure Negros.

The economy is based on agriculture, the main exports being tropical products such as sugar, tobacco, coffee, bananas and cocoa although the mining of bauxite and nickel are both of importance. Approximately 130,000 people are engaged in light industry, mainly connected with the processing of sugar and its byproducts. Imports consist largely of machinery, fuel, chemicals and manufactured goods, including textiles. Although the economy is agriculturally based, production concentrates on a small number of crops and foodstuffs also figure highly among imports.

The island of Santo Domingo later christened La Española and corrupted in English to Hispaniola, was discovered by Columbus in 1492 but it was not permanently colonised until four years later. The importance of Santo Domingo declined with the establishment of Spanish colonies on the mainland of South America and in Mexico and Central America and the island became a colonial backwater. French possession of the western portion of the island, modern Haiti, was recognised in 1697. French revolutionary forces conquered the eastern part of the island in 1794 and Spain ceded Santo Domingo to France. The Haitians then turned on the French and established their own independence, Santo Domingo becoming part of the Negro state of Haiti.

In 1809 the Dominicans revolted and re-established Spanish sovereignty, declaring themselves independent in 1821 and requesting to be admitted to the newly established confederation of Gran Colombia. Before any reaction to this request could be received, the Haitians again invaded Santo Domingo and ruled the whole island until 1844 when the Dominicans declared themselves independent once more. Sporadic Haitian attempts at reconquest continued until 1861 when Spain agreed to re-establish colonial rule in Santo Domingo. Within two years the Dominicans were again in revolt against Spanish rule and a two-year long War of Independence resulted in the expulsion of the Spaniards for the second time in 1865. Following the restoration of independence the country soon lapsed once more into semi-anarchy. In 1916, the United States intervened and until 1924 the country was, in effect, governed by the US Marines.

Rafael Leonidas Trujillo, who had become commander of the constabulary established by the occupying forces, came to power as President in 1930, remaining the absolute master of the Dominican Republic for the following 31 years, ruling either directly or through figure-head puppet Presidents. Following the assasination of Trujillo in 1961, the incumbent Trujillo puppet, Joaquín Balaguer, began to exhibit a surprising degree of political independence, being nevertheless forced to resign in January 1962. He was succeeded as President by Juan Bosch in February 1963, after an interregnum during which the country was ruled by a Council of State. Bosch in turn was deposed by a coup d'etat in September of the same year, being replaced by a civilian triumvirate led by Donald Reid Cabral. In April 1965 the military deposed Reid and full-scale civil war erupted. The United States intervened, landing a total of 21,000 troops but order was not restored for another month, after which the US troops were partially replaced by about 2000 troops from Brazil, Costa Rica, Honduras and Nicaragua, which were combined with the remaining US troops into an Inter-American Police Force under the auspicies of the Organization of American States. This was finally withdrawn in September 1966, following the re-election of Joaquín Balaguer as President. Democratic civilian government has survived to date.

The Dominican Republic is a unitary republic of 26 provinces and a national district. Executive power is in the hands of the President and there is a bicameral legislature.

Dominican foreign policy has traditionally been moulded by fear of invasion by Haiti. Although the population of Haiti is greater than that of the Dominican Republic and is squeezed into little more than half the area of the latter country, a military threat from Haiti is however no longer a serious proposition. More recently, the threat of invasion from Cuba has become something of a preoccupation of Dominican defence planners even though the only two attempts at an invasion by Cuban-based Dominican dissidents during the closing years of the Trujillo regime, were easily dealt with by the Dominican armed forces. Despite some chronic, low-level guerrilla activity in the mountainous regions of the interior, this has been easily contained and the Dominican Republic seems relatively stable since the end of the 1965 civil war. Any tendency to instability is coming from labour agitation rather than political subversion although recent unpopular austerity measures, arising from the debt crisis and the virtual collapse of the economy, have led to rioting and bloodshed.

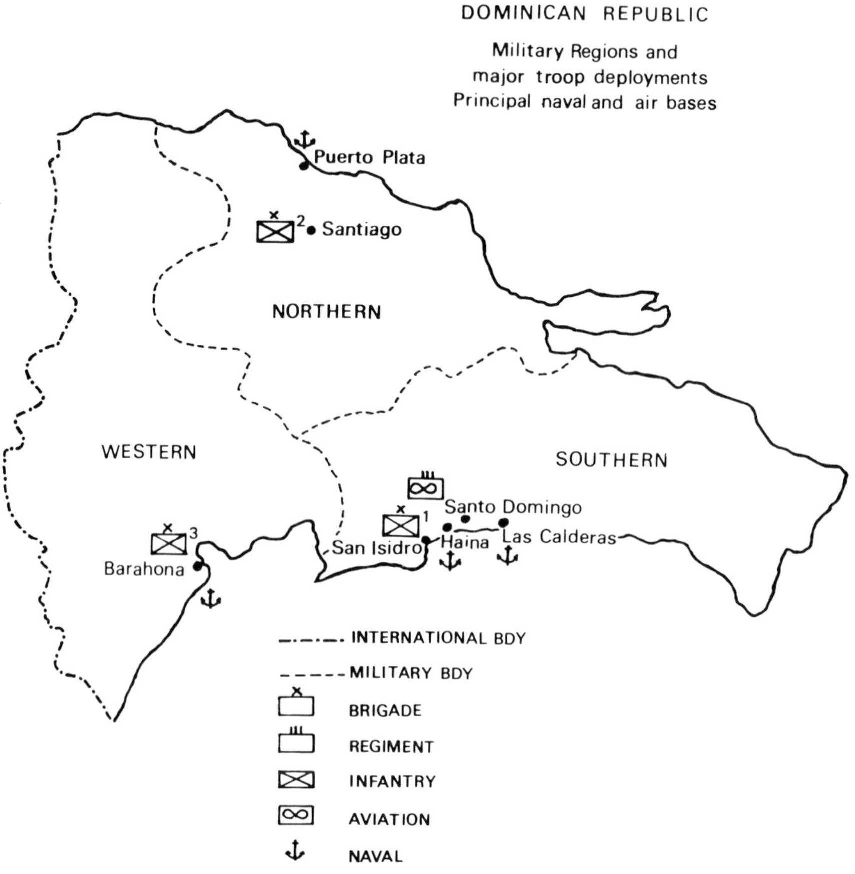

DOMINICAN REPUBLIC
Military Regions and
major troop deployments
Principal naval and air bases

Puerto Plata
Santiago
NORTHERN
WESTERN
SOUTHERN
Santo Domingo
San Isidro
Haina
Las Calderas
Barahona

INTERNATIONAL BDY
MILITARY BDY
BRIGADE
REGIMENT
INFANTRY
AVIATION
NAVAL

Structure of the armed forces

The President is commander-in-chief of the armed forces, the chain of command extending from the President to the Secretary of State for National Defence and from him to the under-secretaries of state for War, Marine and Aviation. The Secretary of State is a member of the cabinet, appointed by the President and is usually an Army officer. The under-secretaries, who are invariably officers of their respective services, are appointed by the Secretary of State, with the approval of the President. Each under-secretary controls his branch of the armed forces by way of a general staff, headed by a chief of staff.

The country is divided into three defensive zones of which the Southern Defence Zone (HQ Santo Domingo) approximates to the provinces of Peravia, San Cristóbal, El Seibo, San Pedro de Macorís, La Romana, La Altagracia and the National District of Santo Domingo. The Northern Defence Zone (HQ Santiago) approximates to the provinces of Puerto Plata, Santiago, La Vega, Espaillat, Salcedo, Duarte, Sánchez Rámirez, María Trinidad Sánchez, and Samana, and the Western Defence Zone (HQ Barahona) covers the provinces of Azúa, Dajabón, Montecristi, Santiago Rodríguez, La Estrelleta, San Juan, Bahoruco, Independencia, Pedernales and Barahona.

Although there is legal provision for compulsory military service, the armed forces are kept up to strength by voluntary enlistment.

Army

Manpower:	15,000
Tactical formations:	3 infantry brigades 1 mechanised combat group:
Major units:	1 Presidential Guard battalion 10 infantry battalions 1 mountain infantry battalion 1 armoured battalion 1 motorised reconnaissance company 4 artillery battalions 1 engineer battalion
AFVs:	AMX-13 light tanks V-150 and Landsverk Lynx armoured cars M3A1 scout cars M3 half-track APCs
Artillery:	US M2A1 105 mm howitzers Bofors M 02/33 75 mm howitzers Bofors L22 105 mm howitzers

During the turbulent early years of Dominican independence and even after the restoration of independence from Spain in 1865, nothing approaching a national army existed. It was not until the presidency of Gregorio Luperón (1879–1882) that any serious attempt at the organisation of a professional national army was made and even then limited funds ensured that this force remained small and of very limited military potential. During the US occupation, the armed forces were abolished, the army was replaced by a US Marine trained Dominican Constabulary Guard and a Military Academy was established at Haina, 30 miles west of the capital, together with a training centre for enlisted men. The dictator Trujillo set about the improvement and strengthening of the Army as his main power base and used the alleged threat of Haitian invasion to justify the maintenance of the most powerful military establishment in the Caribbean, its real function being the control of the Dominican populace and the consolidation of his dictatorship. The armed forces have declined considerably in

AMX-13 tank and Landsverk Lynx armoured car of the Dominican Army at Santo Domingo

both numbers and equipment, though not in efficiency, under the succession of democratic governments since 1966.

The Dominican Army now numbers approximately 15,000 all ranks, organised into three brigades, a mechanised combat group and a number of independent units.

Brigade No 1 (HQ Santo Domingo) covers the Southern Defence Zone and comprises three infantry battalions, a motorised reconnaissance company, an artillery battalion, a signals company, a service company, a transport battalion and a medical company.

Brigade No 2 (HQ Santiago de los Caballeros) covers the Northern Defence Zone and comprises only three infantry battalions and an artillery battalion.

Brigade No 3 (HQ Barahona) covers the Western Defence Zone and also comprises three infantry battalions and an artillery battalion.

At army level there is a mechanised combat group which combines the *Veintisiete de Febrero* Armoured Battalion with a motorised infantry battalion and an artillery battalion at San Isidro. Other army level units are the Presidential Guard Battalion, the 6th Mountain Rifle Battalion, which is in effect a special forces unit, and the Support Command, which includes the 1st Engineer Battalion, a service company, an ordnance battalion and a military police company, all of which are located at Santo Domingo.

The principal small arm is the G3 rifle in 7.62 mm calibre and some M16A1 assault rifles in 5.56 mm calibre were also recently acquired.

Both the locally manufactured Cristóbal and the Beretta 38/49 sub-machine guns are in use and heavier automatic weapons include the Browning M1917 and M1919 0.30-inch calibre and the M2HB 0.50-inch calibre machine guns. Some FN MAGs in 7.62 mm are also in service together with some US M60s. The US M1 81 mm mortar has recently been supplemented by some Hotchkiss-Brandt 120 mm pieces, the US M40A1 106 mm RCL being the standard anti-armour weapon. Some 30 AMX-13 light tanks are the only operational tracked armoured vehicles. There are also six V-150 Commando and about 20 Landsverk Lynx armoured cars, reports of the acquisition of French AML 245 armoured cars remaining unsubstantiated. There are also about 20 examples apiece of the US M3A1 scout car and the M3 half-track. The field artillery is equipped with approximately 20 examples of the US M2A1 105 mm howitzer and 12 examples apiece of the Swedish L/22 105 mm and the M02/33 75 mm howitzers.

The Military Academy at Haina offers a four-year course for aspiring Army officers and Air Force cadets also share the first two years of this course before transferring to the Air Force School for specialist training. The Army conducts a six-month course for company commanders and a ten-month course for battalion commanders, but there are no higher level courses. Under an agreement of 1962, the United States offers command and staff courses to officers of the three Dominican armed forces, either in the United States itself or in the Panama Canal Zone. Other ranks receive both basic and specialist training at the Armed Forces Training Centre at San Isidro air base. There is also the Vocational School of the Armed Forces and National Police at Bani, which trains enlisted men in manual skills prior to their retirement.

Although the strength and military potential of the Dominican Army has declined since the days of Trujillo, it still remains a well-trained and disciplined force, the potential of which is reinforced by the fact that it is composed exclusively of long-serving professional personnel.

Navy

Manpower: 4000 (including Marines)

Major units: 1 frigate
2 corvettes
8 patrol vessels
12 coastal patrol craft
1 LSM

Marines: 1 battalion
frogmen commandos

The turbulent early history of the Dominican Republic prevented the establishment of anything resembling professional armed forces and it was not until 1873 that an attempt was made to establish a Navy which remained insignificant until the disbandment of the Dominican armed forces following the US occupation in 1916. A new Coast Guard was formed in 1938 and by 1941, when it changed its title to Dominican Navy, it consisted of about a dozen small patrol craft. Although the Dominican Republic had no

Flag party of the Dominican Navy

active involvement in the Second World War, several additional patrol craft were transferred by the United States in exchange for base facilities during this period. In the immediate post-war years the Dominican Navy underwent a dramatic expansion with the acquisition of destroyers, frigates, corvettes, additional patrol vessels and amphibious craft and by 1950 it had become the most powerful naval force in the Caribbean. The Navy was involved to some degree in the 1965 civil war, its major units bombarding 'Constitutionalist' strong points in Santo Domingo prior to the landing of the US Marines and the Inter-America Peace-Keeping Force. Some minor vessels were obtained afterwards but much of the original material was beginning to show its age and no replacements were forthcoming for the major units as these were retired from service.

The Dominican Navy has maintained its personnel strength at approximately 4000 but the sea-going fleet has now been reduced to the old 1400 - ton ex-Canadian 'River' class frigate *Mella,* the 650 - ton former US minesweepers *Prestol Botello* and *Tortuguero,* both converted to corvettes with all sweeping gear removed, the 1235 - ton ex-US 'Cherokee' class armed tug *Macorix* and the 534 - ton 'Sotoyomo' class *Caonabo* and *Enriquillo,* plus the three 650 - ton former US netlayers *Cambiaso, Separación* and *Calderas,* which are also used as patrol vessels. There are in addition the old 337 - ton ex-US Coast Guard cutters *Independencia, Libertad* and *Restauración,* all of which are in reserve and unlikely to go to sea, plus the 130 - ton PGM *Betelgeuse,* the 100 - ton *Capitán Alsina* and the 60 - ton *Proción, Aldebarán, Bellatrix* and *Capella* and three unnamed 105 - ton 'Osprey' class patrol craft leased from the US Navy since 1982. A very limited amphibious assault capability is provided by the 734 - ton LSM *Sirio* and two landing craft. There are also the 337 - ton surveying vessel *Capotillo,* the 422 - ton tankers *Capitán Wenceslao Arvelo* and *Capitán Beótegui,* the small auxiliary yachts *Duarte, Atlántida, Nube del Mar, Carite, Atún, Picúa* and *Jurel,* all of which used for training as are the former fishing boats *Alto Velo* and *Saona.* The 70 - ton diving tender *Neptuno* and the tugs *Hércules, Guacangarix, Bohechio, Calderas, Isabela* and *Puerto Hermoso* complete the Dominican naval force.

The Navy operates through three Naval Zones of which the Northern Naval Zone (HQ Puerto Plata) covers the coast from the northern Haitian frontier to the Mona Passage, the Southern Naval Zone (HQ Barahona) covers the coast from the Mona Passage to the southern Haitian frontier and the Santo Domingo Naval Zone (HQ Santo Domingo) administers naval headquarters and the various naval establishments in the national capital and its environs.

The principal naval base is at Las Calderas, which has a 700 - ton synchrolift and there are minor bases at Santo Domingo and Haina.

There is a single battalion of Marines and a unit of frogment commandos. Equipment is the same as that of the infantry units of the Army with the exception of the substitution of the FN FAL for the G-3 rifle.

The Naval Academy at Las Calderas offers a four-year course to aspiring officers. Naval enlisted personnel are also trained at Las Calderas where most naval facilities were located.

The Dominican Navy has gone through over 20 years of sustained neglect which cannot but have had an effect on the morale of its personnel. If it is to remain an effective force it is in urgent need of re-equipment.

Air Force

Manpower:	3500 (including paratroops and anti-aircraft artillery)
Major units:	1 tactical support squadron 1 transport squadron 1 communications squadron 1 helicopter squadron
Tactical support aircraft:	Cessna A-37B
Transports:	Douglas C-47
Communications aircraft:	Rallye Commander Beech Queen Air 80 Cessna 310 Aero Commander Mitsubishi MU-2
Helicopters:	Bell 47 and UH-1H Hughes OH-6A Aérospatiale SA.313B, SA.316 and SA.365
Trainers:	Cessna T-41D Beech T-34D North American T-6G
Ground troops:	1 paratroop group 1 air defence battalion
AA artillery:	Bofors 40 mm L/60

An Aviation Company was formed as part of the Dominican Army in 1933 but this remained a very small force, equipped only with second-line aircraft until 1942 when the Dominican Republic began to receive some communications and training aircraft under Lend-Lease. In 1947 a well-equipped group of Dominican exiles threatened to invade the Dominican Republic from Cuba and Trujillo's agents managed to obtain a number of war-surplus combat aircraft in Britain. With this equipment the *Compañía de Aviación* expanded to become the *Cuerpo de Aviación Militar Dominicana*. As a result of the signature of the Rio Treaty of 1947 by the Dominican Republic the United States also provided some combat and transport aircraft and further aircraft were obtained from commercial sources, including 42 de Havilland Vampire jet fighter-bombers purchased second-hand from Sweden in 1952. By now the *Cuerpo de Aviación Militar Dominicana* had become independent of the Army as the *Fuerza Aéréa Dominicana* and had a total of approximately 240 aircraft. Following the assasination of Trujillo in 1961 the brief golden age of the Dominican armed forces came to an end however. Funds for the replacement of worn-out material became increasingly scarce and by 1963 the *Fuerza Aérea Dominicana* had shrunk to 110 aircraft. Nevertheless it was active in the 1965 civil war, its aircraft strafing 'Constitutionalist' positions in Santo Domingo and two F-51s being lost to ground fire. During the years of democratic rule which have followed the civil war, the Dominican Air Force has continued to decline, aircraft procurements consisting almost exclusively of second-line material.

The Dominican Air Force currently has some 70 aircraft, manned by approximately 3500 all ranks and organised into an Air Command, a Base Defence Command, a Combat Support Command and a Maintenance Command.

The Air Command is responsible for all flying operations and consists of a tactical support squadron with eight Cessna A-37Bs and six Hughes OH-6As, an air transport squadron with seven Douglas C-47s, a communications squadron with a single Beech Queen Air 80, an Aero Commander 500, a Rallye Commodore, a Cessna 310 and a Mitsubishi MU-2J and a helicopter squadron with 11 Bell UH-1Hs, a single SA.316 Alouette III and three SA.313B Alouette IIs. A single SA.365 Dauphin is used as a VIP transport. The Military Aviation School uses ten Cessna T-41Ds, 11 Beech T-34Ds, three North American T-6Gs and two Bell 47 helicopters.

The Base Defence Command includes an air defence battalion with 20 Bofors 40 mm L/60

AA guns and a number of parachute infantry squadrons, which are similarly equipped to the Marines.

Combat Support Command controls all base services, there being military air bases at Azúa, Barahona, La Romana, La Vega, Monte Cristi, Puerto Plata and San Cristóbal, although most aircraft are based at San Isidro (Santo Domingo).

Maintenance Command is responsible for the maintenance of all aircraft, vehicles and buildings.

Air Force cadets pursue the first two years of their four-year course at the Military Academy at Haina before transferring to the *Escuela de Aviación Militar* for specialist training. Other ranks receive all-through training at the *Escuela de Aviación Militar*.

Like the Army and Navy, the Dominican Air Force has suffered from official neglect since the restoration of democratic government and is in urgent need of re-equipment if it is to continue as an effective force.

Paramilitary forces

Manpower: 10,000 (National Police)

The first police force in the Dominican Republic was formed in Santo Domingo in 1844, after the expulsion of the Haitians. Subsequently other municipalities also formed individual police forces. Being essentially civil organisations, these were not affected to any significant degree by the return of Spanish rule between 1861 and 1865 and also continued to operate during the United States occupation of 1916 to 1924. The Dominican Constabulary Guard, subsequently renamed Dominican National Police and ultimately Dominican National Army, formed under the auspicies of the US occupation forces, was essentially a military gendarmerie from its inception, its military functions ultimately eclipsing its functions as a national police force. In 1936, the existing municipal police forces were therefore combined in a new National Police Force, which from the outset also had a paramilitary orientation.

Currently, the Dominican National Police numbers approximately 10,000 all ranks under the overall direction of an Army officer with the title of Director General, who is directly subordinate to the Secretary of State for the Interior. The command structure consists of three sections dealing with administration and support, police operations and special operations, each section being headed by an assistant director general. The country is divided into four police regions with headquarters at Santo Domingo, San Pedro de Macorís, Santiago de los Caballeros and Barahona. The members of the National Police are armed with light infantry weapons in addition to normal police equipment and have co-operated with the armed forces in the suppression of low-level rural guerrilla activities. A National Police Academy was formed after the 1965 civil war and training assistance has also been forthcoming from the United States.

Sources of equipment supply and current requirements

In the past, the Dominican Republic has shopped widely for defence equipment, the principal suppliers being the United States, Britain, France, Germany, Spain and Canada and for a period during the early 1950s, Sweden, no country however enjoying a monopolistic position in this regard. The position of the United States as a supplier of equipment is notably weaker than in the case of many other countries of the region although it has strengthened since the demise of Trujillo.

The equipment of the three Dominican armed forces is obsolescent, replacements failing to keep pace with the withdrawal of obsolete equipment from service. Large-scale re-equipment is becoming more urgent in the case of all three, if they are to continue to retain any military credibility.

Surprisingly for such a small and industrially under-developed country, the Dominican Republic has a small but useful indigenous defence industry. This is centred on the San Cristóbal Arsenal, established by the dictator, Trujillo, after the Second World War. It has developed three models of a sub-machine gun of original conception, in addition to an automatic carbine and an assault rifle, although only the Cristóbal Mk II sub-machine gun was ever produced on a large-scale, even being exported to Cuba during the late 1950s. Projects for the manufacture of mortars and anti-tank weapons did not reach the production stage but the potential for the supply of the requirements of the Dominican armed forces in the area of infantry personal and support weapons exists. Since the fall of Trujillo, the capacity of the San Cristóbal arsenal has been devoted to the manufacture of small arms ammunition and the maintenance and repair of the weapons and equipment of the Army, including AFVs and artillery pieces. The Dominican Republic also has a small local ship-building capacity, which in the past has turned out a number of wooden-hulled small craft of up to 100 tons displacement for the Navy. This facility also has a potential for expansion which to date remains unexploited.

Summary and prospects

During the Trujillo regime, the Dominican armed forces were unequalled by those of any other Caribbean state, it being the boast of the dictator that his Air Force could destroy Havana in three hours and that his Army could overrun Haiti in less than a day, both claims being probably true, at least up to 1960. During the period of democratic government which has followed the civil war of 1965, the armed forces have been consistently neglected and although almost as numerous in manpower as during the Trujillo regime, lack of modern equipment is now a severe and progressive handicap. The Dominican armed forces remain highly trained and professional but have suffered a progressive erosion of their military capacity by the retirement of obsolete equipment without adequate replacement. As the threat of direct military intervention by Cuba has all but vanished and the small amount of low-level internal militant subversion has been easily contained by the armed forces and the National Police and can apparently continue to be controlled with the existing equipment available, any spectacular re-equipment of the Dominican Army, Navy or Air Force seems unlikely in the forseeable future.

ECUADOR

(República del Ecuador)

Area: 106,000 sq miles (274,540 sq km)
Population: 10,408,000 (1986)
Total armed forces: 45,100
Reserves: 150,000
Available manpower: 850,000
Paramilitary forces: 8200
GNP: $12,884 million (1984)
Defence expenditure: $223,871,000 (1984)

Introduction

Ecuador, as its name implies, straddles the Equator and is the second smallest country of South America. To the north, it is bounded by Colombia and to the south and east by Peru. The population consists of approximately 40% full-blooded Amerindians, 40% persons of mixed Indian and European origins, 10% being of predominantly European and 10% of Negro blood.

Until the early 1970s, the economy was based on the cultivation and export of tropical products, principally the banana, but also including sugar, coffee, cocoa and cotton. The discovery of large deposits of petroleum revolutionised the economy and Ecuador currently enjoys the highest economic growth rate in South America, its GNP having continued to grow during the recession which has effected an actual decrease in economic productivity among most of the other countries of the region. Industrial development is receiving active official support but Ecuador still imports not only the majority of its needs in the area of manufactured goods but also petroleum products refined from its own crude oil. The fishing industry is of increasing importance and the country's maritime economic zone is jealously guarded.

An insurrection against Spanish rule in 1809 was suppressed, independence being finally achieved following the defeat of the royalists by a mixed Colombian and Venezuelan army in 1821. From 1822 until 1830 the country, together with Colombia and Venezuela, formed part of the Republic of Gran Colombia. A brief war with Colombia, following but not directly related to Ecuadorian secession, resulted in victory for the Colombians and established the northern frontiers of Ecuador which have endured until the present day. The southern frontier with Peru had already led to hostilities before Ecuadorian secession from Gran Colombia and became the subject of an increasingly bitter dispute over more than a century. As with most of the other countries of Latin America, the first 70 years of Ecuadorian independence were characterised by almost continuous internal disturbance, periods of semi-anarchy being punctuated by the reigns of bizarre dictators and paralleled by sporadic skirmishes between Ecuadorian and Peruvian troops in the disputed frontier region.

The boundary problem with Peru continued and in 1941 Peru invaded southern Ecuador in overwhelming military force, rapidly defeating the less numerous and poorly organised and equipped defenders. After an armistice under the auspicies of Argentina, Brazil and the United States the Protocol of Rio de Janeiro of January 1942, awarded most of the disputed territory, equivalent to 55% of the total area of Ecuador, to Peru. The country remained one of the poorest in the continent until the discovery of oil in the early 1970s and since 1973 Ecuador has been South America's second greatest oil exporter. Ironically, most of the new oil riches lie in the region adjoining the Peruvian frontier and indications are that the former Ecuadorian territory, now occupied by Peru may contain equal or greater deposits. This has exacerbated the bitterness between the two countries which once more erupted into full-scale hostilities in January/February 1981, an all-out war being avoided by the intervention of the Organization of American States.

Ecuador is a unitary centralised republic of 20 provinces, four of which constitute the sparsely inhabited 'Oriente' and one the Galapágos Islands, officially known as the *Archipiélago de Colón*. Executive power is vested in the President who appoints the provincial governors. The *Archipiélago de Colón* is however administered by the Ministry of Defence. There is a bicameral legislature.

Since the 1920s the armed forces have been the dominant power in national politics, generally choosing to rule through an acceptable civilian administration rather than directly. The military held power directly however from 1976 to 1979, ruling the country via a three-man junta and following the adoption of a new constitution, permitted elections which returned a civilian president in August 1979. There were two military uprisings in 1986 which while unsuccessful in overthrowing President Febres Cordero nevertheless resulted in the replacement of part of the military high command by individuals more acceptable to the armed forces than the presidentially appointed incumbents.

Foreign policy is dominated by relations with Peru, the somewhat forlorn aspiration of regaining the territory lost in 1941 and the resolve to prevent further losses of territory. Although the country maintains a pro-Western attitude in international politics it has not hesitated to quarrel with the United States over fishing rights in the 200 mile maritime economic zone. The Ecuadorian Communist party is fragmented and factionalised and the Amerindian peasantry have shown little interest in Communist sponsored subversion. In 1986 relations with the United States had also improved sufficiently to permit the holding of joint military exercises in the province of Guayas.

Structure of the armed forces

The President is commander-in-chief of the armed forces, exercising his authority with the assistance of the Council of National Security and the combined General Staff of the armed forces. The Minister of National Defence, although in the chain of command, occupies a subordinate position to the high command, represented by the President and the above two consultative organs.

The three armed forces and the National Police each divide the country differently for administrative purposes.

The Army divides the national territory into four Zones of Defence of which the 1st (HQ Quito) covers the provinces of Tungurahua, Carchi, Pichincha, Cotopaxi and Imbabura, the 2nd (HQ Guayaquil) the provinces of Guayas, Los Rios, Esmeraldas and Manabí, the 3rd (HQ Cuenca) the provinces of El Oro, Cañar, Azuay, Loja, Chimborazo and Bolívar and the 4th (HQ Puyo) the provinces of Napo, Pastaza, Morona-Santiago and Zamora Chínchipe.

The Navy however divides the country into three Naval Districts of which the 1st (HQ Guayaquil) covers the Pacific coast and the Galápagos Islands, the 2nd (HQ Quito) consists only of the headquarters units stationed at the capital and the 3rd (HQ Puyo) covers the riverine system of the Oriente. The defence of the Galápagos Islands is also the responsibility of the Navy which administers them as a Naval Zone.

The Air Force divides the country into the two Air Force Districts of which the 1st (HQ Quito) covers the 11 Andean provinces and the four jungle provinces of the Oriente, the 2nd (HQ Guayaquil) covering the four coastal provinces and the Galápagos Islands.

The Law of Obligatory Military Service at present in force dates from 1921 although its provisions have been implemented only since 1935 and in practice a system of selective service is employed, the period of compulsory training being two years. Trained reserves are estimated at approximately 150,000 and partial trial mobilisations are periodically carried out.

The three armed forces each maintain their own training institutes although there is a tri-service Institute for Higher National Studies, the curriculum of which embraces economics and politics in addition to specifically military subjects.

Army

Manpower: 35,000

Formations: 6 divisions comprising:-
5 infantry brigades
1 special forces brigade
1 jungle brigade

Major units: 11 infantry battalions and 10 independent infantry companies
2 mechanised battalions
3 jungle battalions
2 special forces groups
3 cavalry groups
3 motorised recce squadrons

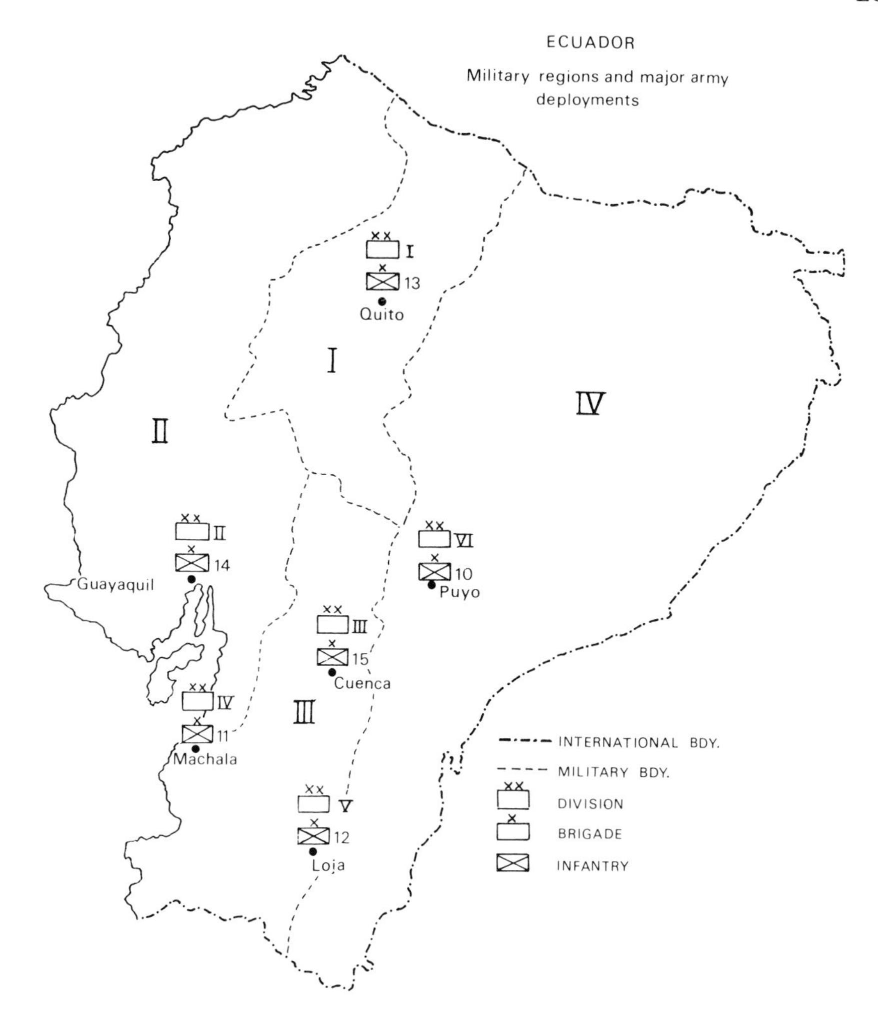

3 mixed artillery groups
1 AA artillery group
2 combat engineer battalions

AFVs: AMX-13 and M3A1 light tanks
AML 245 and EE-9 Cascavel armoured cars
EE-3 Jararacá scout cars
AMX-VCI, M113 and EE-11 Urutú APCs

Artillery: US M101 and Oto Melara Model 56 105 mm howitzers
US M198 155 mm howitzers
French Mk F3 155 mm SPH
Soltam 160 mm mortars

Air defence: Blowpipe SAMs
Vulcan M167 and M163 20 mm
40 mm L/60 and L/70 AA guns

Fixed-wing aircraft: Beech King Air, Super King and Queen Air
Cessna 172, 185 and 206
DHC-5, Learjet, Arava, Pilatus PC-6

Helicopters: SA.315B Lama, SA. 342L Gazelle, SA.330 Puma, AS.332B Super Puma and Bell UH-214

The modern Ecuadorian Army dates from the presidency of Eloy Alfaro (1895–1911). Some French officers were engaged to train the Army during the 1890s, followed by a full-scale Chilean military mission, which commenced its operations in 1903, Chilean officers continuing to operate the Staff College until 1962. An Italian military mission functioned between 1922 and 1940, setting up a Combat Arms School at Quito, expanding and improving the existing infantry, cavalry and engineering schools and establishing a School of Military Aviation. Following its departure in

1940 and the disastrous war with Peru in 1941 a group of US military advisers commenced operations in Ecuador. Ecuador declared war on the Axis powers immediately after the Japanese attack on Pearl Harbor and in 1942 the United States established a full military mission in Ecuador. Lend-Lease military aid also began to flow in 1942. Ecuador continued to receive considerable training and material assistance from the United States until 1971 when increasing tensions over fishing rights in Ecuador's 200-mile Exclusive Economic Zone prompted the withdrawal of the US military missions. Since that date Ecuador has accepted training assistance from Brazil and Israel.

The Ecuadorian Army currently numbers approximately 35,000 all ranks.

The 1st Military Zone (HQ Quito) is garrisoned by the 1st Army Division (HQ Quito) which consists principally of the 13th *Pichincha* Infantry Brigade (HQ Quito) comprising 36th *Mayor Galo Molina*, 37th *Vencedores* and 38th *Esmeraldas* Infantry Battalions, the 13th *Yaguachi* Motorised Cavalry Group, the 13th Mechanised Reconnaissance Squadron, the 13th *Mariscal Sucre* Mixed Artillery Group and the 3rd *Chimborazo* Combat Engineer Battalion.

The 2nd Military Zone (HQ Guayaquil) is garrisoned by the IInd Army Division (HQ Guayaquil), which consists essentially of the 14th *Litoral* Infantry Brigade (HQ Guayaquil) comprising the 5th *Guayas* and 25th *Marañon* Infantry Battalions, the 14th *Teniente Hugo Ortiz* Motorised Cavalry Group, the 14th Mechanised Reconnaisance Squadron, the 14th *Atahualpa* Mixed Artillery Group and the 1st *Montúfar* Combat Engineer Battalion.

The 3rd Military Zone (HQ Cuenca) contains the IIIrd, IVth and Vth Divisions, the IIIrd Army Division (HQ Cuenca) consisting essentially of the 15th *Azuay* Infantry Brigade (HQ Cuenca) comprising the 51st *Cayambe* Infantry Battalion, the 52nd *Galápagos* Mechanised Battalion, the 15th Mechanised Reconnaissance Squadron, and the 15th *Bolívar* Mixed Artillery Group, the IVth Army Division (HQ Machala) consisting primarily of the 11th *El Oro* Infantry Brigade (HQ Machala) comprising the 1st *Constitución*, 3rd *Pichincha* and 9th *Imbabura* Infantry Battalions and the 11th *Machala* Mechanised Cavalry Group, and the Vth Army Division (HQ Loja) made up of the 12th *Loja* Infantry Brigade (HQ Loja) consisting of the 20th *Capitán Díaz* and 21st *Macará* Infantry Battalions and the 23rd *Azuay* Mechanised Battalion.

The 4th Military Zone (HQ Puyo) is garrisoned by the VIth Army Division (HQ Puyo) which is the Ecuadorian Army's jungle division and consists essentially of the 10th *Napo* Jungle Infantry Brigade (HQ Puyo) comprising the 101st *Napo*, 102nd *Pastaza* and 103rd *Zamora* Jungle Infantry Battalions.

Each division also includes communications and logistic support units and each military zone also contains two or three independent infantry companies and a company apiece of signals and military police.

At Army level there is the 1st *Patria* Special Forces Brigade (HQ Quito) comprising the 1st Para-Commando Group at Quito and the 2nd Special Forces Group at San Camilo, the *Granaderos de Tarquí* Presidential Escort Squadron at Quito, the 1st AA Artillery Group, which is divided between Quito and Guayaquil, the 2nd *Cotopaxi* Construction Engineer Battalion, a logistic support battalion and a military police battalion, all located at Quito.

Rifles in service are the FN FAL in 7.62 mm and the SiG-540 in 5.56 mm calibre, the latter being used by the special forces. The standard sub-machine gun is the Uzi in 9 mm. The FN MAG in 7.62 mm is the standard machine gun, used in both the heavy and light roles, although examples of the US M1919 0.30 calibre and M2HB 0.50 calibre are still found, mainly in their vehicle-mounted form. The standard infantry mortar is the US M1 81 mm. Anti-armour weapons comprise the US M67 90 mm and M40A1 106 mm RCLs. Armour consists of 81 AMX-13 and 30 US M3A1 light tanks, 27 AML 245 H60/90 and ten EE-9 Cascavel armoured cars, ten EE-3 Jararacá scout cars, 50 AMX-VCI and 20 M113 tracked and 18 EE-11 Urutú wheeled APCs. Artillery consists of about 30 US M101 and 20 Oto Melara Model 56 105 mm howitzers, ten US M198 towed and a similar number of French Mk F3 155 mm SP howitzers, recently supplemented by a dozen Israeli 160 mm Soltam heavy mortars. Air-defence weapons comprise an unspecified number of US M1 40 mm L/60 and Bofors 40 mm L/70 AA guns, together with ten Vulcan M167 and 18 M163 20 mm systems, the Blowpipe SAM being the only missile system operated.

The AMX-13s and VCIs are operated mainly by the two mechanised battalions, the M3A1s being originally divided between the three mechanised reconnaissance squadrons. More recently they were reported to have been concentrated at Quito where they are presumably operated by the 13th *Yaguachi* Cavalry Group. The 11th *Machala* Cavalry Group is believed to operate the AML 245s and it seems likely that the 12th *Teniente Hugo Ortiz* Cavalry Group, which until the mid-1970s was still horsed, may have received the Brazilian equipment.

The *Servicio Aéreo del Ejercito* consists principally of the *Pichincha* Aviation Group and operates approximately 40 aircraft including three Beech King Air/Super King Air 100/200s, three Pilatus PC-6B Turbo-Porters, a single DHC-5 and five IAI Aravas in the transport role, a Learjet and two Beech Queen Air 80s for aerial survey, four Cessna 172s, two 185s and a 206 on training and liaison duties and five Aérospatiale SA.330 Pumas, ten AS.332B Super Pumas, five of a total order of 26 SA.342L Gazelles and two examples each of the Aérospatiale SA.315B Lama and the Bell UH-1 helicopters. Most aircraft are based at the Mariscal Sucre International Airport, Quito, although nominal groups are attached to the Army's brigades on an ad hoc basis.

Aspiring officers of the Ecuadorian Army pursue a five-year course at the *Eloy Alfaro* Military Academy at Quito which has an average enrollment of approximately 300. The War College, situated some 20 miles from Quito, imparts post-graduate training to field grade officers and its two-year course must be successfully completed to qualify for promotion to senior rank or for appointment to the General Staff.

Conscripts receive their basic training in the units to which they are assigned but there are specialist infantry, cavalry, armoured forces, artillery, engineer and signals schools. The *Escuela de Perfeccionamiento* at Quito offers specialist courses both for officers and time-expired conscripts who volunteer to remain in the Army as potential NCOs. There is a paratroop and special forces school at Salinas and a jungle warfare school in the Oriente.

Following its secession from Gran Colombia, Ecuador does not appear to have maintained any permanent or significant naval force during the next half-century, the Peruvian fleet being able to blockade the Ecuadorian coast with impunity in 1859. A small naval force was established in 1884 and in 1903 a Chilean naval mission was contracted by the Ecuadorian government but the Ecuadorian Navy remained a modest force even after some patrol vessels were transferred by the United States under Lend-Lease during the Second World War. During the post-war years the Navy expanded slowly with the acquisition of some war-surplus vessels from the US and Britain but did not begin to develop any significant military capability until the 1970s when two submarines and six fast attack craft were ordered in Europe.

Navy

Manpower: 5300 (including Marines and Naval aviation)

Major units: 1 obsolete destroyer
1 APD
6 missile corvettes
2 submarines
6 missile attack craft
1 LST
1 LSM

Marines: 3 battalions

Aircraft: IAI Arava, Beech Super King Air 200 and T-34C, Cessna Citation, 172, 177, 320E and 337
SA.316 Alouette III

The Ecuadorian Navy currently numbers about 5300 all ranks including some 1500 Marines and approximately 200 Naval aviation personnel. The largest surface combatants are the 2400-ton ex-US 'Gearing' class destroyer *Presidente Eloy Alfaro* and the 1400-ton APD *Morán Valverde,* both of which have been modified to carry a helicopter. The real combat potential of the fleet however consists of the six 550-ton missile corvettes *Esmeraldas, Manabí, Los Ríos, El Oro, Galápagos* and *Loja* and the two 1300-ton Type 209 '1300' class submarines *Shyri* and *Huancavilca.* Also of importance are the 250-ton missile attack craft *Quito, Guayaquil* and *Cuenca* and the 120-ton *Manta, Tulcán* and *Nuevo Rocafuerte.* There are eight smaller patrol craft and limited sealift

***Ecuadorian missile corvette* Esmeraldas (Breda Meccanica Bresciana)**

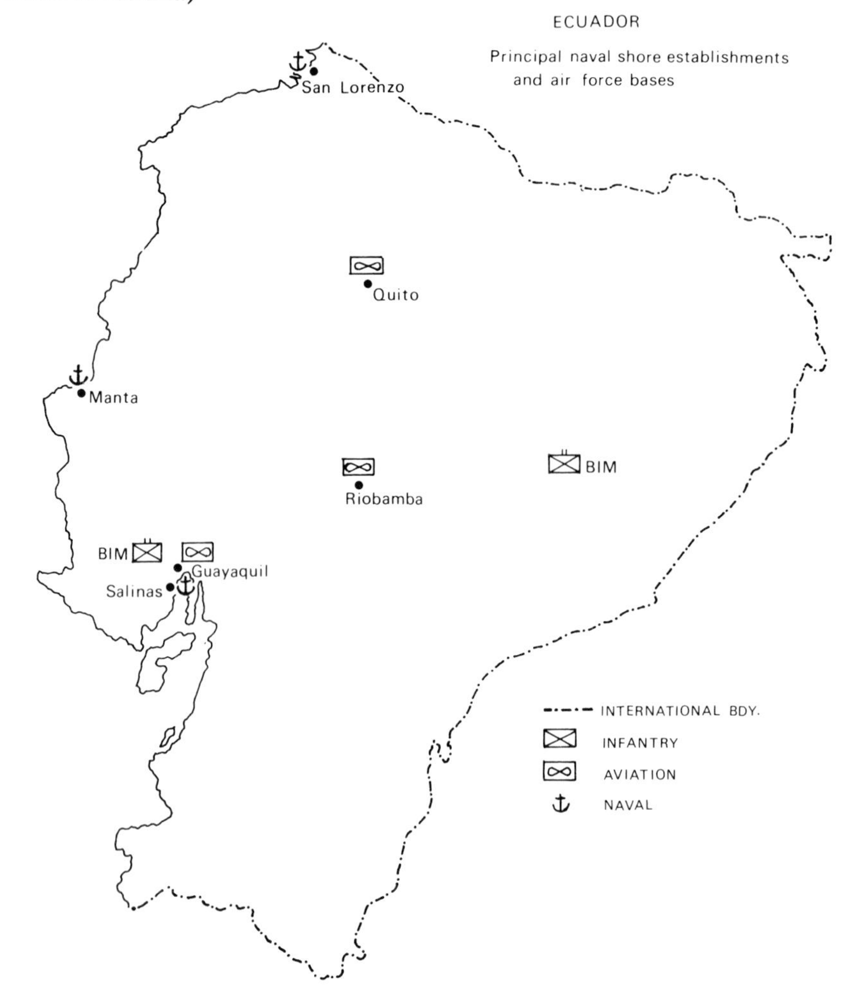

and some amphibious assault capacity is provided by the 650 - ton cargo ship *Calicuchima,* the 1650 - ton LST *Hualcopo* and the 740 - ton LSM *Tarquí,* in addition to the APD *Morán Valverde.* There are also the sail training ship *Guayas* and the surveying vessel *Orión,* both of approximately 1000 tons, the large armed tugs *Cayambe* and *Chimborazo,* three smaller tugs, a repair barge, a water carrier and two ex-US Coast Guard utility boats. Six very small motor launches patrol the inland waterways of the Oriente.

The major naval base is at Guayaquil, with minor bases at Jaramijó, San Lorenzo and in the Galápagos.

The Marines, who are equipped with the same personal and close-support weapons as the Army, are organised in three battalions of which one is located in the Galápagos Islands, one is divided between the naval bases on the Pacific coast and the third is located in the Oriente.

The *Aviación Naval* operates a total of about a dozen aircraft including single examples of the IAI Arava, the Cessna 320E and the Cessna Citation in the light transport role, a Beech Super King Air 200 for maritime reconnaissance, two SA.316 Alouette III helicopters and a pair of Cessna 172s, a single 177 and four 337s for training duties. The acquisition of six Bell 212 helicopters, for operation from the 'Esmeraldas' class corvettes is also projected.

Aspiring officers must successfully complete the four-year course of the Naval Academy at Punta

Missile attack craft* Quito *of the Ecuadorian Navy

Salinas, which has an average enrollment of approximately 120 cadets and midshipmen. There is a Naval War College, at Guayaquil, which conducts a two-year course to prepare candidates for staff appointments or promotion to senior rank. Enlisted personnel receive their basic training at the *Centro de Instrucción Naval* at Salinas which also offers specialist training in marine engineering, gunnery and communications.

One of the 'Esmeraldas' class missile corvettes is reported to be out of commission following a serious fire in 1985 and it is understood that a project for the acquisitions of one or two frigates, either of the Italian 'Lupo' or the Spanish 'Descubierta' class, is receiving attention.

Air Force

Manpower:	4800 troops (including 1 squadron of paratroops)
Major units:	1 combat wing comprising 3 fighter/light strike squadrons 1 fighter wing comprising 2 interceptor squadrons 1 transport group
Interceptors:	Mirage F.1s IAI Kfir C2s
Fighter/ bombers:	BAC Jaguar
Light strike aircraft:	Cessna A-37B and BAC Strikemaster Lockheed AT-33A
Bombers:	Canberra B.6
Transports:	C-130H Lockheed Electra Boeing 707, 720 and 727 DHC-5 and 6 HS.748 Beech King Air E90
Helicopters:	SA.315B Lama, SA.316 Alouette III, SA.330 Puma and AS.332 Super Puma Bell UH-1H, 212 and 214
Trainers:	Lockheed T-33A Beech T-34 Cessna T-41 SIAI Marchetti SF.260C

Ecuadorian military aviation traces its origins to the period of activity of the Italian military mission which established a flying school in 1920.

From 1935 onwards, Italian instructors were gradually replaced by US advisers, operating under individual personal contract to the Ecuadorian government. With the eventual withdrawal of the Italian military mission on the entry of Italy into the Second World War in 1940, an official US aviation mission was established although this did not commence its activities until after the brief but disastrous war with Peru of July 1941. Base facilities had been granted to the

***Jaquar strike aircraft of the 2122nd Fighter Squadron of the Ecuadorian Air Force* (British Aerospace)**

***Ecuadorian Air Force para-commando at Mariscal Sucre International airport, Quito* (Author)**

United States in 1941 and early in 1942 US personnel commenced the expansion and modernisation of the existing airfields and the delivery of small quantities of aircraft to the Ecuadorian Air Force. The Air Force became fully independent of the Army in 1944 and with Ecuador's signature of the Rio Treaty of Mutual Defence of 1947 additional material was acquired from the United States under the Military Aid Program. During the 1950s, Ecuadorian defence spending was largely concentrated on the Air Force and there was a dramatic expansion following the discovery of oil in the 1960s.

The Ecuadorian Air Force currently numbers some 4800 all ranks, manning a total of approximately 160 aircraft and including a squadron of paratroops, and is organised into two wings, a transport group and a flying training school.

Combat Wing 21 (Taura) comprises Combat Squadron 2111, with 11 Sepecat Jaguars, Combat Squadron 2112, with five Cessna A-37Bs and ten Lockheed AT-33As and Combat Squadron 2113, with ten BAC Strikemasters; Fighter Wing 22 (Mariscal Sucre International Airport, Quito) consists of Fighter Squadron 2211 with 16 Dassault Mirage F1JB and Es and Fighter Squadron 2212 with 11 IAI Kfir C2s. The Military Air Transport Group (Mariscal Sucre International Airport, Quito) incorporates the military airline TAME, equipped with four Boeing 707s, a single 720 and three 727s, a Lockheed Electra and two C-130s, a Fokker F.28, two DHC-5s, five DHC-6s, four HS.748s and a single Beech King Air 90.

The *Escuela de Vuelo Militar* (Salinas) is equipped with the first five of 15 Lockheed T-33As, the delivery of whch is scheduled for completion by 1988, 19 Beech T-34Cs, 17 Cessna T-41s, and 12 SIAI Marchetti SF.260Cs.

There are also a number of liaison and rescue flights, equipped with a total of three Aérospatiale SA.315B Lamas, six SA.316 Alouette IIIs, a single SA.330 Puma, two AS.332L Super Pumas, a single Bell 212, two 214s and four Bell UH-1Hs and flying from airfields at Cuenca, Guayaquil, Latacunga, Loja, Manta and Riobamba, in addition to the above major Air Force bases.

The Bomber Squadron, previously based at Mariscal Sucre International Airport, Quito and equipped with three English Electric Canberra B.6s is currently inactive, its equipment being in storage.

The Air Force Paratroop Squadron, which is a rapid-intervention commando unit, equipped with the same personal and support weapons as the Army special forces, is based at Quito but is available for service in any part of the country. For base defence there are also a number of AA batteries equipped with R-550 Magic SAMs.

The Air Force Academy is situated at Quito and offers a five-year course to aspiring officers, aircrew undergoing their flying training at the Military Flying School at Salinas. An Air War College was established at Quito with Brazilian assistance in 1972 and provides a two-year mid-career course which qualifies successful candidates for promotion to senior rank and for staff appointments. A school for air technicians was established at Quito in 1953 and moved to Guayaquil in 1971. Most enlisted personnel undergo some training at this establishment. NCOs either volunteer direct or choose to remain on in the Air Force as a career on completion of their period of compulsory military service.

Paramilitary forces

Manpower: 6800 National Civil Police
700 Customs Police
500 Guayas Traffic Police
200 Coast Guard

A national police force, known as the National Civil Guard, was formed in 1937 under the jurisdiction of the Ministry of the Interior. This force was responsible for both urban and rural policing and incorporated a highway patrol, responsible for traffic control on the national highway system. There was also a separate plain-clothes Investigative Police, also under the jurisdiction of the Ministry of the Interior. A separate Customs Police Force was maintained under the jurisdiction of the Ministry of Finance. In 1948, the province of Guayas was permitted to raise its own Traffic Police force, although this had no law-enforcement function other than traffic control. The National Civil Guard was renamed the National Civil Police in 1951, absorbing the Investigative Police in 1964.

As at present constituted, the National Civil Police numbers approximately 6800 and is the major national law enforcement agency.

The country is divided into four Police Districts of which the 1st (HQ Quito) comprises the provinces of Carchi, Imbabura, Pichincha, Cotopaxi Napo and Pastaza, the 2nd (HQ Riobamba) the provinces of Los Rios, Bolívar, Tungurahua and Chimborazo, the 3rd (HQ Cuenca) the provinces of Cañar, Azuay, Loja, Morona-Santiago and Zamora-Chínchipe and the 4th (HQ Guayaquil) the provinces of Guayas, Esmeraldas, Manabí, El Oro and Galápagos.

Operationally, the National Civil Police is divided into urban, rural, traffic and investigative sections. The police forces of Pichincha and Guayas provinces, which respectively contain the cities of Quito and Guayaquil, are each organised as regiments, that in Pichincha numbering approximately 700 men and that in Guayas, which has a major problem of endemic violent crime, 1200. Elsewhere, the police force is divided into numbered corps, on a provincial basis, the size of each corps varying with the population of the province in which it is located. A specialised unit, established in 1971, is responsible for the security of the oil pipeline and drilling rigs in the Oriente. The Traffic Police, which numbers about 500 and has approximately 200 vehicles at its disposal, is responsible for traffic control throughout the country, with the exception of the province of Guayas. The Criminal Investigative Division of the National Civil Police carries out the functions of the former Investigative Police. There is a Police Academy at Quito, which offers a three-year course for aspiring police offers. Other ranks receive their basic training at the National Police Training Institute, of which the Police Academy forms part.

The 700-man Customs Police comes under the jurisdiction of the Ministry for Finance and performs functions which are self-explanatory at the national ports, airports and major border crossing points.

The province of Guayas is now the only province to maintain a separate police force. The Guayas Traffic Police numbers approximately 500 and has its own training school at Guayaquil.

There is also the Coast Guard, formed in 1980 under the auspicies of the Navy, to which it remains subordinate and numbering approximately 200 manning 14 small patrol launches.

Although the various police forces are essentially civilian in character, all are organised on paramilitary lines and while normally armed only with pistols have a range of light infantry weapons available for use when required.

Sources of defence material supply and current requirements

Historically Ecuador has shopped widely for defence material, Germany, Britain and the Austro-Hungarian Empire being the principal suppliers up to the First World War. In the post-war years, Czechoslovakia occupied the position previously held by the now defunct Dual Monarchy, Italy becoming an important supplier thanks largely to the influence of the Italian military mission which functioned from 1920 to 1940. During the 1930s, the United States became the major supplier of military aircraft to the

Ecuadorian government although not enjoying a complete monopoly in this area. During the Second World War and immediately afterwards, the United States was virtually the sole supplier of military equipment to Ecuador although from the mid-1950s onwards Britain, Canada and Germany came to enjoy an increasing share of the Ecuadorian government's custom. During the 1960s and 1970s, France attained a position of considerable importance as the supplier of armoured vehicles and combat aircraft, the Belgian FN FAL and MAG being adopted as the basic infantry weapons. In recent years, Italy has once again come to be an important supplier of naval vessels and aircraft, Israel being the latest country to benefit from Ecuadorian arms purchases.

Since the discovery of oil in Ecuador, the Ecuadorian armed forces have been extensively overhauled. Probable requirements in the forseeable future include main battle tanks, artillery, both surface-to-air and anti-armour missile systems, medium sized naval surface combatants and both combat and transport aircraft.

As no country enjoys an absolute monopoly in any area of this field, the market is a relatively open one.

Summary and Prospects

Attempted left-wing internal subversion in the early 1960s was easily contained by the armed forces and although both student and labour unrest are virtually endemic, frequently leading to violent protests, the internal situation is relatively stable. Ecuador has also suffered to a lesser degree than many Latin American countries from the effects of the debt crisis, even maintaining its level of economic growth while that of most of its neighbours declined. The frontier dispute with Peru remains the major national problem and failing some highly unlikely diplomatic accommodation, involving the surrender of Peru of at least part of the territory awarded to it by the Protocol of Rio de Janeiro 1942, this area remains a major potential continental flashpoint.

Although inevitably still much weaker than those of Peru, the country's only obvious potential enemy, the Ecuadorian armed forces are now a much more effective deterrent to aggression than was the case in 1941. It is significant that three of the Ecuadorian Army's six divisions and the bulk of its mechanised forces are deployed in the southern region of the country.

THE FALKLAND (Malvinas) Islands

Area: 4698 sq miles (12,168 sq km)
Population: 1800
Total armed forces: nil
Reserves: 100
Available manpower: 150
Paramilitary forces: Nil
GNP: No figures available
Defence expenditure: Nil

Introduction

The Falkland (Malvinas) Islands are not a sovereign state and maintain no armed or paramilitary forces and so would fall outside the scope of this work had they not been the subject of a bloody little war between Argentina and Britain in 1982. As such, they merit a somewhat different treatment to that of the sovereign states which form the bulk of the subject matter of this book.

Although the population of the islands, 60% of which is concentrated in the capital and only town, Port Stanley, is almost exclusively British, the archipelago is geographically part of South America, lying on the extreme south-eastern edge of the continental shelf between 51 and 53 degrees South latitude.

Before the Argentine invasion, the government of the islands was run by a governor appointed from London, assisted by an Executive and a Legislative Council. The Executive Council, effectively the islands' cabinet, consisted of two ex-officio members, two members appointed by the Governor and two members elected from the Legislative Council. The latter body consisted of three appointed members–the Governor, the Chief Secretary and the Financial Secretary–all of whom were British civil servants and six elected members, chosen in practice from the small local land-owning and farm management sectors. Thus while the island government had certain pretensions to relative democracy during the long periods in which Argentina was under military government it compared poorly both to British parliamentary democracy and in relation to the Argentine constitutional system of government during the sporadic periods in which the latter was allowed to function.

Britain maintained a Royal Marine garrison of two platoons prior to the Argentine invasion of 1982 and there was a volunteer part-time local Defence Force equivalent in strength to a weak rifle company.

Historical background

Amerigo Vespucci is given the credit for the discovery of the islands by the Argentines although there is no satisfactory record of his sighting them, much less landing. British tradition attributes their discovery to two separate 16th century navigators, John Davis and Richard Hawkins, but documented proof in support of this claim is equally lacking, the first cartographic reference to the islands being in a Dutch map of 1600. Although lying clearly within the Spanish sphere of influence as defined under the Treaty of Tordesillas of 1494, Spain seems to have made no effort to explore, much less settle the islands.

During the 17th century British, French and Dutch privateers sailed the waters of the South Atlantic, challenging the power of Spain and in 1690 a Captain John Strong was the first Englishman to land on the islands, naming Falkland Sound after his patron, Anthony Cary, Viscount Falkland, then a Commissioner of the British Admiralty. This name, which was subsequently applied to the entire archipelago, thus clearly predates the Spanish appelation Malvinas, which is itself a corruption of the French Malouines given to the islands by Breton sealers, based on Saint Malo, who operated in the region during the early 18th century. The first permanent occupation of the islands was also by France which established a colony at Port Louis on East Falkland in 1764. In 1767 this was transferred to Spain, with which France was then in alliance, in recognition of prior Spanish claims to sovereignty and in exchange for a large financial settlement. In the meantime, the British had established a colony at Port Egmont, on West Falkland. In 1770 the Spanish governor of Buenos Aires ordered an attack on the British settlement but this was not carried out and the British withdrew peacefully in 1774, leaving their flag flying and a plaque affirming British rights to sovereignty.

The Nootka Sound Convention of 1790 bound Britain and Spain to refrain from establishing new colonies in the South Atlantic and on this basis the Spanish colony on East Falkland remained the only one in the archipelago, over the entirety of which the Spaniards continued absolute sovereignty which Britain now appeared to recognize formally. In 1811 Spain abandoned the islands which were not occupied again until 1820 when the United Provinces of Rio de la Plata (Argentina) sent a ship to the archipelago. As successors in title to the Spanish crown, they granted a concession for the development of Isla Soledad (East Falkland) to one Louis Vernet who was officially installed as governor in 1829. Vernet sought to restrict sealing and whaling in Falkland waters, arresting three United States sealing ships in 1830. In response to this the Argentine colony was sacked by a landing party from the United States frigate *Lexington* the following year, its captain declaring the islands "free of all government".

An Argentine garrison and a penal colony were soon re-established but three years later a British force was landed and the Argentine garrison expelled. Despite repeated Argentine protests over the following century-and-a-half Britain continued to occupy the islands until the Argentine invasion of 1982.

British colonisation

After its seizure of the islands in 1833 Britain began the colonisation of the archipelago on a more systematic basis than had previously been undertaken by its various successive occupiers. By 1851 the population stood at 287, rising to 2043 fifty years later and to a peak of 2392 in 1931 after which emigration and a falling birth rate had eroded the population of the islands to 1813 by 1982.

From 1851 onwards the archipelago has largely belonged to the Falkland Island Company, an absentee landlord owning most of the land in the islands. In effect, it also owns most of the islanders who exist in a state close to serfdom, living mostly in company housing, from which they are ejected on retirement and earning an income equivalent on an average to 60% of that of British agricultural workers. In many cases they rarely see the cash content of their meagre wages which they permit the company to hold as an interest-free loan against purchases in the company stores. The company and the nine minor land-owners, for their part, largely repatriate the considerable profits from the islands' one-crop economy, wool, of which little is reinvested locally and have consciously resisted all efforts at the diversification of the local economy.

Until 1971 the Falkland Islands Company maintained a monthly sea link between the islands and Montevideo. Since that year however this service has been replaced by a three-monthly direct sea link between the islands and Britain.

Argentine involvement

Diplomatic negotiations regarding the future of the islands, which had been in progress sporadically for half a century between Britain and Argentina, reached their pinnacle of cordiality during the late 1960s. In 1971 a communications agreement was arrived at by both governments under which Argentina agreed to provide a weekly air service between the archipelago and the South American mainland if Britain would build an air strip in the islands and provide a sea link between them and Argentina. A year later, although Britain had surveyed an appropriate site for the air strip, no construction had commenced nor had the sea link been established and the Argentine government offered to build the air strip themselves if the British would provide the material. This was duly done and from 1972 onwards the main connection between the archipelago and the outside world was the weekly service between Port Stanley and Comodoro Rivadavia provided by the Argentine military airline LADE (Lineas Aéreas del Estado). Two further agreements, signed two years later between the British and Argentine governments, provided for the construction of a permanent airfield by the British to be staffed by Argentine personnel and the supply of fuel oil to the islands by the Argentine state petroleum monopoly YPF (*Yacimientos Petroleros Fiscales*) although the provision of a direct sea link between the islands and the South American mainland remained in abeyance.

With the decline in direct communications between the islands and the remote homeland and the increase in contact with the South American mainland their inhabitants came increasingly to depend upon Argentina for supplies, fuel and advanced medical treatment, all of which successive Argentine governments showed themselves willing to provide. With improved accessibility from the mainland to the islands a limited tourist trade also began to develop providing a welcome element of diversification in an otherwise severely limited economy.

Nevertheless regulations limiting the periods for which Argentine citizens could remain in the islands and absolutely prohibiting their ownership of land and property remained in force even though the British Nationality Bill of 1981 threatened, at a stroke, to deprive 30% of the islanders of any rights to residence in the United Kingdom, a right of which it threatened ultimately to deprive all islanders not actually born in the mother country. When in 1982 it was announced that the last British naval presence in the South Atlantic, the Antarctic supply and research vessel HMS *Endurance*, was to be withdrawn, British disengagement from the Falklands seemed to be virtually complete. The latter action in particular was misconstrued by the then Argentine military regime as a virtual invitation to invade the archipelago and fill the military vacuum left by the British departure.

Strategic importance

The original British annexation of the islands was predicated on their strategic value, first as a victualling station and subsequently as a coaling and telegraphic one. With the contraction of the British Empire from the late 1940s onwards the archipelago became increasingly a colonial anachronism the liability value of which increased as its positive strategic relevance declined. Following the diminution of the strategic importance of the islands, in the context of contracting British overseas responsibilities, the possibility of the existence of deposits of oil and other natural resources within the islands' 200 mile Exclusive Economic Zone, which remained unconfirmed, occasioned a flicker of revived interest in Britain but failed to halt the process of disengagement. At the same time, it reinforced Argentina's resolve to repossess itself of what it had never ceased to consider as its territory.

A new strategic importance for the islands, although one to which Britain was now irrelevant, appeared to present itself during the late 1970s in the context of moves towards the establishment of a South Atlantic Alliance in which Argentina, Brazil and South Africa, together with the United States, would be the principal protagonists. The unequivocal and almost unlimited support by the United States for Britain during the Anglo-Argentine War however not only virtually destroyed the inter-American defence system which had been elaborately built up since the Rio Treaty of 1947 but also stifled all immediate prospects of the development of a South Atlantic Alliance on lines acceptable to the United States. In this context, the maintenance of a major military complex in the South Atlantic by its most reliable ally, Britain, was supremely acceptable to the United States, even if not to a sufficient degree to justify US participation in the cost of its upkeep, which at its peak during 1982–85 amounted to almost 10% of Britain's total annual defence expenditure.

This has diminished to approximately US$ 500 million per annum with the completion of the new military airfield and the contraction of the British garrison from its peak of over 10,000 to a strength of some 2000, made up of an infantry battalion group, an air defence battery equipped with Hawk SAMs and Gepard 35 mm AA guns, an engineer company and an army air squadron, equipped with six Boeing-Vertol CH-47 Chinook helicopters. There is also a naval detachment of three patrol vessels and three Sikorsky S-61B Sea

King helicopters, with a nuclear attack submarine and two frigates on station, and a squadron each of RAF McDonnell-Douglas F-4 Phantom fighters and Lockheed C-130 Hercules transport aircraft, in addition to a squadron of the RAF Regiment equipped with Rapier SAMs.

Summary and prospects

As has been shown, the validity of either Argentine or British claims to the islands is by no means incontrovertible. British claims are based on prescription, or the unarguable fact of occupation for over 150 years. Argentina's claims follow the principle of *Uti Possidetis*: possession as heirs to the Spanish colonial empire at the time of independence, the principle of determining sovereignty universally applied throughout Latin America and the one which has led to almost every war between Latin American states since independence.

While the historical claims of both Britain and Argentina are both flawed, Britain's claim, supported by more than a century and a half of occupation, would appear persuasive, were Britain to show even the remotest interest in developing the islands. The facts of geography remain immutable: Britain is 8000 miles (12,800 kilometres) distant from the archipelago which is only 400 miles (640 kilometres) from Argentina. Despite the atavistic attachment of the Falklanders to their remote motherland, the latter has largely forgotten them and has been traditionally parsimonious in its treatment of them. The fact remains that the 1982 war had been fought as much for the political self-preservation of the contemporary British government as for the defence of the islanders' right to remain British, of which the same government was in the process of depriving them by statute.

By contrast, Argentina has shown itself eager to develop the islands and better the lot of their inhabitants. Health and education services can only be supplied economically to the islands from Argentina yet even prior to the invasion the islanders maintained an almost universal hostility towards both Argentina and its people. The problem of sovereignty appears insoluble without the resettlement of the islanders although the successful integration of the British population of Argentina into Argentine society gives some grounds for cautious optimism in this respect in the event of a solution to the Anglo-Argentine dispute.

Until such solution materialises, despite and perhaps to a certain degree because of Argentina's military defeat in the war of 1982, the area remains a major regional flash-point.

GUATEMALA

(República de Guatemala)

Area: 42,042 sq miles (108,880 sq km)
Population: 8,616,000
Total armed forces: 32,000
Reserves: 100,000
Available manpower: 600,000
Paramilitary forces: 311,000
GNP: $9,397 million (1984)
Defence expenditure: $179,800,000 (1984)

Introduction

Guatemala is the third largest of the Central American republics and is bounded by Mexico to the north, by Belize, which it claims as part of its territory, to the north-east, by the Gulf of Honduras to the east, the Republic of Honduras to the south-east, El Salvador to the south-west and the Pacific Ocean to the west. Its population contains the largest proportion of pure Amerindians – over 53% – of all the Central American republics. Of the remainder, people of mixed Amerindian and European racial origins are by far the most numerous, making up 45% of the total. Less than 2% of the population is of more-or-less pure European origin and there is a small Negro minority, mainly concentrated on the east coast. The population is very unevenly distributed, being largely concentrated in the central highlands, the north-eastern region, in particular, being largely uninhabited and containing less than 1% of the total population.

Agriculture is the main economic occupation, major exports being coffee, bananas, cotton, sugar and meat. Imports consist largely of manufactured goods, textiles, wheat and refined petroleum products although Guatemala has been a small-scale crude oil exporter since 1980. The country is largely self-sufficient in food production and with more modern and better-organised farming methods could be a major food exporter. The mining of zinc, lead, antimony and tungsten is of minor importance but worthy of mention.

Spaniards moving southwards into Central America from Mexico subdued the native Indians and established the first Spanish settlements from 1523 onwards. In 1824, following the fall of the Mexican "Emperor" Iturbide, who had attempted to annexe the five Central American states and the declaration of the Mexican republic, Guatemala, El Salvador, Honduras, Nicaragua and Costa Rica declared their independence as the United Provinces of Central America. The confederation collapsed in 1839 however, its constituent units becoming independent and frequently warring states.

A brief war between Guatemala and El Salvador occurred in 1876, followed by one against all four of the other republics in 1885.

General Manuel Estrada Cabrera who ruled as dictator from 1898 until 1920 and encouraged large-scale United States investment in Guatemala, fought yet another brief war against El Salvador in 1906. General Jorge Ubico, who became President in January 1931 and ruled as absolute despot until 1944, also courted the United States, granting sites for military bases to the US government during the Second World War and declaring war on the Axis powers on 11 December 1941, although Guatemala took no active part in the conflict.

Juan José Arévalo, who became President in March 1945, introduced a programme of cautious reform, coming into conflict with powerful United States business interests. Colonel Jacobo Arbenz Guzmán, who was elected President in 1951, embarked on a collision course with the major US investor in Guatemala, the United Fruit Company of Boston, with which both the contemporary US

Secretary of State John Foster Dulles and his brother, CIA chief Allen Dulles had strong business connections, by the expropriation of portion of its holdings; he also alienated the armed forces by his radical policies. Following the refusal of the US government to sell him military equipment for which he had no apparent need, Arbenz concluded an arms deal with Czechoslovakia which gave an excuse for a US backed invasion of Guatemala from Honduras, in June 1954 and Arbenz was forced to flee into exile.

Colonel Carlos Castillo Armas succeeded Arbenz and ruled Guatemala to the complete satisfaction of US political and business interests from 1954 until his assasination in 1957. He was followed by a succession of conservative military or military-dominated regimes, culminating in 1978 in that of General Lucas García, which repressed the chronic low-level insurgency which had been endemic since the early 1960s with such brutality that the United States threatened to suspend all military aid to Guatemala, provoking a pre-emptive rejection of US assistance by the Lucas García regime. Lucas García was ousted by a coup in March 1982 and replaced by a three-man junta led by General Efraím Ríos Montt whose initial actions to improve the human rights situation, combined with his avowed anti-communism, prompted a renewal of US military assistance. Ríos Montt was overthrown by General Oscar Mejía Víctores in August 1983, after his selectivity in promoting his immediate supporters had antagonised the officer corps. Elections in November 1985 returned Vinicio Cerezo as the first civilian President for almost a generation and the country has enjoyed precarious civilian government to date.

Guatemala is a unitary republic divided into 22 departments. Executive power is in the hands of the President and there is a unicameral legislature.

The politico-strategic situation in Guatemala is one of the most complex in an area of extreme political complexity.

All of the governments which have held office since the overthrow of Arbenz have been more or less reactionary. The adoption of extreme right-wing policies is not however a guarantee of pro-Western orientation in the case of the Guatemalans who are among the most xenophobic peoples in the Americas. A history of commercial exploitation by North American business interests, backed not infrequently by overt meddling by the US in the country's internal affairs, has ensured that even Guatemalans of the extreme political right tend also to violent hostility towards the United States.

A further complication is the fragmentation of Guatemalan society into highly polarised and mutually antagonistic social and ethnic groups. All attempts at the integration of the Amerindian majority into the main stream of Guatemalan life have been abysmal failures, including the faltering steps towards land reform during the Arbenz regime. After four centuries of subjugation and exploitation, the Indian population is unreceptive even to reforms calculated to improve its conditions of everyday life and is apparently incapable of assimilation into modern society.

Chronic guerrilla activity, both urban and rural, appears to have been contained but not suppressed and at the cost of great brutality. The potential for internal instability remains immense.

Another potentially explosive issue, although somewhat diminished since Britain's victory in the Anglo-Argentine War of 1982, is that of Guatemala's territorial claim to the whole of Belize. This is pursued despite the Anglo-Guatemalan Treaty of 1859 whereby Guatemala renounced its claim to Belize in exchange for the construction by Britain of an as yet unbuilt road linking Guatemala City to the Caribbean and is further complicated by Mexico's claim to a large portion of the territory in dispute. Guatemalan claims have not abated since the Mexican government's offer to waive Mexican claims if Guatemala should do likewise although there are indications that the present civilian government may adopt a more reasonable attitude to the problem.

Structure of the armed forces

The Guatemalan armed forces are unusual in that they constitute a single institution with Army, Navy and Air Force elements which, in theory, are equal components of a single entity. The Army, as by far the most numerous, enjoys a certain de facto primacy. All logistic and other supporting services are also provided by the Army which has the effect that the nominal personnel establishments of the Navy and Air Force are less numerous than would normally be the case.

The President has the constitutional status of Commanding General of the armed forces, with the power to decree mobilisation, award commissions, confer decorations and grant special pensions. Only Congress can however declare war or conclude treaties and the military budget must be sanctioned by Congress annually. The President issues instructions through the Minister of National Defence, who is invariably an Army general. The Minister of National Defence is in the chain of command and appoints the commanders of the six military zones into which the country is divided and the commanders of reserves, one of whom is appointed for each of the country's 22 departments and takes over both civil and military authority in case of emergency. The Chief of Staff is third in the chain of command, under the Minister of National Defence and exercises operational command over all units of the armed forces except the Presidential Guard, which receives its orders directly from the President. The President is advised by the Supreme Council of National Defence, which is made up of the Minister of National Defence and the senior commanders of the armed forces and the functions of which are purely consultative although it also acts as the supreme court of military justice.

The six Military Zones approximate to (i) the capital and its immediate environs; (ii) the northern highlands; (iii) the southern highlands; (iv) the Pacific coastal strip; (v) the Caribbean coastal lowlands and Alta Verapaz; and (vi) the jungle department of Petén.

By law, all male citizens between the ages of 18 and 50 are liable for military service. In practice, a selective draft system is employed, only a small proportion of those reaching the age of 18 being chosen for service. The duration of active service varies from one year in the case of elements with low technical requirements, to two years in others such as the mechanised cavalry, artillery, Navy and Air Force. Those not inducted into the regular armed forces must undergo reserve training every week-end during the first year, one weekend per month during the second year, a total of four weekends during the third year and two weekends during the fourth year. This training is administered by regular units stationed in the area. All officers of the three armed forces complete the four-year basic course of the *Escuela Politécnica*, the national military academy. Most officers com- their professional education abroad.

Army

Manpower:	30,300
Formations:	1 Presidential Guard brigade 4 reinforced infantry brigades 1 COIN battalion group
Major units:	2 Presidential Guard battalions 12 infantry battalions 1 counter-insurgency battalion group 1 paratroop battalion 4 special forces companies 1 armoured battalion 4 mechanised reconnaissance squadrons 4 groups of field artillery 1 anti-aircraft group 1 engineer battalion
AFVs:	US M4 medium and M3A1 light tanks AMX-13 light tanks M8 and V-150 Commando armoured cars M3A1 and RBY-1 scout cars M113 and M3 half-track APCs

Artillery: US M101 105 mm, M116 75 mm and German LeIG 18 75 mm howitzers

Air defence weapons: US M1A1 40 mm guns

General Justo Rufino Barrios established the Army on a solid professional basis in 1871. The foundation of the Military Academy in 1874 is also an important milestone in the development of Guatemala's armed forces. At the turn of the century, a French military mission imparted a distinctively French orientation to the Guatemalan Army. Under Manuel Estrada Cabrera (1898–1920) the Army expanded and received much new equipment. With his fall it however declined in importance. Somewhat surprisingly, the military dictatorship of Jorge Ubico saw no dramatic expansion of the armed forces although some equipment was obtained under Lend-Lease following the granting of base facilities to the United States during the Second World War. A United States military mission was established in 1945 and additional equipment continued to be acquired during the post-war period, US military assistance ceasing only during the presidency of Jacobo Arbenz. The reported 2000 tons of Czech arms, ordered by Arbenz and delivered in May 1953, consisted largely of obsolescent material of Second World War vintage and was of little avail to him in the absence of support from the Army for his regime. During the period of reinforced US political influence which followed the collapse of Arbenz, military assistance was resumed and increased.

Guatemalan paratroops **(M. English)**

The intensely xenophobic Guatemalan Army suffered the supreme humiliation of having to request the assistance of US special forces in the suppression of guerrilla activity in the late 1960s and early 1970s and US military aid continued on a massive level. However, Guatemala renounced all further US military aid in 1978, after the Carter administration attempted to relate military assistance to the performance of the Guatemalan government in the human rights field. Israel, which had become an increasingly important supplier of defence equipment from the mid-1970s onwards, stepped readily into the breach as Guatemala's main supplier of defence material and training aid. Although the Reagan administration in the United States is more inclined to turn a blind eye to human rights infringements in basically friendly countries and has recommenced the sale of military equipment to Guatemala, Israeli influence remains strong and the Guatemalan Army is now primarily equipped with personal weapons and equipment of Israeli origins.

The Guatemalan Army currently numbers some 30,300 all ranks, its tactical and operational organisation being only coincidentally ralated to the six Military Zones which however form the infra-structure of the Army's reserve organisation. The principal tactical formation is the brigade, of which there are four. Two of these, the *Mariscal Zavala* and *Guardia de Honor* Brigades have their headquarters at Guatemala City. A third, the *General Barrillas* Brigade is deployed along the Pacific coast, with its headquarters at Quetzaltenango, while the *Capitan General Carrera* brigade is principally deployed along the frontier with Belize, with its headquarters at Zacapa. The brigades, which do not appear to have numerical designations, each consist of three infantry battalions, a reconnaissance squadron and an artillery group, with an operational headquarters and a logistic support company. Recently each has also acquired at least one company of special forces.

Army level troops include the two-battalion

Presidential Guard (not to be confused with the *Guardia de Honor* Brigade) which effectively forms a fifth brigade, the *Agrupación Táctica de Seguridad del Ejército*, which is a battalion group with a counter-insurgency function and which together with the Paratroop/Special Forces Battalion and the special forces companies attached to the brigades are collectively known as "*Kaibiles*", an armoured battalion, an anti-aircraft group and an engineer battalion and are all normally based at or in the vicinity of Guatemala City, being temporarily deployed elsewhere in accordance with operational necessity.

The infantry are equipped with the Israeli Galil and US M16 assault rifles, both in 5.56 mm calibre. The Uzi sub-machine gun, in 9 mm calibre, has become the preferred light automatic weapon although Madsen M46/53, Beretta Model 12 and MAC-10 sub-machine guns are also encountered. The US M1919 machine gun, in 0.30-inch calibre, remains the main infantry support weapon, together with some 0.50-inch calibre M2HBs and US M2 60 mm, M1 81 mm and M2 4.2-inch mortars, the latter acquired via Israel as also was the 106 mm M40A1 RCL, used in the anti-armour role. The single armoured battalion is nominally equipped with ten obsolete US M4 Sherman and a similar number of M3A1 Stuart tanks, plus eight French AMX-13s, together with 15 US M113 tracked and ten M2 half-track APCs, not all of these vehicles being in serviceable condition. The reconnaissance units are heterogeneously equipped, having a mixture of Israeli RBY-1 scout cars, of which there is a total of ten, US Cadillac-Gage V-150 Commando armoured cars, of which there are seven and both US M8 Greyhound armoured cars and M3A1 White scout cars, of which there are eight and six respectively. The artillery groups are equipped with an estimated 12 US M101 105 mm howitzers, 24 M116 75 mm pack howitzers and 12 German Le IG 18 75 mm infantry guns, the latter being the only significant element of the Arbenz purchase still in general service. The single anti-aircraft group is believed to have 12 US M1A1 towed 40 mm AA guns. Some twin 20 mm Oerlikons of pre-Second World War vintage may also remain on inventory.

All officers are graduates of the four-year course of the National Military Academy and are initially commissioned into the infantry for two years, regardless of the subsequent specialisation to which they may aspire. Specialist training for both officers and other ranks is provided by the *Escuela de Aplicación*. There is a series of NCO schools. Most officer and senior NCO personnel undergo some training outside the country, usually either in the Panama Canal Zone or in the continental United States. Selected officers are also sent for further studies to Mexico, Venezuela, Argentina, France, Germany, Italy and Spain. Contact with these latter countries increased during the period of estrangement from the United States.

Since the early 1960s, the Guatemalan Army has developed a specific counter-insurgency orientation. This tendency seems likely to continue for the foreseeable future, a lack of modern heavy equipment militating against its conventional military potential.

Navy

Manpower: 1000 (including Marines)

Major units: 8 coastal patrol craft

Marines: 4 companies

Largely due to its short Caribbean coast and the lack of natural harbours on the longer Pacific coast, Guatemala never developed a maritime tradition and was slow to establish any form of naval force. In 1959 however, following extensive poaching by Mexican fishing boats in Guatemalan territorial waters, it was announced that a Navy was to be established. During the past three decades the Guatemalan Navy has acquired a number of small patrol craft and expanded to include a small element of marine infantry but remains essentially a coastal patrol force of very limited military potential.

The largest unit of the Guatemalan Navy is the 90-ton patrol craft *Kukulkán*, besides which there are the 60-ton *Utatlán* and *Subteniente Osorio Sanabria* and the 30-ton *Tecunumán*, *Kaibilbalam*, *Azumanche*, *Tzacol* and *Bitol*. There are also six very small motor launches and 30 river patrol craft, none of which displaces more than 10 tons, an unnamed 30-ton surveying launch, the 8-ton armoured transport launches *Picuda* and *Barracuda*, two LCMs, the small tugs *Escuintla*, *Maza-*

tenango and *Retalhuleu* and the training yacht *Mendieta*.

The majority of these vessels are stationed on the Caribbean coast, based at Santo Tomás de Castilla, which has a 230-ton synchrolift and limited repair and maintenance facilities. The Pacific coast base is at Sipicate. Personnel strength is approximately 1000 which includes four companies of Marines.

Naval officers receive their basic training at the *Escuela Politécnica* and subsequent specialist training, including sea service, with the Argentinian and Venezuelan Navies. Specialist non-commissioned personnel also receive supplementary training abroad.

In over a quarter of a century of existence, the Guatemalan Navy, although it has expanded considerably, has not developed beyond an inshore patrol force, carrying out essentially coast guard type functions. Any further expansion of the scope of its operations seems somewhat unlikely in the forseeable future.

Air Force

Manpower:	700
Major units:	1 fighter-bomber squadron 1 tactical support squadron 1 transport squadron
Tactical support aircraft:	Cessna A-37B and T-37C Pilatus PC-7
Transports:	Douglas DC-6B, C-54 and C-47, IAI Arava
Communications aircraft:	Beech Super King Air 200, Cessna 170B, 172K, 180 and U206C
Helicopters:	Bell UH-1D, 206B, 212 and 412
Trainers:	Potez CM.170 Lockheed T-33A, Pilatus PC-7 Cessna T-41

A French military aviation mission arrived in Guatemala in 1920 and a flying training school was established but little progress was made until 1929, when the *Cuerpo de Aviacion Militar de Guatemala* was established. In 1934 the dictator Ubico decided on a relatively ambitious expansion programme, ordering 30 assorted aircraft in the United States. The outbreak of the Second World War hindered any further immediate expansion until 1942, when Guatemala began to receive Lend-Lease military assistance from the United States. A US military air mission arrived in Guatemala in 1945 and following Guatemala's signature of the Rio Treaty of 1947 US military aid again increased considerably, the title of the force being changed to *Fuerza Aerea Guatemalteca* in 1948. The hostility of the United States government towards the Arbenz Guzman regime however virtually closed off the Guatemalan Air Force's main source of equipment supply during the period 1951/54. The Air Force took no part in the hostilities during the coup which overthrew Arbenz in 1954 but aircraft deliveries from the US resumed soon afterwards. Following the suspension of US military aid in 1978 Guatemala turned to Israel and Europe as suppliers of defence material. The election of Ronald Reagan as President of the United States brought with it a mellowing of US foreign policy, as a direct result of which spares were made available for existing US-built aircraft and some limited deliveries of new material were made.

The Guatemalan Air Force currently numbers approximately 700, operating about 100 aircraft and is organised in one nominal fighter-bomber squadron based at San José and equipped with eight Cessna A-37Bs and three T-37Cs, a tactical support squadron at Santa Elena, equipped with six Pilatus PC-7s, a transport squadron based at La Aurora Airport, Guatemala City and equipped with nine C-47s, six IAI Aravas and single examples of the C-54 and DC-6. The *Escuela de Aviación Militar* at Los Cipresales has three Potez CM.170 Magisters, three Lockheed T-33As, four Pilatus PC-7s and six Cessna T-41s. There is also a Presidential flight equipped with the sole Beech Super King Air 200 and based at La Aurora. The remaining four Cessna 170s, eight 172s, three 180s and two U206s are based at either any of the above or at Retalhuleu, Quezaltenango, Escuintla, Puerto Barrios, San José or Flores as operational necessity demands, as are the nine Bell UH-1D, ten Bell 206, three Bell 212 and six Bell 412 helicopters. The fighter-bomber and tactical sup-

***Pilatus PC-7 trainer/light-strike aircraft of the Guatemalan Air Force* (Pilatus Aircraft Ltd)**

port squadrons are also redeployed to some of the airfields in eastern Guatemala during periods of tension on the frontier with Belize.

Officers are trained at the *Escuela Politécnica,* receiving their flying training at the *Escuela de Aviación Militar*. Most officers also receive advanced training abroad, either in the United States or in Mexico or Venezuela. Specialist ground crews and other support personnel receive their training either at the *Escuela de Aplicación* or in the *Escuela de Aviación Militar*.

Probable developments in the immediate future include the further expansion of the helicopter force and the possible acquisition of a token force of interceptors, the most likely type being the Israeli Kfir, the United States having consistently refused to supply six Northrop F-5s since first requested to do so in 1978.

Paramilitary forces

Manpower: 9500 (National Police)
2100 (Treasury Police)
300,000 "Civil Defence" Militia

There are two major paramilitary police forces: the National Police and the Treasury Police or Border Patrol. Although officially civilian police forces, both are paramilitary in character, are officered largely by either retired army officers or by active officers on secondment and in time of national emergency would come under the jurisdiction of the Ministry of National Defence.

The National Police was established in 1881 as the Urban Police. Following the coup which overthrew the dictatorship of Jorge Ubico in 1944 and until 1955 the force was known as the *Guardia*

Civil. The present title was adopted in 1955, following the overthrow of the Arbenez Guzmán regime. This force comes under the jurisdiction of the Ministry of the Interior and is usually commanded by a senior army officer on secondment, with the title of director-general. It is the principal law enforcement agency in the country, although with the escalation of violent political subversion since the early 1960s, the Army has increasingly assumed responsibility for internal security. Approximately 60% of its effectives are stationed at Guatemala City, the remainder being distributed principally between the capitals of the remaining 21 departments. Approximately 100 of the remaining major population centres have a permanent police presence and there are 14 mobile detachments which form a police rapid intervention force. For administrative purposes, the National Police divides the country into zonal commands, which approximate to the six military regions. The force is armed principally with revolvers and US M1 carbines in 0.30-inch calibre. Some light automatic weapons are also available.

The *Guardia de Hacienda* was established in 1954 under the Ministry of Finance, to serve primarily as customs police on the frontiers and at air and sea ports. In 1967, the force was transferred to the jurisdiction of the Ministry of the Interior, in an effort to rationalise police administration under a single Ministry. Detachments are located in each of the 22 departmental capitals with a stronger presence in the frontier and coastal departments. The *Guardia de Hacienda* has similar equipment to that of the *Policía Nacional.*

Long-standing plans for the establishment of a national Police Academy remain unrealised but most officer personnel of the two forces have been trained abroad, either in the United States or in neighbouring Latin American countries.

In an only partially successful attempt to curtail rural insurgency, the Amerindian peasants of the country districts have been conscripted into a so-called "Civil Defence" Militia which is estimated to number approximately 300,000. Lacking adequate leadership, equipment, training and motivation, the existence of this force may be regarded rather as a political gesture than the establishment of an effective para-military organisation.

Sources of defence material supply and current requirements

Until recently Guatemala had no indigenous defence industry and all military equipment was imported. During the first 40 years of the 20th century, Germany was the main source of defence material although the Air Force was initially equipped with a mixture of French and British aircraft and from the mid-1930s until the early 1970s, all aircraft acquired were of US origins. During the latter stages of the Ubico regime, Guatemala turned increasingly towards the United States and considerable quantities of Lend-Lease material were acquired during the Second World War. Since the end of the Second World War the United States has been the principal source of supply, although the purchase of large quantities of principally Czech arms from the Soviet bloc by the Arbenz Guzman regime in 1954, provided the principal rationalisation for its overthrow by a CIA engineered invasion.

Following the refusal of the Carter administration in the United States to supply the type and quantity of material required, Guatemala turned increasingly to alternative sources of supply, mainly Israel. During this period, aircraft were also purchased in France, Switzerland and Italy, although the Italian government embargoed the delivery of aircraft in the early 1980s thereby cutting off a potential market. While the first vessel of the Guatemalan Navy was a second-hand Swedish minesweeper and three small patrol craft were ordered in Denmark in 1979, the United States has supplied the overwhelming majority of the vessels of the Navy and seems likely to continue to do so.

Despite the fact that the Israelis have made significant inroads into the Guatemalan military equipment market and seem assured of continuing opportunities, since the resumption of US military sales to Guatemala the latter country would seem to be destined to continue to supply a high proportion of Guatemala's needs in the field of defence equipment. For the forseeable future, these are likely to be largely confined to material with a definite counter-insurgency potential although the Army needs modern armoured vehicles as well as anti-armour and air defence material, the Navy needs additional patrol craft and the Air Force continues to show an interest in the acquisition of at least a token force of modern interceptors.

Since 1983 Guatemala has become the only Central American country to supply any of its own small arms needs, assembling the Israeli Galili rifle under licence at the Guatemalan Army's central arsenal. Small arms ammunition is also produced and the production of other equipment, including mortars, is planned.

Summary and prospects

Next to El Salvador, Guatemala has the most serious and longest standing problem of armed internal subversion in Central America. The social problems giving rise to this situation are more complex and hence more difficult to resolve even than those in the neighbouring republic. In addition to the almost universal Latin American problem of the concentration of most of the country's wealth in the hands of a very small minority, this minority, in the case of Guatemala, consists largely of foreign and principally US based multi-national corporations. The racial mix of the Guatemalan population adds a further dimension of complexity inasmuch as in the somewhat remote eventuality of an enlightened and benevolent government attempting to tackle the problems of wealth distribution and land reform, the Amerindian majority would apparently be unable to deal with the situation. The modest attempts at land reform, made by the Arévalo and Arbenz Guzmán regimes between 1945 and 1954, were an almost unmitigated disaster, the Indians rapidly destroying the redistributed land with primitive farming methods. The underlying problems giving rise to Guatemala's endemic internal instability thus appear to be almost insoluble.

For the forseeable future the Guatemalan armed forces seem destined to continue to face a problem of chronic low-level insurgency, which they can at best hope to contain but have no hope of eliminating. Fortunately, the country has no serious external military threat, either actual or potential. Sabres will continue to be rattled over the often reiterated territorial claim to Belize, the sole rationalisation of which appears to be the failure of Britain to build a highway linking Belize with Guatemala which was a key condition of the treaty of 1859. While successive Guatemalan governments will continue to make warlike noises regarding the annexation of the former British colony, not only does the internal security situation promise to continue to occupy most of the energies of the Guatemalan armed forces but the ignominious defeat of Argentina, a country of infinitely greater military potential than that to which Guatemala could ever hope to aspire, in the Falklands War of 1982, should continue to reinforce the deterrent value of the small British military presence in Belize.

The Guatemalan Army is traditionally the most powerful in Central America, although probably less efficient than that of El Salvador and certainly less politically motivated than that of Nicaragua, which now not only completely outclasses it in the abundance and quality of its equipment but also outnumbers it by a wide margin as does that of El Salvador. The Guatemalan Navy remains an insignificant force, but as such conforms to the Central American norm. The Guatemalan Air Force does not stand comparison with the air forces of either Honduras or El Salvador. All three arms appear adequate for their current counter-insurgency role but would offer little effective opposition to land, sea or air forces equipped with modern material and adequately trained in its use.

GUYANA

(Co-operative Republic of Guyana)

Area: 83,000 sq miles (214,970 sq km)
Population: 870,000
Total armed forces: 5500
Reserves: 3000
Available manpower: 70,000
Paramilitary forces: 5000
GNP: $461,900,000 (1985)
Defence expenditure: $44,874,000 (1985)

Introduction

Guyana, formerly British Guiana, is bounded on the north by the Atlantic ocean, on the west by Venezuela, on the south by Brazil and on the east by Suriname. The population comprises some 51% East Indians, 43% Negros and 1% Europeans, the remaining 5% being divided between Chinese, Amerindians and various racial mixes.

The major economic products are bauxite, alumina, diamonds, hardwoods and sugar and its by-products. The country is potentially self-sufficient in food production but due to political mismanagement of the economy currently imports most foodstuffs, in particular wheat and dairy products, in addition to petroleum and most manufactured goods, including clothing.

Guyana was not colonised to any extent until 1616 when the Dutch West India Company established some settlements in the region of the Essequibo river. These colonies were captured by the British in 1796 and alternated between Dutch and British rule for almost 20 years, being finally ceded to Britain in 1814. The colonies were united, as British Guiana, in 1831. Limited self-government was established in 1938 and full independence was due to be granted in 1957 when the constitution was suspended by Britain, following allegations of Communist subversion. Full internal self-government was finally granted in 1961 but in 1964 British troops were brought in again following a period of violent internal unrest. In 1966, Guyana became an independent state within the British Commonwealth and in 1970 was proclaimed a republic.

Executive power is vested in the President, the senior of the five vice-presidents having the title of prime minister. There is a single-chamber National Assembly.

The country is a co-operative republic, the world's first and as such is institutionally well to the left of the political spectrum. Both major political parties are Marxist-Leninist in orientation, the ruling People's National Congress

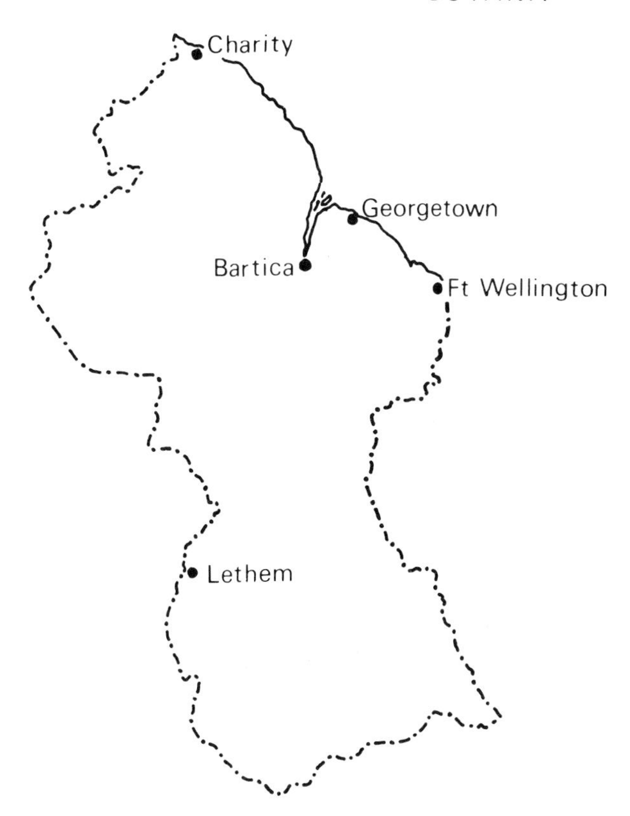

having its power base in the black population and the People's Progressive Party, which forms the main opposition, being supported by the East Indian element.

Internal politics thus break down on a racial rather than an ideological basis. The political history of the country has been stormy since the early 1950s.

There are serious frontier disputes with Suriname, which claims some 6000 sq miles of bauxite-rich territory and Venezuela, which claims fully 60% of the entire territory of the republic. There was a brief armed clash with Suriname in 1969, in which year there was also a revolt by the Amerindian minority. The dispute with Venezuela was temporarily defused by the Protocol of Trinidad of 1970, whereby both parties agreed to refrain from pressing their conflicting territorial claims for a period of 12 years. Although the period provided for under the protocol has passed, the dispute remains apparently in abeyance. Guerrilla incidents occurred in the remote area adjoining the Brazilian frontier in 1972.

Armed forces

Personnel:	5500 all ranks (incl 300 Marine and 200 Air Defence Force elements)
Ground force units:	1 Presidential Guard battalion 2 infantry battalions 1 special forces battalion 1 field artillery battalion 1 engineer company
AFVs:	EE-9 Cascaval armoured cars Shorland scout cars
Artillery:	Soviet M 1946 130 mm howitzers
Air defence:	Soviet SA-7 SAMs.
Naval units:	1 patrol vessel 5 motor torpedo boats 9 small patrol craft
Aircraft:	Britten-Norman BN.2A-6 and BN.2A-27 Islander and Defender, Cessna U206F, Beech Super King Air 200 and DHC-6 light transports, Bell 206B, 212 and 214 helicopters

The armed forces form a single unified service: the Guyana Defence Force, which has land, sea and air elements. The Guyana Defence Force is under the direct command of the President. Recruitment is on a voluntary and increasingly racialist basis with a preference for Negro recruits. Before independence, the Guyana Defence Force was trained by British personnel. It seems probable that some Cuban training assistance may have been received more recently. Officer personnel are largely British trained.

The land force element is by far the largest component of the Guyana Defence Force and consists of a Presidential Guard battalion, two infantry battalions, each comprising a headquarters, three rifle companies and a support company, a special forces battalion, a nominal artillery battalion and an engineer company. The few armoured vehicles are operated by the Presidential Guard, the artillery battalion operating both field and air defence artillery equipment.

The basic personal weapon is the German G3 rifle although quantities of British SLRs are also in use. It seems likely that some Soviet small arms, including AK-47 rifles have also been acquired. Machine guns in service include the British L7A2 and Bren, both in 7.62 mm calibre. Mortars include the British 81 mm, of which 12 are available and the Chinese T-55 120 mm, 20 examples of which are believed to be on inventory. Four British Shorland scout cars have recently been joined by a half dozen Brazilian EE-9 Cascaval armoured cars as the only AFVs known to be operated. A battery of six Soviet M 1946 130 mm howitzers is believed to have been acquired from Cuba. The only air-defence weapons known to be in service are a small number of Soviet SA-7 SAMs. Further quantities of AFVs and missiles are reputedly on order.

The largest unit of the maritime element of the Guyana Defence Force is the 100-ton patrol vessel *Peccari*. There are also five North Korean "Sin Hung" class motor-torpedo boats (apparently delivered without torpedo tubes) and nine very small coastal patrol craft. Two former shrimp boats, an LCU, a harbour tug and a fuel lighter perform subsidiary functions. The above vessels are manned by a total of approximately 300 all ranks, with bases at Georgetown and New Amsterdam.

The Guyana Defence Force Air Command operates six Britten-Norman Islanders and Defenders, two DHC-6 Twin Otters, a Beech Super King Air 200, a Cessna U206F and two examples of the Bell 206, three of the Bell 212 and two of the Bell 214, with no apparent squadron organisation. Personnel strength is about 300 and all aircraft are based at Timehri Airport, Georgetown.

There are also two paramilitary forces: the 3000-strong Guyana People's Militia and the 2000-man Guyana National Service, both effectively the military arms of the ruling People's National Congress and equipped only with small arms. There is an unarmed civil police force of 3140 members.

As a former British colony, the formative influences on the Guyana Defence Force were naturally British. The political orientation of all governments since independence has led to closer links with Cuba. The Soviet arms recently acquired appear to emanate from Cuban sources and Guyana is also now believed to be the recipient of Cuban training assistance. This influence may be expected to increase.

No major training facilities appear to have been established.

Sources of defence material supply and current requirements

In the early post-independence period, equipment procurement, particularly for the ground element of the Guyana Defence Force, was primarily from British sources. More recently, suppliers, including China, North Korea, Germany and Brazil, have benefitted from the Guyanese custom. The current trend appears to be primarily towards the Soviet Union, via Cuba, as the main but not exclusive supplier of ground defence material.

There has been considerable expansion of the Army element of the Guyana Defence Force in recent years. This has not been matched by any comparable expansion of the military capabilities of the naval or air elements, the latter having actually contracted. The latter two forces may be expected to acquire additional material of more advanced military potential in the medium term although the prevailing economic circumstances continue to militate against any immediate major acquisitions of defence equipment. The Marine Section of the Defence Force may possibly acquire small quantities of larger patrol vessels and perhaps additional quantities of more modern fast attack craft. The Air Command also seems likely to expand its helicopter element and possibly to acquire some tactical support aircraft as soon as economic circumstances permit.

Summary and prospects

The government of Forbes Burnham, which ruled Guyana from 1964 until his death in 1985, developed an increasingly Marxist orientation which was matched by the increasing political predominance of the Negro element of the population. Burnham's Co-operative Socialism, a weird mixture of Marxism, liberal democracy, racism and militarism, wrecked the Guyanese economy, transforming the country from a major food exporter to a nett importer of foodstuffs, increased racial frictions and discouraged foreign investment. Although the economic crisis has forced some degree of both political and commercial liberalisation on Burnham's successors, an economic situation which continues to worsen and racial and demographic pressures have a potential for internal disruption. Externally there is a potential threat from Venezuela, but despite its strong support for the Argentine invasion of the Falkland islands, the possibility of military action to support Venezuelan claims to more than half of the country's total area seems unlikely.

HAITI

(République d'Haití)

Area: 10,712 sq miles (27,713 sq km)
Population: 5,543,000 (estimated 1986)
Total armed forces: 7000
Reserves: 3000
Available manpower: 450,000
GNP: $2,130 million (1985)
Defence expenditure: $30 million (1984)

Introduction

The Republic of Haiti occupies the western third of the island of Hispaniola and is thus bounded on the north by the Atlantic Ocean, on the west by the Windward Passage, which separates it from Cuba, on the south by the Caribbean and on the east by the Dominican Republic. The population is overwhelmingly black, 95% being pure Negro and the remainder Mulattos. There are no significant racial minorities. The population is concentrated in the fertile 30% of the country, the mountainous remainder being virtually uninhabited. Haiti is the only independent French-speaking state in the Western Hemisphere.

The major exports are coffee, sugar, sizal and bauxite. Due to extremely low labour costs, there has been a degree of industrialisation in recent years and light industrial products and sporting goods are now also important exports. Although the overwhelming majority of the work force is engaged in agriculture, Haiti does not produce sufficient food for domestic consumption and food figures highly among imports, together with machinery, manufactured products and fuels.

Hispaniola was discovered by Columbus in 1492 and the first European settlements in the Americas were established there. In 1697 the region corresponding to modern Haiti was ceded to France by Spain. In 1791, the slaves rose in revolt, massacring the whites. A French army, unsuccessfully attempting to reconquer the country, was defeated two years later and eventually the French revolutionary government declared the emancipation of the slaves. In 1798, a combined French and Haitian army overran the Spanish-speaking eastern part of the island. Although a civil war broke out two years later a second French attempt to reconquer the island was successfully resisted and independence was declared in 1804.

The country rapidly lapsed into a semi-tribal state as blacks and mulattos struggled for dominance. The internal political situation remained extremely turbulent, drifting towards total anarchy in 1905 when the United States took control of the customs service after Haiti had defaulted on payment of its foreign debts. The situation continued to deteriorate until 1915 when the United States took complete control of the country. Haiti remained under US rule until 1934. Two mulatto Presidents held office between 1934 and 1946 when the Negro Dumarsais Estimé assumed power with the assistance of the Army. Estimé was in turn overthrown in 1950 and replaced by Colonel Paul Magloire who in his turn was overthrown by the Army in 1956 and after some months of chaos Dr François Duvalier was elected President.

Duvalier created a militia and an irregular police force – the *Tonton Macoutes* – as a counterbalance to the armed forces and maintained a mesmeric power over the people of Haiti by a combination of conventional police-state terror tactics and voodoo, declaring himself President for life in 1964 and successfully resisting five invasions by Haitian dissidents and some low-level insurgency in the latter years of his 15-year reign of terror. Duvalier died in 1971 and was succeeded, also as President for life, by his son Jean-Claude, who continued to rule as absolute despot until he was forced to flee the country in 1986. The Duvalier regime was replaced by a mixed military-civilian junta which continues to rule the country.

Structure of the armed forces

The armed forces, which combine the functions of national defence with those of internal security, form a single unified defence force with distinct land, sea and air elements although each is described respectively as the Army, Navy and Air Force, the Army containing a large identifiable police element.

The President is commander-in-chief of the armed forces and exercises personal control of the Presidential Guard and the Déssalines Battalion, the only two units with any real military capability. The Secretary of State for the Interior and National Defence is next in the chain of command and the Chief of the General Staff is the senior military officer and Commander of the armed forces.

The country is divided into six regional Military Departments: North, North-West, Artibonite, West, Centre and the South. There are three additional military departments at the capital, Port-au-Prince. These are: the Presidential Guard, the Déssalines Battalion and the Port-au-Prince Police.

Recruitment is entirely voluntary and is generally a life-long career, officers retiring at the age of 60 and enlisted men at 50.

Officers are trained at the Military Academy at Fréres, which offers a three-year course and usually has a student body of approximately 60. There is also an NCO School, the *Camp d'Application*.

HAITI

Military Departments

Army

Manpower: 6400

Major units: Presidential Guard
1 tactical battalion
1 special forces group

AFVs: M3A1 and M5A1 light tanks
V-150 armoured cars
M2 half-track APCs

Artillery: US M116 75 mm howitzers
US M2A1 105 mm howitzers

Air defence weapons: Israeli RAMTA TCM-20 20 mm
US M1 40 mm/L60

At the time of the US occupation the Haitian Army remained the partizan force which it had been since the end of the Wars of Independence. The Army and Navy were immediately disbanded by the occupying forces. Primarily to deal with the resistance of nationalist guerrillas, the United States occupation forces established a paramilitary police force, the *Gendarmerie d'Haití* in 1916. This force, with considerable assistance from the US occupation forces, had successfully contained guerrilla resistance by 1920 and the succeeding 14 years, until the departure of the US Marines in 1934, were among the most tranquil in Haitian history. A US Marine training mission was active from 1939 to 1945, establishing a Military Academy in 1941, by which time the force was known as the *Garde d'Haití*. Some material assistance was also forthcoming from the United States during the war years. In 1963 the title of the force was again changed to *Armée Haitien*. In 1971 a new 569-man special forces unit, known as the "Leopards", was also established and trained by a US-based private security company.

The Haitian Army currently numbers approximately 6400 all ranks. Of the three Military Departments based at Port au Prince, the Presidential Guard consists of four companies, the Déssalines battalion and headquarters troops total seven companies and the Port-au-Prince Police has six companies. The six other Military Departments, which in some respects approximate to battalions as a level of command, contain a total of 21 companies, operating principally as district police. The three companies of the Leopards are directly responsible to the Chief-of-Staff and both the Port-au-Prince Fire Brigade and the Prison Guard Company also form part of the armed forces.

The M1 Garand rifle remains the principal small arm although small quantities of both the German G3 and the US M16 rifle have been acquired to equip the elite units and the Israeli Uzi sub-machine gun has largely superseded the Thompson as the principal light automatic. Infantry support arms, confined in effect to the Presidential Guard, the Dessalines Battalion and the Leopards, consist of Browning M1919 and M2HB machine guns in 0.30 and 0.50 calibres respectively, M18 57 mm and M40 106 mm RCLs and M2 60 mm and M1 81 mm mortars. A few M3A1 and M5A1 Stuart light tanks, from a total of six and three units respectively originally acquired, remain in serviceable condition, the effective armoured force consisting of six V-150 armoured cars and a similar number of M2 half-track APCs. Artillery consists of four US M116 75 mm howitzers and s x M2A1 105 mm pieces and there are about half-a-dozen examples apiece of the Israeli RAMTA twin mounted TCM-20 20 mm and the US M1 single 40 mm AA guns. Ten examples apiece of the totally obsolete US M3 37 mm and M1 57 mm towed anti-tank guns also remain on inventory. There are no separate armoured or artillery units, the few AFVs and artillery pieces being operated by either the Presidential Guard or the Dessalines Battalion.

The Haitian Army remains basically an internal security force with very limited military potential.

Navy

Manpower: 325

Major units: 1 patrol vessel
9 small patrol craft
1 Presidential yacht

A Haitian Navy was formed in 1860 and by 1911 the Navy, which was largely manned by foreign mercenaries, was theoretically the most powerful naval force in the Caribbean. Haiti's period as a major local naval power was however strictly limited and with the US military occupation in 1915, the Navy ceased to exist. A coastguard section of the *Garde d'Haiti* was formed in the late 1930s with the title *Garde Cotiére Haitienne*. Some small vessels were transferred by the United States during the 1940s and a US naval mission arrived in Haiti in 1948. In April 1963, following the suppression of an unsuccessful mutiny, the Coast Guard was renamed *La Marine Haitienne* (Haitian Navy).

The Haitian Navy currently consists of only the armed tug *Henri Christophe*, nine small patrol craft built in the United States between 1976 and 1981 and the old Presidential yacht *Sans Souci*. This small force is manned by 45 officers and 280 other ranks and based at Port-au-Prince.

Air Force

Manpower: 300

Units: 1 light strike squadron
1 transport squadron
1 helicopter squadron

Light strike aircraft: Cessna 337

Transports: Beechcraft Baron
Cessna 401 and 402
Curtiss C-46 Commando
Douglas C-47
DHC-2 and DHC-6

Helicopters: Sikorsky S-58
Hughes 269C and 369C

Trainers: SIAI S-211 and
SIAI-Marchetti SF.260TP
Beechcraft Bonanza
Cessna 150, 172 and 310

An aviation section of the *Garde d'Haiti*, known as the *Corps d'Aviation d'Haiti*, was established with the help of a US Marine Corps aviation mission in 1943. During the years immediately following the Second World War small quantities of second-line types were acquired and in 1950 a US Air Force mission arrived in Haiti and the first combat unit was formed shortly afterwards with six North American F-51D Mustangs.

Recent acquisitions have been confined to second-line types and the *Corps d'Aviation* currently consists of a combat unit with seven Cessna 337s, a transport unit with three C-47s, one C-46, two DHC-2s, one DHC-6 and single examples of the Beechcraft Baron, the Cessna 401 and 402, and a helicopter unit with four S.58s and two examples apiece of the Hughes 269Cs and 369C. Training is carried out on four SIAI S-211s and four SIAI-Marchetti SF-260TPs, three Cessna 152s, a 172 and a Beech Bonanza. All aircraft, a high proportion of which are unserviceable, are based at Bowen Field, Port-au-Prince and personnel strength is approximately 300 all ranks.

Sources of defence material supply and current requirements

Until recently almost all equipment was of United States origins, even when not obtained directly from the US and was largely obsolete. The first major exception to this rule was a quantity of Uzi sub-machine guns purchased from Israel in the mid-1970s, following which some German G3 rifles were obtained, followed in turn by some Italian training aircraft and Israeli anti-aircraft guns. Much equipment is unusable due to poor maintenance and the lack of spare parts. Haiti's poor economic position makes the acquisition of any significant quantities of material highly unlikely within the forseeable future.

Summary and prospects

The end of the Duvalier regime came suddenly and unexpectedly. There had been a limited degree of liberalisation under the younger Duvalier, leading to a considerable diminution in the power of the *Tonton Macoutes* which had been the major apparatus of institutionalised state terror maintained by Duvalier senior. Nevertheless, the regime had made no tangible effort to curb human rights abuses which continued at a level which could not be ignored. Refusal by the United States Congress to sanction the economic aid upon which the country had become increasingly dependent led to an outbreak of rioting from the end of 1985 onwards and the US government finally withdrew all support from the regime, providing an aircraft for the departure of the dictator and his immediate entourage. Following the flight of Jean-Claude

Duvalier from the country in February 1986, the *Tonton Macoutes* were disbanded although the new civilian-military junta did not appear to be markedly more liberal than the bizarre hereditary dictatorship which it replaced. Haiti seems blessedly free from immediate external threat although demographic pressures in a country which already has an effective population density of 2000 per square mile and which is being rapidly turned into a desert by primitive farming methods may eventually provoke some major internal cataclysm even among a population which is at once the poorest, least-educated, most disease-ridden and most chronically under-nourished in Latin America.

HONDURAS

(República de Honduras)

Area: 43,300 sq miles (112,150 sq km)
Population: 4,507,000 (1986)
Total armed forces: 19,200
Reserves: 50,000
Available manpower: 350,000
Paramilitary forces: 5000
GNP: $3,360 million (1985)
Defence expenditure: $90 million (1984)

Introduction

Honduras, the second largest country in Central America, is bordered on the west by Guatemala, on the north by the Caribbean Sea, on the east and south-east by Nicaragua and on the south-west by El Salvador. Approximately 90% of the population is of mixed European and Amerindian racial origins, pure aboriginal Indians account for 7% of the population with a Negro minority of 2% concentrated largely on the Caribbean coast. Less than 1% of the population is of pure European origins. The population is concentrated in the mountain valleys, to the west of the country, parts of the remainder being virtually uninhabited.

The economy is based on agriculture, the major exports being bananas, coffee and meat. Lumbering is also of economic importance. Imports consist largely of manufactured products, machinery, fuel and chemicals. The country is largely self-sufficient in food production. Mineral resources, which are not fully exploited, include gold, silver, lead, tin and mercury.

From independence in 1824 until 1838 Honduras formed part of the United Provinces of Central America. Honduras combined in a new federation with El Salvador and Nicaragua in 1842 but this disintegrated in 1845 when war broke out between Nicaragua and an alliance of Honduras and El Salvador. In 1895 another attempt at federation between Honduras, El Salvador and Nicaragua collapsed almost immediately and both Honduras and El Salvador were involved in a brief war with Nicaragua again in 1907, hostilities ending after the intervention of Mexico and the United States. From just before the turn of the century, the economy had passed largely into the hands of United States commercial interests, principally the United Fruit Company of Boston, which had an important influence on subsequent Honduran domestic politics. The *caudillo* period lasted longer in Honduras than in almost any other country of Latin America, the country enjoying its longest period of internal stability under the dictatorship of General Tiburcio Carías between 1933 and 1949. In 1969 Honduras was involved in a short but disastrous war with El Salvador and relations between the two countries remained strained for many years afterwards, mediation attempts, under the patronage of the President of Peru, finally bearing fruit and after prolonged negotiations a peace treaty was signed in November 1980. The current internal problems in El Salvador render a further outbreak of hostilities in the forseeable future highly unlikely.

Honduras is a unitary republic of 18 departments. Executive power is in the hands of the President, who chooses his own cabinet but is restricted to an unusual degree by the requirement to refer specific matters to the single chamber legislature.

Honduras occupies a pivotal position in one of the most unstable regions in the world and to date, is relatively unaffected by the chronic armed subversion which has plagued Guatemala since the early 1960s. However, it has become peripherally involved in the current civil war in El Salvador when Salvadorean guerrillas have strayed into its territory and has also carried out joint security operations with the Salvadorean armed forces in the frontier region. It has also permitted the United States to train the military personnel of its recent enemy in its territory.

With the signature of the Panama Canal Treaty between Panama and the United States whereby the former country will assume full responsibility for both the administration and defence of the Canal in 1999 Honduras also seems set to take over from Panama as the major focus of United States military power in Central America.

The US military mission in Honduras, which had less than 30 members up to 1980, has more than trebled in strength and in addition to the military mission itself there are now approximately 1700 US military personnel more or less permanently based in the country. On an average, an additional 4000 are also present on a transient basis at any one time in connection with the succession of "training exercises" in which US and Honduran forces have been engaged almost continuously since February 1983. United States military assistance to Honduras increased from $3.98 million in 1980 to $87 million in 1986/87 and during 1983 three times as many Honduran military officers as from any other Latin American country were trained in the US Army "School of the Americas" in the Panama Canal Zone. Honduras was being regarded as a likely site for the relocation of this establishment when it closed down at the end of 1984 under the terms of the treaty between the United States and Panama. Despite the decision to relocate the school in the continental United States, US military involvement in Honduras has continued on a massive level.

Approximately 180 US "Green Berets" run the special forces training establishment at Puerto Castilla where 1500 Salvadorean troops were also trained during 1983, this number more than doubling in subsequent years. US military engineer construction teams have also to date completed six new airfields at El Aguacate, Cucuyagua, La Lima, Palmarola, Puerto Lempira, and San Lorenzo, improved existing Honduran Air Force air base facilities at La Ceiba and Trujillo and are completing a major air base at Jamastram. A major army base has also been built at Puerto Castilla while base facilities for the US Navy at La Ceiba, Puerto Castilla and Puerto Lempira and US-manned radar stations at Tegucigalpa, the Honduran capital and at El Zope on Honduras's short Pacific coast have also been constructed.

Inevitably, due both to its geographic position and its traditional subservience to United States interests, Honduras has in the past been used as a jumping-off point for such adventures as the CIA inspired invasion of Guatemala in 1954 and the abortive invasion of the Bay of Pigs in Cuba in 1961. Currently, it also forms the major base for the US-supported right-wing guerrillas actively engaged in the destabilisation of Nicaragua.

Structure of the armed forces

The President of the republic is commander-in-chief of the armed forces and may declare war, make peace, send Honduran troops outside the country or invite foreign troops into it without reference to Congress. The President may also appoint officers up to and including the rank of captain without reference to Congress but must obtain congressional approval for the appointment of officers of higher rank. The Honduran constitution contains a peculiar provision which exorts its citizens, as a matter of national duty, to rebel against a President who is held to have acted in violation of the constitution and this greatly circumscribes the apparently far ranging powers enjoyed by the President. The Secretary of Defence is a member of the cabinet but is concerned only with the administrative control of the armed forces, this office generally being held by a relatively junior army officer. The chief of the armed forces is the most powerful figure in the chain of command and has almost absolute control over the armed forces, on an operational level. An important collegiate body is the Superior Council of National Defence, comprising the President of the republic, the chief of the armed forces, the chief of staff of the armed forces, the Secretary of Defence and all senior officers of the Army, Navy and Air Force. There is a combined Armed Forces General Staff.

The country is divided into six Military Zones, three of which adjoin the frontier with El Salvador.

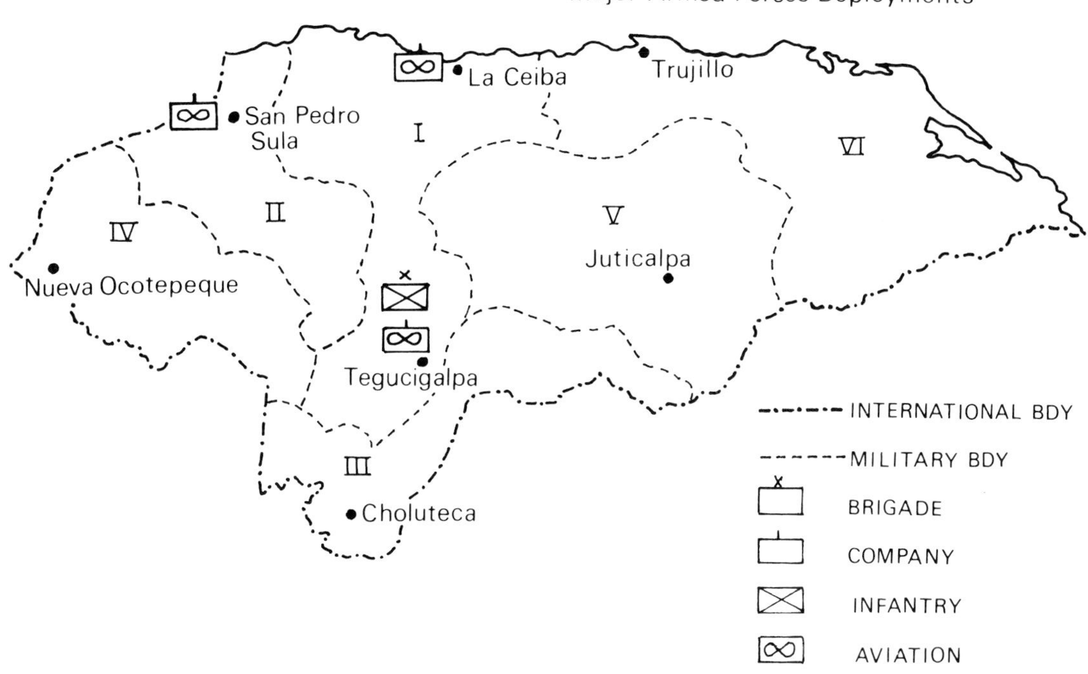

Legislation provides for an 18 month period of compulsory military service between the ages of 18 and 32 and for continuing service in the reserves until the age of 55. In practice, most of the ranks of the armed forces are filled by volunteers. With the dramatic increase in strength since the 1969 war with El Salvador and particularly in the context of the major military build-up since the early 1980s, an increasing number of conscripts serve for eight months of military training.

The National Military Academy, the *Escuela Militar Francisco Morazán* at Tegucigalpa, provides a comprehensive five-year course for aspiring officers of the three armed forces, almost all of whom undergo some continuation training abroad.

Army

Manpower: 17,000

Tactical formations: 3 infantry brigades
1 Presidential Guard brigade

Major units: 2 Presidential Guard battalions
9 infantry battalions
1 special forces battalion
1 armoured regiment
4 artillery battalions
1 engineer battalion

AFVs: Scorpion and Scimitar light tanks
Saladin and Staghound armoured cars
RBY-1 and M3A1 scout cars

Artillery: M116 75 mm, M101 105 mm and M198 155 mm howitzers

Honduras was unusually slow to develop its Army as an organised, professional force and until the 1920s there was little identifiable as a Honduran National Army. The Second World War brought limited military assistance from the United States and with the signature of the Rio Treaty of Mutual Defence of 1947, Honduras became eligible to receive increased US military aid. The brief war with El Salvador of 1969 however found Honduras ill-prepared and showed

***Honduran Presidential guard at Tegucigalpa* (M. English)**

up many defects in the organisation, training and equipment of its Army. The military government immediately set out to remedy these as quickly as possible in the conditions of tension between the two countries which were to endure for the next 11 years.

Little is published about the deployment of the units of the Honduran Army which currently numbers approximately 17,000 all ranks and is organised in three infantry brigades, of which the 1st (HQ San Lorenzo) comprises the 7th, 9th and 11th Infantry and the 1st Artillery Battalions and is deployed in the vicinity of the frontier with El Salvador, the 2nd, located in the region adjoining the Nicaraguan frontier, comprises the 2nd, 3rd and 8th Infantry and the 3rd Artillery Battalions and the 3rd, which is believed to be located in the southern part of the country, comprises the 4th, 6th and 10th Infantry and the 2nd Artillery Battalions. At Army level there is the Presidential Guard, with its headquarters at Las Tapias, near Tegucigalpa and comprising the 1st and 5th Infantry Battalions and a military police unit; the 1st Armoured Regiment, the 4th Artillery Battalion, the 1st Engineer Battalion and the 1st Signals Battalion. No separate air defence units have been identified and it is possible that these are incorporated into the artillery battalions. The existing special forces unit has been expanded to a battalion and is now known as the *TESONES*, an acronym for *Tropas Especiales para Operaciones Nocturnas y en la Selva*. Sub-units of the elements found at army level are deployed in support of the three brigades in accordance with operational requirements. Of these, the tank squadron of the 1st Armoured Regiment is believed to be on semi-permanent attachment to the 2nd Brigade.

The Honduran infantry is currently armed with either the FN FAL or the US M14 rifle in 7.62 mm calibre, or the US M16 Armalite in 5.56 mm. Second-line units still use the M1 Garand rifle and the German HK MP5 supplements the Israeli Uzi as the standard sub-machine gun. A variety of automatic weapons are in service including FN MAGs and US M60s in 7.62 mm calibre and Browning M1919s and M2HBs in 0.30-inch and 0.50-inch calibres respectively. The Browning Automatic Rifle and the Madsen Model 1937 remain on inventory and the M16A1HB is also used as a squad weapon. Mortars in use include French Hotchkiss-Brandt models, in both 60 mm and 81 mm and 30 Soltam 120 mm mortars are also reported to be in service. The main anti-armour weapons are the US M18 57 mm and M40A1 106 mm RCLs, now supplemented by the 84 mm Swedish Carl Gustav. AFVs in service include 16 Alvis Scorpion and Scimitar light tanks, 72 Alvis Saladins and the survivors of 15 T17 Staghound armoured cars. A total of 14 Israeli RBY-1 and a similar number of M3A1 White scout cars complete the armoured force, while the small number of M24 light tanks formerly operated appear to have been retired from service. The artillery is equipped with 12 US M116 75 mm, 44 M101 105 mm and 12 M198 155 mm howitzers. Nothing is known concerning any air defence weapons which may be in use although it seems remotely possible that six Breda and Madsen 20 mm pieces, in service during the late 1930s, may remain on inventory, if not actually on issue to units.

Almost all officers commissioned since 1957 are graduates of the *Escuela Militar General Francisco Morazán* at Tegucigalpa, which offers a five-year course, leading to a commission in the rank of second lieutenant. Most officers have also pursued some additional training abroad, either in the United States, the Panama Canal Zone or in other Latin American countries. More recently, some officers have also undergone training in the German Federal Republic. The *Escuela Básica de Armas* provides specialist training for both officers and non-commissioned personnel of the combat arms.

The Honduran Army now appears to be a smart and well trained force and has made quite spectacular progress since the 1969 war with El Salvador, representing one of the most efficient armed forces in Central America.

Navy

Manpower:	700 all ranks
Major units:	3 patrol vessels 7 coastal patrol craft 8 river patrol craft

An attempt to form a naval force was made 30 years before the Army was established on a firm organisational basis but by the early 1920s it ceased to exist. The dictator Tiburcio Carías created a small coastguard force during the Second World War which remained of extremely modest dimensions, although it changed its title to Honduran Navy in 1977. All vessels of the Honduran Navy were stationed on the Caribbean coast, with a base at Puerto Cortés. As part of the increased US military aid to Honduras a group of naval instructors arrived from the United States in August 1981 and two new base facilities were established at Puerto Castilla and Caratasca, a naval presence also being established on the Pacific coast.

The Honduran Navy currently consists of the three 100-ton patrol vessels *Guaymuras*, *Honduras* and *Hibures*, seven smaller coastal patrol craft of 30 to 50 tons, eight small river patrol craft, a surveying launch, the 989-ton buoy tender *Hogal* and six armed fishing boats used for subsidiary duties. Personnel total 700, including 450 conscripts in training.

Officer personnel are trained at the *Escuela Militar* at Tegucigalpa. Other ranks receive their preliminary shore training at the *Escuela Básica de Armas*.

Air Force

Manpower:	1500
Major units:	1 fighter squadron 1 fighter-bomber squadron 1 light strike squadron 1 transport squadron 1 communications squadron 1 helicopter squadron
Fighters:	Super Mystére B.2
Fighter-bombers:	North American F-86E and K
Light strike aircraft:	Cessna A-37B
Reconnaissance aircraft:	Lockheed RT-33A
Transport:	Lockheed C-130 Lockheed Electra Douglas DC-6, C-54 and C-47 IAI Arava and Westwind
Communications:	Cessna 180 and 185 Beechcraft Baron Piper Cheyenne
Helicopters:	Sikorsky S-76 Bell UH-1B and H Hughes 500
Trainers:	Fouga Magister CASA C-101 EMBRAER EMB-312 Tucano Cessna T-41 North American T-6

The Honduran Air Force is unusual in that its formation predates that of the Honduran Army as an organised force. A military flying school was established in 1921, expanding to become the Military Aviation Service in 1934. In 1954, the *Aviacion Militar* became independent of the Army as the *Fuerza Aérea Hondureña*. At the beginning of the Honduras–El Salvador war, Honduras had Central America's best air force and gained complete control of the air at an early stage, although its ground forces had to retreat in the face

Cessna A-37B light-strike aircraft of the Honduran Air Force's fighter-bomber squadron **(Cessna Aircraft Corpn.)**

of the superior Salvadorean Army. A considerable build-up, including the replacement of obsolete piston-engined operational material with jet aircraft, took place during the 1970s. Since the early 1980s the Honduran Air Force has also received considerable material and training assistance from the United States which has however declined to supply modern first-line combat equipment.

The Honduran Air Force currently consists of approximately 1700 military personnel and 400 civilian employees, manning about 130 aircraft and organised into a fighter squadron, a fighter-bomber squadron, a light strike squadron, a transport squadron, a communications squadron and a helicopter squadron.

The fighter squadron is based at *Base Aérea Coronel Héctor Caracciollo* at Moncada, La Ceiba and is equipped with 12 ex-Israeli Dassault Super Mystéres. The fighter-bomber squadron, which is equipped with ten F-86E, F and K Sabres and the light strike squadron, with 15 Cessna A-37Bs, are both based at *Base Aérea Coronel Armando Escalón Espinal* at San Pedro Sula, together with the transport squadron, which is equipped with a single Lockheed C-130, a Douglas DC-6, a C-54 and eight C-47s, plus two IAI Aravas, two Westwinds and a Lockheed Electra. The communications squadron, which is equipped with two Cessna 180s, two 185s, a Beechcraft Baron and a Piper Cheyenne and the helicopter squadron which has a single Sikorsky S-76, 22 Bell UH-1Bs and Hs and eight Hughes 500s, are both based at *Base Aérea Teniente Coronel Hermán Acosta Mejía* at Toncontin, Tegucigalpa, where the *Escuela de Aviación Militar* with three Lockheed RT-33As, four Fouga Magisters, four CASA C-101s, 12 EMBRAER EMB-312 Tucanos, six North American T-6s and eight Cessna T-41s is also located.

Officers receive their initial training at the Escuela Militar at Tegucigalpa and their subsequent specialised training at the *Escuela de Aviación Militar* at Toncontin. The Air Force provides ab initio training for its non-commissioned personnel. As in the case of the Army, most officer and certain selected non-commissioned personnel also receive continuation training abroad.

Current plans envisage the replacement of the remaining F-86 Sabres in the fighter-bomber role by about a dozen more modern aircraft, the preferred types being the Northrop F-5 or the IAI Kfir, the weight having apparently come down in favour of the former type with the announcement in May 1987 that four examples of the F-5 would be delivered to Honduras by the end of the year.

Paramilitary forces

Manpower: 5000

In 1959, President Villeda Morales raised a paramilitary national police force, the *Guardia Civil*, as a counter-balance to the political power of the armed forces. In 1965 this force was abolished and replaced by the *Cuerpo Especial de Seguridad*, an almost identical force except that it was commanded by army officers and under direct military control. This force, which now numbers some 5000 all ranks, is the main nationwide law-enforcement agency and also serves as a back-up force to the Army in times of national emergency. Its members are normally armed with sidearms and truncheons but have available a full range of light infantry weapons, mainly of obsolescent type passed on from the Army.

***Honduran National Police at Tegucigalpa* (Author)**

Sources of defence material supply and current requirements

In the past Honduras has shopped widely for defence material, purchasing equipment from Germany, Denmark, Italy, France, Britain and the United States. From the mid-1930s until the 1969 war with El Salvador equipment of US origins came to predominate. During the following decade war material was purchased from France and Yugoslavia, in addition to the United States, and Israel also became an important supplier of the Honduran armed forces. Since the election of Ronald Reagan as President of the United States, the US has once more come to the fore although Israel continues to supply much of Honduran equipment needs and Spain and Brazil have both benefitted from Honduran orders for aircraft.

Although now reasonably well equipped as regards infantry weapons and artillery and having almost trebled its armoured force with recent acquisitions of wheeled equipment, the Honduran Army still lacks sufficient tracked armour and is notably deficient as regards APCs. A further notable defect in the current equipment of the Honduran Army is the apparent lack of adequate anti-armour and particularly air-defence weapons and the total absence of any missile capability.

The small Navy apparently does not aspire to anything more than a paramilitary coast guard role and the fact that its potential adversaries are principally organised and equipped on a similarly limited level makes it unlikely that this force will attempt any dramatic expansion in the forseeable future.

The Air Force has been the premier national air arm in Central America since the late 1940s. Although largely equipped with obsolescent material it remains as well equipped as any of its immediately potential adversaries, with the exception of the Mi-24 helicopters operated by Nicaragua which are unmatched by any comparable equipment in any other Latin American air arm apart from that of Cuba.

Future acquisitions of defence material by Honduras will probably be largely conditioned by developments in Nicaragua and the United States may be expected to provide most of the additional equipment required to match any spectacular acquisitions by the Nicaraguan revolutionary government.

Summary and prospects

Although Honduras is the second poorest country in the Western Hemisphere (after Haiti) and its exaggerated social and economic problems might be expected to have produced violent social tensions, the country's internal situation has been relatively stable in recent years and it has avoided the chronic guerrilla problems which threaten the stability of Guatemala and have caused both a violent civil war in El Salvador and a successful left-wing revolution in Nicaragua. This may be due in some part to the relative ethnic cohesion of its population compared with that of Guatemala and social equilibrium in relationship to that of El Salvador. The various authoritarian regimes since the fall of Carías have also avoided both the extreme blood-thirstiness and blatant and pervasive corruption of that of the Somozas in Nicaragua.

During the 1970s, the military government took a definite step towards the political left, initiating a limited degree of land reform, permitting the formation of trade unions and expropriating major foreign business interests such as the banana monopoly hitherto enjoyed by United States-based multi-national corporations. The success of the Sandinista revolution in Nicaragua and its rapid progress towards the extreme political left however occasioned a reverse in the orientation of the contemporary Honduran government and its successors.

The continuing tension with El Salvador and the threat of a further outbreak of hostilities with that country, which was the major preoccupation of Honduran foreign policy from 1969 to 1980, was removed by the treaty of 1980 and the current civil war in El Salvador makes any further threat from that quarter relatively unthinkable for the forseeable future. The Honduran armed forces have even co-operated with those of El Salvador in preventing the flight of Salvadorean refugees into Honduran territory and large numbers of Salvadorean troops have been trained by the United States within Honduras. The real or imagined threat of left-wing subversion, based in Nicaragua, has taken over as the major preoccupation of the Honduran government, which as a direct consequences has allowed the United States to use its territory, more or less openly, as a base for military attacks on Nicaragua by CIA-sponsored right-wing guerrillas.

The virtual military occupation of Honduras by the United States, despite being matched by relatively bountiful economic and military aid, has caused some resentment. In particular the training of troops of its traditional enemy, El Salvador, on Honduran territory has occasioned a mild nationalistic backlash in the Honduran armed forces as has the increasingly unwanted presence of the anti-Sandinista Nicaraguan Contra guerrillas. Ironically, the effective conversion of Honduras into a US protectorate has led to a considerable increase in the hitherto negligible left-wing guerrilla activity within the country, which while it has been relatively easily containable to date, has an inherent potential for destabilisation.

JAMAICA

Area: 4231 sq miles (11,422 sq km)
Population: 2,350,000 (1986)
Total armed forces: 2150
Available manpower: 200,000
Paramilitary forces: 4900
GNP: $2,132 million (1984)
Defence expenditure: $25,557,000 (1984)

Introduction

Lying some 90 miles to the south of Cuba and a similar distance to the west of Haiti, Jamaica is the third largest of the Greater Antilles. Over 75% of the population is of African origins, with substantial Chinese, Indian and European minorities.

The island contains important deposits of bauxite, the export of which, together with such tropical produce as sugar and its by-products, including rum, coffee, cocoa and fruit forms the basis of an economy also heavily dependent on tourism. Although the island is highly fertile, overpopulation necessitates the importation of large quantities of food. Almost all manufactured products must also be imported.

The island was colonised by Spain from 1505 onwards, the aboriginal population being rapidly exterminated and replaced by Negro slaves. Jamaica was occupied by Britain in 1658, the Spanish inhabitants being driven out. The island remained a British possession until 1962, slavery being abolished in 1833 and self-government introduced in 1944. From 1959 to 1962, Jamaica formed part of the short-lived Caribbean Feder-

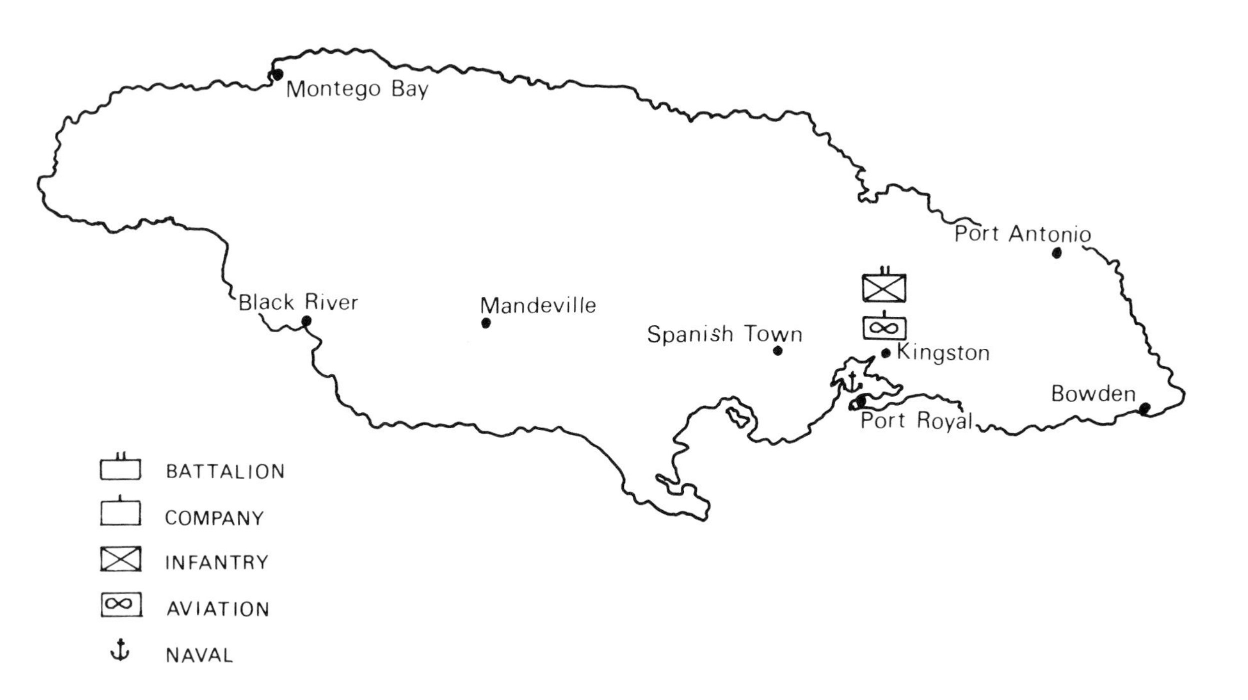

ation. Since 1962, Jamaica has been an independent state within the British Commonwealth.

The Crown, as head of state, is represented by a Governor General who is assisted by a Privy Council of six members. The government is a parliamentary democracy with a bicameral legislature. Executive power is vested in the cabinet, led by the Prime Minister, as head of government.

Ostensibly non-aligned in international affairs, Jamaica moved towards the extreme political left and closer links with Cuba during the 1970s, but this tendency was reversed after the Jamaica Labour Party replaced the People's National Party in the 1980 elections. Currently, Jamaica is the most solid ally of the United States among the former British colonies of the Caribbean. Internal demographic pressures, arising from overpopulation, large racial minorities and unequal distribution of wealth, exacerbated by the conspicuous consumerism of wealthy tourists however have a continuing potential for internal instability.

Armed forces

Manpower:	2150 all ranks (1780 land, 170 sea and 200 air)
Major ground force units:	2 infantry battalions 1 support battalion
AFVs:	Ferret scout cars V-150 APCs
Major naval units:	2 large and 4 small patrol craft
Fixed-wing aircraft:	Britten-Norman Islander Beech King Air 100 Cessna 337G
Helicopters:	Bell 206, 212 and 222

The armed forces are known as the Jamaica Defence Force and comprise both land, sea and air elements. The Prime Minister is also Minister of Defence and commands the Jamaica Defence Force through a major general. Recruitment is entirely voluntary.

The Jamaica Regiment, the predominant element in the Jamaica Defence Force, traces its origins to the West India Regiment, founded in 1798. The West India Regiment formed the nucleus of the defence forces of the short-lived Caribbean Federation, the 1st and 3rd Battalions being allocated to Jamaica on the break-up of the Federation and being renamed 1st and 3rd Battalions of the Jamaica Regiment. The 1st Battalion, together with a recently activated 2nd Battalion, forms the ground force element of the Jamaica Defence Force, the few armoured fighting vehicles being operated by these two units. There is also a Support and Service Battalion, which provides engineer and signals elements in addition to providing logistic support. Equipment is almost exclusively of British origins and includes the SLR rifle, the Sterling sub-machine gun, the GPMG general-purpose machine gun and the 81 mm mortar. There are also a small number of Ferret scout cars, recently supplemented by 15 US Cadillac-Gage V-150 Commando wheeled APCs. The 3rd Battalion of the Jamaica Regiment, manned by part-time volunteers, constitutes the ground force reserve.

A Coast Guard, established on independence in 1962 with technical assistance from the Royal Navy and material assistance from the USN, forms the naval element of the Jamaica Defence Force. The Jamaican Coast Guard currently operates two patrol craft in the 100-ton range, the *Fort Charles* and the *Paul Bogle* and three in the 60-ton range named *Discovery Bay*, *Holland Bay* and *Manatee Bay*, plus one unnamed 40-foot patrol craft and a sail training yacht. There is a naval base at Port Royal and current personnel strength consists of approximately 170 officers and ratings on the active list and a reserve of approximately 50 officers and other ranks.

An Air Wing of the Jamaica Defence Force was formed in 1963 and currently operates two Britten-Norman Islanders and single examples of the Beech King Air 100 and the Cessna 337G in a fixed-wing flight based at Manley International Airport, Kingston and four Bell 206As, three Bell 212s and a single Bell 222 in a helicopter flight, which operates from Up Park Camp, Kingston. There is also an air strip at Montego Bay, which is not permanently manned by JDF elements.

Both officers and other ranks of the Jamaican Defence Force now receive their basic training at the JDF Depot at Kingston. All officers however continue to receive their advanced training abroad, either in Britain, the United States, Canada or the German Federal Republic.

Paramilitary forces

Manpower: 4920 (Jamaica Constabulary)
1500 (Special Constabulary)

In addition to the Jamaica Defence Force, there is an armed national police force, the Jamaica Constabulary, formed in 1867 and with a current establishment of 4920 men and women. This is supplemented by the 1500-man Special Constabulary, formed in 1938, together with a total of 1700 District Constables, who serve as local police. They are equipped with side arms, shotguns and riot equipment, including CS gas projectors.

Sources of defence equipment supply and current requirements

Most of the equipment of the ground force element of the Jamaica Defence Force is of British origins although the recent acquisition of US-built APCs is an interesting departure. The United States has also given Jamaica military aid to the value of $1,100,000 since 1950, mainly in the form of patrol craft for the Coast Guard and the latter force is equipped with material exclusively of US origins. The Air Wing also has predominantly US equipment. There is no local defence industry. Although the Jamaica Defence Force, as at present constituted, is totally inadequate for the country's defence, for its small size it appears to have as much equipment of appropriate type as it can conveniently handle.

Summary and prospects

Jamaica is fortunate in that its geographical position permits it to maintain defence forces of an insignificance totally incommensurate with its population. The ground force element, even in conjunction with the police forces, would be inadequate both in numbers and equipment to contain any significant internal disturbances, such as demographic pressures may cause in the forseeable future, much less to resist foreign military aggression. The latter seems likely only in the context of the former and then is most likely to come from Cuba.

The Coast Guard is scarcely adequate even for the effective policing of the 600 mile coastline. Until recently, the Air Wing was probably the most adequately equipped element of the Jamaica Defence Force for its present modest role of support for the ground and marine elements and of civilian agencies, but it has no potential even for effective tactical support and has actually contracted in recent years as the deteriorating economic situation has prevented the replacement of worn-out material.

In the present state of the Jamaican economy, any expansion of the Defence Force seems unlikely, unless the country should become the recipient of significantly increased military assistance from the United States in the context of the present highly unstable condition of the Caribbean area.

MEXICO

(Estados Unidos Mexicanos)

Area: 764,000 sq miles (1,978,000 sq km)
Population: 81,162,000
Total armed forces: 139,500
Reserves: 1,500,000
Available manpower: 6,750,000
Paramilitary forces: 120,000
GNP: $175,410 million (1984)
Defence expenditure: $659,616,000 (1986)

Introduction

The third largest country in Latin America, Mexico is bounded by the United States to the north, the Gulf of Mexico to the east, Belize to the south-east, Guatemala to the south and the Pacific Ocean to the west. About 60% of the population is of mixed Indian and European blood, 30% is pure Indian, 9% white and the remaining 1% includes Negro and Chinese minorities. Almost 50% of the total population occupies the Central Meseta, surrounding Mexico City. Population is sparsely and unevenly distributed throughout the remainder of the country.

Mexico is believed to contain the world's largest reserves of petroleum, most of which remain unexploited. The major exports are cotton, coffee, sugar, lead and zinc, together with petroleum products, sulphur, salt, meat and shell-fish. Industry is developing and the country is on the road to self-sufficiency in the production of consumer goods. Imports include machinery, motor vehicles, chemicals, maize, wool and fertilizer.

American aboriginal culture had its finest flowering in the territory corresponding to modern Mexico. The Maya empire in the south reached its peak between the 4th and 10th centuries AD and had already disappeared before the arrival of the first Europeans. The Aztec empire was however at its zenith, controlling all of the central and much of northern Mexico, at the time of the arrival of the first Spaniards in 1519. During the next three centuries, Spanish rule extended southward throughout Central America and northward into the region corresponding to the south-western United States and Texas.

There were unsuccessful peasant uprisings in 1811 and 1813 and the Liberal rising in Spain in 1820 provoked fears of a similar development in Mexico among the Mexican Conservatives, who, led by Augustín Iturbide, initiated an armed revolt which was aimed mainly at the preservation of their own privileges. This attracted widespread support due to the failure of the mass of the population to appreciate its true motivation, quickly overcoming Spanish resistance and in 1822 Iturbide proclaimed himself Emperor. The Empire lasted less than a year, Iturbide being forced to abdicate in March 1823 and in 1824 Mexico adopted a federal republican constitution. In 1828 a Spanish invasion was easily repelled although by now Mexico was beginning to colapse into anarchy. The largely North American settlers in Texas rose in revolt in 1836, establishing a separate republic the annexation of which by the United States in 1845 provoked the disastrous war of 1846–48 between Mexico and its northern neighbour. A bitter civil war, known as the Reform War, occurred between Liberals and Conservatives in the period 1858 to 1861, resulting in the establishment of the Liberal, Benito Juárez, as President.

Continuing economic problems caused the Mexican government to default on repayments of its foreign debts and Britain, France and Spain landed a joint military force at Vera Cruz in 1861/62 to safeguard their financial interests. Although the British and Spanish forces soon withdrew, the French marched inland to Mexico City, ejecting the government of Juárez in 1863 and establishing a puppet kingdom ruled over by Archduke Maximilian of Austria, with the title of Emperor Maximilian I. On the conclusion of the American Civil War the United States began to give active support to the Mexican republicans who had been driven into a small enclave adjoining the frontier with Texas, causing the French to withdraw in 1867. Deprived of French support, Maximilian was defeated in battle at Querétaro and subsequently executed. Juárez now set about the conversion of Mexico into a modern nation, giving the country its first truly stable government since independence. Re-elected President in 1871 he died the following year.

A rebellion against the next President gave Porfirio Díaz, a prominent general of the war against the French, the opportunity to establish himself as President, ruling Mexico as absolute dictator from 1876 to 1911. Although autocratic and corrupt, Díaz provided 34 years of stable government during which the economy flourished and foreign investment increased. Popular disaffection grew during the early years of the 20th century, inflamed by the polemical works of Francisco Madero who unsuccessfully challenged Díaz for the Presidency from prison during the 1910 election and subsequently provided the ideological background to the revolts of Emiliano Zapata in the south and Pancho Villa in the north. The successes of the rebels sparked off army revolts and rioting and Díaz fled the country in May 1911. Madero was elected President in November 1911 but proved to be inept if well-meaning and was overthrown by General Victoriano Huerta and murdered in February 1913.

Mexico now sank back into virtual anarchy as rival revolutionary factions struggled for supremacy and Huerta, who had made himself President after the murder of Madero, was forced to flee the country in 1914. Later the same year representatives of the four principal revolutionary leaders, Villa, Zapata, Carranza and Obregón, met in an unsuccessful attempt to form a government. Continued civil war ensued, with the Carranza–Obregón factions gaining the upper hand towards the end of 1914. Villa's raids into US territory provoked the dispatch of a punitive expedition under General "Black Jack" Pershing in 1916, the US forces being withdrawn the following year on the eve of the entry of the United States into the First World War.

By the early 1920s all of the principal revolutionary leaders except Obregón were dead and he became President in 1920, presiding over the final pacification of the country. The succession of presidents during the late 1920s and 1930s consolidated the basis of the revolution – land reform and free universal education – although the original revolutionary fervour rapidly declined. Nevertheless, the successive Mexican governments supported the Spanish Republicans in the civil war of 1936 to 1939, expropriated foreign oil holdings in 1938 and declared war on the Axis in 1942.

Mexico is a federal republic of 31 states and one federal district. Executive power is vested in the President and there is a bicameral Congress. Each state has an elected governor and its own legislature and judiciary.

Mexican foreign policy is probably the most independent in Latin America, Mexico having resisted US pressures to break off diplomatic relations with Cuba following the Cuban revolution of 1958 and being among the most trenchant critics of current US policies in Central America. Since the end of the revolutionary period, Mexico has also been the most politically stable country in Latin America, limited urban guerrilla activity in the 1960s and early 1970s being easily contained by the armed forces. Sporadic student unrest found its most violent expression in the riots which preceded the Olympic Games in 1968 and there have been occasional disturbances during elections.

Structure of the armed forces

Although the Mexican armed forces played as critical a role in national politics as elsewhere in Latin America up to and during the revolution of 1910/20, they are now the least politicised in Latin America and their function has been reduced to that of an internal constabulary, the country relying implicitly on the United States for its defence against external enemies.

The President is commander-in-chief of the armed forces and has very far-reaching powers with regard to the declaration of war, mobilisation,

the suspension of constitutional guarantees and the promotion of officers. The President exercises day to day control over the Army and Air Force through the Ministry of National Defence and over the Navy via the Ministry of Marine. Both Ministers are in the chain of command and the respective force commanders report directly to them. Each of the three armed forces has its own general staff but there is no joint general staff.

All male citizens must undergo military training at the age of 18. In practice, although the conscripts are organised in National Service Brigades with a total nominal strength of 250,000, the obligation for military service is discharged by attendance at Sunday morning drills, supervised by the regular armed forces. The armed forces are in fact recruited by voluntary enlistment for a period of three years, re-enlistments being common and a large proportion of the personnel of the three armed forces being professional, long-service regulars.

The Army is deployed on a pattern established in 1924, shortly after the end of the revolution. There are 35 military zones, which correspond essentially to the 31 states of the Mexican Confederation, plus one for the Federal District, the states of Oaxaca, Guerrero and Vera Cruz each being divided into two zones. The Navy divides the coast into 17 Naval Zones, corresponding to the 17 coastal states.

Army

Manpower: 105,000

Tactical formations: 2 infantry brigades
1 paratroop brigade
1 mechanised brigade
1 motorised cavalry brigade
1 rapid intervention (COIN) brigade

Major units: 75 infantry battalions
3 Presidential Guard mechanised battalions
2 paratroop battalions
1 special forces battalion
22 mechanised cavalry regiments
1 horsed cavalry regiment
3 artillery regiments
(9 battalions)
1 combat engineer battalion

AFVs: M4 Sherman medium tanks
M3 and M5 light tanks
ERC-90, M8, Humber Mk IV and MAC-1 armoured cars
Panhard VBL and M3A1 scout cars
M3 half-track and
HWK-11 APCs
DN-3, DN-4, DN-5 and
Sedena 1000 AFVs

Artillery: M116 75 mm pack howitzers
M101 105 mm howitzers
M8 75 mm SPH

***Presidential guards at Mexico City* (Author)**

In the peculiar conditions under which Mexico gained its independence the Creole-officered Spanish colonial army became overnight its army as an independent state. A Military Academy was set up in 1822 but the professionalisation of the Army was not completed until over a century later. Despite the confused political situation, the Spanish invasion of 1828 was repelled with relative ease. The Army however suffered humiliating defeats in both the War of Texan Secession in 1836 and the disastrous war of 1846–48 against the United States. The Reform War of 1857–60 was followed almost immediately by the French intervention, during which the Mexican Army effectively ceased to exist. The final defeat of the Franco–Mexican forces in 1867 was accomplished by a vast popular army which bore little resemblance to a conventional military force and most of which was subsequently demobilised by Juárez who set about the recreation of a formal Mexican Army. The Military Academy was re-established in 1867 and an arms factory was set up at Mexico City.

From 1910 to 1920 Mexico was rent by civil war, various forces claiming to be the legitimate national Army existing simultaneously for most of the period. The revolution effectively came to an end in 1920 and in 1924 President Calles reformed the *Colegio Militar*, established a staff college and divided the country into 32 military zones corresponding to the 29 states then existing plus the 2 national territories and the Federal district, each of which was to be garrisoned by one or two infantry battalions and at least one cavalry regiment. An officers' revolt, in which less than 25% of the officer corps participated, occurred in 1927, a final military revolt being suppressed with relative ease in 1929 and since then the Mexican armed forces have become the most apolitical in the region.

Mexico declared war on the Axis powers in May 1942, receiving considerable US military aid as a result. With the end of the Second World War and Mexico's signature of the Rio Treaty of 1947 additional equipment was acquired both by transfer from the United States and by purchase in Europe. Although some new units were formed the Army stagnated, with progressively obsolescent equipment, until the late 1970s when the discovery of vast oil reserves off the Gulf coast occasioned a reassessment of Mexico's defence policies. However, the country's increasing economic crisis curtailed plans for the acquisition of new equipment.

The Mexican Army currently numbers approximately 105,000 all ranks and remains essentially organised and deployed on the basis established in 1924. Three of the original military zones have however been divided in two to produce a total of 35 which are still mainly garrisoned by one to three infantry battalions each, the majority also having at least one cavalry regiment and a variable complement of tactical and logistic support elements.

There are now a total of 75 infantry battalions. A new armoured reconnaissance regiment has recently been formed and five existing cavalry regiments have been converted into armoured infantry battalions, while all but one of the remaining 23 cavalry regiments, most of which remained horsed as recently as 1981, have now been motorised. The artillery is organised in three regiments and no separate air defence units appear to exist. The engineers consist of one combat engineer battalion, plus a number of construction battalions, believed to number at least 19 and a number of independent companies.

Army level units based at Mexico City provide the only effective tactical manoeuvre force comprising the three-battalion Presidential Guard Armoured Brigade, the *José María Morelos y Pavón* Paratroop Fusiliers Brigade, which combines the 1st and 2nd Paratroop Fusilier Battalions with the Air Force Paratroop Battalion, the 1st Infantry Brigade, comprising the 2nd and 3rd Infantry Battalions and the 1st Armoured Reconnaisance Squadron, the 2nd Infantry Brigade, with the 59th and 67th Infantry Battalions and the 2nd Armoured Reconnaissance Squadron, the *José Antonio Torres* Motorised Cavalry Brigade, with the 25th, 26th and 29th Motorised Cavalry Regiments and the Rapid Intervention Brigade with the Assault Troops Battalion and the 1st and 2nd Military Police Battalions. Further army level troops deployed at or in the vicinity of the capital include the 1st Construction Battalion, 1st Transport Regiment and 1st Transport Battalion.

Other troops deployed within the 1st Military Zone (HQ Mexico City) conform to the prevailing pattern throughout the remaining 34 military zones and include the 53rd and 66th Infantry Battalions, the 1st Armoured Reconnaisance Regiment, the 1st Artillery Battalion and the 1st Engineer, Supply and Medical Companies. Among other zonal garrisons the IXth Military Zone (HQ Durango) is garrisoned by the 58th, 71st and 72nd Infantry Battalions and the 50th Mechanised Cavalry Regiment, the XVIIIth (HQ Comitán, Chiapas) by the 24th and 32nd Mechanised Cavalry Regiments and the XXIst (HQ Puebla) only by the 12th Cavalry Regiment.

The principal rifle in service is the HK 33 in 5.56 mm calibre, Mexican-assembled FN FALs in 7.62 mm calibre still being fairly frequently encountered, while the US M1 in 0.30-inch calibre is still to be found in the hands of second-line troops. The HK 53 sub-machine gun in 5.56 mm calibre and the locally-developed Mendoza HM-3 in 9 mm are both in use, some old Thompson M1921s, M1s and M1A1s in 0.45-inch also being on inventory. The principal machine guns in service are the FN MAG in 7.62 mm calibre, the Mendoza RM-2 and both the Browning M1917 and M1919, all in 0.30-inch calibre as well as the Browning M2HB in 0.50-inch calibre and the Mendoza B-1933 and the Madsen M-1934, both in 7 mm. Anti-armour weapons in service include the obsolete US 37 mm M3 anti-tank guns, the M40A1 106 mm RCL and the Milan ATGW. Mortars in use include Hotchkiss-Brandt 60 mm, 81 mm and 120 mm and US M2 4.2-inch pieces.

The current status of the 25 US M4 medium and the 15 M3 and ten M5 light tanks formerly in service is unclear although the 50 US M8 armoured cars have been rearmed and re-engined. Likewise, it is not certain whether the 15 examples apiece of the MAC-1 and Humber Mk IV armoured cars formerly in service remain active or have ben replaced by the 41 Panhard ERC-90 armoured cars acquired during the mid-1980s. Many of the 100 US M3A1 scout cars certainly do remain in service, together with 27 Panhard VBL scout cars and 40 HWK-11 APCs. Several locally-developed types, including the DN-3, DN-4 and DN-5 and the Sedena 1000 are also now in service.

Artillery is limited and largely obsolescent and includes 48 US M101 105 mm and 18 M116 75 mm howitzers, plus six M8 75 mm SPHs. The only anti-aircraft weapons positively identified include some 40 13.2 mm Hotchkiss AA machine guns dating from the late 1930s and an indeterminate number of US M55 quadruple 0.50 calibre machine guns.

All officers are trained at the *Colegio Militar*, which offers a basic four-year course and graduates 300 to 350 second lieutenants annually. Officers continue professional training at specific stages throughout their careers, specialist training being provided by the *Centro de Aplicacion para Oficiales de las Armas*. The *Escuela Superior de Guerra* trains officers for superior rank and for staff appointments. There is also a comprehensive system of specialist schools for other ranks, all training establishments being located at Mexico City.

Plans exist for the superimposition of a corps structure on the Army's combat units, the majority of which are at present organised only at battalion level and dispersed throughout the country's 35 military zonal commands. These will in due course be grouped into brigades although the formation of divisions as an intermediate level of command does not appear to be immediately envisaged. It is estimated that the total number of brigades will be of the order of 36 of which two will continue to be located in the vicinity of Mexico City, together with the existing armoured brigade, which is formed by the Army component of the Presidential Guard, the Motorised Cavalry Brigade and the Paratroop Fusilier Brigade. While the latter three formations and the internal security orientated Rapid Intervention Brigade seem likely to remain under the direct control of Army Headquarters the remaining brigades will probably be subordinate to five new army corps. For the moment, the Mexican Army still remains essentially an armed constabulary with only limited military capacity and economic considerations seem destined to perpetuate this situation for the forseeable future.

Navy

Manpower:	23,632 (including 3810 Marines and approximately 500 Naval aviation)
Major units:	2 destroyers 1 destroyer escort 4 APDs 2 gunboats 34 patrol vessels 37 large patrol craft 7 small patrol craft 20 river patrol craft 2 LSTs 3 transports
Marines:	1 brigade 1 Presidential Guard group 31 security companies

***OPV* Comandante Virgilio Uribe *of the Mexican Navy* (Bazan)**

***Mexican "Azteca" class patrol vessel* Felix Romero (F. Calzada)**

Naval aviation:	1 patrol squadron 1 communications squadron 1 helicopter squadron
Maritime patrol:	Grumman HU-16 Albatross CASA-212
Communications:	Beechcraft Baron and Bonanza, Cessna 150, 180, 310, 337G and 402, DHC-5, Douglas C-47, Fairchild F.27, Learjet 24D, Tonatiuh
Helicopters:	Bell 47 and UH-1, MBB Bo 105, SA. 316B Alouette III
Trainers:	Beech T-34

After Mexico became independent from Spain a small Navy was established. Most of the Mexican fleet was lost however in the short naval war against France in 1838. Further attrition occurred during the Texan War of Independence and by the time of the outbreak of the war with the United States in 1846 the Mexican Navy had been reduced to a few small craft which spent the entire war blockaded in port. No spectacular additions were made during the next 20 years and the remaining ships disappeared during the French intervention of 1862–67. After the expulsion of the French, the Mexican armed forces were laboriously rebuilt. The expansion and modernisation of the Navy however proceeded at a very leisurely pace and it played a relatively small part in the Mexican revolution. The outbreak of the Second World War found Mexico still with a very modest fleet although a few small patrol craft were acquired from the United States and Canada during the war years and a respectable fleet of frigates, corvettes and patrol vessels was built up during the immediate post-war period. Sporadic purchases of mainly US surplus material maintained the growth of what remained essentially a coastal patrol force with few military pretensions over the next three decades.

The Navy, which currently has a total establishment of 23,632 all ranks, including Marines and Naval aviation, is organised in two commands comprising a total of 17 zones and 14 sectors.

Gulf Command controls the Gulf and Caribbean Naval Force (HQ Veracruz) and consists of the 1st Naval Zone (HQ Ciudad Madero, Tampico) which contains the Matamoros sector, the 3rd (HQ Vera Cruz) containing the Tuxpán and Coatzcoalcos sectors, the 5th (HQ Frontera, Tabasco), the 7th (HQ Ciudad del Carmen, Campeche) which contains the Champotón and Lerma sectors, the 9th (HQ Yucalpetén, Yucatán) which contains the Progreso sector and the 11th (HQ Chetumal, Quintana Roo) which contains both the Isla Mujeres and San Miguel sectors.

Pacific Command controls the Pacific Naval Force (Acapulco) and comprises the 2nd Naval Zone (HQ Ensenada, Baja California Norte), the 4th (HQ La Paz, Baja California Sur) which contains the Santa Rosalía and Puerto Cortés sectors, the 6th (HQ Guymas, Sonora) which contains the Puerto Penasco sector, the 8th (HQ Mazatlán); the 10th (HQ San Blas), the 12th (HQ Puerto Vallarta), the 14th (HQ Manzanillo) which contains the Isla Socorro Sector, the 16th (HQ Lázaro Cárdenas, Michoacán), the 18th (HQ Acapulco) which contains the Ixtapa-Zihuatanejo sector, the 20th (HQ Salina Cruz) which contains the Puerto Angel sector and the 22nd (HQ Puerto Madero, Chiapas).

The major units of the Mexican Navy are the two 2425-ton "Gearing" class destroyers *Quetzalcoatl* and *Netzahualcoyotl*, the 1200-ton "Edsall" class destroyer escort *Comodoro Manuel Azueta*, the four 1400-ton APDs *Tehuantepec*, *Usumacinta*, *Coahuila* and *Chihuahua* and the old 1600-ton Spanish-built transport-gunboat *Durango*. There are also the six 900-ton "Halcón" class OPVs *Cadete Virgilio Uribe*, *Teniente José Azueta*, *Capitán de Fragata Pedro Sainz de Baranda*, *Comodoro Carlos Castillo Bretón*, *Vice Almirante Othón P. Blanco* and *Contralmirante Angel Ortiz Monasterio*, four slightly larger vessels being under construction locally, the old 1300-ton gunboat *Guanajuato*, the 17 former US "Auk" class minesweepers *Leandro Valle*, *Guillermo Prieto*, *Mariano Escobedo*, *Manuel Doblado*, *Sebastián Lerdo de Tejada*, *Santos Degollado*, *Ignacio de la Llave*, *Juan*

Mexican Marines with FN MAG machine gun (F. Calzada)

N. Álvarez, *Manuel Gutiérrez Zamora*, *Valentín Gomez Farías*, *Ignacio M. Altamirano*, *Francisco Zarod*, *Ignacio L. Vallarta*, *Jesús González Ortega*, *Melchor Ocampo*, *Juan Aldama* and *Hermenegildo Galeana* and the 12 unnamed 650-ton "Admirable" class vessels numbered *D-01*, *D-03*, *D-04*, *D-05*, *D-11*, *D-12*, *D-13*, *D-14*, *D-15*, *D-17*, *D-18* and *D-19*, all of which serve as patrol vessels with minesweeping gear removed.

The construction programme of the 130-ton "Azteca" class patrol craft seems to have ground to a halt, at least temporarily, with the construction of 31 vessels of an initially projected total of 36. In addition to the above sea-going vessels, there are the two 80-ton "Azueta" class and five 37-ton "Polimar" class coastal patrol craft, together with the six 37-ton "Rio" class and the eight 18-ton "Olmeca" class units so far completed.

Auxiliaries include the surveying vessels *Mariano Matamoros*, *Alejandro Humboldt*, *Altair*, *Onjuko*, *El Puma*, *Justo Sierra* and *D-20*, the 1200-ton sail training ship *Cuauhtémoc*, the 1653-ton LSTs *Pánuco* and *Manzanillo*, the 2500-ton transports *Huasteco* and *Zapoteco* and the 785-ton *Zacatecas*, the depot ship *Vicente Guerrero* (a converted LST), the 400-ton oilers *Aguascalintes* and *Tlaxcla*, the unnamed 1863-ton tugs *R-2* and *R-3* and the 1675-ton *Otomi*, *Yaqui*, *Seri* and *Cora*.

The Marines are currently organised into a paratroop brigade, a Presidential Guard group, 31 Marine security companies and three companies of Naval Police and have an established strength of 3810 all ranks. These are equipped with the HK 33 assault rifle and the HK 53 sub-machine gun, both in 5.56 mm calibre, the Walther MP-K sub-machine gun in 9 mm and the FN MAG machine gun in 7.62 mm. Support weapons include Stokes-Brandt 81 mm mortars.

Naval aviation has a personnel strength of approximately 500 operating a total of almost 80 aircraft. The 1st Naval Air Squadron (Tampico) is a communications unit operating four Fairchild F.27s, two Beechcraft Barons, two examples of the Cessna 150, three apiece of the Cessna 180 and 310, two Cessna 337Gs, two Cessna 402s, seven examples of the locally-developed Tonatiuh and single examples of the DHC-5 and Learjet 24D. The 2nd Naval Air Squadron (Mexico City) is the helicopter element of the force with four examples of the Aérospatiale SA.316 Alouette III, two Bell UH-1Hs, two Hiller UH-12Es and twelve MBB Bo 105Cs. The 3rd Naval Air Squadron (La Paz, Baja California) is the maritime reconnaissance element with 12 Grumman HU-16B and D Albatrosses and ten CASA-212 Aviocars. The *Escuela de Aviación Naval* at Vera Cruz has five Beech T-34As, one North American AT-6 and four Bell 47 helicopters.

Vera Cruz and Salina Cruz are the principal naval bases on the Gulf and Pacific coasts respectively, with minor bases at Tampico, Guaymas, Manzanillo and Ciudad del Carmen. The Naval Academy is at Vera Cruz and incorporates courses for Marine and Naval aviation officers. There are schools for seamen at Vera Cruz and Mazatlán and for engineering, armament fitter, communications, marine and Naval aviation other ranks at the former centre.

The Mexican Navy is ultimately to build 19 additional patrol launches of the "Azteca", "Olmeca" and "Águila" classes in local shipyards, although it seems unlikely in the prevailing economic conditions that the project for the acquisition of 12 Swedish "Spica" class fast attack craft and the construction of a further 24 in Mexican yards, which was announced in 1981, will proceed in the immediate future. While the breakdown of the current order has not been made public it seems likely that at least nine of the new vessels will be of the "Azteca" class.

Air Force

Manpower: 6500 (including paratroops)

Major units: 9 groups comprising
2 fighter squadrons
6 tactical support squadrons
1 tactical training squadron
2 heavy transport squadrons
2 medium transport squadrons
1 light transport squadron
1 executive transport squadron
1 Presidential transport squadron
1 helicopter squadron

***Pilatus PC-7 trainer/light-strike aircraft of the Mexican Air Force* (Pilatus Aircraft Ltd)**

Fighters:	Northrop F-5E and F Lockheed AT-33A
Tactical support aircraft:	Pilatus PC-7 North American T-28A
Transports:	Douglas C-47, DC-6, DC-7 and C-54, Boeing 727 and 737, Lockheed Electra, Fairchild F.27, IAI Arava Short Skyvan
Helicopters:	Bell 47G, 205, 206B and 212, Aérospatiale SA.316 Alouette III, SA.330 Puma and AS.332 Super Puma
Trainers:	Piper Aztec, Beech Bonanza and Musketeer, CAP-10B, Pilatus PC-7
Ground forces:	1 paratroop battalion

The Carranza government set about the establishment of an air arm in 1914. The war in Europe had however cut off all external sources of supply and Mexico therefore had to start the development and production of aircraft from scratch. By 1920 the *Arma Aérea* had a total of approximately 50 locally-built aircraft and by 1930 it had changed its name to *Fuerza Aérea Mexicana*, although it was still subordinate to the Army and little new equipment was acquired during the 1930s. Mexico declared war on the Axis on 29 May 1942 and considerable amounts of Lend-Lease aid began to be received. The first combat types arrived in 1944 and later the same year the *Fuerza Aérea* also became independent from the Army. A fighter squadron operated against the Japanese in the Philippines during 1945, being the only element of the Mexican armed forces to see active service abroad during the Second World War. During the late 1950s the first jet aircraft were acquired but acquisitions during the 1960s and 1970s were largely confined to second-line types. In the early 1980s the Mexican government attempted to purchase 36 examples of the Northrop F-5 fighter from the United States, running into the usual refusal of the US Government to sanction the sale of modern military equipment to Latin American countries. After Mexico had entered into negotiations with Israel for the supply of at least two-dozen Kfirs, the United States agreed to part with ten F-5Es and two F-5Fs.

The Mexican Air Force currently numbers approximately 6500 all ranks operating some 350 aircraft and is organised into nine groups comprising 19 squadrons and flying from nine bases.

Military Air Base No 1 is located at Santa Lucía, in Mexico State, Military Air Base No 2 is at Ixtepec, Oaxaca, Military Air Base No 3 at El Cipres, Baja California, Military Air Base No 4 at Cozumel, Quintana Roo, Military Air Base No 5 at Zapopán, Jalisco, Military Air Base No 6 at Puebla, Military Air Base No 7 at Pie de la Cuesta, Guerrero, Military Air Base No 8 at Mérida and Military Air Base No 9 is at La Paz, Baja California.

The 1st Air Group (HQ Santa Lucía) comprises Communications Squadron 208 with ten IAI Aravas and three Short Skyvans and Helicopter Squadron 209 with ten Bell 47s, five Bell 205s, ten Bell 206s, eight Aérospatiale SA.316 Alouette IIIs and three SA.330F Pumas, both units being based at Santa Lucía, plus the unnumbered Mixed Tactical Training Squadron at Zapopán with 15 North American T-28As.

The 5th, 6th, 7th and 9th Groups are also based at Santa Lucía.

The 5th Air Group comprises Communications Squadron 101 and the unnumbered Photo-Reconnaisance Squadron, each equipped with eight Aero Commander 500s, the 6th Group is made up of Heavy Transport Squadron 301, equipped with two DC-6s and one DC-7 and Heavy Transport Squadron 302 with five C-54s, the 7th Group consists of Jet Fighter Squadron 202 with ten AT-33As and Defence Squadron 401 with nine Northrop F-5Es and two F-5Fs, while the 9th Group comprises Medium Air Transport Squadrons 311 and 312, each with six C-47s.

The 2nd Air Group (HQ Puebla) comprises Fighter Squadrons 206 (Puebla) and 207 (Ixtepec) each with 12 Pilatus PC-7s and six North American T-28As.

The 3rd Air Group (HQ La Paz) comprises Fighter Squadrons 203 (La Paz) and 204 (El Cipres) each with 12 PC-7s and six T-28As.

The 4th Air Group (HQ Cozumel) comprises Fighter Squadrons 201 (Cozumel) and 205 (Merida) each with 12 PC-7s and six T-28As.

The 8th Air Group (Benito Juárez International Airport, Mexico City) comprises the Executive Transport Squadron with one Boeing 737, four 727s, one Jetstar 8 and seven Sabreliners and the Presidential Transport Squadron with one Boeing 737 and three 727s, three Fairchild F.27s, a single Lockheed Electra, seven Bell 212s and two AS.332L Super Pumas.

The *Escuela Militar de Aviación* is at Zapopán and is equipped with three Piper Aztecs, 20 Beech Musketeers, 40 F33C Bonanzas, 20 CAP-10Bs and eight PC-7s, both the *Colegio del Aire* and the *Escuela Militar de Especialistas de la Fuerza Aérea* being also located at Zapopán while the other main non-flying elements are at Balbuena. The Air Force Paratroop Battalion is stationed at Campo Militar No 1 at Mexico City.

Officer cadets pursue a four-year course at the *Colegio del Aire* before commissioning as second lieutenants and most officers receive some post-graduate training abroad, principally in the United States. Air Force officers attend the Army's *Escuela Superior de Guerra* for senior post-graduate studies, leading to promotion to field rank or to staff appointments. Enlisted personnel receive their training at the *Escuela de Especialidades de la Fuerza Aérea* at Zapopán.

Immediate expansion plans involve the acquisition of 21 additional Beech Bonanzas and 25 Pilatus PC-7s. There are no concrete proposals for the acquisition of additional combat aircraft in the forseeable future.

Paramilitary forces

Manpower: 23,400 Federal Police
120,000 Rural Defence Corps

There are federal, state and municipal police forces, all of which are organised and equipped on a paramilitary basis.

The main federal police force is the 22,000-strong *Dirección General de Policía y Tránsito*, which comes under the jurisdiction of the Ministry of the Interior and includes the Preventive Police, Riot Police, Traffic Police and the Division of Investigations. The Judicial Police, who have a supervisory function over the other police forces and the 1400-man Federal Highway Police also function on a country-wide basis.

Each of the 31 states and the federal district has its own police force, the equipment, training and general efficiency of which varies considerably relative to the size of the force. Special units, such as Tourist Police, are found in the larger cities. Many large commercial organisations, such as banks, mines etc maintain private armed police forces, which sometimes consist of elements of the local police force, the salaries and operating costs of which are borne by the organisations to which they are assigned.

The *Dirección General de Policía y Tránsito* operates a Police Academy which provides both elementary and advanced training for its own members and the Federal Highway Police also operates its own training school. Some of the states also operate police training schools, but there is no national standard of police training.

Although the *Guardia Rural*, the rural paramilitary police force of the Porfirio Díaz era, was disbanded during the revolution, a part-time rural militia was formed in the immediate post-revolutionary period, mainly to protect the peasants, among whom land had been divided under the agrarian reform policies of the revolution, against the hired thugs of reactionary landowners. In 1929, this force was officially incorporated into the Army with the title of *Cuerpo de Defensa Rural*. It was extensively reorganised as an auxiliary police force in 1955 and during the early 1970s numbered some 80,000 mounted and 40,000 dismounted members, armed with obsolete small arms. The members of this force do not wear uniforms or receive pay but are eligible for free medical care in respect of wounds or injuries received while on duty. Membership of the force is open to male citizens between the ages of 18 and 50 and carries with it a certain social prestige. The units of the *Cuerpo de Defensa Rural* come under the jurisdiction of the commanders of the military zones in which they are located and cannot be used outside the area in which they are raised without the permission of the military zone commander.

Sources of defence equipment and current requirements

Germany and France were the traditional sources of Mexican defence material, although some naval vessels were obtained in Britain, the United States, Italy and later Spain. During the revolution, arms were obtained from whatever sources offered themselves. Following the Second World War most equipment was obtained second-hand from the United States, although from the late 1960s onwards some equipment began to be obtained in Europe once more and some aircraft were purchased in Israel. No country may be said to have a monopoly of the Mexican defence material market.

Very little new material has been obtained since the mid-1950s and the equipment in service is largely obsolete. A re-equipment programme was launched in the late 1970s but was curtailed with the country's growing economic crisis. The Mexican Army needs modern infantry support weapons, anti-armour and air defence weapons, tanks and artillery. Most of the vessels of the Navy are nearly 40 years old and must be approaching the end of their useful lives. The small quantity of F-5 fighters recently obtained by the Air Force constitutes its entire combat equipment. The Air Force also needs heavy tactical transports, such as the C-130. In the country's present economic condition, any spectacular re-equipment seems unlikely during the forseeable future.

Surprisingly for a country which has maintained only very modest and poorly equipped armed forces for over 50 years, Mexico has a small but long-established and flourishing defence industry.

Small arms of various types, some of them of original conception and developed locally, have been manufactured since the turn of the century, General Manuel Mondragón being especially prolific as a weapons designer in the early 1900s and being credited with an involvement in the design of the famous Schneider M97 75 mm field gun. The short-lived military re-equipment programme of the late 1970s and early 1980s envisaged a considerable expansion of the country's existing manufacturing capacity with the licence production of both wheeled and tracked AFVs in collaboration with the German, Israeli and Brazilian defence industries. At least for the moment, this seems largely to have been the victim of economic cut-backs although the development of some APCs of original conception is proceeding.

Shipbuilding is relatively underdeveloped, although some small patrol and auxiliary craft were built from the 1940s onwards. Ten units of the "Azteca" class patrol vessels were built locally with British technical assistance and the programme calls for the construction of 27 more. It was also hoped to build fast attack craft locally with Swedish assistance, but this programme also appears to have become a casualty of the prevailing economic conditions.

The Mexican aircraft industry, although never large, carried out much pioneering work during the first quarter of the century and kept up a steady stream of production into the 1960s. It was intended to expand this with the collaboration of the Brazilian and Israeli aerospace industries and to manufacture such types as the Xavante trainer/light strike aircraft and the Arava light tactical transport in Mexico under licence from Imbraer and Israeli Aircraft Industries. This project also seems to have been at least temporarily shelved although a light general-purpose aircraft is in limited production for the Navy.

Summary and prospects

Despite its turbulent early history, since the revolution Mexico has become one of the least militaristic countries in Latin America, the weakness of its armed forces being inconsistent both with the country's size and international importance and the highly independent line which it has taken in foreign policy. The discovery of enormous off-shore oil reserves during the 1970s appeared to have occasioned something of a reappraisal of the country's defence policies and Army and Navy manpower increased by about 50%. However, in the early 1980s the relatively modest re-equipment programme of the armed forces was an early victim of the spending cut-backs necessitated by a deteriorating economic situation. For the foreseeable future, the Mexican armed forces appear to be destined to remain limited to the internal security role adopted since the end of the revolution.

NICARAGUA

(República de Nicaragua)

Area: 57,145 sq miles (147,900 sq km)
Population: 3,317,000
Total armed forces: 53,000
Reserves: 150,000
Available manpower: 250,000
Paramilitary forces: 7000
GNP: $5,340 million (1984)
Defence expenditure: $598 million (1984)

Introduction

Nicaragua, the largest country of Central America, is bounded by Honduras to the north and north-west, by the Caribbean Sea to the east, by Costa Rica to the south and south-west and by the Pacific Ocean to the west. Of the total population, over 69% is of mixed European and Amerindian origins, under 17% is pure white, approximately 9% is Negro and the remainder Amerindian. Over 90% of the entire population lives in the western lowland region, large tracts of country being completely uninhabited.

The economy is agriculturally based, the main products being coffee, cotton, meat, sugar and bananas. Lumber, particularly hardwoods, is also of importance and there are exploitable deposits of gold, silver, copper and tungsten. Industry is underdeveloped, the principal imports being fuels and manufactured products. Despite the activities of anti-government guerrillas and a partial economic blockade the economy grew by approximately 2% during 1984–85, the most recent period for which figures are available.

The Spaniards first reached the country in 1519 and colonised the eastern lowlands during the first half of the 16th century. The Caribbean coastal region however attracted no interest from the Spaniards, being partly colonised by the English from the early 18th century onwards and the Mosquito Coast actually being a British protectorate from 1780 to 1860. The early history of Nicaragua is that of the remainder of the region until the break up of the United Provinces of Central America in 1838. For most of the remainder of the 19th century, Nicaraguan history was dominated by the continual feuding between the Conservatives and Liberals, with a brief interlude between 1855 and 1857, when a North American adventurer, William Walker, succeeded in making himself President, provoking intervention by a combined British and US naval force and his expulsion. After a second attempt at intervention in Nicaraguan internal politics, Walker was captured by the British, who handed him over to the Hondurans by whom he was executed. In the latter part of the 19th century, a project for the construction of an inter-oceanic canal, via Lake Nicaragua, came to nothing although US commercial investment in the country began in the 1870s, intensifying towards the turn of the century.

The Presidency of José Santos Zelaya (1893–1909) brought Nicaragua its first period of relative stability but antagonised North American commercial interests and led to his overthrow by the Conservatives, with US backing, in 1909. The new government virtually mortgaged the country to United States bankers, to protect whose investment US Marines were landed during a rebellion in 1912. The country collapsed into civil war within months of the departure of the Marines, provoking further US intervention in 1927. This time, the Marines remained until 1933, handing over power to an elected government in 1932.

A sustained campaign of guerrilla resistance had been carried out throughout the occupation by General Augusto César Sandino and shortly after the departure of the Marines he was lured into a parley with the new President, Juan B.

Sacasa, emerging from which he was kidnapped and murdered. Sacasa was overthrown by the US trained National Guard in 1936, its commander, General Anastasio "Tacho" Somoza, succeeding to the Presidency after the formality of a rigged election and ruling Nicaragua as absolute despot until his assasination in 1956. Somoza was succeeded by his son Luís who displayed unexpectedly liberal tendencies but died in mysterious circumstances in 1963, being succeeded in turn by his younger brother, Anastasio Junior, known as "Tachito", who it was widely believed had arranged his murder. In 1979, the 43-year long regime of the Somozas finally collapsed when, following almost seven years of increasingly bloody civil war, Somoza fled the country, to be subsequently assassinated while in exile in Paraguay. Somoza was replaced by a junta of the Sandinista National Liberation Front, the provisional government representing a wide spectrum of political opinion.

Following efforts on the part of the United States to destabilise the revolutionary government, culminating in support for armed attacks on Nicaraguan territory by exiled supporters of the Somoza regime, the Marxist elements of the Sandinista government began to gain the ascendancy at the expense of its more moderate members. Nevertheless, elections held in 1984 and pronounced as fair and honest by delegations of European parliamentarians who had been invited to the country to observe them, confirmed the rule of the Sandinista revolutionary government and the Presidency of its leader, Dr Daniel Ortega.

Nicaragua is a unitary, centralised republic of 16 departments. There is a single chamber legislature but as in most countries of a Marxist orientation both legislative and executive power is mainly in the hands of the Council of Ministers or cabinet, the National Directorate of the Sandinista National Liberation Front occupying an unofficial but de facto position of predominance analagous to that of the Soviet Communist Party relative to that of the government of the USSR. While external pressures by the United States, both directly and through its surrogate guerrillas, have facilitated the rise to predominance of the Marxist elements in the Sandinista revolutionary government, the politico-economic system of the country remains a pluralistic mixture of capitalist democracy and socialism, although there are disturbing signs of a move towards the development of a totalitarian Marxist state.

Structure of the armed forces

The President is titular commander-in-chief of the armed forces although both command, administrative and operational control are effectively in the hands of the Minister of Defence who is theoretically answerable to the Council of Ministers but in practice enjoys great autonomy. The Minister is advised by a general staff.

The country is divided into seven Military Regions of which the 1st Region (HQ Estelí) covers the departments of Estelí, Madriz and Nueva Segovia, the 2nd Region (HQ Chinandega) the departments of Chinandega and León, the 3rd Region (HQ Managua) the department of Managua, the 4th Region (HQ Matagalpa) the departments of Matagalpa, Boáco, Jinotega and part of Zelaya, the 5th Region (HQ Puerto Cabezas) the northern half of the department of Zelaya, the 6th Region (HQ Granada) the departments of Granada, Carazo, Masaya and Rivas and the 7th Region (HQ Bluefields) the departments of Chantales, Río San Juan and the southern part of Zelaya.

The present external threats have resulted in the registration for military service of all men between the ages of 17 and 50 and all women between 18 and 40, conscripts serving for two years active service before passing to the reserve. Popular enthusiasm still results in widespread membership of the militias by those not on full-time active service.

Army

Manpower: 50,000

Formations: 2 mechanised brigades
6 infantry brigades
1 artillery brigade

Major units: 22 infantry battalions
(incl 4 mechanised)
11 rapid reaction battalions

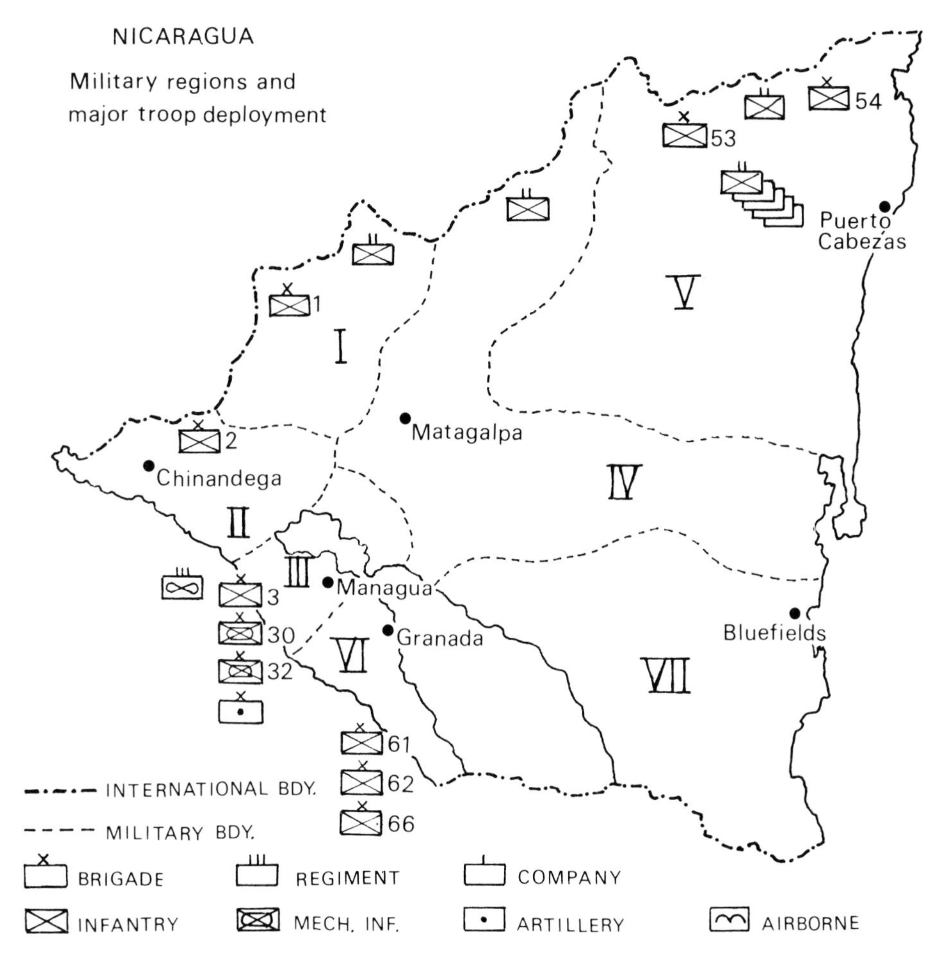

6 rifle battalions
3 armoured battalions
3 field artillery battalions
1 engineer battalion

AFVs: T-54, T-55 and PT-76 tanks
BRDM-2 armoured cars
BTR-60 and BTR-152 APCs

Artillery: M-1942 76 mm guns
D-30 122 mm and D-20 152 mm howitzers

Anti-armour weapons: ZIS 57 mm towed guns
ASU-85 tank destroyers

Air-defence weapons: ZPU-1, ZPU-2 and ZPU-4 machine guns

Nothing approaching a formally constituted Nicaraguan Army existed until 1893 when President Santos Zelaya made the first attempts to organise the armed forces on a regular basis and a Military Academy was established. The Army however was never a numerous or powerful force and during the military occupation of 1927–33 the United States persuaded the Nicaraguan government to abolish it and replace it with a new force to be known as the National Constabulary. It finally emerged as the *Guardia Nacional*, combining the functions of an army and police force. Within three years of the end of the US occupation, this force had overthrown the President, making its own commander the absolute tyrant of Nicaragua and serving him and his descendents faithfully as the most effective repressive force in Latin America.

Nicaragua declared war on Japan on 9 December 1941 and on Germany and Italy two days later and thus qualified for Lend-Lease military aid in exchange for base facilities on its Pacific coast, although it avoided any active participation in hostilities. In 1947 Nicaragua signed the Rio Treaty of Mutual Defence, a US Army mission being established in 1953. In 1957, a year after the assasination of "Tacho" Somoza, a brief frontier conflict with Honduras was defused by the intervention of the Organization of American States. The *Guardia Nacional* took part in its only overseas operation when an infantry company participated in the US-sponsored OAS peace-keeping force sent to the Dominican Republic in 1965.

The first 20 years of the Somoza regime had seen no organised opposition. In 1958 however, the *Frente Sandinista de Liberación Nacional* was founded, low level guerrilla activity being initially contained with relative ease by the *Guardia Nacional*. Following "Tachito" Somoza's blatant misappropriation of the relief funds which poured in from all over the world after the disastrous earthquake of 1972 the middle classes began to support the FSLN, the Somoza regime becoming almost totally isolated within the country. US military assistance was withdrawn in 1976 when Somoza's excesses became too much for the Carter administration and the balance finally began to tip in favour of the guerrillas. Although militarily still undefeated, the *Guardia Nacional* rapidly collapsed after its abandonment by its leader in 1979, most of its members fleeing into exile in neighbouring countries or the United States.

The new Sandinista Revolutionary Army, which replaced the *Guardia Nacional*, was planned to consist of nine infantry battalions, one armoured battalion, two field artillery batteries, one air-defence battery and one engineer battalion, with a strength of approximately 15,000 all ranks.

From the outset the high profile presence of supporters of the extreme political left in the new regime had aroused the suspicions of the United States government. This attitude turned to one of overt hostility with the assumption of the Presidency by Ronald Reagan in 1981, creating economic difficulties for the new Nicaraguan government and with them an enhanced problem in replacing military equipment lost during the civil war. This problem assumed increased urgency with the escalation of efforts to destabilise the new Nicaraguan regime by counter-revolutionaries, including former members of the *Guardia Nacional*, based in Honduras and given both encouragement and material support by the United States government.

In December 1981 Nicaragua signed a contract for the supply of defence equipment to the value of approximately $17 million by France. However, the continued active hostility of the US administration, demonstrated by the implementation of a naval blockade, a massive military presence in neighbouring Honduras, together with greatly increased guerrilla activity and finally raids by unidentified aircraft on Managua, the Nicaraguan capital and the mining of Nicaraguan territorial waters, blocked the acquisition of further defence material from Western countries. These events prompted the delivery of substantial quantities of additional equipment from Cuba and the Eastern Bloc from 1982 onwards.

The *Ejército Popular Sandinista* currently numbers approximately 50,000 and consists of two mechanised and six infantry brigades, comprising 18 infantry, four APC-mounted and two armoured battalions, an artillery brigade, with three field artillery battalions, an independent armoured battalion and a single engineer battalion. There are also 11 counter-insurgency units, known as Irregular Warfare Infantry Battalions and six light

***T-55 tank of the Sandinista Revolutionary Army* (US Dept. of Defense)**

***Nicaraguan PT-76 tank and BTR-60 APCs* (Jane's Defence Weekly)**

rifle battalions, which also have a primary counter-insurgency orientation. The bulk of the active Army however consists of mobilised elements of the Sandinista People's Militia, which includes at least 20 brigades and approximately 100 battalions. The infantry brigades consist essentially of three infantry battalions without organic combat support units, the mechanised brigades comprising a single tank battalion and two APC infantry battalions, artillery support being supplied by sub-units of the artillery brigade on an ad hoc basis in accordance with operational requirements.

Few details of the current deployment of the Nicaraguan Army are available although it is known that the 1st to 6th Military Regions have been grouped in pairs into three Military Zones for operational purposes. The 1st Military Region is known to be the normal station of the *Adán Gómez* Light Rifle Battalion while the 2nd Military Region normally houses the 21st Infantry Brigade (HQ Chinandega). The 3rd Military Region contains both the 30th and 32nd Mechanised Infantry Brigades and the 214th and 233rd Militia Brigades, the 4th Military Region containing the 301st and 312th Militia Brigades and the *Cristóbal Vanegas* Frontier Battalion. The 5th Military Region houses the 53rd and 54th Infantry Brigades, plus the *Rigoberto Cruz, Oscar Benávides*, *Modesto Duarte*, *Edgar Murguía* and *Gaspar García Laviana* Light Rifle Battalions, the 6th Military Region being the normal station of the 61st, 62nd and 66th Infantry Brigades. No units normally assigned to the 7th Military Region have been identified.

BTR-60 APC on parade at Managua
(US Dept. of Defense)

The *Farabundo Martí, Ramón Raudales, Francisco Estrada, Germán Pomares, Santos López, Pedro Altamirano, Súcrates Sandino, Simón Bolívar, Juan Pablo Umanzor, Juan Gregorio Colindres* and *Rufo Marín* Irregular Warfare Battalions come under the control of Army headquarters and are deployed in accordance with operational requirements. Also subordinate to Army HQ are the *Managua* Tank Battalion, the *General Omar Torrijos Herrera* Artillery Brigade and the Engineer Battalion. There are also at least two female units, the *Batallones Femininas Cernín Guevara* and *Aslinda López* and the six Frontier Guard battalions come under army control during the present emergency.

Equipment of Soviet and Eastern Bloc origins now predominates. Infantry weapons consist mainly of AK-47 and AKM assault rifles, SVD sniper rifles, RPD and RPK light machine guns, all in 7.62 mm calibre, DShK 38/46 12.7 mm machine guns, AGS-17 30 mm grenade launchers and Soviet 60 mm, 82 mm and 120 mm mortars. Quantities of US M16A1 and Israeli Galil rifles in 5.56 mm calibre and both 7.62 mm M60 and 0.50 calibre Browning M2HB machine guns were inherited from the National Guard, together with quantities of M1 Garand rifles and M1 carbines, both in 0.30-inch calibre and some of these may remain in service with second-line units. Armour now includes about 100 Soviet T-54 and T-55 tanks, 30 PT-76 light tanks and 50 BRDM-2 scout cars, together with 20 BTR-60 and 100 BTR-152 APCs. Three US M4 Sherman tanks, approximately 20 T17 Staghound armoured cars and about six US M3A1 half-track APCs, inherited from the National Guard together with six US M2A1 105 mm howitzers are probably no longer in service. The artillery is equipped with some M-1942 76 mm guns, about 30 Soviet D-30 122 mm and a similar number of D-20 152 mm howitzers. There are also believed to be about 20 BM-21 122 mm multiple rocket launchers and an unknown number of ASU-85 SP 85 mm anti-tank guns. About 100 obsolete Soviet ZIS-2 57 mm towed anti-tank guns are deployed with infantry battalions, approximately 100 ZPU-1, ZPU-2 and ZPU-4 single, twin and quadruple 14.5 mm machine guns being used for close-range AA defence.

The major training establishments are the

Escuela Carlos Agüero Hechevarría, which is the officer training school, the *Centro de Estudios Militares Comandante Hilario Sánchez Vázquez*, which provides technical and specialised training for both officers and other ranks and the *Centro de Entrenamiento Militar Eduardo Contreras*, which is the basic conscript training school, all three institutions being located at or near Managua. Considerable training assistance has been received from Cuba but the usually quoted figure of 3000 Cuban military personnel, allegedly present in Nicaragua, is a gross exaggeration. About 90% of this number are engaged in civilian occupations although all physically fit Cubans are military reservists.

Navy

Manpower: 1000

Major units: 2 motor torpedo boats
18 coastal patrol craft
6 inshore minesweepers
1 LCM

The military reforms of 1893 also called for the formation of a Navy, which although never large, was for some years the most powerful in Central America. Although the Navy seems to have lasted throughout the First World War, it ceased to exist very shortly afterwards. Nicaragua was without any naval force until 1938 when a small coast guard section was established within the *Guardia Nacional*. During the Second World War, the United States established a naval base, with coastal defences, at Corinto and thus Nicaragua's naval defence was effectively in the hands of the US throughout this period. In 1947, with Nicaragua's signature of the Rio Treaty of Mutual Defence, the Nicaraguan Coast Guard received some additional patrol craft from the United States and a number of other small craft were acquired over the next 30 years. Following the downfall of the Somoza dynasty, the Coast Guard was renamed Sandinista Revolutionary Navy. The new force inherited 16 small craft operated by the former Coast Guard. Two 57-ton patrol vessels formed part of the contract for the supply of defence material signed between the Nicaraguan and French governments in December 1981, one of these, named *El Tayacán*, being seriously damaged by a mine in February 1984. Over the past five years a number of small craft have been acquired from the Soviet Union, Cuba and North Korea.

***Patrol vessel of the Sandinista Revolutionary Navy* (Jane's Defence Weekly)**

The personnel strength of the Nicaraguan Navy has increased about five-fold since the revolution and currently numbers approximately 1000 all ranks, manning two 35-ton North Korean "Sin Hung" class motor-torpedo boats, two 57-ton French-built patrol craft (of which only one is believed to be operational), three 50-ton Soviet "Zhuk" and four 35-ton Israeli "Dabur" class patrol boats and ten other patrol craft of 25 to 100 tons, two 90-ton Soviet "Yevgenya" and four 26-ton "K8" class inshore minesweepers, a 40-foot utility craft and an LCM.

There are naval bases at Corinto and Puerto Cabezas.

Training is carried out at the central complex of training establishments of the Sandinista Revolutionary Armed Forces, some specialist training assistance being also received from Cuba.

Air Force

Manpower: 2000 (including air defence)

Major units: 1 ground attack squadron
1 transport squadron
2 helicopter squadrons

Counter-insurgency aircraft: Cessna 337

Transports: Douglas C-47
CASA 212
IAI Arava
An-2 and An-26
Dassault-Breguet Falcon 20

Communications: Cessna 180

Helicopters: Hughes OH-6A
Mil Mi-2, Mi-8 and Mi-24
Aérospatiale SA.316 Alouette III

Training/light-strike aircraft: Lockheed AT-33A
Aero L-39Z
SIAI Marchetti SF.260W

Ground forces: 1 air defence artillery battalion

Air defence weapons: ZU-23 23 mm, M-1939 37 mm and KS-19 100 mm guns

Missiles: SA-7 SAMs

The *Fuerza Aérea de la Guardia Nacional* was formed in 1938 but little progress was made until the receipt of material and training assistance from the United States commenced in 1942. From 1942 onwards small quantities of trainers and light transports were acquired and by 1945 a total of 20 aircraft were on strength. In 1952 a US aviation mission arrived in Nicaragua and subsequently additional quantities of trainers and transports were received, followed by P-38, P-47 and P-51 fighters. For some years the Nicaraguan Air Force was the strongest in Central America, although it was shortly to cede this position to Honduras. Numbers of aircraft fell victim to rebel ground fire during the civil war which finally toppled the Somozas and others were flown into exile by their pilots. Among aircraft known to have survived the civil war were four Lockheed AT-33As, two North American T-28s, two CASA 212s, a single IAI Arava, three C-47s, four Cessna 337s, seven Cessna 180s, three Cessna U-17Bs, four Hughes OH-6As, and two Sikorsky CH-34As.

The supply of two SA.316 Alouette III helicopters formed part of the French arms deal of 1981 and according to repeated reports emanating from official US sources at least a dozen MiG-23s were to be transferred from Cuba during the same year. Neither these latter aircraft nor the six MiG-21s which were supposed to have been delivered in 1985 have so far materialised although Nicaraguan pilots have undergone training on these types in Bulgaria and Cuba. Material more suitable to Nicaragua's immediate requirements and which has been received from countries of the Eastern Bloc includes numbers of Mil Mi-2, Mi-8 and Mi-24 helicopters, An-2 and An-26 transports and Aero L-39Z trainer/light-strike aircraft. Some SIAI Marchetti SF.260W trainer/light-strike aircraft and a single Dassault-Breguet Falcon 200 transport aircraft have also been received from Libya.

The 2000-man Sandinista Revolutionary Air

Nicaraguan troops with Mi-8 helicopter **(Jane's Defence Weekly)**

Force currently operates a total of approximately 70 aircraft in a single counter-insurgency squadron equipped with three AT-33As and four Cessna 337s, a transport squadron with three C-47s, two An-26s and six An-2s, two CASA 212s and an Arava, a helicopter attack squadron with eight Mi-24s, a general purpose helicopter squadron with about a dozen Mi-8s, six Mi-2s, two Alouette IIIs and two Hughes 500s and a training/light strike squadron with six examples apiece of the SF.260W and the L39Z. The sole Falcon 20 serves as a VIP transport and the surviving Cessna 180s perform various subsidiary duties. The continuing serviceability of so many of the US types is surprising.

A major new military air base is under construction at Punta Huete near Managua and existing facilities at Bluefields, Montelimar, Puerto Cabezas and Puerto Sandino are being upgraded.

Following the Soviet and Cuban models the Air Force is also primarily responsible for air

***Mi-25 helicopter gunship of the Sandinista Revolutionary Air Force* (US Dept. of Defense)**

defence, its single anti-aircraft artillery battalion and several independent batteries operating 30 ZU-23 23 mm, 36 M-1939 37 mm and 18 KS-19 AA guns, plus 30 SA-7 SAM systems. Some 40 mm L/60 Bofors guns, inherited from the *Guardia Nacional*, are reported to be unserviceable.

Personnel receive their basic training in the central school system of the Sandinista Revolutionary Armed Forces, supplemented by both basic and advanced training in Cuba or Eastern Europe in the case of aircrew and specialists.

Paramilitary forces

Manpower:	5000 Frontier Guard 2000 Ministry of the Interior troops
Units:	6 Frontier Guard battalions

President Santos Zelaya made the first attempts at establishing the Nicaraguan police on a formally organised, professional footing. In 1925, the United States persuaded the Nicaraguan government to establish a National Constabulary to combine the functions of the Army, Navy and Police and ultimately to supersede these forces. Internal instability delayed the development of this force and in 1928 it was, in its turn, supplanted by the *Guardia Nacional*. Under the Somoza regime the National Guard combined defence and internal security functions and the constitution permitted the existence of no separate military or police force. The police element of the *Guardia Nacional* was always predominant and although subject to the overall command of the *Guardia* was responsible to the Ministry of the Interior rather than to the Ministry of War and Marine and wore distinctive uniforms to those of the military units.

Following the downfall of Somoza the *Guardia Nacional* was disbanded and nothing is known of the size or structure of the Sandinista Revolutionary Police Force which replaced it in its main internal security functions. Following Soviet and Cuban practice, the Nicaraguan Ministry of the Interior maintains its own paramilitary forces, the 2000-strong *Tropas Pablo Ubeda*, of which likewise no details are known. There are also six Frontier Guard battalions, of which only the *Cristóbal Vanegas* Battalion has been identified. This 5000-strong force is currently under the control of the Army but would be subordinate to the Ministry of the Interior in peacetime conditions. Although sometimes referred to as paramilitary forces, the 100,000-strong Sandinista People's Militias are part of the armed forces structure and are subordinate to the Ministry of Defence.

Sources of defence material and current requirements

During the Somoza regime, the United States was the principal but by no means the sole source of Nicaraguan defence material. Thus second-hand US-built armoured vehicles were purchased from Israel and US-built fighter aircraft were acquired, also second-hand, from Sweden. With the withdrawal of US military assistance in 1976, Nicaragua turned to Israel and Spain as its main suppliers. Since the fall of the Somozas and the establishment of the Sandinista revolutionary government Nicaragua has turned to France, Cuba, the Soviet Union, Czechoslovakia, East Germany and North Korea for military supplies. In the present situation of cold war between Nicaragua and the United States the Eastern Bloc states have become almost the exclusive suppliers of military equipment to the Nicaraguan government, a situation which seems likely to continue.

Summary and prospects

Despite the efforts of the United States government to brand it as Communist, the Nicaraguan Sandinista revolutionary government was originally nothing of the kind, even incorporating two Roman Catholic priests as Ministers of Foreign Affairs and Culture, respectively. US hostility, combined with the active support of the Reagan administration for right-wing exile forces, has however diminished the influence of the more moderate members of the revolutionary government, with a corresponding increase in the influence of its hard-line left-wing members. Increasing dependency on the Eastern Bloc for essential supplies and defence equipment cannot but increase such influence.

The Sandinista Revolutionary Armed Forces are incontrovertibly the most powerful in Central America, being more than six times more numerous than the *Guardia Nacional* was at its peak strength and the range and type of ground forces equipment at their disposal being in excess of the immediate requirements of the counter-insurgency type war of attrition which the US government, through its surrogates, has inflicted upon them. It can however be argued that this equipment forms a necessary deterrent to any temptations to overt military action against it by its universally hostile neighbours. In this respect, the concentration of most of the armoured forces and artillery of the Nicaraguan Army in the vicinity of the capital and away from the frontiers is notable. It is significant that the Soviet Union has avoided the ultimate provocation of the United States inherent in the supply of modern combat aircraft to Nicaragua, concentrating instead on the provision of such eminently more suitable material, in the context of counter-insurgency operations, as helicopters. The Nicaraguan Air Force thus remains purely a tactical support force, with no real air-to-air combat capability, being totally outclassed in this respect by the Air Forces of Honduras and El Salvador. The Nicaraguan Navy likewise remains an insignificant force, consistent in size and capabilities with the other naval forces of the region.

The Sandinista armed forces appear to be winning the guerrilla war against the US-supported "Contras" and having once done so the Nicaraguan revolutionary government will be too fully occupied in rebuilding a country ravaged by over a decade of war to engage in any foreign military adventures even should it be so inclined. Being almost absolutely dependent on the Soviet Union and the Eastern Bloc for arms supply and logistic support, both of which can be easily interdicted by the US, the repeated allegations of aggressive intentions towards its neighbours fail to convince.

PANAMA

(República de Panamá)

Area: 29,208 sq miles (75,650 sq km)
Population: 2,147,000 (1986)
Total armed forces: 4500
Reserves: 1500
Available manpower: 175,000
Paramilitary forces: 5000
GNP: $4,677 million (1979)
Defence expenditure: $100 million (1985)

Introduction

The Republic of Panama is bordered on the north by the Caribbean, on the west by Costa Rica, on the south by the Pacific and on the east by Colombia. The country is roughly bisected by the canal of the same name which connects the Atlantic and Pacific oceans. Over 70% of the population are of mixed European, Negro and Amerindian blood, 14% are more or less pure Negro, 9% European and of the remainder less than 3% are pure Amerindians. Of the pure Negro element in the population, the overwhelming majority are of British West Indian origins. There are small Chinese and East Indian minorities. Approximately 40% of the total population live in the vicinity of the two major cities of Panama and Colón and the majority of the remainder occupy the coastal strip between the mountains and the Pacific coast, the Caribbean coastal region being extremely sparsely inhabited.

The canal dominates the economy of the country. The major exports are tropical products, mainly bananas, sugar and coffee and refined petroleum. The major imports are manufactured goods of all kinds, raw petroleum and foodstuffs. Panama has also become an important centre for offshore banking operations.

Panama was first explored by the Spaniards in 1502. In the immediate post-independence period it was part of Colombia and its history until 1903 is that of the latter republic. Preliminary studies for the construction of an inter-oceanic canal were carried out in 1881 and the construction of such a canal was commenced by a French company the following year. A combination of factors caused the bankruptcy of this company in 1893 and the Colombian government authorised the sale of its remaining assets to United States interests. In 1903, these prompted the small Panamanian successionist movement to declare independence from Colombia, the success of the insurrection being ensured by active US official support. The new Panamanian government granted the United States perpetual sovereignty over a zone extending five miles on either side of the route of the proposed canal, the construction of which was immediately commenced, the first ship passing through the completed canal on 15 August 1914.

Although internal disturbances prompted direct US intervention in 1904, 1917 and 1918, Panama was subsequently spared the turbulence which characterised the remainder of the region throughout most of the 20th century and ther republic developed as a virtual dependency of the United States. Nevertheless, a growing aspiration towards full sovereignty over the Canal Zone began to develop. Colonel José Antonia "Chichi" Remón, the commander of the National Police and effective ruler of Panama from 1947 until his assassination in 1953, pursued progressively radical policies although these were effectively reversed by his successors. A small-scale Cuban invasion was easily defeated in 1959 and outbreaks of rural unrest during the early 1960s were also suppressed with relative ease. In 1964 however there was major rioting against continued US presence in the Canal Zone.

By 1969 Colonel Omar Torrijos had emerged as effective dictator, ruling the country through a succession of civilian puppet administrations. On

1 October 1979 a treaty was signed between Panama and the United States whereby the Canal Zone would be handed over to Panama, by stages, between December 1979 and December 1999. Following the death of Torrijos in an aircraft accident in 1981, no comparable strongman emerged although the endorsement of the military remained a prerequisite for the survival of any government. During the latter part of 1987 there was growing public opposition to this situation, manifested in strikes and rioting demanding the resignation of Manuel Noriega, the commander of the Defence Forces.

Panama is a unitary republic of nine provinces. Executive power is in the hands of the President who selects his own cabinet. There is a two-tier Legislative Assembly which cannot be strictly classified as bi-cameral.

Relations between the Panamanian and United States governments are conditioned by the impending transfer of sovereignty over the Canal Zone. Nevertheless, Panama has demonstrated considerable independence in its foreign policy, having been one of the most vocal supporters of Argentina in the Anglo-Argentine War of 1982 and has also joined with Mexico, Colombia and Venezuela in the Contardora Group which is strongly critical of United States policies in Central America.

Structure of the armed forces

The President of the republic is commander-in-chief of the Defence Forces, to whom the commanders of the individual land, sea and air elements are directly responsible. The country is divided into 10 military zones, corresponding to the nine provinces and an additional zone covering the capital city. Recruitment is entirely voluntary although legal provisions exist for the introduction of universal compulsory military service. Defence expenditure has trebled since the ratification of the Canal Treaty.

Army

Manpower: 3500

Major units: Presidential Guard
7 light infantry companies
1 cavalry squadron

AFVs: Cadillac-Gage V-150 and V-300 APCs and armoured cars

A small Army was formed on independence but was soon disbanded after an abortive attempt at a military coup. The Army was replaced by the

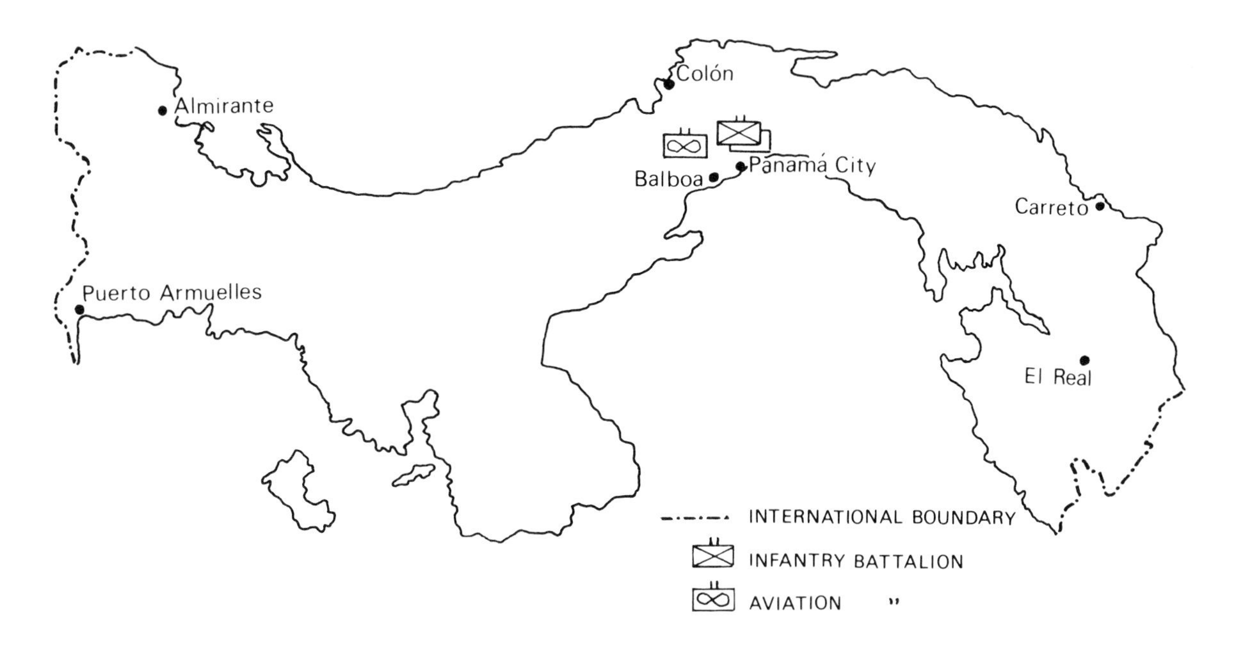

National Police which began to develop a subsidiary military element during the early 1950s. After changing its name to the National Guard in 1953 the importance of the military element increased and when in 1984 its defence and internal security functions were split the military elements of the Guard became the ground element of the Panamanian Defence Forces.

Currently the ground defence element of the Panamanian Defence Forces numbers approximately 3500 officers and men but its strength may be expected to grow considerably during the next ten years. Its major units are the battalion-sized Presidential Guard, a cavalry squadron and seven overstrength fusilier companies, of which the airmobile 1st *Tigre* Company is stationed at Panama Viejo. The 2nd *Pumas* Company is air-transportable and is based at Tocumén airport, Panama City, together with the 7th *Macho de Monte* Company, which is a ranger unit. The 4th *Urraca* Company is also stationed at Panama City, the 3rd *Diablo Rojo* Company being located in Chiriqui province, the 5th *Victoriano Lorenzo* Company at Fort Amador in the Canal Zone and the 6th *Expedicionaria* Company at Rio Hato.

These are equipped with US M16A1 5.56 mm, Belgian FN FAL 7.62 mm rifles and Israeli Uzi 9 mm sub-machine guns, support weapons being the FN MAG 7.62 mm, the US M1919A4 0.30 calibre and the M2HB 0.50 calibre machine guns, together with US M20 3.5-inch RCLs and both US M2 and Israeli Soltam 60 mm mortars. The only heavy equipment in service consists of four Cadillac-Gage V-150 armoured cars, plus 12 APC variants of the same vehicle and 12 V-300 fire support vehicles, mounting 90 mm guns. An order for 60 Argentine TAM tanks and APCs, which was announced in 1984, has so far failed to materialise as has the formation of any unit or units capable of operating such material. There is no known artillery equipment nor are there any air defence weapons.

The Orientation School, established in 1954 with the assistance of a Venezuelan military mission, trains recruits who receive a basic training course of three months duration. A Police Academy for officers and an NCO School were both established in the early 1960s, the latter now having become the Panama Defence Forces Academy but most officers continue to receive the bulk of their training abroad, principally in the United States. Many officers have also followed post-graduate courses in the military schools of other Latin American countries including Chile, Mexico, El Salvador and Venezuela.

Navy

Manpower: 500 all ranks

Major units: 2 patrol vessels
7 small patrol craft
3 landing ships
1 logistic support vessel

A small Navy was established on independence and continued in existence for some time after the abolition of the Army, finally disappearing in the early 1920s. A coast guard was formed as an adjunct of the National Police during the Second World War but this continued to be a very modest force even after the National Police became the National Guard. The Coast Guard element of the National Guard was renamed Panamanian Naval Force in 1984. Currently it consists of the two 100-ton Vosper patrol craft *Ligia Elena* and *Panquiaco*, the 35-ton *Comandante Torrijos*, *Presidente Poras*, *Ayanasi* and *Zarti*, the 10-ton *Marte* and *Jupiter* and the unnamed *GNT 8*. There are also a 600-ton logistic support vessel, the former US LSM *Tiburon*, two "Batral" class landing ships, three LCMs and a former shrimp boat which is used as a troop transport. The Panamanian Naval Force operates on both the Caribbean and Pacific coasts, using US naval facilities in the Canal Zone for maintenance and repair.

Air Force

Manpower: 500

Light strike aircraft: Cessna A-37B

Transports: Pilatus-Britten-Norman Islander BN.2A,
DHC-6, DHC-3, Short Skyvan,
Piper Navajo, Cheyenne and Cherokee,
CASA C-212 Aviocar

Light aircraft: Cessna U-17B, 172 and U206

Helicopters: Bell UH-1 and Fairchild-Hiller FH-1100

A small air service was established as part of the National Police in 1933 but was disbanded in 1945. A second attempt to establish an air arm was made during the early 1960s and in 1969 this force became known as the Panamanian Air Force remaining a part of the National Guard. Although still small, the Air Force has expanded to a greater degree than the other elements of the Panamanian Defence Forces.

Currently, the Panamanian Air Force is primarily a transport and helicopter force operating a total of some 50 aircraft, all of which are based either at Tocumén International Airport or Albrook Air Force Base, Panama City. Additional airstrips are at Boca del Toro, David, Santiago, Chitre and La Palma, none of which are normally manned on a permanent basis. A number of Cessna A-37B light strike aircraft were obtained from the United States in 1983/84 as the first combat equipment of the Air Force which now consists of a single tactical squadron with about ten A-37Bs, a transport squadron with three CASA C-212s, two DHC-6s, a single Pilatus-Britten-Norman Islander, a Short Skyvan and two DHC-3s, a VIP transport flight with two Boeing 727s, a Dassault-Breguet Falcon 20 and a single Aérospatiale AS.332L Super Puma helicopter, plus a helicopter squadron with three Fairchild-Hiller FH-1100s and 21 Bell UH-1A, H and Ns, most of which are assigned to the 1st *Tigre* Airmobile Company of the Ground Defence Force. Most of the transport aircraft also carry out coastal patrol functions.

Agreements existed until recently whereby all training was carried out by the Colombian and Venezuelan Air Forces on behalf of the Panamanian government but the Panamanian Air Force now carries out its own primary training with two Cessna U-17Bs, three 172s and single 402, single examples of the Piper Cherokee, Navajo and Cheyenne doubling in the liaison/training roles. Both air ground crew continue to receive their advanced training abroad.

Paramilitary forces

Manpower: 5000

The police elements of the former National Guard have become the National Police and are distributed throughout the ten military zones. There are in addition a number of specialised elements including the Bay Guard (a harbour police unit), the Tocumén Airport Guard, the Public Order Company (a rapid intervention police unit) and the National Department of Investigation, known colloquially as the "Secret Police" and which is believed to number approximately 1500 in addition to the uniformed members of the force. The police are organised on paramilitary lines and are equipped with sidearms and obsolescent small arms of mainly US origins, including the M1 Garand rifle in 0.30-inch and the M1928A1 sub-machine gun in 0.45-inch calibres. Training facilities are shared with the Defence Forces.

Sources of defence material and current requirements

The equipment of the Ground Defence Force is largely of United States origins although in recent years quantities of Belgian and Israeli material have also been obtained. The major units of the Navy and some of the transport aircraft used by the Air Force are of British, Canadian and Spanish origins. No defence equipment is produced locally. Fairly substantial acquisitions of equipment for the land, sea and air elements of the Panama Defence Forces may be expected during the next ten years.

Summary and prospects

The Canal Treaty with the United States represents the realisation of the country's main foreign policy objective. There are no significant frontier disputes and outbreaks of the internal armed subversion have been effectively dealt with by the security forces. Despite the separation of the military and internal security functions of the former National Guard, the Panama Defence Forces are still primarily equipped only on a paramilitary level. As the date for the assumption of full responsibility for the defence of the Panama Canal approaches they seem certain both to expand and to acquire quantities of heavier equipment. This will most probably include mortars, modern anti-armour weapons, additional armoured fighting vehicles, field artillery pieces and air defence weapons, including some form of surface-to-air missile systems. The Navy may be expected to acquire additional patrol craft and possibly some fast attack craft and mine warfare vessels. The Air Force, which has already taken the first steps towards acquiring some operational potential, may also be expected to acquire at least a token force of interceptors as well as some anti-submarine warfare aircraft and sufficient training aircraft to enable it to undertake this function without continuing to rely on foreign governments to train its air crew.

The main challenge currently facing Panama is that of demonstrating the ability to administer, operate and defend the canal before these become its sole responsibility in December 1999. The strategic situation and military importance of the Panama Canal confer on the Panamanians the dubious distinction of being the only worthwhile target for thermonuclear weapons in Central America. This situation will not change with the transfer of sovereignty of the Canal Zone and it is extremely doubtful that Panama will be able to develop an adequate independent defence capability once the last United States troops leave the country. Some assistance in this respect may be forthcoming from Venezuela, with which Panama has very close and cordial relations, but there is an attendant risk that in accepting it Panama may effectively exchange the dependent status which it has suffered relative to the United States, throughout its entire independent existence, for a similar status relative to the nearest regional military power.

PARAGUAY

(República del Paraguay)

Area: 157,039 sq miles (406,630 sq km)
Population: 3,487,000
Total armed forces: 26,200
Reserves: 160,000
Available manpower: 300,000
Paramilitary forces: 8000
GNP: $5,808 million (1985)
Defence expenditure: $78,138,000 (1986)

Introduction

Paraguay is the third smallest of the ten originally independent republics of South America and is bordered by Argentina to the south and south-east, by Brazil to the east and by Bolivia to the north-west and north. The population is homogeneous and largely rural, 95% being a mixture of European and Guaraní Indian, only about 3% being pure white and less than 1.5% pure and largely unassimilated Amerindian. There is also a small Japanese minority. Unlike other countries with a comparable racial mix, the pure white minority does not form a separate oligarchy, the population being remarkable for its social cohesion. The Guaraní Indian language has coequal official status with Spanish and is the preferred medium of communication of the majority of the population, most of whom are nevertheless to a greater or lesser extent bilingual.

Having no significant deposits of minerals, although oil is believed to exist in the Chaco, which separates it from Bolivia, the economy is totally based on agricultural production, the principal exports being meat and meat products, hides, leather, tobacco, cotton and coffee. Although predominantly agricultural, Paraguay is not self-sufficient in food production, food figuring among imports, together with fuels, chemicals, finished textiles and manufactured products. Industry is largely related to the processing of agricultural products and is underdeveloped. Paraguay is however a large-scale exporter of hydro-electric power, the hydro-electric complexes on the Upper Paraná being among the largest in the world.

Paraguay was first visited by Europeans in 1524 and the first steps towards colonisation were made in 1537. Largely neglected by Spain for most of the colonial period, Paraguay's War of Independence was fought against Argentina rather than Spain, independence being declared after the Paraguayans defeated an Argentine army, sent in 1811 to compel the country to submit to the authority of the junta of Buenos Aires. After a brief experiment with a type of republicanism based on that of ancient Rome, Paraguay passed into the hands of Gaspar Rodriguez de Francia, an eccentric despot who ruled the country as his personal estate, totally cut off from the rest of the world, until his death in 1840. After four years of semi-anarchy, Carlos Antonio López was elected as constitutional President in 1844. Re-elected for a ten-year term in 1854, López ruled relatively benevolently until his death in 1862. Under López, Paraguay became one of the foremost nations in Latin America, external trade flourished, the first railway and telegraph system in South America being inaugurated in 1852.

After the death of López, his son, Francisco Solano, was elected to succeed him as President. The younger López unfortunately embarked on a suicidal, five-year long conflict against the Triple Alliance of Argentina, Brazil and Uruguay in an ill-starred attempt to consolidate Paraguay's position as the premier power in South America. Lasting from 1865 to 1870, during which time the population fell from 525,000 to 221,000, of whom only 28,000 were males, the Triple Alliance War reduced Paraguay to a state of total national prostration. Large tracts of territory in the north-east and south-west were also ceded to the victorious allies under the terms of two separately negotiated peace treaties.

In an effort to rebuilt the shattered economy, successive governments sold off large tracts of land in the largely unexplored and commercially unexploited Chaco to foreign investors. Friction with Bolivia over the possession of this region, the frontier between the two countries having never been properly defined, let to sporadic hostilities from 1927 onwards, culminating in the Chaco War of 1932-35. Paraguay emerged victorious from the Chaco War, but at the cost of 36,000 dead and economic ruin.

In the wake of the Chaco War, political instability culminated in the civil war of 1947. Continuing instability ended with a *coup d'etat* by the Army in 1954 which placed General Alfredo Stroessner in power as President. With his mandate confirmed by all subsequent elections General Stroessner has ruled Paraguay ever since. Although condemned for human rights violations, the Stroessner regime has brought Paraguay a measure of stability unknown since the era of the elder López. This has encouraged economic development, the Paraguayan currency being one of the most stable in the Americas and the country having until recently largely escaped the scourge of inflation which has bedevilled most of Latin America during the past decade.

Paraguay is a unitary, centralised republic of 16 departments. Executive power is vested in the President. There is a bicameral legislature. The departments are supervised by a *Delegado*, who is appointed by the central government.

The Stroessner regime appears to enjoy the tacit support of most of the population although there has been a large-scale flight of its opponents into voluntary exile. Stroessner has had to face only two major challenges to his authority since 1954, both in the late 1950s. Low level left-wing guerrilla activity has been easily controlled by the armed forces.

Since the end of the Triple Alliance War, Paraguayan foreign policy has been aimed at striking an advantageous equilibrium between the influences of its two larger neighbours. Argentina and Brazil. Although the Chaco War was one of the most bitter in history and the territorial distribution achieved by the Buenos Aires Treaty of 1938, which officially ended the war, equally failed to please Bolivian and Paraguayan extremists, relations between the former enemies are relatively cordial and the possibility of further hostilities between the two countries seems remote.

Structure of the armed forces

The President is commander-in-chief of the armed forces. As a professional soldier and a hero of the Chaco War, the memory of which is still vivid in Paraguay, General Stroessner has also retained the office of commander-in-chief of the Army. The Minister of National Defence is not in the direct chain of command and performs functions which are primarily administrative. In the peculiar conditions prevailing under the present regime, the role of the Minister of Defence is even more circumscribed than its constitutional position would indicate. Directly subordinate to the commander-in-chief of the armed forces is the chief of the general staff of the armed forces, who is invariably an Army general, the Army thus having a certain institutionalised primacy over the Navy and Air Force. The General Staff has sections dealing directly with the Army, Navy and Air Force. The commander-in-chief of the three armed forces are directly subordinate and answerable to the General Staff of the armed forces. Each force also has its own general staff.

The country is divided into six Military Regions of which the 1st Region (HQ Asunción) covers the capital, the Central department and the departments of Cordillera and Paraguarí, the 2nd Region (HQ Villarica) covers the departments of Guairá, Caazapá and Itapúa, the 3rd Region (HQ San Juan Bautista) the departments of Misiones and Neembucú, the 4th Region (HQ Concepción) the departments of Concepción, Amambay and San Pedro, the 5th Region (HQ Puerto Presidente Stroessner) the departments of Alto Paraná and Caaguazú and the 6th Region (HQ Mariscal Estigarribia) the departments of Boquerón, Olimpo and Presidente Hayes.

Military service is compulsory for all male citizens, who serve for two years (in practice reduced to 18 months) from the age of 18, spending the next nine years in the reserve, followed

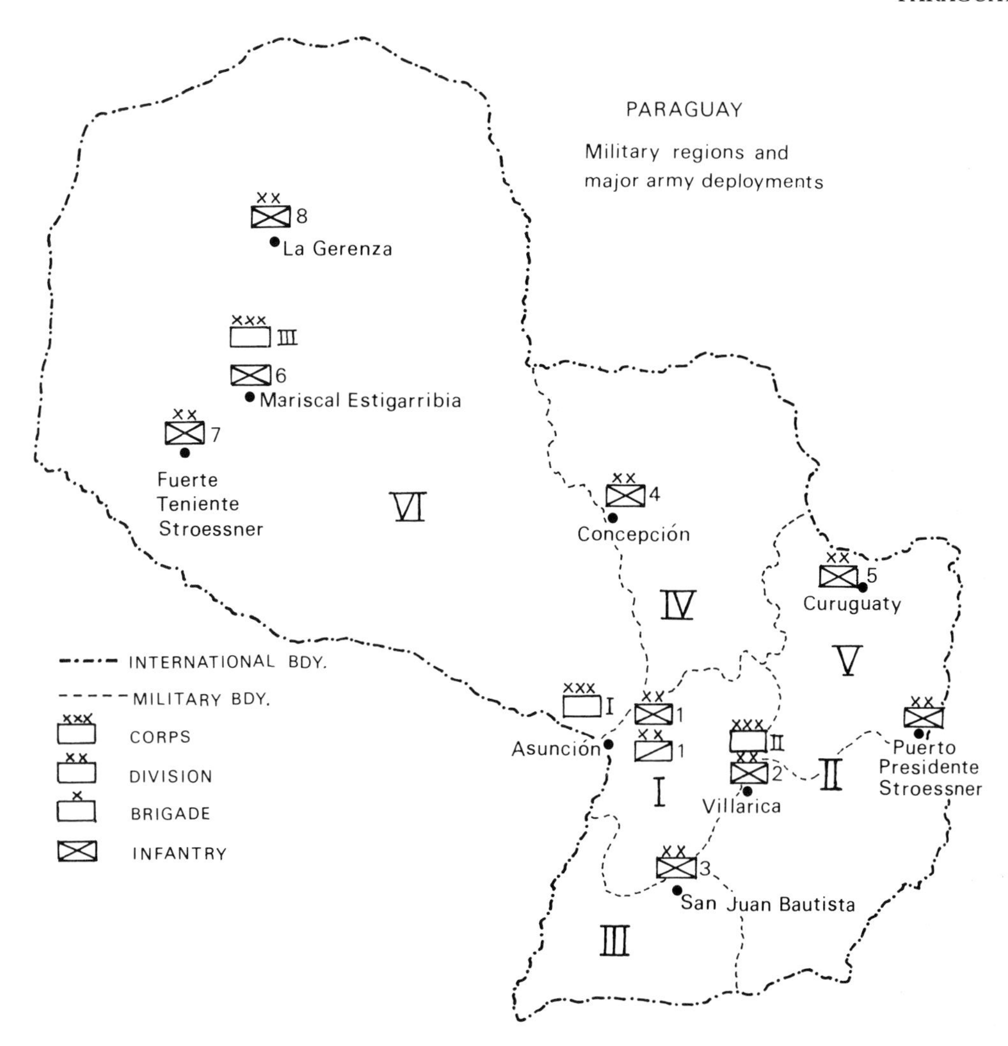

by ten years in the National Guard and then passing to the Territorial Guard until the age of 45. Unlike most Latin American countries, there is a well-organised and effective reserve system although the National and Territorial Guards seem to be largely paper organisations. The obligation for military service is not only rigorously enforced but is considered a patriotic duty, but there are many legal exemptions and the annual conscript intake of approximately 10,000 is lower than the population figures would indicate.

Officers of the Army, Navy and Air Force receive their basic military education at the *Mariscal Francisco Solano López* Military College at Asunción, which provides a four-year tri-service course leading to a commission in the chosen arm. Specialist training continues in the respective services and many officers complete their training abroad. The Navy has a long-standing arrangement with the Argentine Navy whereby midshipmen receive sea training aboard units of the Argentine fleet. The National War College, also a tri-service institution established in 1968, provides advanced level training for officers of the Army, Navy and Air Force. There is also a Reserve Officers School, which provides a compressed course for aspiring reserve officers.

Army

Manpower: 20,600

Formations: 3 army corps comprising 8 infantry divisions and 1 partly mechanised cavalry division

Major units: 1 Presidential Guard regiment
10 infantry regiments
2 frontier battalions
4 cavalry regiments
(2 mechanised and 2 horsed)
1 artillery regiment
5 engineer battalions

AFVs: US M4 Sherman and
Sherman Firefly medium tanks
US M3A1 light tanks
US M8 and Brazilian EE-9
Cascavel armoured cars
US M2 half-track and
Brazilian EE-11 Urutú APCs

Artillery: Bofors 75 mm L/40 Model 1935
field guns
Schneider 75 mm Model
1927 mountain guns
Schneider 105 mm Model
1927 mountain howitzers
Vickers 6″ (152 mm) Mk V
coastal guns

The Paraguayan Army owes its origins as an organised professional force to Carlos Antonio

***Cadet of Paraguay's* Mariscal Francisco Solano López Military College (Author)**

***M3A1 light tanks of the 1st* Valois Rivarola *Cavalry Regiment of the Paraguayan Army on parade at Asunción* (Col R. J. Icks)**

López. Francisco Solano López reorganised and expanded it, making it the second strongest in South America. In the Triple Alliance War the Paraguayans fought until they were almost annihilated and for the rest of the 19th century the Army consisted of only a few small and widely dispersed units for the defence of the frontiers and security and ceremonial duties at the capital. A Military School was set up in 1905 and a German military mission functioned for less than a year before the outbreak of the First World War. As war with Bolivia became more inevitable the armed forces were expanded, reorganised and re-equipped and a French military mission functioned between 1926 and 1930. During the Chaco War the Paraguayans took the initiative from the outset and although less numerous and more poorly equipped than their adversaries maintained it for most of the three-year long conflict. The Paraguayan Army entered a period of virtual stagnation during the 1940s, only token Lend-Lease aid being received from the United States during the Second World War. Limited amounts of new equipment were acquired in the immediate post-war period and Paraguay's signature of the Rio Treaty of 1947 had little immediate impact. Following the seizure of power by General Stroessner several new units were established and quantities of largely obsolescent equipment were received as gifts from Argentina and Brazil. Since the mid-1960s, United States military aid has also increased and more recently some modern equipment has been acquired from Israel.

The Paraguayan Army currently numbers approximately 20,600 all ranks. A new tactical organisation, adopted in 1980, grouped the six existing infantry and one cavalry divisions under three army corps and added two more infantry divisions, bringing the total to eight.

The Ist Army Corps (HQ Asunción) covers the 1st and 3rd Military Regions with the 1st Infantry Division (HQ Asunción) which consists principally of the 14th *Cerro Corá* Infantry Regiment, the 3rd Infantry Division (HQ San Juan Bautista) which has the 8th *Pirebebuy* Infantry Regiment (San Juan Bautista) as its major embodied unit and the 1st Cavalry Division (HQ Ñú Guazú, Asunción) which consists of the 1st *Valois Rivarola*, 2nd *Coronel Toledo*, 3rd *Coronel Mongelós* and 4th *Aca Carayá* Cavalry Regiments, plus an artillery nucleus approximating to a single battery. At corps level there is also the 1st Frontier Battalion at Pilar.

The IInd Army Corps (HQ Villarica) covers the 2nd, 4th and 5th Military Regions with the 2nd Infantry Division (HQ Villarica) which consists essentially of the 27th *General Garay* Infantry Regiment, the 4th Infantry Division (HQ Concepción) which is built around the 5th *General Díaz* Infantry Regiment and the 5th Infantry Division (HQ Curuguaty) which has the 15th *Lomas Valentinas* Infantry Regiment as its major embodied unit. At corps level there are also the 2nd Frontier Battalion at Puerto Presidente Stroessner and two cavalry detachments, based at Encarnación and Pedro Juan Caballero respectively.

The IIIrd Army Corps (HQ Mariscal Estigarribia) covers the 6th Military Region, which approximates to the theatre of operations of the Chaco War, with the 6th Infantry Division (HQ Mariscal Estigarribia) consisting essentially of the 6th *Boquerón* Infantry Regiment, the 7th Infantry Division (HQ Fuerte Teniente Stroessner) which is built around the 10th *Sauce* Infantry Regiment and the 8th Infantry Division (HQ La Gerenza) the principal unit of which is the 4th *Curupayty* Infantry Regiment. This corps also includes the Pilcomayo and Cerrito military detachments, based at Villa Hayes and Benjamín Aceval respectively.

Army troops include the Presidential Escort Regiment which consists of two battalions, a motorised unit and a military police unit at Asunción, the anomalously named *Regimiento Batallón Cuarenta*, which is an infantry unit organised on the same lines as a cavalry regiment, at Pilar, the 16th *Mariscal López* Infantry Regiment and the 1st *General Bruguez* Artillery Regiment (the three constituent groups of which are deployed in support of the army corps and divisions in accordance with operational requirements) both at Paraguarí. In addition, there are the Army Engineering Command (HQ Asunción) with five engineer battalions distributed throughout the country and a signals battalion at Asunción.

The establishment of each infantry division consists of a headquarters, three regiments and a logistic support battalion, combining supply, transport and medical units. In peacetime each division normally contains only one active infantry regiment of one or two battalions, the other two regiments being in reserve. Each cadre division however also includes a special forces unit, a military police company and logistic units.

The principal rifles in service are the FN FAL in 7.62 mm calibre, the SiG 540 in 5.65 mm and the US M1 in 0.30-inch. Various models of the Mauser rifle in 7.65 mm calibre are also still found in the hands of second-line troops. Sub-machine guns include the Danish Madsen Models 46, 50 and 54 and the Israeli Uzi, all in 9 mm. The principal machine guns used by the Paraguayan Army are the Browning M1917 in 0.30-inch and M2HB in 0.50-inch and the Madsen Model 1924 in 7.65 mm. The only anti-armour weapon observed in use is the US M20 75 mm RCL. Mortars in service include the Stokes-Brandt 81 mm and the US M2 and M32 4.2-inch. Armour consists of some nine M4 Sherman and six Sherman Firefly medium tanks, 12 US M3A1 light tanks, 24 EE-9 Cascavel and 12 modified M8 armoured cars, plus ten EE-11 Urutú wheeled and 12 M2 half-track APCs. The most modern artillery pieces in service are 12 Bofors 75 mm L/40 Model 1934 field guns, received second-hand from Argentina. There are also some 20 Schneider Model 1927 75 mm mountain guns, six Schneider Model 1927 105 mm howitzers and a battery of six Vickers Mk V 6-inch mobile coastal guns, the latter obtained third-hand from Brazil and employed as field artillery.

Aspiring officers pursue the basic four-year course of the Marshal Francisco Solano López Military College at Asunción. Specialist training follows graduation and intermediate grade officers must successfully attend courses at the National War College to qualify for staff appointments or promotion to higher rank. The Army maintains an NCO School, an Armoured Forces School, a School of Military Engineering, a Communications School, a School for Armaments Mechanics, a Motor Drivers' School, an Army Medical School, a Veterinary School and a School of Physical Education. Conscripts, who account for approximately 40% of the total manpower strength, receive non-specialist military training in the units to which they are assigned.

Navy

Manpower:	3500 (including Marines, Naval aviation and Coast Guard)
Major units:	3 river gunboats 3 minesweepers 1 helicopter tender

River gunboats Paraguay *and* Humaitá *at Asunción* (Author)

	1 patrol vessel 6 patrol craft
Marines:	1 commando battalion and 3 security detachments
Aircraft:	North American AT-6 Cessna 150M, U206 and 210 Douglas C-47 Bell 47G and Helibras HB.350B helicopters

Although Paraguay is totally landlocked, it is bisected by the river from which it derives its name and most of its frontiers are also delimited by navigable rivers. The country therefore established a navy upon achieving its independence. The Paraguayan fleet was annihilated during the Triple Alliance War and was not re-established until 1887, remaining a small force of armed merchant vessels until 1930 when two armoured gunboats were completed in Italy as part of the preparations for the forthcoming conflict with Bolivia. As Bolivia possessed no navy, no naval actions, as such, took place during the Chaco War. The Navy however played an important subsidiary role, forming a vital link in the tortuous logistic system in support of the field army in which the navigable rivers formed the first phase, garrisoning the upper Paraguay river with its Marines and operating an impressive industrial system at its arsenal at Asunción. The Second World War had little impact on the Paraguayan Navy although as a result of the Mutual Defence Agreement with the United States some patrol launches were received. Having backed the losing side in the 1947 civil war, the Navy continued to stagnate during the 1950s. Nevertheless, some material was acquired from both the United States and particularly Argentina from the mid-1960s onwards.

The personnel strength of the Paraguayan Navy is approximately 3500, including Coast Guard, Marines and Naval aviation.

The veteran 745-ton gunboats *Paraguay* and *Humaitá*, both refitted in the mid-1970s, remain the major units of the river fleet, together with the new 300-ton Brazilian-built "Roraíma" class gunboat *Itaipú*, the 450-ton ex-Argentine minesweepers *Nanawa*, *Capitan Meza* and *Teniente Fariña*, the 180-ton armed tug *Capitán Cabral*, built in 1907, the 1000-ton so-called "helicopter carrier" *Boquerón*, which is actually a converted LSM acquired second-hand from Argentina and six 10-ton patrol craft. There are also the 150-ton river transport *Presidente Stroessner*, the 700-ton sea-going transport *Guaraní*, which is operated under commercial charter between Asuncion and north-western Europe, a surveying launch, a buoy tender, two LCUs used as ferries and two small tugs.

The *Prefectura de Puertos*, which is an integral part of the Navy, functions as a harbour police force and coast guard, regulating the activities of the Merchant Marine and maintaining navigational aids. The 800-man *Cuerpo de Defensa Fluvial* is a Marine corps consisting of the *Boquerón* Commando Battalion and three security companies and is mostly deployed on the Upper Paraguay, its personnel being divided between Bahía Negra and Olimpo, with a small nucleus at Asunción and detachments at Encarnación and Puerto Presidente Stroessner.

The *Aviación Naval* deploys four armed T-6G Texan trainers in a nominal figher squadron, a single C-47, three Cessna U206s and a single 210 in the transport and communications role and four Cessna 150Ms as primary trainers, plus four Bell 47 and two Helibras HB.350B Esquilo helicopters. Fixed-wing aircraft are based at Chaco-Í, the helicopters being stationed at Puerto Sajonia when not embarked aboard the helicopter tender *Boquerón* which normally carries two Bell 47s.

The main naval base is at Puerto Sajonia, Asunción, with a minor base for small craft at Chaco-Í, on the other side of the Paraguay river. There are also bases at Bahía Negra, on the Upper Paraguay and at Encarnación and Puerto Presidente Stroessner on the Paraná.

Approximately 25% of the Navy's enlisted personnel are conscripts, these receiving their basic training at the *Escuela de Especialidades de la Armada* at Puerto Sajonia. A long-standing project for the establishment of a Naval Academy remains unfulfilled, naval officers continuing to receive their preliminary training at the Military College, pursuing the same basic four-year course as Army and Air Force officers and receiving their subsequent specialised training as midshipmen in Argentine naval training establishments and aboard units of the Argentine fleet.

Air Force

Manpower:	2100 (including paratroops)
Major units:	2 fighter/light strike squadrons 1 transport squadron
Fighter/light strike aircraft:	EMBRAER EMB-326 Xavante North American AT-6
Transports:	Convair CV-240 Douglas C-47 and DC-6 DHC-3 and DHC-6 CASA C-212
Helicopters:	Bell 47G Hiller UH-12
Liaison aircraft:	Cessna 185, 337 and 421
Trainers:	Aerotec Uirapurú Neiva Universal Cessna T-41 Fokker S.11
Ground troops:	1 paratroop regiment 3 AA batteries

A flying school was formed in 1924, several aircraft having been operated in a desultory fashion by the Army from 1912 onwards. The air arm expanded somewhat over the next seven years but remained a small force when hostilities with Bolivia erupted in 1932. Although the Paraguayan air arm was inferior both in numbers and quality of equipment to that of Bolivia and sensibly largely avoided air-to-air combat it performed valuable logistic and tactical support functions during the Chaco War. During the three years which elapsed between the Armistice which effectively ended the Chaco War and the Peace Treaty of 1938, which formalised the cessation of hostilities, numbers of additional aircraft were acquired but by the time of the signature of the Mutual Defence agreement with the United States in 1940 the Paraguayan military air arm had been reduced to little more than a token force. US Lend-Lease aid during the Second World War was concentrated largely on the air arm, over 40 training and transport aircraft being transferred. An independent Air Force was established in 1946, incorporating the existing personnel and material of the *Aviación Militar*, although the Navy retained its own separate air service. With the signature of the Rio Treaty of 1947 some additional military assistance was received from the United States, mainly in the form of transport aircraft. At about this time, Argentina and Brazil began to compete for the ascendancy of influence in Paraguay by the transfer of surplus military equipment, the

C-47 transport aircraft of the Paraguayan Air Force

***Private of the* Silvio Pettirossi *Paratroop Regiment of the Paraguayan Air Force* (Author)**

Paraguayan Air Force thereby more than doubling its effective strength, although it continued to lack first-line combat types.

The Paraguayan Air Force currently numbers approximately 2100 all ranks (including paratroops and air defence units) manning a total of approximately 80 aircraft and is organised into a tactical group and a transport squadron.

The Tactical Group, based at Presidente Stroessner International Airport, Asunción, comprises one squadron equipped with nine EMBRAER EMB.326 Xavantes and a second squadron with 12 North American AT-6s. The Transport Squadron, based at Ñú-Guazú, outside Asunción, is equipped with four CASA 212s and single examples of the DHC-3 and DHC-6, the latter aircraft being used as a VIP transport, a single Convair PBY-5A amphibian being out of service. A military airline, the *Transporte Aéreo Militar*, with its headquarters at Asunción, is equipped with 14 Douglas C-47s, two DC-6s and a single Convair C-240. There are also ten Bell 47G and two Hiller UH-12 helicopters and single examples of the Cessna 185, 337 and 421 liaison aircraft, not assigned to any of the above units and used primarily for co-operation with the Army.

The *Escuela de Aeronáutica Militar* at Ñú-Guazú is equipped with five Neiva Universals, eight Aerotec Uirapurús, eight Fokker S.11s and five Cessna T-41s.

Stroessner International Airport and Nu-Guazu are the only bases with permanently assigned flying units. In addition however there are airstrips at Yacy-Retá, Puerto Presidente Stroessner, Capitán Meza, Nueva Asunción, Teniente Prats Gil, Mariscal Estigarribia, Concepción, Pilar, San Ignacio, Villarica and San Pedro, some of which are manned by permanent Air Force detachments.

The paratroops, numbering about 500, are organised in the single active battalion of the *Regimiento de Paracaidistas Silvio Pettirossi* based at Luque, outside Asunción, with a Paratroop School at Ñú-Guazú which trains approximately 200 paratroops annually. The Air Force is also responsible for anti-aircraft defence deploying ten US M1A1 40 mm and 20 vintage single and twin-mounted 20 mm Oerlikon AA guns in three batteries.

Aspiring officers pursue the four-year course of the *Escuela Militar* before commissioning and transfer to the main Air Force base at Ñú-Guazú for specialist training. All officers return to the *Escuela Superior de Guerra* for post-graduate training at least twice during their service careers. The Air Force maintains its own system of schools for NCOs and enlisted personnel.

Paramilitary forces

Manpower: 8000 (National Police)

During the late 19th century the police force was divided into urban and rural elements, this arrangement surviving, with little material change, until the present day.

The National Police is under the jurisdiction of the Ministry of the Interior but is in all respects a paramilitary force and conscripts may be drafted into it to fulfil their obligation for military training. The force numbers approximately 8000 all ranks, of whom slightly more than 55% are deployed at the capital and its immediate environs which constitute the *Departmento Central*. This number includes a battalion-sized unit known as the *Guardia de Seguridad*, which includes a mounted squadron and is used both as a rapid intervention police reserve and for ceremonial functions. There is also a plain-clothes unit of about 100 members, known as the Police of the Presidency and employed as bodyguards to the President and senior members of the government. The police detachment at the capital also includes the Fire Service, which has a secondary riot control function and a plain-clothes criminal investigation department. The police detachments in each of the other 15 departments are administered by a government-appointed *Delegado*, each of whom is in turn responsible to the Minister of the Interior and is assisted, for operational purposes, by a chief of police.

Police officers are either graduates of the five-year course of the Police School at Asunción or are seconded from the armed forces. Police NCOs are also trained at the Police School, enlisted personnel receiving their training "on the job".

The National Police is equipped primarily with sidearms, apart from the guards on public buildings, who usually carry sub-machine guns, but has a range of light infantry weapons, including machine guns, at its disposal.

***Officer and ratings of Paraguay's* Prefectura de Puertos (Author)**

Sources of defence equipment and current requirements

In the past, Paraguay has purchased defence material from a wide variety of sources including Germany, France, Spain, Denmark, Italy, Argentina, Brazil, Chile, Great Britain and the United States. During the Chaco War, such enormous quantities of equipment were captured from Bolivia that further acquisitions of equipment were minimal during the next two decades. The existing material became progressively antiquated however, a situation not helped by the transfer of large quantities of already obsolescent material from Argentina and Brazil from the early 1950s onwards. Despite US military aid amounting to a total value of $14,900,000 received between 1950 and 1977, equipment of US origins, apart from that received as third-hand gifts from Argentina and Brazil, was less visible than in almost any other country of Latin America. Until as late as the mid-1970s, most equipment in service with the Army appeared to date from the Chaco War. This situation has been only partly ameliorated by the adoption of the already obsolescent FN FAL rifle as the standard infantry small arm during the late 1970s and the more recent acquisition of quantities of more modern small arms and infantry support weapons from the United States, Switzerland and Israel. Responding to the fairly significant gifts of equipment received from Argentina and Brazil over the past 30 years, most major recent orders for heavy equipment such as aircraft and naval vessels have gone to these countries, a trend which seems likely to continue. The only exception are four CASA 212 light transports acquired from Spain in the mid-1980s.

Although all three of the armed forces are in fairly urgent need of new material, including armoured vehicles, artillery pieces, modern anti-armour and air defence weapons, including missiles, patrol vessels and combat aircraft, both the poor financial situation of the country and the probability of continuing donations of equipment from its larger neighbours makes the purchase of significant quantities of modern equipment, from any source, rather unlikely in the foreseeable future. The only major purchases of new equipment during the past 25 years constituted the AFVs acquired from Brazil in the mid-1980s and the new river gunboat, *Itaipu*, built in Brazil during the same period.

From colonial times onwards, Paraguay has produced a surprising proportion of its own requirements in the field of armaments, especially in the context of its otherwise underdeveloped industrial base. Thus, during the Triple Alliance War, much of the artillery used by the Paraguayan Army was produced in the country's own cannon foundries. Although the growing complexity of modern weapons caused the country to shop elsewhere for its requirements during the period between the Triple Alliance and Chaco Wars, the Naval Arsenal continued to produce small vessels for the Navy at irregular intervals, several small patrol craft being completed in the period immediately preceding the Chaco War. During the latter conflict, the arsenals were particularly busy, a work force of 22,000 being employed round the clock to provide many of the requirements of the armed forces in the areas of ammunition, grenades, aircraft bombs and motor transport in addition to personal equipment, even producing radio transmitters of original design. Since the Chaco War, the resources of the arsenals have been principally devoted to the maintenance of progressively antiquated equipment. A considerable unexploited potential for expansion remains however and could be turned to good account should the necessity arise.

Summary and prospects

Paraguay has the most uncompromisingly martial history of any country in Latin America, having resisted the Triple Alliance of Argentina, Brazil and Uruguay for almost five years between 1865 and 1870, only succumbing when over half of its total population and almost all of its adult males had been killed. In the Chaco War it also took on a country with three times its manpower and many times its economic resources, defeating it resoundingly in three years of bloody warfare which cost the lives of 8% of its total male population. In both wars, the Paraguayan soldier proved to be a redoubtable opponent, comparable in many respects to the Gurkha. In the Chaco War in particular, the country produced many competent military leaders, some of whose mastery of the art of war reached the level of genius.

While the human material remains the same, the three decades of peace since General Stroessner's assumption of the Presidency have deprived the Paraguayan soldier of today of the practical experience gained by his predecessors during the endemic military rebellions which characterised the period between the 1890s and the 1950s. The Paraguayan armed forces of the 1980s are probably less well equipped, relatively speaking, than those of the 1930s and the current organisation of the Army, in particular, would appear to owe as much to political as to military considerations.

Despite being classified as repressive by foreign observers, the Stroessner regime would appear to have at least the passive support of the majority of Paraguayans, although an unexpected recent threat has come from the radicalisation of the Paraguayan Catholic Church. Currently, Paraguay would appear to be reasonably safe from any threat of potential foreign aggression or internal subversion, the only major long-term political problems being the question of succession when eventually General Stroessner, who was born in 1912 and is in declining health, hands over the reins of power.

PERU

(República de Peru)

Area: 496,093 sq miles (1,284,640 sq km)
Population: 20,342,000 (1986)
Total armed forces: 127,000
Reserves: 300,000
Available manpower: 1,700,000
Paramilitary forces: 52,500
GNP: $16,979 million (1984)
Defence expenditure: $640,605,000 (1985)

Introduction

Peru is the third largest country in South America and is bordered on the west and south-west by the Pacific Ocean, on the north-west by Ecuador, on the north and north-east by Colombia, on the east by Brazil, on the south-east by Bolivia and on the south by Chile. More than 46% of the population is pure Amerindian, 38% mixed Indian and white, 15% of European origins and the remainder is made up of small minorities of Negro and Asian racial origins.

The most important exports are both raw and refined metals, principally copper, lead, silver, zinc and iron. The country is self-sufficient in petroleum production, with a small surplus for export. Imports consist largely of manufactured goods, including machinery, pharmaceuticals, clothing and foodstuffs. Although the majority of the workforce is engaged in agriculture and certain agricultural products, including sugar, cotton and coffee, are important exports, Peru is a nett food importer. Fishing, once of great economic importance, has declined due to overfishing and abnormal marine conditions. Industry is of increasing importance and after a decline during the Morales-Bermúdez military regime of 1975-80, is once more developing.

Independence from Spain was achieved in 1824, with the assistance of an Argentino-Chilean expeditionary force and Bolívar's Colombian army. A period of internal turbulence ensued, culminating in the union of Peru and Bolivia in a confederation which was broken as the direct result of a war with Chile in 1936-39. A brief war ensued between Peru and Bolivia, resulting in the victory of the latter. In 1859 friction with Ecuador led to a Peruvian naval blockade of the Ecuadorian coast and there was a brief naval war with Spain in 1865-66. Frontier tensions with Chile led indirectly to the Pacific War of 1879-83 which resulted in a Peruvian defeat and the loss of provinces of Tarapacá. Tacna and Arica.

From the end of the Pacific War until 1939 Peru was ruled by a succession of oligarchic administrations. A significant event was the establishment of the radical nationalist *Alianza Popular Revolucionaria Americana*, generally known by its initials APRA, during the late 1920s. A frontier incident in 1932 led to a brief conflict with Colombia from which Peru emerged as the loser, national pride being salvaged somewhat by a short but successful war with Ecuador in 1941. A series of civilian presidents held office, frequently with military support, from 1939 until 1948 when an APRA sponsored naval mutiny provoked a reaction by the Army which replaced the incumbent civilian president by General Manuel Odría, a hero of the war with Ecuador, who ruled as dictator until 1956.

In 1962 the armed forces once more seized power, after an inconclusive election, ruling through a three-man junta until the following year when Fernando Belaúnde Terry was elected President. Belaúnde was overthrown by yet another military coup in 1968, bringing in Latin America's first left-wing military government which continued in power until 1980. The military government embarked on a programme of land reform and the nationalisation of foreign business undertakings, developed relations with the Soviet

Union and Cuba and embarked on a massive arms build-up with material purchased both from the Soviet bloc and western countries. With increasing economic problems, the regime took a turn back towards the political right after the accession of General Morales Bermúdez to the Presidency in 1975, elections held in 1980 ironically resulting in the return to the Presidency of Belaúnde Terry. In 1985 Belaúnde was succeeded as President by Alan García, leading an administration in which the APRA party predominated.

Peru is a unitary, centralised republic of 23 departments. Executive power is vested in the President who appoints his own Council of Ministers. There is a bicameral legislature.

In the late 1960s, relations with the United States deteriorated following the seizure of US fishing boats operating within Peru's 200-mile exclusive economic zone, a concept largely pioneered by Peru and now receiving widespread acceptance. The decline in tuna fishing, following the alteration of the direction of ocean currents in the early 1970s, removed this cause of friction. Nevertheless, since the military regimes of 1968-80 Peru has assumed a non-aligned rather than distinctly pro-Western stance in international affairs.

Although Cuban-sponsored low-level insurgency in the south east of the country appeared to have been brought under control by the late 1970s the development of a guerrilla movement, known as the "*Sendero Luminoso*" or "Shining Path" from the early 1980s onwards, is causing problems. For long identified as Maoist, this movement, with its popular base in the 46% of the Peruvian population who are pure-blooded Quechua Indians, combines elements of Inca nationalism and anarchic nihilism with a rather confused version of Chinese-style Marxism as its ideological base. By 1982 it had become such a menace that a two-year long state of emergency was declared in the area comprising the provinces of Ayacucho, Apurímac and Huancavelica and following a major outbreak of related urban terrorism in Lima itself a 60-day state of emergency was also declared in the Peruvian capital on 20 August 1982. President García has attempted with some success to combat the terrorists by eradicating the widespread poverty, ignorance and disease in the areas in which they were strongest but has been frustrated by the country's growing economic crisis, provoked by an external debt in excess of US $14 billion, largely incurred by extravagant purchases of military equipment during the regimes of Generals Velasco Alvarado and Morales Bermúdez. The prevailing economic conditions are also a source of chronic labour unrest, manifesting itself in sporadic strikes, frequently accompanied by bloodshed.

Peru has been at the forefront of Third World protest against the debt crisis, unilaterally rescheduling its repayments to foreign bankers from 1985 onwards.

Structure of the armed forces

Under the 1979 Constitution, the chain of command runs directly from the President of the republic to the commanders-in-chief of the Army, Navy and Air Force. Although, in the past, the commander-in-chief of the Army also held the office of Minister of War under President Belaúnde, the latter office became purely an administrative one, outside the direct chain of command. Traditionally the Ministers of War, Marine and Aviation had also been serving officers. President Belaúnde also broke with this tradition, naming retired officers who had opposed the 1968 coup to these Ministries. More recently, President García has created a single Ministry of Defence, which is held by a civilian.

The Joint Command is an advisory group, consisting of the chiefs of staff of the Army, Navy and Air Force, plus their assistants. Each of the armed forces appoints five or six officers of the rank of colonel (in the cases of the Army and Air Force) or captain (in the case of the Navy) to assist their respective chiefs of staff on the Joint Command, which is a planning group rather than an operational staff. The presidency of the Joint Command rotates annually amongst the three chiefs of staff.

In addition to their primary function of protecting the country from external aggression, the armed forces may, in specified emergencies, assume the responsibility for the maintenance of internal order, taking precedence over the police in this respect.

The country is divided into five Military

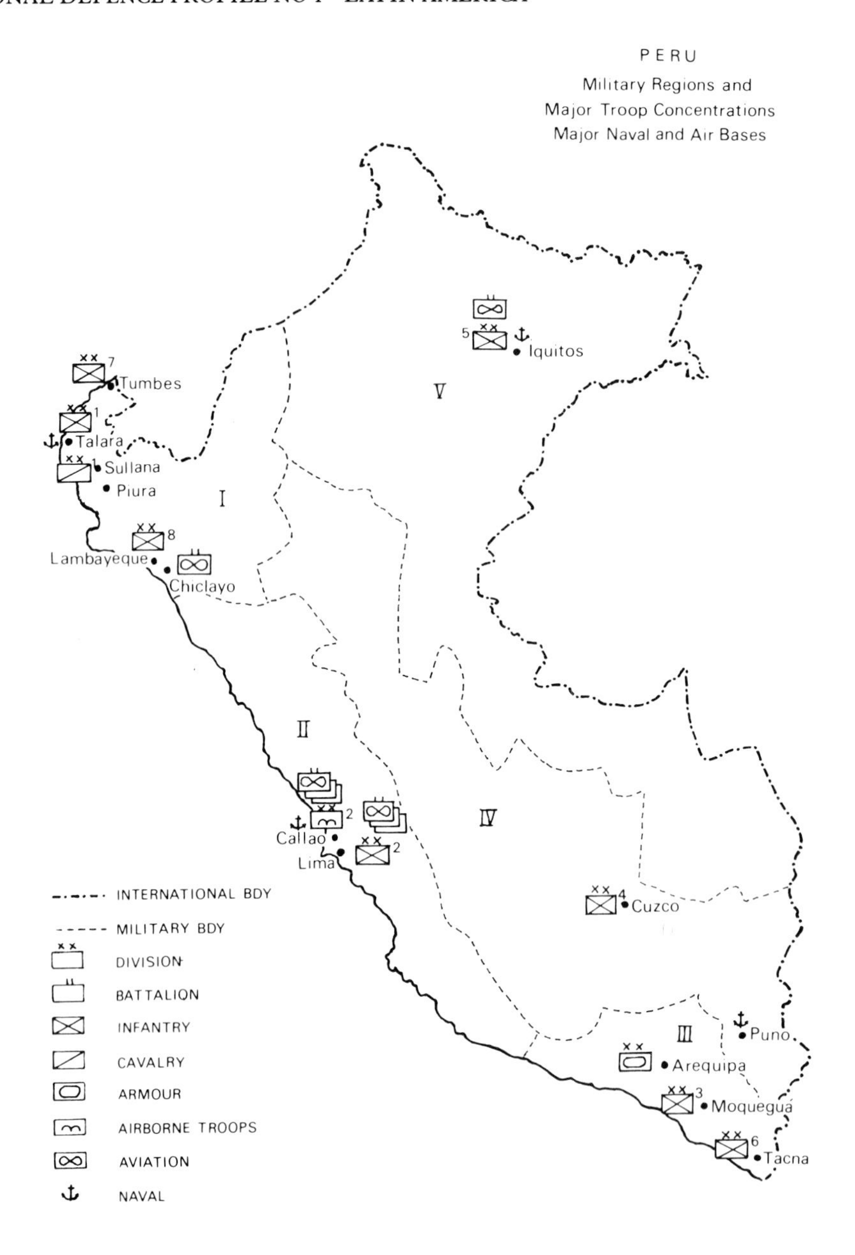

Regions of which the 1st (HQ Piura) covers the departments of Tumbes, Piura, Lambayeque, Cajamarca and Amazonas, the 2nd (HQ Lima) the national capital and the departments of La Libertad, Ancash, Lima, Huancavelica, Ica and Callao, the 3rd (HQ Arequipa) the departments of Arequipa, Moqueguá and Tacna, the 4th (HQ Cuzco) the departments of Puno, Cuzco, Apurímac, Junín, Pasco, Huanuco, San Martín, Ayacucho and Madre de Dios and the 5th (HQ Iquitos) the jungle departments of Loreto and Ucayalí.

The bulk of the manpower of the Army and to a lesser extent that of the Navy and Air Force, is provided by two-year conscripts. All male citizens are liable for military training between the ages of 20 and 25 but in practice a selective draft system is employed. After completing their two years service, conscripts pass to the reserve for the next ten years and then to the National Guard, a second-line reserve. No formal system of reserve mobilisation appears to exist although a partial mobilisation was carried out during the border tension with Ecuador at the beginning of 1981.

Officers are trained in the schools of their

respective services. There is also a joint service Centre for Higher Military Studies, established in 1958, which has a largely civilian faculty under a director appointed by the Joint Command of the armed forces. The centre is divided into academic, strategic and research and development departments. Peru also trains military personnel from several of the smaller Latin American countries, by arrangement with their respective governments.

Army

Manpower:	85,000
Formations:	1 armoured division 1 cavalry division 1 airborne division 8 light divisions (incl 1 jungle)
Major units:	24 infantry battalions (incl 2 motorised, 1 airborne, 2 commando and 2 jungle battalions) 6 independent infantry companies 1 special forces group 3 armoured battalions 1 mounted escort regiment 7 (mechanised) cavalry regiments 11 artillery groups 1 anti-aircraft artillery group 6 combat engineer battalions
AFVs:	T-54 and T-55 MBTs US M4 medium tanks (in storage) AMX-13 light tanks US M6 and Fiat 6616 armoured cars M113, Mowag Roland and UR-416 APCs
Artillery:	US M101 and Oto Melara Model 56 105 mm howitzers Soviet M-46 122 mm and M-54 130 mm howitzers US M114 155 mm howitzers US M109 and French Mk F.3 155 mm SPH
Air defence weapons:	Soviet SA-3 and SA-7 SAMs Soviet ZSU-23-4 23 mm SP Bofors and US M1 40 mm L/60
Aircraft:	Beech Queen Air light transport Cessna 185 liaison Bell 47, Mil Mi-6 and Mi-8 and Aérospatiale SA.318C Alouette II helicopters

Peruvian Presidential guards at Lima
(M. English)

Peruvian independence was largely won by the intervention of the Argentino-Chilean Army of Liberation, supported by the Chilean Navy, from the south and Bolívar's Army of Gran Colombia from the north and no identifiably Peruvian armed forces existed until after the successful conclusion of the War of Independence. The new Peruvian Army received its baptism of fire in a series of disastrous wars with Gran Colombia, Chile and Bolivia in quick succession and was finally professionalised under President Ramón Castilla (1848-

51), being subsequently virtually destroyed in the Pacific War of 1879-83. The Peruvian military establishment was painfully rebuilt during the late 1880s and in 1895 a French military mission was engaged to reorganise and train the army. A military academy was established at Chorrillos in 1896, followed by an NCO school and branch schools for the combatant arms and logistic support services. A succession of French military missions operated in Peru continuously until the outbreak of the First World War and again from 1919 to 1939. Peru engaged in an unsuccessful military adventure against Colombia in 1932 and a successful one against Ecuador in 1941. From the Second World War onwards French influence was replaced by that of the United States, some limited Soviet influence, almost exclusively in the technical field, also being absorbed during the military regime of 1968-80 following the purchase of large quantities of equipment from the USSR. Although US influence remains predominant some vestigial French influence is noticeable in such items as ceremonial uniforms and rank insignia.

The Peruvian Army numbers approximately 85,000 all ranks, its basic tactical formation being the light division which consists nominally of four infantry battalions and an artillery group, to which may be added a cavalry regiment and/or an engineer battalion. Currently each division appears to average only three units of infantry or cavalry. There are eight such formations which therefore resemble brigades rather than divisions in normal military usage. There is also an armoured division, a cavalry division and an airborne division, all of which also would appear to resemble brigades rather than divisions in their strength and organisation.

The 1st Military Region (HQ Piura) contains the 1st Light Division (HQ Talara) which comprises the 7th, 8th and 31st Infantry Battalions and the 1st Artillery Group, the 7th Light Division (HQ Tumbes) with the unnamed 5th and 33rd and the 51st *Ayacucho* Infantry Battalions, the 7th Artillery Group and the 1st Combat Engineer Battalion, the 8th Light Division (HQ Lambayeque) with the 3rd, 11th and 20th Infantry Battalions and the 8th Artillery Group and the

Peruvian infantry with M113 APC

1st Cavalry Division (HQ Sullana) with the 5th, 6th and 7th Cavalry Regiments and the 9th Artillery Group. This region also accommodates the *Marañón* Construction Engineer Group at Bagua and a supply and a medical battalion, both at Piura.

The 2nd Military Region (HQ Lima) contains the 2nd Light Division (HQ Lima) made up of the 1st *Legión Peruana* and the unnamed 17th and 25th Infantry Battalions, the 1st *Húsares de Junín* Cavalry Regiment, the 2nd Artillery Group and the 2nd *Huascarán* Combat Engineer Battalion. This region also accommodates the unnumbered Airborne Division (HQ Callao) which comprises the 19th and 39th Commando and the 61st Paratroop Infantry Battalions, plus the 10th Artillery Group.

The 3rd Military Region (HQ Arequipa) contains the 3rd Light Division (HQ Moqueguá) comprising the unnamed 6th and the 41st *San Pablo* Infantry Battalions, the 2nd Cavalry Regiment, the 3rd Artillery Group and the 3rd *José Olaya* Combat Engineering Battalion, the 6th Light Division (HQ Tacna) with the 35th *General Salaverry* Motorised Infantry and 45th Infantry Battalions, the 3rd Cavalry Regiment, the 6th Artillery Group and the 6th *Teniente Coronel La Rosa* Combat Engineer Battalion, and the 1st Armoured Division (HQ Arequipa) with the 1st, 211th and 311th Tank Battalions, the 13th Motorised Infantry Battalion, the *Bolognesi* Artillery Group and the 3rd Armoured Engineer Battalion. This region also contains the *Puma* Special Forces Group at Arequipa, the *Dos de Mayo* Construction Engineer Group, also at Arequipa and the *La Breña* Construction Engineer Battalion at Moqueguá.

The 4th Military Region (HQ Cuzco) contains only the 4th Light Division (HQ Cuzco) made up of the 9th and 10th Infantry Battalions, the 9th Cavalry Regiment, the 4th Artillery Group and the 4th Combat Engineer Battalion, plus the *Ollantaytambo* Construction Engineer Battalion.

The 5th Military Region (HQ Iquitos) contains the 5th Light Division (HQ Iquitos) which is the Peruvian Army's jungle division and is made up of the 21st and 23rd Jungle Infantry Battalions, at least 6 independent infantry companies, the 5th Artillery Group and the 5th Combat Engineer Battalions.

The Military Regions, each of which appears to approximate to an army corps as a level of command, would seem to include at least one battalion each of logistic support and medical troops apiece, in addition to signals and military police units. Each division appears to have at least a company each of signals, logistic support and medical troops.

Army level troops, most of which are located within the 2nd Military Region, include the *Mariscal Nieto* Presidential Escort Regiment, the 1st Anti-Aircraft Artillery Group, the 501st Communications Battalion, the 511th and 512th Supply and Maintenance Battalions, the 511th Intendance Battalion, the 511th Transport Battalion, and the 512th Maintenance Battalion.

The Peruvian Army has an abundance of equipment, acquired from a wide variety of sources, much of which is in storage. Rifles in use are the FN FAL, the G3 and the AK-47, all in 7.62 mm calibre. Sub-machine guns include the Uzi, the locally-manufactured MGP-79 and the Argentine FMK, all in 9 mm calibre. The Peruvian Army uses a variety of machine guns including the FN MAG and the Soviet DShK 38/46, both in 7.62 mm, the Czech ZB30 in 7.65 mm and both the Browning M1917 0.30 calibre and the M2HB 0.50 calibre. All mortars in use are of French origins and include various marks of the Hotchkiss-Brandt 81 mm and 120 mm. Anti-armour weapons are the US M40A1 106 mm RCL and the German Cobra ATGW.

Combat armour consists mainly of the Soviet T-54/55 medium tanks, of which there are some 280 in service. There are also about 110 examples of the French AMX-13 light tank, while approximately 50 US M4 Sherman medium tanks are in storage. Some 60 US M8 armoured cars are in use, mainly for internal security purposes and there are approximately 300 US M113 tracked APCs (about half of which were obtained from Argentina) and 228 examples of the UR-416 wheeled APC in service. A relatively recent acquisition consists of 20 Fiat 6616 scout cars although the reported acquisition of 100 SPz-12-3 armoured cars does not seem to have materialised.

Artillery consists of 130 US M101 and 50 Oto-Melara Mod 56 105 mm howitzers, 30 examples apiece of the Soviet M-46 122 mm and the M-54 130 mm howitzer, 36 US M114 155 mm towed howitzers (obtained via Argentina), six US M109 and 12 French Mk F.3 155 mm SPHs.

Air-defence weapons in service include some 40 examples of the Bofors 40 mm L/60 and the similar US M1 40 mm, 36 examples of the Soviet ZSU-23-4 quadruple 23 mm SP AA gun and both SA-3 and SA-7 shoulder-fired SAMs.

The *Servicio de Aviación del Ejercito*, formed in 1971, opperates a single Beech Queen Air light transport, five Cessna 185 general-purpose aircraft, six SA.318C Alouette II helicopters and eight Bell 47s. About 20 Soviet Mi-6 and 40 Mi-8 helicopters are reported to be in storage.

Officers receive their training at the Military Academy at Chorrillos, which offers a four-year course leading to a commission as a 2nd lieutenant. Lieutenants must also successfully complete at least two specialised courses before promotion to captain. A further two-year course at the *Escuela Superior de Guerra* must be completed before promotion to field rank. There is a comprehensive system of specialised schools, almost all of which are located in the environs of Lima and include the infantry, armoured, parachute, commando, mountain warfare, cavalry, artillery, engineering, communications, services and medical schools. There is a Jungle Warfare School at Iquitos.

The modern Peruvian Army is extremely well-equipped and led by a highly-trained and professional officer corps. It has successfully contained recent attempts at internal subversion, although it has so far failed to eliminate guerrilla activity and voluntarily handed power back to civilian politicians after running the country for 12 years. The quality of its rank and file is more debatable. Peru has engaged in more foreign wars since independence than any other Latin American country but, with the exception of the Zarumilla campaign of 1941, in which Peru enjoyed an overwhelming qualitative and quantitive superiority over Ecuador, these were almost uniformly disastrous in their outcome. Despite the profusion of modern equipment available to the present-day Peruvian Army, its very diversity must be something of a liability to its owners.

Navy

Manpower:	27,000 (including Marines and Naval aviation)
Major units:	1 obsolete cruiser 2 missile destroyers 6 obsolete destroyers 4 missile frigates 12 submarines 6 missile attack craft 4 LSTs 2 LSMs 5 river gunboats
Marines:	1 amphibious brigade plus local defence units
Heavy equipment:	Chaimite V-200 APC US M42 twin 40 mm SP AA gun
Naval aviation:	Fokker F.27 maritime patrol aircraft Grumman S-2E Tracker ASW Douglas C-47 Beech Super King Air 200 and Piper Aztec transport Agusta-Bell 212AS Agusta-Sikorsky S-61D Bell 47, UH-1H and 206 helicopters Beech T-34C trainers

A Navy was formed shortly after independence, most of its units being captured by Chile in the war of 1836-39. The war with Spain of 1865-66 brought home the importance of sea power to the Peruvian government and a programme of naval expansion was embarked upon. By 1879 the Peruvian Navy was the fourth most powerful in Latin America. Most of the fleet was again lost however during the Pacific War against Chile and Peru did not regain its historic fourth position in the Latin American naval league until the mid-1920s. No major naval actions took place in either the Leticia campaign against Colombia in 1932 or the brief 1941 war with Ecuador. Despite considerable acquisitions of war surplus material following the end of the Second World War, the Peruvian Navy lost its traditional position to Venezuela during the 1950s. By the end of the 1960s however Peru had again regained it and the 1970s were a period of dramatic expansion for all of the Peruvian armed forces. By the early 1980s the Peruvian Navy had outstripped that of Chile to become the third regional naval power and was challenging Argentina for the second position. A French naval

***Peruvian "Lupo" class missile frigate* Villavicencio**

mission functioned between 1905 and 1912 and a US naval mission arrived in Peru in 1920 and has functioned almost continually since that date.

The Peruvian Navy is organised into two major operational entities: the Pacific Naval Force and the Amazon River Force. There are also three subsidiary elements: the Lake Titicaca Patrol Force, the Naval Air Service and the Marine Infantry Force.

The largest unit of the Peruvian fleet is the Netherlands-built 9500-ton cruiser *Almirante Grau* (ex-*Aguirre* and formerly *De Ruyter*). A sister ship has been under reconstruction in the Netherlands since 1985 but interim payments for the work rapidly fell into arrears and finally stopped early in 1986 so that the future of this vessel is now very much in doubt. There are two 2800-ton modernised ex-British "Daring" class destroyers, *Ferré* and *Palacios*, which have been armed with Exocet SSMs, and four 2200-ton "Lupo" class missile frigates, *Melitón Carvajal*, *Manuel Villavicencio*, *Montero* and *Mariátegui*, the latter two of which were built in Peru. The other major surface units are the six survivors of eight "Holland" and "Friesland" class destroyers which were acquired by Peru between 1978 and 1982. These are the 2200-ton *Bolognesi*, *Castilla*, *Quiñones*, *Villar*, *Gálvez* and *Diez Canseco*. Being still essentially as built in the late 1950s, these are of limited value as well as very expensive in manpower and may be expected to pass from the scene, together with the cruiser *Almirante Grau*, in the near future. Superficially less impressive but potentially far more useful are the six 470-ton missile corvettes *Velarde*, *Santillana*, *De Los Héroes*, *Herrera*, *Larrea* and *Sánchez Carrión*.

Peru has the largest submarine fleet in South America with six Type 209 "1200" class boats: *Casma*, *Antofagasta*, *Pisagua*, *Chipana*, *Islay* and *Arica*, the modified US "Mackerel" type *Dos de Mayo*, *Abtao*, *Angamos* and *Iquique* and the "Guppy 1A" class *Pacocha* and *La Pedrera*. Although the latter two boats date from the mid-1940s both these and the four "Mackerel" type craft, all of which are more than 30 years old, have been recently modernised and are expected to remain in service for several years more.

The 12,000-ton transport *Ilo*, together with the 6200-ton *Independencia* (currently used as a training ship), the 2600-ton LSTs *Pisco*, *Paita*, *Callao* and *Etén* and the 500-ton LSMs *Lomas* and *Atico* furnish more than adequate sea-lift and amphibious assault capacity for the single brigade of Marines.

Five replenishment tankers provide a useful logistic back-up which considerably extends the range of the Peruvian Navy's combat units and there are also two surveying vessels, five inshore surveying craft, a salvage tug, two harbour oilers, two water carriers, a torpedo recovery vessel and three harbour tugs, in addition to a number of small miscellaneous service craft.

The Amazon River Force patrols over 2000 miles of inland waterways and consists of the 365-

ton river gunboats *Marañón* and *Ucayalí*, the 250-ton *Amazonas* and *Loreto* and the slightly smaller *América*, in addition to the 150-ton river hospital craft *Morona*, six patrol launches, a water carrier and a tug.

Six small launches patrol Lake Titicaca.

The *Servicio Aeronaval* currently deploys ten Grumman S-2E Trackers, a single Fokker F.27 Maritime and four Agusta-Sikorsky S.61Ds in a maritime reconnaissance/ASW squadron based at Jorge Chávez International Airport, Lima, a transport squadron with four C-47s, six Beech Super King Air 200s and a single Piper Aztec, also based at Jorge Chavez, a helicopter squadron based at Callao, with six Agusta-Bell 212As, ten Bell 206 Jet Rangers and six Bell UH-1D Iroquois and a training unit, also based at Callao, with six Beech T-34Cs and four Bell 47s. As many as 40 Soviet Mi-8 helicopters are reported to be in storage.

The Marine infantry consists of an amphibious brigade of three battalions, plus local security units. In addition to personal and infantry support weapons, which include the FN FAL rifle, the MGP-79 sub-machine gun, the FN MAG general-purpose machine gun, 81 mm and 120 mm mortars and M40A1 106 mm RCLs, the Marines are equipped with about 40 Portuguese Chaimite V-200 amphibious APCs and with an unknown number of M42 twin 40 mm SP AA guns.

Naval HQ is located at Lima while by far the most important shore installation is the Callao Naval Base with one dry dock, three floating docks, a floating workshop and a floating crane of 120-ton lift capacity. Here are also the Naval Academy, the Naval War College and the Naval Technical and Training Centre. The submarine force is based at San Lorenzo and there is a minor naval base at Talara. The Amazon River Force has its main base at Iquitos, with repair facilities and a floating dock and a subsidiary river base at Madre de Dios. The Lake Titicaca Patrol Force is based at Puno.

The Naval Academy at La Punta, Callao, offers

"Type 209" submarine **Pisagua (Dr R. Scheina)**

Cessna T-34C trainer of the Peruvian Navy

four and five year courses (depending on previous educational qualifications) to aspiring officers and the courses of the Naval War College must be successfully completed for promotion to senior rank or for staff appointments. The Naval Technical and Training Centre provides specialist courses for both officers and ratings, as well as basic training for the latter.

Air Force

Manpower: 15,000

Major units: 1 fighter group (4 squadrons)
1 fighter-bomber group (3 squadrons)
1 bomber group (3 squadrons)
1 helicopter group
1 attack helicopter squadron
2 transport groups (3 squadrons)
1 communications group (2 squadrons)
1 Presidential transport flight
1 aerial photograph unit

Fighters: Sukhoi Su-22

Fighter-bombers: Dassault Mirage 5P and 2000
Cessna A-37B

Bombers: Canberra B(I).68, B.52, B.56 and T.54
Cessna A-37B
Aermacchi MB.339AP

Photo-reconnaissance aircraft: Learjet 25B and 36A

Transports: Antonov An-26
Douglas DC-6 and DC-8
DHC-5 and 6
Fokker F.28
Falcon 20
Lockheed C-130
Pilatus PC-6

Communications aircraft: Beech King Air and Queen Air

Helicopters: Aérospatiale Alouette III
Bell 47, UH-1H, 206, 212 and 214
Mil Mi-6, Mi-8 and Mi-25

Mirage 5P fighter of the 13th Fighter Group of the Peruvian Air Force

Trainers: Beech T-34A
Cessna T-37, T-41 and 150
Pitts S.2A

The Peruvian Army initiated flying training in 1910 but the outbreak of the First World War prevented further development and the *Servicio de Aviación Militar* did not get going until January 1919. A French military aviation mission arrived in November 1919 and the US naval mission, which functioned from 1920 onwards, also included an air element, under the stimulus of which a naval air arm was set up. The French air mission was replaced by a British one in 1921, it in its turn, being replaced by a US mission and in 1929 the air services of both the Army and Navy were amalgamated as the *Cuerpo de Aeronáutica del Perú*. This force was active during the Leticia conflict of 1932 and in 1935 the Peruvian government contracted the services of an Italian air mission to reorganise and modernise its air arm. This mission functioned for only five years and from 1938 onwards Peru turned increasingly towards the United States for material and training assistance. The *Cuerpo de Aeronáutica* was heavily involved in the conflict with Ecuador in July 1941 and in November of that year an independent Ministry of Aviation was set up, the *Cuerpo de Aeronáutica* becoming an independent force, equal in status to the Army and Navy. In July 1950 the *Cuerpo de Aeronáutica* changed its title to *Fuerza Aérea del Perú*, since when it has maintained its position as one of the premier military air arms of Latin America, oscillating between third and fifth place amongst South American air forces.

The *Fuerza Aérea del Perú* currently has a strength of approximately 15,000, operating some 350 aircraft organised into eight groups.

Fighter Group No 12 (HQ Lima Tambo) consists of Squadrons Nos 121, 122, 123 and 124, equipped with a total of 46 Su-22s.

Fighter-Bomber Group No 13 (HQ Chiclayo) consists of Squadron No 131, equipped with 17 Mirage 5Ps, Squadron No 132 with 12 Mirage 2000s and Squadrons Nos 133 and 134 with a dozen A-37Bs apiece.

Bomber Group No 21 (HQ Lima Jorge Chávez) comprises Squadrons Nos 211 and 212 equipped with a total of 22 Canberra B(I).68s, B.52s, B.56s and T.54s and Squadron No 213 with 13 Aermacchi MB.339APs.

Transport Group No 41 (HQ Lima Jorge Chávez) comprises Squadron No 411 with eight Lockheed C-130s and two Douglas DC-8s,

Squadron No 412 with 14 DHC-5s, and Squadron No 413 with 15 Antonov An-26s which are to be replaced by An-32s. There is also a Presidential Flight based at Lima Jorge Chávez, with one Fokker F.28 and one Falcon 20F, the *Servicio Aerofotográfico Nacional* based at Las Palmas, with one squadron equipped with two Learjet 25Bs, two 36As and two Beech Queen Airs, and an aerobatic unit with six Pitts S.2As.

Transport Group No 42 (HQ Iquitos) operates *Transportes Aéreos Nacionales de la Selva* – National Jungle Air Transports, a military operated civil airline with 19 DHC-6s and 12 Pilatus PC-6s.

Helicopter Group No 3 (HQ Callao) with no squadron organisation and flight elements detached throughout the country, is equipped with a total of 15 Bell 47Gs, eight Bell 206Bs, 12 Bell UH-1Hs and five examples apiece of the Bell 212 and 214, plus eight Aérospatiale Alouette IIIs. There is also a helicopter gunship squadron, with 12 Mil Mi-25s, six Mi-6s and a similar number of Mi-8s, which comes under the operational control of the Army.

Communications Group No 8 (HQ Callao) consists of Squadron No 81 equipped with three Beech King Air 90s and five Queen Airs and Squadron No 82 with eight Queen Airs.

The *Academia del Aire* is at Las Palmas, its flying element being Training Group No 51 which comprises Squadron No 511 with 26 Cessna T-37Bs and Cs, Squadron No 512 with 15 T-41Ds, Squadron No 513 with six Beech T-34As and four Cessna 150Fs and Squadron No 514, still in formation with the first of 20 EMBRAER Tucanos.

All training establishments are concentrated under the Aeronautical Instruction Centre Command which embraces the Air Force Academy,

C-130 transport of the Peruvian Air Force's 41st Transport Group
(Lockheed Aircraft Corpn)

the Air University and the Air Technical Training School. Aspiring officers must complete a four or five year course at the Air Force Academy, its length depending on academic qualifications, before receiving a commission as a second lieutenant. The Air University provides squadron officers' courses for lieutenants and captains, command and staff courses for majors and lieutenant colonels and an Air War College course for colonels, all of which must be successfully completed for promotion to the next highest rank. Many officers also pursue post-graduate courses abroad and Peru trains air force officers from some of the smaller Latin American countries. Enlisted specialists follow courses at the Air Technical Training School.

The Peruvian Air Force is currently the third largest in Latin America.

***Members of the Peruvian Republican Guard at Lima* (M. English)**

Paramilitary forces

Manpower:	36,000 (Civil Guard) 15,000 (Republican Guard) 1500 (Coast Guard)
Heavy equipment:	Mowag Roland APCs (Civil Guard) 20 patrol vessels (Coast Guard)

There are two paramilitary police forces, the Republican Guard and the Civil Guard. Five police regions cover identical areas to those of the five military regions. The present police system was established in 1924, the *Guardia Civil* becoming the main national police force. The existing *Guardia Republicana* retained its specialised functions but investigative and forensic functions were handed over to a new plain-clothes organisation, the *Policía de Investigaciones del Peru.*

The Republican Guard, established in 1919, is recruited entirely on a voluntary basis, numbers about 15,000 and is equipped with light infantry weapons, including carbines and sub-machine guns, in addition to riot control gear. The force patrols the country's land frontiers, guards public buildings and furnishes prison guards at penal institutions. In 1963 a parachute squadron was formed. A Republican Guard Superior School for the advanced training of the senior officers of the force was opened in 1973 and there is now a Republican Guard Centre of Instruction for the comprehensive training of all ranks which will ultimately incorporate the former institution.

The Civil Guard is currently organised into 59 "*Comandancias*" and includes a special anti-terrorist unit, the *Sinchi* battalion, based at Lima but available for service throughout the country. The Guard is equipped with light infantry weapons and has a number of armoured vehicles, including 112 Argentine-built versions of the Mowag Roland APC, at its disposal. It currently numbers approximately 36,000 all ranks, recruited entirely by voluntary enlistment. There is a Civil Guard Centre of Instruction at Chorrillos which includes the Officers' School, which provides a four-year course for aspiring officers of the force. There are also training schools for enlisted ranks and NCOs and like the armed forces, mid-career courses are provided for both officers and NCOs and must be successfully completed before the candidates are eligible for promotion to higher rank. Numbers of *Guardia Civil* officers also attended the International Police Academy in the United States between 1963 and 1974.

Many of the larger urban centres maintain municipal police forces, the functions of which are principally confined to parking control and the enforcement of hygiene regulations.

In addition to the above internal security forces, all of which come under the jurisdiction of the Ministry of the Interior, there is a Coast Guard, established in 1975 as an adjunct of the Navy and under the jurisdiction of the Ministry of Marine. Entrusted primarily with coastal patrol, fishery protection, harbour security, life-saving and the maintenance of navigational aids, this force numbers about 1500 and consists of some 20 patrol craft, the largest of which are the 300-ton *Rio Nepena*, *Rio Tambo*, *Rio Ocona*, *Rio Huarmey*, *Rio Sana* and *Rio Canete*, the two 130-ton US "PGM" type *Rio Sama* and *Rio Chira* and the four 100-ton Vosper fast patrol boats *Rio Chicama*, *Rio Pativiloa*, *Rio Locumba* and *Rio Vito*. There are also over a dozen smaller patrol craft of 30 tons or less, six of which are based on the navigable river systems of the Peruvian Oriente. Coast Guard personnel are recruited from and trained by the Navy.

Sources of defence material supply and current requirements

France and to a lesser degree Germany and Italy, were Peru's main suppliers of military equipment from the last quarter of the 19th century until the outbreak of the Second World War. The United States had however established itself as a supplier of naval vessels and aircraft from the mid-1920s onwards and in the years following the Second World War, the United States was the principal supplier of arms and defence equipment. In the mid-1960s, French influence, always strong in Peruvian military circles, began to assert itself once more and quantities of equipment were also acquired from Belgium and Switzerland. During the early 1970s, with the growth of ties with Argentina, some quantities of largely second and third-hand material were also received from the latter country, followed by quantities of material of Argentine manufacture or assembly. The military regime, which held power from 1968-80, underlined its independence of the United States by engaging in massive purchases of Soviet equipment, while continuing to purchase material from Western countries, including the United States. Since the return of civilian government, Peru has returned to Western countries as its major suppliers although the US no longer enjoys a monopoly and the Netherlands, in particular, for a while became a major supplier of second-hand naval vessels. Despite the poor serviceability record of much of the Soviet material in hand, in particular the large numbers of helicopters, most of which are in storage, some aircraft continue to be purchased from the Soviet Union.

Although in the past Peru has produced some of its own defence material, military production is surprisingly limited for a country of its size and political aspirations. The assembly of aircraft was established during the 1930s and a number of primarily Italian designed aircraft types have been manufactured in Peru at various times during the past 50 years. The project to build a batch of 66 Aermacchi MB.339 light strike aircraft for the Peruvian Air Force by the newly established Indaer-Perú company was postponed in 1984 due to economic stringency. Military production is otherwise confined mainly to small arms, notably the MGP-79 and MGP-84 sub-machine guns and ammunition. Some Mowag Roland APCs have also been assembled from parts manufactured in Argentina under licence from the parent firm in Switzerland. Despite the current economic crisis and in part because of it, in an effort to save on foreign exchange, Peruvian defence production may be expected to develop to a significant degree during the next ten years.

Peru's existing arsenal, which is impressive, must suffer from the extraordinarily heterogeneous origins of its equipment, the maintenance of which must pose a logistic nightmare. Almost alone among Latin American countries, Peru has more defence equipment than its peacetime armed forces can use and in the context of the present economic crisis future procurements seem assured to remain limited. Certain gaps occur in the Peruvian arsenal however, notably in the areas of anti-armour and air defence weaponry and acquisitions in the immediate future seem likely to be confined to these areas.

Summary and prospects

Fear and resentment of Chile, dating back to the Pacific War and earlier, has conditioned Peruvian politico-military policies for over 100 years. Despite the relinquishment of all legal claim to the province of Arica, lost to Chile in 1883 under the terms of the Treaty of Tacna-Arica of 1929, its recovery remains, at least nominally, the cornerstone of Peruvian foreign policy. Hostility against Ecuador even predates the emergence of the latter country as an independent entity and has manifested itself in sporadic hostilities between the two countries, the most recent of which was in January/February 1981. Although the latter country presents no conceivable military threat to Peru, the largest concentration of Peruvian military force is in the vicinity of the Ecuadorian frontier.

Hostility between Peru and Chile parallels that between Chile and Argentina and the emergence of close times between Peru and Argentina was thus almost inevitable. This was demonstrated, on a tangible level, by the transfer of military equipment from Argentina to Peru during the late 1960s and 1970s and was reciprocated by Peru's active support of Argentina in the South Atlantic War of April/June 1982, which took the form of the loan and subsequent outright sale of Mirage aircraft and SA-7 surface-to-air missile systems to Argentina by Peru and the transfer of Exocet missiles from the Peruvian to the Argentine navy.

While Peru retains a healthy respect for the Chilean armed forces and is unlikely to engage in any military adventure against the latter country on a unilateral level. Peruvian support for Argentina would be certain in the event of any escalation of the Argentino-Chilean frontier dispute. A combination of the domestic political and international economic circumstances of all three countries, particularly in the context of the Beagle Channel Treaty between Argentina and Chile, would however seem to rule out any probability of conflict between them in the medium term at least. Peruvian armed aggression against Ecuador, for which a precedent exists in 1941, cannot however be totally discounted.

While internal guerrilla activity during the 1960s and 1970s appeared to have been contained, the activities of the Maoist "*Sendero Luminoso*" guerrilla movement have continued to escalate during the 1980s and have a potential for serious internal destabilisation.

EL SALVADOR

(República de El Salvador)

Area: 8260 sq miles (21,400 sq km)
Population: 5,622,000
Total armed forces: 42,640
Reserves: 200,000
Available manpower: 450,000
Paramilitary forces: 8700
GNP: $5,606 million (1985)
Defence expenditure: $177,778,000 (1986)

Introduction

El Salvador, which is bounded by Guatemala to the west, by Honduras to the north east and south-east and by the Pacific Ocean to the south is the smallest of the original, independent states of Central America. It is also the most densely populated and the only one which does not have coastlines on both the Pacific and the Caribbean. Of the population, which is evenly distributed, 92% are of mixed European and Amerindian blood, 6% pure Indians and only 2% pure whites.

The economy is principally based on the exportation of coffee and to a lesser degree cotton, sugar and lumber. Primarily agricultural, El Salvador is also the most highly industrialised country in Central America, both food and manufactured goods figuring highly among imports, together with fuels of all kinds and particularly petroleum products.

The first Spaniards penetrated into El Salvador from Honduras in 1522 and its early history is that of the remainder of Central America. With the break-up of the United Provinces of Central America in 1839, El Salvador became an independent entity, a republic being formally established in 1841. The country was involved in wars with Guatemala in 1876, 1885 and 1906. In the brief interludes of freedom from external threat the constant power struggle between the Conservative and Liberal factions ensured that its early years as an independent republic were as turbulent as in any other country of the region. Despite this background of strife, national institutions, including the armed forces, developed more rapidly in El Salvador than elsewhere in Central America and by the mid-1860s had been securely established. In the 1880s the cultivation of coffee was introduced and El Salvador rapidly emerged as the most prosperous and advanced of the Central American republics. The Great Depression of the 1930s caused a catastrophic fall in coffee prices, sparking off major peasant revolts in 1930 and 1931. These were ruthessly suppressed by the Army and in 1931 General Maximiliano Hernández Martínez seized power and ruled as absolute dictator until he was ousted by a general strike in 1944. Since 1944 an almost unbroken succession of military governments has continued.

In 1969, El Salvador was involved in a brief frontier war with Honduras, from which it emerged victorious, but branded as the aggressor and with a major problem in the resettlement of thousands of Salvadorean emigrants expelled from the neighbouring country. Tension with Honduras continued until the ratification of a peace treaty between the two countries in 1980. Although the war with Honduras and the continuing tension between the two countries had a certain unifying effect during the early 1970s, the progressive erosion of the already abysmal living standards of the mass of the population, as demographic pressures increased, saw a revival of armed internal subversion and from the end of 1978 onwards chronic low-level insurgency developed into a full-scale civil war.

The guerrilla movement was originally fragmented between the *Fuerza Armada de Resistencia Nacional* (FARN), the *Ejército Revolucionario Popular* (ERP) and the *Farabundo Martí Fuerzas Populares de Liberación* (FMFPL), each of which demonstrated various and progressive degrees of left-of-centre political orientation. These, in their turn, provoked two extreme right-wing reactionary groups, opposed to the limited degree of liberalisation and land reform which the government was prepared to offer. These were the *Falange* and the *Unión Guerrera Blanca* (UGB), together with *Órden*, a semi-official counter-terror group organised by the Salvadorean government as far back as 1968 to combat subversion, particularly in rural areas. Initially, the civil war was characterised largely by terror and counter-terror between these opposing groups. Since early in 1979, the *Farabundo Martí* organisation has succeeded in uniting all left-wing guerrilla groups in the Farabundo Martí National Liberation Front (FMFLN), named after the Communist leader of the 1931 peasant uprising.

Blatantly fraudulent elections, held in 1982, led to the defeat of the Christian Democrat President José Napoleón Duarte and the strengthening of the extreme political Right, led by Roberto d'Aubisson, who as President of the constituent assembly was the real power behind the figurehead President Alvaro Magaña. The 1984 Presidential elections returned Duarte to power although effectively as the puppet of the United States upon which the beleaguered Salvadorean government had come to rely for its military and economic survival. Despite continuing massive US financial and military assistance the Duarte administration has been able to establish only a fragile equilibrium between its forces and those of the guerrillas.

El Salvadore is a unitary, centralised republic, divided into 14 departments.

Executive power is vested in the President and there is a single-chamber legislature.

As the most densely populated country in Central America, El Salvador has always been looked upon with suspicion by its neighbours whose fears of Salvadorean expansionism were underlined by massive Salvadorean emigration to Honduras during the 1960s, this in turn being a major causative factor in the brief war between the two countries in 1969. In the period following the 1969 war, Salvadorean foreign policy was dominated by the continuing tensions between the two countries. Since the signature of the peace treaty with Honduras, internal problems have occupied the attentions of successive Salvadorean governments to the exclusion of other considerations. A major and perennial internal problem is the concentration of wealth in the hands of a tiny minority of the population at the expense of the pauperisation of the overwhelming majority. This has led to the dedication of most of the agricultural land to the cultivation of economically attractive non-food products, the benefits of which are not felt by the majority of the peasants, among whom malnutrition is widespread. The position is exacerbated by the 3.3% annual population growth rate which already gives El Salvador a population density greater than that of the Netherlands. Despite President Duarte's centre-left political origins, the US supported government and armed forces have become increasingly identified with the political Right, although its more extreme exponents, including Major d'Aubisson, are currently in exile.

Structure of the armed forces

The command structure of the armed forces is the conventional Latin American one in which the President is commander-in-chief. The Minister of National Defence is however in the chain of command and executes the President's command functions on a day-to-day basis. A Deputy Minister of National Defence fulfils the purely administrative role assigned to the minister in many other countries of the region. The Chief of the General Staff of the Armed Forces is the senior serving officer and is also Chief of the Army with operational control over the chiefs of the Navy and Air Force and of the three security forces: the National Guard, National Police and Treasury Police.

Prior to the present civil war the country was divided into three Defence Zones of which the Western Zone (HQ Santa Ana) covered the departments of Santa Ana, Sonsonate and Ahuachapán, the Central Zone (HQ San Salvador) the departments of San Salvador, La Libertad, La Paz, Cabañas, Chalatenango and San Vicente and the Eastern Zone (HQ San Miguel) the departments of San Miguel, Morazán, Usulután, Cuscatlán and La Unión. A Northern Defence Zone (HQ El Paraíso, Chalatenango) has now

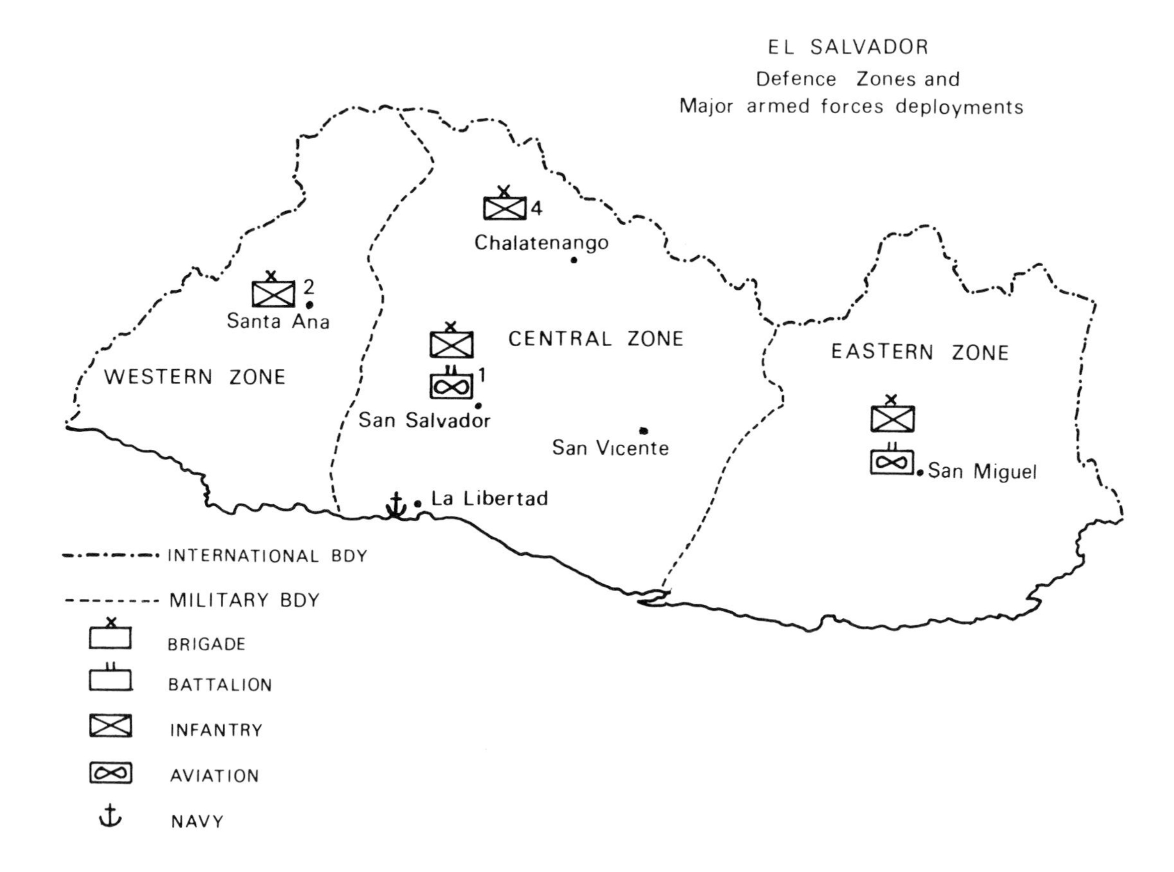

been established to embrace the region adjoining the frontier with Honduras, including the entire departments of Chalatenango, Cabañas and Morazán and parts of Santa Ana, San Miguel and La Unión. Subordinate to these are 15 Military Regions, corresponding to the 14 departments, plus the national capital, each of which is, in theory, the recruiting area of an infantry regiment. In practice, recruiting to the regular armed forces is carried out on a national level and this arrangement applies only to the reserve forces.

The law provides for compulsory military service for all male citizens between the ages of 18 and 60 and the minimum strength of the Army is set at 3000 all ranks. Prior to the current civil war, military service was a relatively attractive career and selective compulsory military service had to be resorted to only rarely. The expansion of the armed forces, from 1979 onwards, has however led to recourse to increasingly widespread application of this obligation, conscripts serving 18 months at the ages of 18 or 19, on completion of which they revert to "active reserve" status until the age of 30. From the ages of 30 to 60 reservists are assigned to the second-line Territorial Service, which principally provides the manpower for the rarely mobilised 2nd and 3rd battalions of the 15 infantry regiments.

Army

Manpower:	386,500
Tactical formations:	4 infantry brigades
Major units:	8 infantry regiments (1 bn each)
	2 + independent infantry battalions
	6 immediate-reaction battalions
	14 rifle battalions
	1 mechanised cavalry regiment
	1 artillery regiment (3 bns)
	1 engineer battalion

AFVs: AMX-13 light tanks
AML 245 armoured cars
M113, M114 and UR-416 APCs

Artillery: US M101 and Yugoslav M-56 105 mm howitzers
US M114 155 mm howitzers

While the first 50 years of Salvadorean independence were as turbulent as those of any of the other states of Central America, the limited dimensions of the country ensured that, for reasons of national survival, the Army should develop as a competent national defence force earlier than elsewhere in the region. A French military mission was active for most of the 1860s, establishing the Military Politechnic School as Central America's first military academy in 1867. In the 1890s a German military mission was contracted and during this period an NCO school was also established. Further German influence was absorbed at second-hand from the series of Chilean military missions which functioned from 1901 to 1957. During the 1930s small groups of Italian specialists were also active in training Salvadorean military personnel in the handling of various items of equipment obtained from that country. A Command and Staff School was set up, under Chilean auspicies, in 1941 and remained staffed by Chilean personnel until 1957. Foreign training assistance has since been exclusively in US hands but Prusso-Chilean influence remains strong, being readily discernible in such outward manifestations as the continued use of the "goose-step" and the cut of ceremonial uniforms.

The outbreak of the Second World War halted the further development of the Salvadorean armed forces and although quantities of military equipment were acquired from the United States from the mid-1940s onwards, the immediate impact of the country's signature of the Rio Treaty of 1947 was slight. The Salvadorean Army however continued to be regarded as the best in Central America and in the 25-day long war of 1969 it demonstrated its clear superiority over that of Honduras. During the subsequent ten-year period of extreme tension between the two countries the Salvadorean armed forces embarked on a massive re-equipment programme, material being acquired principally from France, Germany, Israel and Yugoslavia. US military assistance, withdrawn in protest against human rights violations by the government of General Carlos Humberto Romero in 1977, was restored after his overthrow in October 1979. Following the election of Ronald Reagan as President of the United States this has increased to a massive level.

Prior to the present civil war each of the three Defence Zones was garrisoned by an infantry brigade of two regiments, of which the 1st Brigade (HQ San Salvador) garrisoned the Central Zone with the 1st Infantry Regiment at San Carlos Barracks, San Salvador and the 4th at Chalatenango, the 2nd Brigade (HQ Santa Ana) garrisoned the Western Zone with the 2nd Infantry Regiment at Santa Ana and the 5th at Ahuachapán and the 3rd Brigade (HQ San Miguel) garrisoned the Eastern Zone with the 3rd Infantry Regiment at San Miguel and the 6th at Usulután. In 1981 a 4th Brigade was formed from the existing 4th and the recently mobilised 7th Infantry Regiments, with its headquarters at El Paraíso in Chalatenago Department, the 8th Infantry Regiment being mobilised to replace the 4th Regiment in the 1st Brigade. In practice only the first battalions of the traditional infantry regiments are mobilised, each being approximately 650 strong and are referred to interchangeably as "regiments" or "battalions".

Three 1000-strong immediate-reaction battalions, each with seven companies instead of the usual four, were also formed during 1981/82 and named *Atlacatal*, *Atonal* and *José Ramón Belloso* In March 1983 it was announced that the United States was to train a fourth counter-insurgency battalion and that 14 light infantry battalions, each of 350 men, would be raised for local security purposes. Two further immediate-reaction battalions were formed during 1984/86, together with some independent battalions and the delivery of additional artillery equipment from the United States permitted the formation of a third artillery battalion within the existing artillery regiment.

The Salvadorean Army currently numbers 38,650 all ranks and continues to expand.

The Central Zone (HQ San Salvador) which has been reduced to the departments of La Libertad, San Salvador, Cuscatlán, La Paz and San Vicente, is now garrisoned by the *San Salvador, Cuscatlán, La Libertad, La Paz* and *San Vicente* Rifle Battalions, its tactical manoeuvre element continuing to be the 1st Infantry Brigade (HQ San Salvador) which however is now composed

UR-416 APC of the Salvadorean Army
(Jane's Defence Weekly)

of the 1st and 8th Infantry Regiments.

The Western Zone (HQ Santa Ana) is now reduced to the departments of Ahuachapán and Sonsonate, plus the southern part of Santa Ana and is garrisoned by the *Santa Ana, Sonsonate* and *Ahuachapán* Rifle Battalions, the 2nd Infantry Brigade (HQ Santa Ana) still composed of the 2nd and 5th Infantry Regiments, continuing to be its main tactical manoeuvre element.

The Eastern Zone (HQ San Miguel) which has been reduced to the department of Usulután and the southern parts of San Miguel and La Unión,

Salvadorean artillerymen with Yugoslav M-56 105 mm howitzer

is now garrisoned by the *San Miguel, Usulután* and *La Unión* Rifle Battalions, its tactical manoeuvre element being still the 3rd Infantry Brigade (HQ San Miguel) with the 3rd and 6th Infantry Regiments.

The new Northern Zone (HQ El Paraíso, Chalatenango) comprises the entire departments of Chalatenango, Cabañas and Morazán, plus the northern parts of the departments of Santa Ana, San Miguel and La Unión and is garrisoned by the *Chalatenango, Cabañas* and *Morazán*, Rifle Battalions and the *Ronald Reagan* and *Jaguar* Independent Infantry Battalions, its tactical manoeuvre element being the 4th Infantry Brigade (HQ El Paraíso) with the 4th and 7th Infantry Regiments.

Army level troops include the *Atlacatl, Atonal, José Ramón Belloso, Lenca, Manual José Arce* and *Bragamonte* Immediate Reaction Battalions. Most of the combat support units are also directly subordinate to Army headquarters and are based in the 1st Military Defence Zone, the single cavalry regiment being based at San Andrés, the sole artillery regiment at El Zapote barracks, San Salvador and the one engineer battalion at Zacatecoluca. Squadron elements of the cavalry regiment and batteries of the three field artillery battalions are deployed in support of the brigades in accordance with operational requirements. The independent infantry units are also formed into brigades, on an ad hoc basis, in response to operational requirements, units also being lent between the four zones as required although the four regular infantry brigades normally remain in their parent zones.

Quantities of Israeli Galil and US M16 Armalite rifles, together with some Austrian AUG assault rifles, have recently supplemented the German G3 as the standard infantry small arm. The principal sub-machine gun in use is the Uzi although many examples of the Madsen M/50 are also encountered. The US M60 machine gun is also beginning to supplant the heterogeneous collection of automatic weapons in use which include the Browning M1919 0.30-inch calibre and M2HB 0.50-inch calibre and the 7.62 mm Madsen Model 1954 machine guns. The US M79 grenade launcher is now widely used and the main mortar in service is the 81 mm Hotchkiss-Brandt, supplemented by some Yugoslav UBM-52

120 mm pieces. Anti-armour weapons include both the US M18 57 mm and M20 75 mm RCLs, together with both US M72 66 mm and Israeli 80 mm rocket launchers. Armour consists of 12 AMX-13 light tanks 18 AML 245 H-90 armoured cars, ten US M113 APCs and an unknown number of M114s, most of which have been modified locally, plus 20 UR-416s and various types of locally-built armoured trucks. The artillery is equipped with approximately 18 US M101 and a similar number of Yugoslav M-56 105 mm howitzers, plus a dozen recently-acquired M114 155 mm howitzers. Some of the above armoured and artillery equipment has been lost in action.

All officers of the Salvadorean Army, Navy and Air Force receive their basic training at the *Escuela Militar Capitán General Gerardo Barrios* at San Salvador, the four year course of which leads to graduation with a bachelor's degree and commissioning in the rank of subteniente. Specialist training for both officers and other ranks is provided by the *Escuela de Armas y Servicios*, also located at San Salvador. This establishment also provides an advanced six-month course for field grade officers. The Command and Staff College provides courses in advanced military science for officers of the rank of lieutenant colonel and above and aspiring staff officers. Most officers however pursue additional post-graduate studies abroad. Regular NCOs are trained at the NCO School and at the Arms and Services School and in many cases are also sent abroad for additional training. There is a Special Forces School at San Francisco Goitera, the existence of which pre-dates the present civil war, although most of the Immediate Reaction Battalions have received their training either in the United States or in Honduras, with US instructors.

The *Capitán General Gerardo Barrios* Military Academy, which also trains cadets from other Central American countries, has a normal student body of about 150, only 60% or so of the annual graduating class being destined for the Salvadorean armed forces. Both the overall numbers and the proportion of Salvadorean students have increased with the dramatic expansion of the Army during the present civil war.

Navy

Personnel: 1290 all ranks

Major units: 6 patrol craft
1 tug

Marines: 1 commando battalion

An attempt at the formation of a Navy was made in 1890 with the açquisition of a single small gunboat. This vessel formed El Salvador's entire naval strength until it was sold to Panama in 1910 and with its disposal, the Salvadorean Navy appears to have come to an end. A Coast Guard was formed in 1913 but it seems to have been confined to the administration of the country's four ports and the maintenance of the rudimentary navigational aids then in existence. After a lapse of more than 40 years, the Navy was revived in 1952 and over the years a number of small craft were acquired. Although the new Navy absorbed the functions of the existing Coast Guard, expanding them to include coastal patrol and fishery protection, it remained a very modest force.

Since the escalation of the civil war there has been a considerable expansion in the strength of the Navy which now numbers 1290 all ranks, including a Marine commando battalion equipped with M16 rifles, M60 machine guns, M79 grenade launchers and 81 mm mortars. The largest and only named unit is the 150-ton tug *Libertad*, besides which there are three patrol boats of about 100 tons numbered *GC6*, *GC7* and *GC8*, the 30-ton *GC5*, two 20-ton craft, two Coast Guard utility boats and more than 20 small undecked motor launches equipped with outboard motors.

The principal base of the Salvadorean Navy is at La Unión, although repair and maintenance facilities are rudimentary. There is a minor naval station at La Libertad and a Naval School at Army HQ in San Salvador.

Air Force

Manpower: 2700
1 fighter-bomber squadron
1 light strike squadron
1 transport squadron

Fighter-bombers: Dassault Ouragan

Light strike aircraft:	Cessna A-37B and Potez Magister 170
Counter insurgency aircraft:	Cessna O-2A Douglas AC-47
Transports:	Lockheed C-130 Fairchild C-123 Douglas DC-6 and C-47 IAI Arava
Light aircraft:	Cessna 180, 182 and 185
Helicopters:	Aèrospatiale SA.315 and SA.316 Hughes 500M Bell UH-1H and M
Training aircraft:	Potez Magister 170 North American T-6 Texan Beech T-34A Cessna T-41A and C
Ground forces:	1 paratroop battalion 1 anti-aircraft battalion
Air defence weapons:	Yugoslav M-55 triple 20 mm guns

El Salvador formed a Military Aviation Service in 1922. The service remained a modest force however and the outbreak of the Second World War cut off the supply of further equipment until its closing stages when a few training aircraft were transferred from the United States. Following its signature of the Rio Treaty of 1947, El Salvador benefitted from the activities of a US air mission and increased transfers of aircraft under the Mutual Defence Assistance Program and the Military Aviation Service was renamed *Fuerza Aérea Salvadoreña* as an independent component of the armed forces.

Although the Salvadorean Army was clearly superior to that of Honduras during the war of 1969, the inferiority of the Salvadorean Air Force was painfully demonstrated and its reorganisation and re-equipment was an immediate priority following the close of hostilities. Israel now became a major supplier of aircraft, four Arava transports being delivered in 1974/75, followed by a total of 24 fighter and trainer/light aircraft over the next four years. The internal situation was now becoming critical and with the signature of the peace treaty with Honduras in 1980 the attentions of the Salvadorean armed forces became increasingly focussed on internal security. The United States has transferred large quantities of helicopters and some fixed-wing aircraft with a distinct counter-insurgency orientation to El Salvador since 1981, more than making good both combat attrition and the crippling losses sustained in a successful guerrilla raid on the main base of the Salvadorean Air Force at Ilopango, near San Salvador, in January 1982.

The Salvadorean Air Force, which currently has a personnel strength of approximately 2700 all ranks operating some 126 aircraft, consists of a fighter-bomber squadron with eight Dassault Ouragans, an attack (COIN) squadron equipped with four Potez CM.170 Magisters, nine Cessna A-37s, five Cessna O-2As and two Douglas AC-47s and a transport squadron equipped with a single Lockheed C-130, two Fairchild C-123s, a Douglas DC-6, six C-47s and three IAI 201 Aravas, all based at Ilopango which also houses the *Escuela de Aviación Militar* equipped with three Potez CM.170 Magisters, three Beech T-34s, four Cessna T-41s and five North American T-6s. The growing helicopter arm is equipped with at least 40 Bell UH-1Hs, a dozen UH-1M gunships, four Hughes 500Ms, three Aérospatiale SA.315 Lamas and three SA.316 Alouette IIIs. There are also six Cessna 180 light aircraft and single examples of the Cessna 182 and 185.

In addition to the main base at Ilopango, there are airstrips at San Miguel, Ahuachapán, Sonsonate, Zacatecoluca, San Vicente, Chalatenango and Usulután which are used by the Air Force in accordance with operational requirements.

The Air Force includes a battalion of paratroops and an anti-aircraft battalion, the former being equipped with Steyr AUG and M16 rifles, M60 machine guns, M79 grenade launchers and 81 mm mortars and the latter with about 20 Yugoslav M-55 towed triple 20 mm AA guns and ten SP versions of the same weapon mounted on M114 APC chassis.

Officer personnel complete the four year course of the National Military Academy before commencing flying training at the *Escuela de Aviación Militar* or other specialist training at the *Escuela de Especialización*, both of which are located at Ilopango. Specialist other ranks receive their training at the latter establishment. Most officer personnel also pursue some additional training abroad.

Paramilitary forces

Manpower: 4300 (*Guardia Nacional*)
2900 (*Policía Nacional*)
1500 (*Policía de Hacienda*)

There are three police forces, the paramilitary nature of which is underlined by their being under the jurisdiction of the Minister of National Defence, even in peacetime. Of these, the *Policía Nacional* is principally an urban police force, the *Guardia Nacional* functions mainly in rural areas and the *Policía de Hacienda* is concerned principally with the prevention of smuggling.

The *Policía Nacional* derives from the *Guardia Civil* founded in 1867 and was reorganised in its present form in 1945. It numbers approximately 2900 uniformed members and is divided into the *Policía de Linea*, which functions as an ordinary urban police, the *Policía de Tránsito*, which acts as traffic police in urban areas, the *Policía de Caminos* or Highway Patrol, the plain-clothes *Departamento de Investigaciones* or detective force and the *Cuerpo de Vigilantes Nocturnos y Bancarios* which provides bank guards and night watchmen at key installations. The force is armed with Smith and Wesson revolvers in 0.38-inch calibre and 0.30-inch calibre M1 carbines and has a large number of patrol cars and motorcycles.

***Member of the National Police at San Salvador* (M. English)**

The *Guardia Nacional* was formed in 1912 and was initially trained by Spanish officers, being modelled closely on the Spanish *Guardia Civil.* Its current strength is approximately 4300 all ranks armed with light infantry weapons, including G3 rifles and equipped with a number of Unimog trucks, in addition to jeeps and motorcycles. It is organised in 14 companies, one for each of the country's 14 departments, upon which a tactical organisation of five "Commands" or battalions can be superimposed. This force bore the brunt of the earlier anti-guerrilla operations and although highly efficient, earned a reputation for extreme blood-thirstiness and unnecessary brutality.

The *Policía de Hacienda,* formed in 1926, functions mainly as a frontier guard and customs force. It is armed and equipped on a similar level to that of the *Policía Nacional* and numbers approximately 1500.

Until 1980, internal security was principally in the hands of the three police forces. The escalation of left-wing guerrilla activity and right-wing counter-terrorist violence has however involved an increasing level of participation by the armed forces in counter-insurgency operations.

Sources of material supply and current requirements

Germany was originally the main supplier of military equipment to El Salvador, supplemented during the 1920s and 1930s by France, Denmark and Italy. Some US manufactured aircraft were also acquired in the 1930s, followed by additional quantities, together with some ground forces equipment, during the 1940s and 1950s. Subsequent to its signature of the Rio Treaty of 1947, El Salvador turned increasingly towards the United States as a source of defence equipment, and the Air Force in particular became equipped almost exclusively with aircraft of US origins. Following the 1969 war with Honduras El Salvador sought military equipment from wherever it could be obtained. France and Israel becoming important suppliers. The infantry was completely re-equipped with the German G3 rifle during the 1970s and quantities of wheeled APCs were also obtained from this source. Some mortars and both field and anti-aircraft artillery pieces were also purchased from Yugoslavia during this period. Since the escalation of the civil war and the virtual destruction of the economy, the country has become essentially a client state of the US, upon which the government is dependent for its survival. Transfers of US military equipment have come to dwarf all others although it suits US policies to channel some of its financial military aid into additional purchases from Israel. Market opportunities for other than US or US approved suppliers seem destined to remain effectively non-existent for the forseeable future.

Although El Salvador possessed nothing approaching a local defence industry, from an early stage of the civil war various improvised armoured vehicles based both on commercial truck chassis and on the M114APC, of which the Salvadorean Army had managed to obtain a considerable number during the 1970s, were noted in service. A recent and interesting development by the Central Workshops of the Salvadorean Army is that of a wheeled APC/reconnaissance vehicle, based on the chassis of the US M37 4 × 4 light military truck of which the Salvadorean Army has over 100 examples. An initial series of 66 vehicles is entering service and the entire programme extends to about 90 vehicles. Further tentative developments towards the development of a limited defence industry may be expected.

Summary and prospects

El Salvador has been defined by President Reagan as the main battlefield between democracy and communism in the Western Hemisphere. This is however a dangerously simplistic view of what appears to have become a conflict between a US supported oligarchy and the majority of the Salvadorean people, waged on an increasingly genocidal level and with overtones disturbingly reminiscent of the war in Viet-Nam. While the anti-government guerrillas in El Salvador contain significant Marxist and Communist elements, to which, to a great extent, they owe their political cohesiveness and military efficiency and their blanket organisation bears the name of the Communist hero of the 1931 peasant uprising, it is a mistake to categorise all anti-government activists as belonging to the extreme political left. The fact that the Catholic Church, normally an extremely conservative institution and a staunch supporter of the status quo, is prominent in its opposition to the regime is significant. Thus, Archbishop Oscar Romero of San Salvador was assasinated by right-wing terrorists while celebrating Mass in March 1980.

The strength of the Salvadorean armed forces has increased more than three-fold since the outbreak of the present civil war. In June 1981 the Army numbered 12,000, the Navy 350 and the Air Force 450. By November 1981 Army strength had risen to 14,000, with 700 in the Navy and 600 in the Air Force and by June 1983 the strength of the Army was 26,688 and that of the Air Force 1287. Currently the Army numbers 38,650, the Navy 1290 and the Air Force 2700. These face an estimated 10,000 military active guerrillas and about as many active supporters who engage in sporadic acts of terrorism and sabotage, mainly in urban areas.

The civil war in El Salvador, the death toll of which had risen to an estimated 60,000 by 1986, cannot however be won on a military level alone and the political level upon which the US government initially decided to conduct it seemed destined to polarise all opposition to the series of regimes which it supported further towards the left. The political nadir occurred during the figurehead presidency of Alvaro Magaña between 1982 and 1984, when the real power was seen to be the ultra-rightist Major Roberto d'Aubisson. Despite, or perhaps because of, a spectacular increase in counter-terror, of which the administration was only barely covert in its support, the military initiative swung to the guerrillas. For a while during the first half of 1983 they controlled large tracts of the departments of Chalatenango and Morazán and were fielding a reinforced brigade, supported with captured armoured vehicles and artillery and engaging the Army in conventional set-piece battles. They could not however match the massive build-up in both manpower and equipment of the government forces and towards the end of 1983 were forced to revert to conventional guerrilla hit-and-run tactics, supported by a sustained campaign of sabotage against economic targets such as bridges and power lines. Although the armed forces appear to have won back the military initiative and the administration of President Duarte has a vastly more wholesome image than that of his immediate predecessors, a political solution to El Salvador's problems seems no closer.

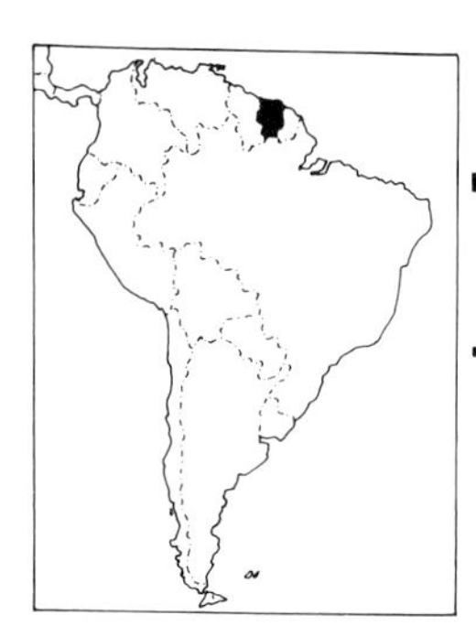

SURINAME

(Republiek van Suriname)

Area: 55,212 sq miles (142,709 sq km)
Population: 384,900
Total armed forces: 2535
Reserves: 3000
Available manpower: 30,000
Paramilitary forces: 900
GNP: $1,013,000 (1979)
Defence expenditure: $75 million (1984)

Introduction

Suriname is bordered by the Atlantic Ocean to the north, by the Republic of Guyana to the west, by French Guiana to the east and by Brazil to the south.

The population is highly cosmopolitan and heteregeneous consisting of 35% East Indians, 32% Creoles (persons of mixed European and either Indian or Negro racial origins), 16% Indonesians, 10% Bush Blacks (descended from escaped slaves), 3% Amerindians, 2% Europeans and 2% Chinese. About 90% of the population is concentrated in the coastal zone, principally in the vicinity of the capital, Paramaribo.

The major exports are bauxite, alumina and tropical woods. Most food and manufactured products are imported.

The country was first colonised by the English in 1630 and remained an English possession until 1667 when it was conquered by the Dutch, reconquered by the English and finally passed to the Netherlands by the Peace of Breda, all within the same year. The colony was reconquered by the English in 1799 and restored once more to the Netherlands by the Peace of Amiens of 1802. It was seized by Britain, yet again, in 1804 and was not finally restored to Netherlands rule until the Treaty of Vienna of 1815. Slavery was abolished in 1863 and in 1950 the colony became self-governing, full independence being finally obtained in 1975. Following independence, there was large scale emigration, the population falling by almost 35%. A left-wing military coup in February 1980 was followed by a more centrist one in August of the same year. There have been several subsequent unsuccessful attempts to overthrow the military government.

Suriname is a unitary, centralised republic. Executive power is vested in the President, who selects the Council of Ministers. There is a unicameral Legislative Council.

Suriname retains close relations with the Netherlands and is theoretically non-aligned in international politics. The exotic racial mix of the population has a potential for internal instability. Suriname also has frontier disputes with both Guyana and French Guiana.

Armed forces

Manpower: 2570 (Army 2350, Navy 160, Air Arm 60)

Infantrymen of the Suriname Defence Force

Ground force units: 1 Guard battalion
1 reinforced infantry battalion
1 Military Police battalion

AFVs: EE-9 Cascavel armoured cars
EE-11 Urutú and DAF YP-408 APC

Major naval units: 3 small patrol vessels
4 coastal patrol craft
3 river patrol craft

Aircraft: Britten-Norman BN-2A-21 Defender
Cessna U206

The Suriname Armed Forces consist of a single unified defence force with land, sea and air elements. The commander-in-chief is the President. Executive power rests with the Prime Minister, who is also Minister of Defence.

The land force element of the Suriname Armed Forces consists of a Guard battalion, a single reinforced infantry battalion and a military police battalion, most of the effectives of which are concentrated in the vicinity of the capital. Current strength is approximately 2350 all ranks with a volunteer reserve of about 3000. There is also a paramilitary National Militia numbering approximately 900. Equipment includes the FN FAL rifle in 7.62 mm calibre, the US M3A1 submachine gun in 0.45-inch and the FN MAG general-purpose machine gun in 7.62 mm. Support weapons comprise 81 mm mortars and 106 mm RCLs. The only heavy equipment in use consists of six Brazilian EE-9 Cascavel armoured cars, plus 15 EE-11 Urutú and nine Dutch DAF YP-408 APCs.

The armed forces include a Marine Section based at Paramaribo and manning the three 140-ton patrol vessels *S410*, *S402* and *S403*, the three 65-ton patrol craft *C301*, *C302* and *C303* and the three 15-ton river patrol craft *Bahadder*, *Fajablow* and *Korangon*, which appear to be the only named vessels in service. There is also a 10-ton coastal patrol craft, the number of which is unknown.

An air element is equipped with three Britten-Norman Defender multi-purpose tactical aircraft and a single Cessna U206.

Recruitment for the armed forces is entirely voluntary, the personnel being drawn almost exclusively from the Creole section of the population. Officers are trained in the Netherlands.

Sources of material supply and current requirements

Most of the equipment in use by the ground element of the Suriname armed forces has been acquired second-hand from the Netherlands, although by no means all of it is of Dutch manufacture. All vessels of the Marine Section were also built in the Netherlands. The recent acquisition of Brazilian manufactured armoured vehicles and of British and US aircraft may indicate a new departure in arms procurement policies.

The armed forces, as at present constituted, are inadequate either for effective internal security or for the defence of the country against external aggression. Some steps to remedy this situation may be expected in the forseeable future although economic stringency may continue to militate against the acquisition of artillery pieces, air defence weapons and helicopters, all of which are needed if the Suriname armed forces are to retain any credibility either as the guarantors of internal stability or the defenders of national sovereignty.

Summary and prospects

With an unbalanced economy, an extraordinarily heterogeneous population and frontier disputes with two of its three neighbours, the auspicies even for the survival of Suriname as an independent state seemed singularly unpromising, prompting the emigration of over a third of its population in the period immediately preceding and following independence. After its initial growing pains, the country, under its present military government, is grappling with its formidable problems and given reasonable freedom from outside interference, seems to be emerging as a viable political entity. Despite having no common frontiers with any of the Spanish-speaking countries of the South American continent, Suriname appears to be staking its future on cordial relations and commercial intercourse with these, even to the extent of attempting to phase in Spanish as the main business language in a hitherto predominantly Dutch-speaking country.

TRINIDAD AND TOBAGO

(Republic of Trinidad and Tobago)

Area: 1980 sq miles (5218 sq km)
Population: 1,350,000
Total armed forces: 2136
Reserves: 700 (estimated)
Available manpower: 100,000
Paramilitary forces: 4000
GNP: $8,792 million (1983)
Defence expenditure: $75 million (1984)

Introduction

The Republic of Trinidad and Tobago consists of the two islands of these names which lie off the north-east coast of Venezuela, from which Trinidad is only some 15 miles distant at its closest point. Trinidad, the larger, has an area of 1,864 sq miles and a population of approximately 1,300,000 of whom 45% are Negro and 35% of East Indian origins with substantial Chinese and European minorities. Tobago, 21 miles north-east of Trinidad, has an area of only 116 sq miles and a population of 50,000 which is overwhelmingly black.

The main economic activity is oil refining, both from Trinidad's own wells and of imported Venezuelan crude. Asphalt is an important product and tourism is also economically important. Some tropical products, including sugar, rum and cocoa are exported but although the soil is extremely fertile, over-population ensures that the republic must import most of its food.

Both islands were visited by Columbus in 1498, a Spanish colony being established in Trinidad in 1532. This suffered from almost continuous harrassment by pirates and privateers and from raids by the British, Dutch and French. The island was seized by Britain in 1797, British sovereignty being formally acknowledged by the Treaty of Amiens of 1802. Tobago attracted little attention until Latvian settlers from the Duchy of Courland established a colony in 1642. After the Swedish occupation of Courland the island was taken over by the Dutch, who held it from 1658 until 1662 when it passed to the French crown. Tobago was ceded to Britain by the Treaty of Paris of 1763, but it was not until 1804 that British rule was fully established, the island becoming a Crown Colony in 1877. From 1888 to 1959 Trinidad and Tobago were united as a British colony, becoming a member of the short-lived West Indian Federation in the latter year. When the Federation collapsed in 1962 Trinidad and Tobago became an independent state within the British Commonwealth, becoming a republic within the Commonwealth in 1976.

Executive power is vested in the President, who selects the cabinet, the senior minister in which has the title of Prime Minister. There is a bicameral legislature.

Demographic pressures and the decline in oil prices have a potential for serious internal instability, already manifested in rioting in 1970 and 1971 and leading to the declaration of a state of emergency in 1972. The republic takes an

independent stand on many international issues and requested the closure of US bases, established in 1941, the United States abandoning the last of these in 1967.

Armed Forces

Manpower: 2136 (Army 1500; Coast Guard 586; Air Service 50)

Ground force units: 1 infantry battalion
1 support battalion

Naval units: 2 patrol vessels
4 large and 7 small patrol craft
1 sail training ship

Light transport aircraft: Cessna 402

Helicopters: Sikorsky S-76

The armed forces form a single entity, the Trinidad and Tobago Defence Force, which is under the direct command of the Prime Minister. Recruitment is entirely voluntary, most officers continuing to be trained in Britain.

The ground force element of the Trinidad and Tobago Defence Force consists of the 1st Battalion of the Trinidad and Tobago Regiment, formerly the 2nd Battalion of the West India Regiment, the 1st and 3rd Battalions of which went to form the Jamaican Army on the break-up of the West Indian Federation. The Trinidad and Tobago Regiment also has a volunteer reserve battalion and supporting units. Equipment is exclusively of British origins and includes the L1A1 SLR rifle, the L2A3 Sterling sub-machine gun, the Bren light machine gun and the L7A1 GPMG general-purpose machine gun, plus a few 81 mm mortars. No heavy equipment or armoured vehicles are known to exist.

The Coast Guard which forms the naval component of the Trinidad and Tobago Defence Force, is militarily its most important element. It currently consists of the two 210-ton patrol vessels *Barracuda* and *Cascadura*, the four 100-ton patrol craft *Chaguramas*, *Buccoo Reef*, *Trinity* and *Courland Bay*, the 20-ton *Plymouth*, *Caroni*, *Galeota* and *Moruga* and the smaller *El Tucuche*, *Naparima* and *GC9*. There is also the small sail training ship *Humming Bird II*, the surveying launch *Meridian* and two unnamed research launches. Personnel numbers 45 officers and 541 ratings and there is a naval base at Staubles Bay.

The Trinidad and Tobago Coast Guard, which

***Patrol vessel* Barracuda *of the Trinidad and Tobago* (Bofors AB)**

was then subordinate to the Ministry for Home Affairs, formed an air element in 1966. The current aircraft inventory comprises one Cessna 402 fixed-wing aircraft, plus two Sikorsky S-76 and two Aérospatiale SA.341 Gazelle helicopters, manned by about 50 all ranks and operating from two bases at Piarco, Trinidad and Crown Point, Tobago.

Paramilitary forces

Manpower: 4000 (Police)

Heavy equipment: 6 patrol launches

A police force was formed in Trinidad towards the end of the 18th century. Controlled by the Minister of Home Affairs, this currently numbers some 4000 men and women. Although it has a para-military organisation, weapons are not normally carried. Small arms are available for use in an emergency and the police includes a marine section with six small patrol craft, based at Chaguaramas.

Sources of equipment supply and current requirements

Although the ground element of the Trinidad and Tobago Defence Force is equipped exclusively with British material, the Coast Guard has purchased equipment from the United States and Sweden as well as the UK and the Air Wing uses equipment of US and French origins. Trinidad and Tobago is thus clearly not bound by its colonial past nor its continuing membership of the British Commonwealth in the formulation of its defence material procurement policies.

The ground force element of the Trinidad and Tobago Defence Force needs some light armoured vehicles, anti-armour and air defence weapons and may be expected eventually to require some artillery. The Coast Guard seems unlikely to expand significantly in the forseeable future, although for effective coast defence the acquisition of some fast attack craft would make sense. Likewise, the air element of the Defence Force could usefully employ some additional light fixed-wing aircraft and helicopters even if the acquisition of combat equipment seems highly unlikely.

Summary and prospects

Although superficially the most prosperous of the former British Caribbean colonies, Trinidad and Tobago has suffered from the decline in world oil prices. Severe overpopulation and a highly heteregeneous population mix have an inherent potential for internal disorder which is explosive in the medium term. The country's own oil resources and its proximity to Venezuela's oil fields give it a high strategic importance which must make it a prime target for Cubano-Soviet subversion.

As is demonstrated by both the foreign policy of the republic and the material procurement policies for its Defence Force, exercised since independence, Trinidad and Tobago feels far less bound by traditional loyalties than do other former British colonies in the region. Future equipment procurement policies and outside influences remain therefore highly unpredictable.

Although the Coast Guard is showing signs of developing into something approaching a Navy, both the ground and air elements of the Trinidad and Tobago Defence Force are inadequate both in size and equipment for any serious internal security functions, much less the defence of the country against an external agressor. At present, the republic trusts implicitly in Britain and the United States and possibly to a certain largely subconscious degree to Venezuela, for its defence from any external threat, which effectively means Cuban intervention in the event of acute internal disturbance. The potential for the latter continues to grow and despite the country's declining economic situation some expansion of the ground and air forces may be forced on the government of the republic within the forseeable future.

URUGUAY

(República Oriental del Uruguay)

Area: 72,172 sq miles (186,998 sq km)
Coastline: 410 miles (660 km)
Population: 3,000,000 (estimated)
Total armed forces: 31,600
Reserves: 100,000
Available manpower: 250,000
Paramilitary forces: 3170
SNP: $5,050 million (1985)
Defence expenditure: $124,442,000 (1986)

Introduction

Uruguay is the smallest of the original independent states of South America and is bounded by Argentina to the west, by Brazil to the north and north-east, by the Atlantic Ocean to the south-east and by the River Plate estuary to the south and south-west. More than 90% of the population is of European origins, mainly Spanish and Italian, the remainder being largely of mixed white and Negro blood. There are no aboriginal Indians. More than 50% of the total population is concentrated in the vicinity of Montevideo, the capital city, less than 15% of the total population being rural.

Despite the concentration of population in the urban areas, the economy is almost totally dependent on stock raising and its by-products. The country is self-sufficient in food production but must import all fuels and most manufactured products although manufacturing industry is developing, with active government support.

In 1811 the Uruguayans declared their independence from Spain, resisting an attempt at annexation by Argentina during 1814/15. Brazil annexed the country from 1821 to 1825 but a three-year long war between Argentina and Brazil finally resulted in the recognition of Uruguayan independence by both countries in 1828. The early years of independence were characterised by an almost incessant struggle between nationalist and the pro Argentine factions, which attracted British and French intervention in 1852. From 1854 to 1857, Brazilian troops were stationed in the country at the request of the Nationalist President Flores to prevent annexation by Argentina. In 1865, the Paraguayan dictator, Francisco Solano López, intervened in Uruguayan internal politics provoking an extraordinary bloody war with the Triple Alliance of Argentina, Brazil and Uruguay between 1865 and 1870, from which the allies emerged victorious.

The internal political situation remained extremely turbulent until the two presidencies of José Battle y Ordóñez, from 1903 to 1907 and from 1911 to 1915, which brought peace and democracy to Uruguay, establishing the country as the first welfare state in Latin America. In the early 1950s the country was menaced by the expansionist plans of Argentina's Juan Domingo Perón, receiving active US support in resisting Perón's overtures.

An epidemic of urban terrorism by the "*Tupamaro*" guerrilla movement from the mid-1960s onwards provoked the seizure of power by the armed forces, hitherto the least politicised in Latin America, in 1973. The armed forces successfully contained the guerrilla threat but incurred much international opprobrium by alleged human rights violations. Following elections in 1984, the armed forces handed over power to a civilian government while specifically retaining the right to intervene if politics should once more take an unacceptable turn towards the Left.

Uruguay is a unitary republic of 19 departments. Executive power is in the hands of the President, who selects his own cabinet. There is a bicameral legislature.

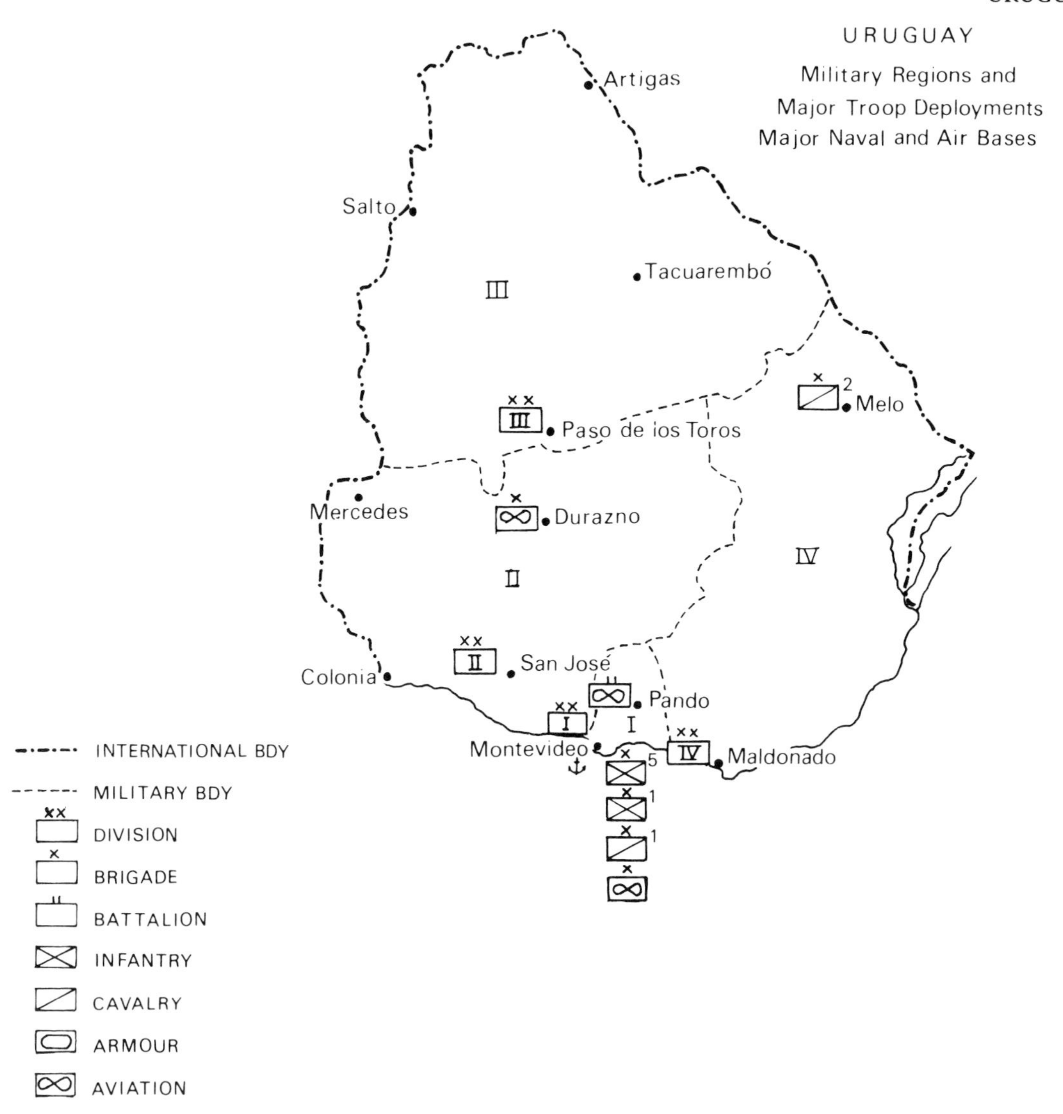

Structure of the armed forces

The President is commander-in-chief of the armed forces, although his powers, as such, are greatly circumscribed by Congress. The Minister of National Defence exercises administrative control over the Army, Navy, Air Force and the Maritime Police. Each of the armed forces has its own general staff but there is no joint staff.

The country is divided into four military regions.

Región Militar I (HQ Montevideo) covers the national capital and the departments of Montevideo and Canelones, *Región Militar II* (HQ San José) covering the departments of Durazno, Florida, San José, Flores, Colonia and Soriano, *Región Militar III* (HQ Paso de los Toros) the departments of Río Negro, Paysandú, Salto, Artigas, Rivera and Tacuarembó and *Región Militar IV* the departments of Cerro Largo, Treinta y Tres, Rocha, Lavalleja and Maldonado.

Unusually in Latin America, recruitment is entirely voluntary, recruits contracting to serve for periods of one or two years although suitable candidates may complete up to 27 years service between the ages of 18 and 45.

Each of the armed forces has its own schools for the training of officers and a comprehensive system of branch schools for the training of specialist other ranks. There is a tri-service Institute of Superior Studies for senior officers.

Army

Manpower: 22,300

Tactical formations: 4 divisions comprising:-
5 infantry brigades
3 cavalry brigades
1 engineer brigade
1 signals brigade

Major units: 15 infantry battalions (including 1 armoured, 1 paratroop and 2 motorised)
9 cavalry regiments (including 1 ceremonial, 4 armoured and 1 motorised)
5 artillery groups
1 anti-aircraft group
5 engineer batallions

AFVs: M41, M24 and M3A1 light tanks
FN 4RM/62 and EE-9 Cascavel armoured cars
EE-3 Jararacá and M3A1 White scout cars
M113, M2 half-track and Condor APCs

Artillery: Mod.81 155 mm, M101 and M102 105 mm howitzers
Bofors M.1902 75 mm guns

Air defence: M1 40 mm L/60
Vulcan M167 20 mm

The development of organised, professional armed forces was slower in Uruguay than in the case of its immediate neighbours. A degree of professionalisation followed the Triple Alliance War at 1865–70 but depoliticisation did not occur until during the first administration of Battle y Ordónez in 1904. Following the First World War the Uruguayan Army came under the influence of a succession of French military missions and officers were sent for post-graduate training to the various specialist schools of the French Army. The outbreak of the Second World War occasioned the recall of the French military mission and with it the almost simultaneous substitution of United States for French influence in the Uruguayan armed forces. US influence has continued to be predominant despite the period of rejection of US military assistance between the mid-1970s and 1980s.

The Army currently numbers approximately 22,300 all ranks.

Each of the four Military Regions is garrisoned by a nominal division of identical numerical designation. Each division consists of a single infantry brigade of three battalions, at least one cavalry regiment, an artillery group and an engineer battalion, plus logistic and medical units.

The Ist Division (HQ Montevideo), covering the 1st Military Region, consists of the 1st Infantry Brigade (HQ Montevideo), with the 1st *Florida*, the unnamed 2nd and the 3rd *Veinticuatro de Abril* Infantry Battalions, the 3rd Cavalry Brigade (HQ also Montevideo), with the 6th *Antanizaldo Suárez* Horsed, the 4th Armoured, which is equipped with EE-9 Cascavel armoured and EE-3 Jararacá scout cars, and the 9th Motorised Cavalry Regiments, an Artillery Command comprising the 1st and 5th Field Artillery Groups, the latter equipped with 155 mm howitzers, and the 1st Anti-Aircraft Artillery Group, plus the 1st Engineer Battalion, 1st Signals Company and logistic support units.

The IInd Division (HQ San José), which covers the 2nd Military Region, consists of the 2nd Infantry Brigade (HQ Colonia), made up of the 4th, 5th and 6th Infantry Battalions, the 2nd *General Pablo Gallarza* Armoured Cavalry Regiment equipped with M41 tanks and M113 APCs, the 2nd Field Artillery Group and the 2nd Engineer Battalion, 2nd Signals Company and logistic support units.

The IIIrd Division (HQ Tacuarembó), covering the 3rd Military Region, consists of the 3rd Infantry Brigade (HQ Salto), comprising the unnamed 7th, the 8th *Leandro Gómez* and the unnamed 9th Infantry Battalions, the latter equipped with Condor APCs, the 1st Cavalry Brigade (HQ Rivera), made up of the 3rd and 10th Horsed and the 5th Armoured Cavalry Regiments, the latter equipped with M3A1 light tanks and White scout cars, the 3rd Field Artillery Group and the 3rd Engineer Battalion, 3rd Signals Company and logistic support units.

The IVth Division (HQ Minas) comprises the 4th Infantry Brigade (HQ Minas), with the 10th, 11th and 12th Infantry Battalions, the 2nd Cavalry Brigade (HQ Melo), with the 7th Horsed and 8th Armoured Cavalry Regiments, the latter equipped with FN 4RM/62 armoured cars and Condor APCs, the 4th Field Artillery Group and the 4th Engineer Battalion, 4th Signals Company and logistic support units.

Army troops, almost all of which are deployed at or in the vicinity of Montevideo, include the 1st *Blandengues de Artigas* Cavalry Regiment, which serves as the Presidential bodyguard, performing largely ceremonial duties at the capital, the 5th Infantry Brigade (HQ Montevideo), an administrative rather than a tactical or operational formation, which comprises the 13th Armoured Infantry Regiment equipped with M24 tanks and M2 half-tracks, the 14th Airborne and the 15th Motorised Infantry Regiments, the latter equipped with Condor APCs, the 1st Engineer Brigade, which comprises the 5th and 6th Engineer Battalions and the 1st Signals Brigade with the 1st and 2nd Signals Battalions.

Rifles in service are the FN FAL in 7.62 mm calibre, the US M16 in 5.56 mm and the 0.30 calibre M1 Garand. The US M3A1 sub-machine gun in 0.45-inch calibre and the Israeli Uzi in 9 mm are both in use as are the FN MAG machine gun in 7.62 mm, the Browning BAR and M1919, both in 0.30 calibre, the Madsen Model 1937 in 7.62 mm and the Browning M2HB 0.50 calibre. Anti-armour weapons in service are the US M40A1 106 mm RCL, the M18 57 mm rocket projector and the obsolete M1 57 mm towed anti-tank gun. Mortars are all of US origins and include both 81 mm and 4.2-inch models, the latter obtained via South Korea. Armour consists of 22 US M41 light tanks obtained second-hand from Belgium, 17 M24 and 28 reconditioned M3A1 light tanks. Fifteen Scorpions are also reputedly on order. There are also 12 Belgian FN 4RM/62 and 15 Brazilian EE-9 Cascavel armoured cars, 18 Brazilian EE-3 Jararacá and ten White M3A1 scout cars, plus 18 US M113 tracked, ten M2 half-track and 55 German Condor wheeled APCs. Artillery equipment comprises six Argentine Mod.81 L/33 155 mm, 28 US M101 and 8 M102 105 mm howitzers and 12 ex-Argentine Bofors M1902 L/40 75 mm field guns. Air-defence weapons in service consist of an undisclosed number of US 40 mm M1 and six M167 Vulcan 20 mm equipments.

The Uruguayan Army remains one of the very few in Latin America to rely on voluntary enlistment for recruitment and the rank and file continue to be composed largely of long-service professionals. Officers are trained at the Military Academy which offers a four year course leading to a commission in the rank of 2nd lieutenant. Both junior officers and other ranks receive specialist training in the School of Arms and Services. The Command and Staff School provides post-graduate training for officers at mid-career, leading to promotion to field rank or to staff appointments.

Navy

Manpower:	6300 (including Marines and Naval aviation)
Major units:	3 destroyer escorts 1 corvette 4 patrol vessels 1 training ship
Marines:	1 battalion
Naval aviation:	1 light strike unit 1 patrol/ASW unit 1 communications flight 1 helicopter flight
Aircraft:	Beech Super King Air 200 Sud Aviation T-28S Fennec Grumman S-2A and G Sikorsky SH-34J; Bell 47 Bell 222 Beech TC-45; Piper PA-18 Beech T-34B and C; North American SNJ-5

As an organised force the Uruguayan Navy dates only from the second half of the 19th century and has always remained quite a small service, although during the 1950s Uruguayan Naval Aviation grew out of all proportion to the surface units of the force and for a period was the second most powerful naval air arm in Latin America.

The Uruguayan Navy is currently made up largely of somewhat antiquated material and comprises an Escort Division with the 1240-ton Second World War vintage "Cannon" class destroyer escorts *Uruguay* and *Artigas* and the 10-year younger 1450-ton "Dealey" class *Diez y Ocho de Julio*, together with the 1090-ton corvette *Comandante Pedro Campbell* (formerly a US

***Destroyer escort* Diez y Ocho de Julio *of the Uruguayan Navy* (US Navy)**

"Auk" class ocean minesweeper of Second World War vintage) and a Patrol Division, with the 375-ton former US coastal minesweeper *Rio Negro* and the three 190-ton French-built fast patrol craft *Quince de Noviembre*, *Veinticinco de Agosto* and *Comodoro Coe*, completed in 1981, as the only modern units of an otherwise rather geriatric fleet.

The 57-year old Spanish-built surveying vessel *Capitán Miranda* has now been converted to a schooner-rigged sea-going sail training ship and the old Italian-built patrol vessel *Salto* is used for training purposes, the former US "Cohoes" class

***Grumman S-2 Tracker ASW aircraft of Uruguay's* Aviación Naval**

netlayer *Huracán* doubling as a salvage vessel and for hydrographic survey. About half a dozen small landing craft furnish a limited amphibious assault capability for the single battalion of the *Fusileros Navales* (Marines), who are equipped with the same personal and close support weapons as the Army. The 131,000-ton tanker *Juan A. Lavalleja* is on semi-permanent commercial charter as is the small transport *President Oribe*, although both vessels are owned by the Navy.

The only naval base in operation is at Montevideo and has fairly extensive ship repair facilities, including a drydock and a slipway.

The *Aviación Naval Uruguaya* is currently but a shadow of its former glory, with a combat unit equipped with the survivors of nine ex-Argentine T-28S Fennecs, an ASW/SAR unit equipped with six Grumman Tracker S-2A and Gs, a single Beech Super King Air 200T and two Sikorsky SH-34Js, a communications flight with three Beech TC-45Js and two Piper PA-18 Super Cubs, a helicopter element with two Bell 47s and a single Bell 222 and a training element with three Beech T-34B and Cs and three North American SNJ-5s, all based at the *Base Aeronaval Capitán de Corbeta Carlos A. Curbelo* at Laguna del Sauce on the River Plate estuary.

Total naval personnel strength is approximately 6300, including 500 marines and 400 naval aviation.

Naval officers follow a five-year course at the Naval Academy, which also trains officers for the maritime police and the merchant marine. There is also a Naval War College, which provides advanced post-graduate training for senior officers, preparing them for promotion to the higher ranks or for staff appointments. The Navy's enlisted personnel receive their training at the School of Naval Specialiation. All naval training establishments are located at the Naval Training Centre in the Montevideo port area.

Air Force

Manpower: 3000

Units: 2 air brigades, comprising
1 fighter/ground attack squadron
3 transport squadrons
1 helicopter squadron
1 training squadron

Fighter/ground attack aircraft: Cessna A-37B
Lockheed AT-33A
IA-58 Pucará
North American AT-6G

Fokker F.27 transport of the 4th Aviation Group of the Uruguayan Air Force **(A. J. Risseeuw)**

***Uruguayan CASA-212 Aviocar light transport* (Author)**

Transports:	Beech Queen Air 80 CASA C-212 Aviocar Douglas C-47 EMBRAER EMB.110 Fokker F.27 Learjet 35A
Liaison aircraft:	Piper PA-18 Super Cub Cessna U-17A
Helicopters:	Bell UH1-B and H Bell 212 FH-227
Trainers:	Beech T-34A and B Cessna T-41D and 182

Uruguayan military aviation dates from 1916 when a flying training school was established at Paso de Mendoza, near Montevideo. It remained a modest force until the Second World War during which the *Aeronáutica Militar Uruguaya* was the recipient of fairly lavish US military assistance. In 1947 a US air mission arrived in Uruguay and set about the reorganisation of the Uruguayan military aviation service and in 1953 the *Aeronáutica Militar* became the *Fuerza Aérea Uruguaya*, a completely autonomous service co-equal in status with the Army and Navy. With the retirement of most of the equipment received under US military assistance programmes during the 1940s and 1950s the Uruguayan Air Force once more contracted and has remained of modest proportions with limited and largely obsolescent equipment.

The *Fuerza Aérea Uruguaya* currently has a total personnel strength of approximately 3000 all ranks, operating about 100 aircraft and is organised into two flying and one non-flying commands.

Tactical Air Command controls Air Brigade No 1 (*Base Aeronáutica* No 1 *Capitán Boiso Lanza* at Paso de Mendoza) which comprises Aviation Group No 3 (Transport) with five CASA C-212 Aviocars, six Beech Queen Air 80s and six Douglas

C-47s, Aviation Group No 4 (Transport) with a single Gates Learjet 35A, two Fokker F.27s and two Fairchild-Hiller FH-227Ds, Aviation Group No 5 (Search and Rescue) with eight Bell UH-1B and Hs, two Bell 212s and six Cessna U-17s and Aviation Group No 6 (Transport) with five EMBRAER EMB.110 Bandeirantes, plus Air Brigade No 2 (*Base Aeronáutica No 2 Teniente 2° Mario Walter Parallada* at Durazno) which consists of Aviation Group No 1 (Training) with ten Beech T-34As, three Cessna 182s and two Piper Super Cubs and Aviation Group No 2 (Fighter) with six IA-58s, six Cessna A-37Bs, four Lockheed T-33As and three North American AT-6Gs.

Air Training Command controls the *Escuela Militar de Aeronáutica* (*Aéropuerto Militar General Artigas* at Pando) with 20 Beech T-34Bs and six Cessna T-41Ds as its sole flying unit, the *Escuela Técnica de Aeronáutica*, also at Pando and the *Escuela de Comando y Estado Mayor* at Carrasco, Montevideo.

Air Material Command exercises control over the Maintenance and Supply Brigade, the Communications and Electronics Brigade and the Directorate of Airfields.

Aspiring officers must successfully complete the four-year course at the *Escuela de Aeronáutica* before receiving their commissions in the rank of second lieutenant. The *Escuela Técnica de Aeronáutica* gives specialist training to both officers and other ranks. The *Escuela de Comando y Estado Mayor* prepares officers for staff appointments or promotion to the higher levels of command. The *Escuela Técnica de Aeronáutica* also includes the parachutists school although the sole paratroop battalion is part of the Army.

There are a number of airfields suitable for the operation of military aircraft throughout the country which are not permanently occupied by units of the *Fuerza Aérea Uruguaya*. Most important of these is the *Aerodromo Angel S. Adami* at Melilla, which is staffed by the Air Force although no flying units are permanently deployed there.

The Air Force is also responsible for civil aviation, controlling the *Dirección General de Aeropuertos Nacionales* and since 1974 the civil airline PLUNA and the military airline TAMU operate their domestic routes on a joint basis.

Paramilitary forces

Manpower: 520 (Republican Guard)
650 (Metropolitan Guard)
2000 (Maritime Police)

Heavy equipment: 12 patrol craft (Maritime Police)

Operationally, the 17,000-man National Police, which is subordinate to the Minister of the Interior and which was established in 1829, is divided between the Montevideo Police, the Interior Police, the Highway Police and the National Corps of Firemen, the latter being a somewhat unusual institution as in Uruguay fire-fighting is organised at national level and is a police function. Each section recruits separately and although recruits are trained together, they usually follow the same specialisation throughout their careers.

The National Police performs essentially civil police functions, but the Montevideo Police also includes two distinctly paramilitary forces: the Republican Guard and the Metropolitan Guard. The Republican Guard is a mounted ceremonial unit of two squadrons which has a subsidiary riot control function and a total strength of 520. The Metropolitan Guard is a unit of about 650 all ranks which provides guards at public buildings, embassies, banks etc. The Montevideo Police also includes a quick-action anti-terrorist unit and a small force of policewomen.

The paramilitary units are recruited and trained identically to the civilian units of the National Police, receiving specialist training from the Army.

Officer candidates must be between the ages of 17 and 23, enlisted personnel must be between the ages of 21 and 35 and have reached a prescribed educational level, as well as being physically fit. The Police Training Academy, established in 1943, has separate schools for officers and other ranks. Basic training for enlisted personnel lasts for three months and that for non-commissioned officers one year. The officer cadet program lasts for two years. In-service courses for promotion to the next highest rank last for three months in the case of both officers and NCOs. The senior ranks are usually held by either retired army officers or officers on the active list seconded to the National Police.

The Republican Guard adds sabres to the

pistols and truncheons carried by the civilian units of the National Police and the Metropolitan Guards usually carry sub-machine guns. A range of infantry weapons is also available.

In addition to the National Police, there is the *Prefectura Nacional Marítima*, established in 1925. This force is subordinate to the Navy and performs coast guard functions including coastal patrol, life saving, the maintenance of navigational aids and the supervision of the ports and of the merchant marine. It also functions as harbour police and has a strength of approximately 2000 manning the 70-ton patrol craft *Carmelo*, the 60-ton *Paysandú* and the 30-ton *Colonia*, all of which nominally belong to the Navy, together with about ten small unnamed patrol craft and the buoy tender *Vanguardia*. Both the officers and ratings of the Maritime Police are trained by the Navy.

Sources of defence material supply and current requirements

Germany, France and Italy were Uruguay's traditional sources of defence material up to the Second World War. During the 25 years after the end of the war, the United States became the almost exclusive purveyor of defence material to the Uruguayan government. Following Uruguay's rejection of US military aid during the latter stages of the Carter administration, the county turned elsewhere, notably to Belgium, France and Spain, for its requirements. Argentina has also provided some second-hand material and Uruguay was the first foreign country to order the Argentine Pucará aircraft. Armoured vehicles, motor transport equipment and aircraft have recently been purchased from Brazil and quite a large consignment of artillery and air defence weapons has recently been purchased from South Korea. The Uruguayan Army also notably lacks either anti-tank or anti-aircraft missiles and systems of this type must figure on its shopping list in the foreseeable future.

While for most of the 20th century the Uruguayan armed forces were starved of new equipment, the military regime predictably took some measures to modernise and improve the equipment of the Army. The Navy however remained largely equipped with obsolescent material of Second World War vintage and the two Type 209 submarines, rumoured to have been ordered in the late 1970s, have failed to materialise. The Navy could also usefully employ half-a-dozen or so fast attack craft and several additional maritime patrol and anti-submarine warfare aircraft while the small Marine Corps notably lacks an adequate sea-lift or amphibious assault capability. The Air Force also has suffered from the lack of modern combat aircraft in recent years and at least a token force of modern interceptors could well figure on the Uruguayan military shopping list in the forseeable future.

Although several small craft have been built locally for the *Prefecture Marítima*, Uruguay cannot be said to have anything classifiable as a local defence industry.

Summary and prospects

Uruguay owes its independent existence to its geographical position as a buffer state between Brazil and Argentina, both of which have made sporadic attempts to annexe it. Currently the country seems blessedly free of any immediately potential external threat. The Uruguayan military government of 1973/84 appears likewise to have successfully contained the activities of the various terrorist forces which brought the country to the verge of social and economic disintegration in the mid-1970s. The economy is recovering, despite the current debt crisis which afflicts all the countries of the region to varying degrees and although under military rule active political opposition appeared to have ceased to exist, a very active political life commenced again once the military government consented to the holding of elections in 1984.

Although the Uruguayan armed forces experienced great difficulty in disengaging from their self-imposed but largely unwanted political role, they now seem effectively to have done so and while spelling out the conditions under which they were prepared to hand over power to civilian politicians appear to have returned to their traditionally apolitical status.

As an entirely professional force, which is in the process of replacing a largely obsolescent equipment inventory with more modern material, the military potential of the Uruguayan Army should be superior to that of most of its neighbours. Having engaged in no foreign war since 1870, its true potential is however difficult to assess.

The Uruguayan Navy remains a modest force of very limited military potential. Its composition of exclusively professional personnel however gives it a certain qualitative edge over many larger forces in the region.

The Air Force is likewise highly professional but lacks modern combat equipment, having become largely an internal security, transport and training force.

VENEZUELA

(República de Venezuela)

Area: 352,143 sq miles (911,680 sq km)
Population: 18,911,000
Total armed forces: 66,000
Reserves: 250,000 (estimated)
Available manpower: 1,500,000
Paramilitary forces: 22,000
GNP: $49,654 million (1984)
Defence expenditure: $1,069 million (1984)

Introduction

Venezuela, the sixth largest country in South America, is bounded on the north by the Caribbean Sea, on the west by Colombia, on the south by Brazil and on the east by Guyana. Some 67% of the population are of mixed European and Amerindian racial origins, approximately 21% are pure white, 10% Negro and 2% unassimilated Indians. Over 75% of the population is concentrated in the main urban centres, much of the country being virtually uninhabited.

As the world's third largest oil exporter, the Venezuelan economy is dominated by the export of petroleum products although iron ore, coffee and cocoa are also important exports. There are also largely underexploited deposits of gold, diamonds, bauxite, manganese, nickel and coal. Imports consist mainly of machinery and manufactured goods. Due mainly to the large-scale migration of population from the countryside to the major population centres, food production is insufficient to meet demand and foodstuffs also figure amongst imports.

Independence from Spain was established in 1821, following a bloody struggle which cost the lives of 300,000 out of a total population of 800,000.

From 1821 until 1829 Venezuela joined with Colombia and Ecuador in the Federation of Gran Colombia, Venezuela withdrawing in the latter year and Ecuador a year later. Notable as the cradle of South American independence, the period of instability which followed independence in most of the countries of Latin America lasted considerably longer in Venezuela than elsewhere, the country emerging as a modern nation state only in the late 1930s. Despite a return to military dictatorship between 1948 and 1958, hard-won democracy, once established, has however survived on apparently firmer grounds in Venezuela than in almost any other country of Latin America and has successfully weathered concentrated attempts at subversion and destabilisation throughout the 1960s and early 1970s. Recently the country has developed an increasingly independent foreign policy and while remaining essentially pro-Western, supported Argentina in the South Atlantic War of 1982 and has joined with Mexico, Colombia and Panama in the "Contadora Group" to oppose United States policies in Central America. A long history of cordial relations with Panama would appear also to indicate a potential role for Venezuela as a guarantor of Panamanian sovereignty when that country assumes full responsibility for the Panama Canal at the end of the current century.

Venezuela is a federal republic of 20 states, a federal district and two federal territories. Executive power is vested in the President, who selects his own cabinet. There is a bicameral federal legislature and each state elects its own governor and legislature.

The country's strategic importance is two-fold, stemming both from its geographical position and its enormous oil reserves. Relations with its neighbours until recently were relatively friendly despite frontier disputes with both Colombia and Guyana, Venezuela claiming almost 60% of the total territory of the latter country. A series of frontier incursions during 1987 however led to tension with Columbia.

Structure of the armed forces

Venezuela adds to the three traditional armed forces a fourth, the *Fuerzas Armadas de Cooperación*, a national paramilitary police force colloquially and semi-officially known as the "National Guard", which has full co-equal status with the Army, Navy and Air Force.

The President is commander-in-chief of the armed forces, exercising control on a day-to-day basis through the Minister of National Defence, to whom all major units of the four armed forces report directly. The Minister of Defence is traditionally a senior officer, not necessarily of the Army, which enjoys no special position of primacy over the other armed forces. The Minister is advised by the Joint Staff and by the Inspector General of the armed forces but enjoys great autonomy under the overall authority of the President of the republic. The Joint Staff is a purely advisory body although, in practice, it usually combines the general staffs of the Army, Navy, Air Force and National Guard, each of which is an autonomous entity.

The Ministry of Defence directly controls a number of multi-service command, security and logistic support units, including the Presidential Guard Regiment.

The country is divided into six military areas of which *Area Militar 1* (HQ San Cristóbal) covers the states of Táchira, Mérida, Barinas and western Apure, *Area Militar* 2 (HQ Maracaibo) the state of Zulia and western parts of Falcón and

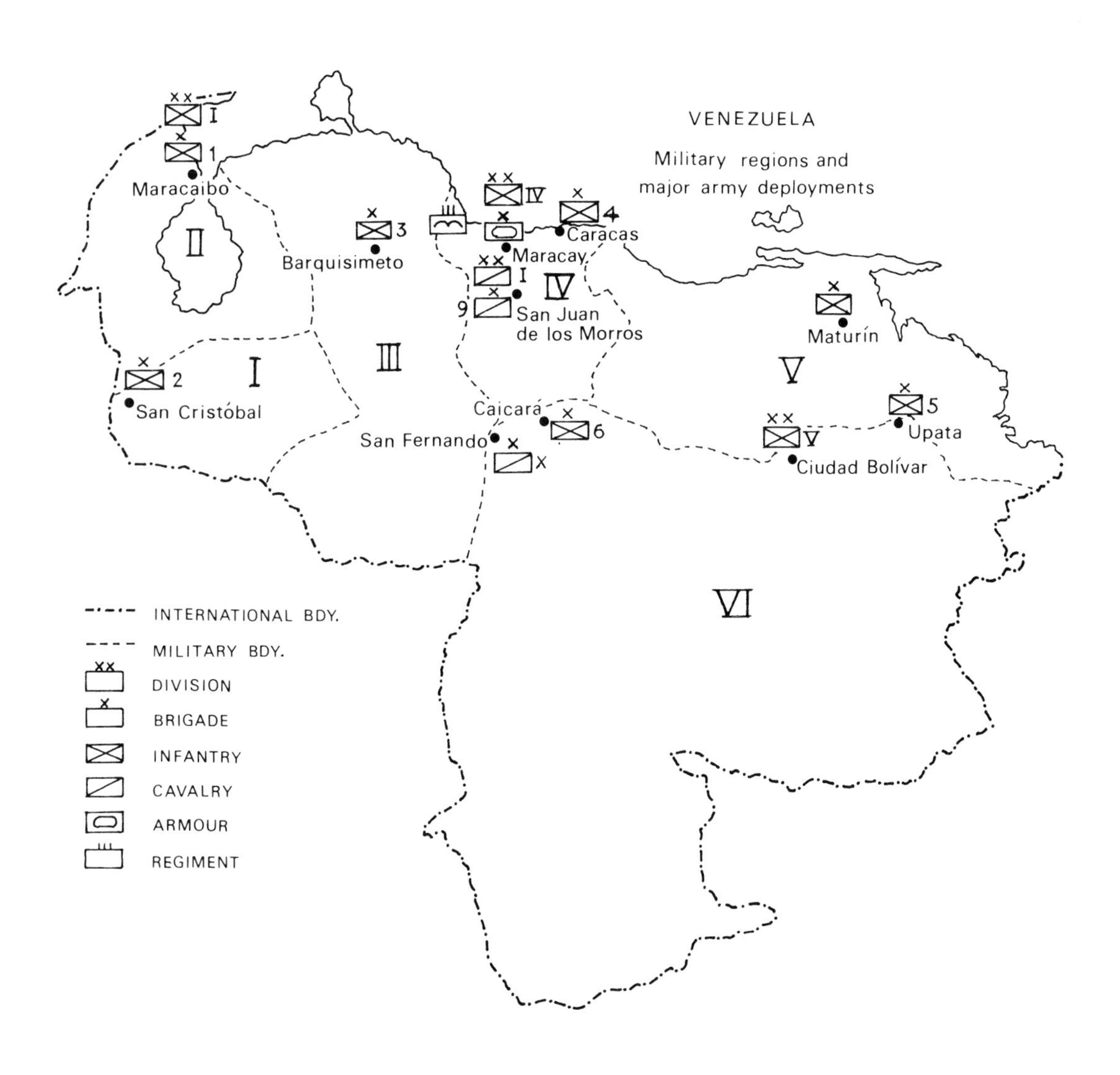

Trujillo, *Area Militar 3* (HQ Barquisimeto) the states of Lara, Yaracuy, Portuguesa, Cojedes, Carabobo, most of Falcón and eastern Trujillo, *Area Militar 4* (HQ Maracay) the federal capital and the states of Aragua, Miranda, Guárico and most of Apure, *Area Militar 5* (HQ Maturín) the states of Nueva Esparta, Sucre, Monagas, Anzoátegui and the Delta Amacuro Territory and *Area Militar 6* (HQ Ciudad Bolívar) the state of Bolívar and the Amazonas Territory.

Military service is theoretically obligatory for all male citizens although in practice a selective draft system is employed, conscripts, of whom there are approximately 20,000 at any given time, serving for two years from the age of 18. On completion of their service conscripts revert to reserve status until the age of 45 but no formal reserve organisation appears to exist. Recruitment to the National Guard is entirely voluntary, many conscripts choosing to enlist in this force on the completion of their term of military training. NCOs are time-expired conscripts who re-enlist voluntarily for extended periods of service and generally make the armed forces their careers. All four armed forces also include female elements.

Each of the armed forces has its own comprehensive system of schools for officers, NCOs and specialists. There is also a joint service Institute of Higher Studies for National Defence at Caracas, at which high ranking officers and selected civilians pursue studies in overall security and defence strategy.

Although Venezuelans played a prominant part in the wars of independence in the northern and north-eastern parts of South America the professionalisation of the Venezuelan armed forces dates only from the 1890s. The original significant foreign influence during their formative years was that of Germany, later consolidated, at second-hand, by a Chilean military mission which functioned in the early years of the present century. Following the First World War, French and later Belgian influence became important and officers were also sent to study in Peru, from which further French influence was absorbed at second-hand. During the Second World War all other external influences were superseded by that of the United States which remains predominant.

Venezuela now trains officers and subordinate military personnal from some of the smaller Latin American countries, including Panama.

Army

Manpower: 47,000

Formations:
3 infantry divisions
(plus another to form)
1 jungle division
1 mechanised cavalry division
1 armoured brigade
1 ranger brigade
1 airborne regiment
(to expand to a brigade)

Major units:
20 infantry battalions (of which
2 mechanised, 1 motorised,
1 mountain and 6 jungle)
6 ranger battalions
2 paratroop battalions
3 armoured battalions
1 armoured cavalry group
1 motorised cavalry group
3 motorised cavalry squadrons
7 artillery groups (one SP)
1 artillery rocket group
5 heavy mortar batteries
2 air defence groups
(plus two forming)
3 air defence batteries
4 combat engineer battalions
1 aviation regiment

AFVs:
AMX-30 medium tanks
AMX-13 light tanks
M18 tank destroyers
AMX-VCI APCs
V-150 Comando AFV

Artillery:
Oto Melara Model 56 and
M101 105 mm howitzers
M114 155 mm howitzers
Mk F.3 155 mm SPH
LAR 160 mm MLRs

Missiles: SS-11 ATGW and Roland SAM

Air defence:
Bofors 40 mm L/60 and
Breda-Bofors 40 mm L/70
M42 twin 40 mm SP and
AML S.530 twin 20 mm SP

Aircraft:
Beech Queen Air and
Super King Air,
Pilatus-Britten-Norman
Islander, Aeritalia G222 and

IAI Arava transport aircraft
Cessna Skylane and Stationair light aircraft
Agusta A109 and AS-61N, Bell 47, UH-1H and 206B helicopters

Following the Wars of Independence, the Venezuelan Army declined in importance political chaos which prevailed for most of the 19th century, being revived only by the series of dictators who ruled the country from the late 1880s until 1935 and used the armed forces as their power base. The Pérez Jiménez dictatorship of 1948–58 was also characterised by lavish investment in the armed forces which nevertheless overthrew it and restored democratic government which they have continued to support to date. Widespread guerrilla insurgency during the 1960s however led the Venezuelan Army once more to develop an internal-security/counter-insurgency orientation.

Until recently each of the six Military Areas was garrisoned by a nominal infantry division of identical numerical designation, each of which was organised into one or two brigades and a variable complement of combat and logistic support units. There was also an armoured brigade, a regiment of paratroops and an independent ranger brigade, all subject to the strategic command of the Ministry of Defence. In addition there was an air defence group subordinate to the Air Defence Command of the Ministry of Defence, which controlled both Army and Air Force units.

Under the *Plan Carabobo*, adopted in 1975 with a view to the restoration and amplification of conventional military capabilities, the ground forces were to be divided into a Territorial Defence Force of five infantry and one cavalry divisions and an Immediate Intervention Force comprising the remaining tactical formations and combat units. Economic considerations have delayed its full implementation, only four of the infantry divisions of the Territorial Defence Force having been established and each having only one or two of its scheduled three brigades while the cavalry division also remains incomplete.

The Army currently numbers some 47,000 all ranks.

The Territorial Defence Force consists of the 1st, 2nd and 4th Infantry Divisions, the 5th Jungle Infantry Division and the 1st Mechanised Cavalry Division and will ultimately also include a new 3rd Infantry Division.

The 1st Infantry Division (HQ Maracaibo) covers the 2nd Military Area and consists primarily of the IInd Infantry Brigade (HQ Maracaibo) consisting of the 1st *Venezuela, 23rd Aramendi* and 52nd *Santiago Mariña* Infantry Battalions and the 2nd Motorised Cavalry squadron, the 51st *Freites* Field Artillery Group, a heavy mortar battery, the 2nd Air Defence Battery, a combat engineer battalion and a signals company, plus a frontier detachment and a group of SP missile artillery at division level. The second and third brigades of this division will be formed in the medium term to cover the areas immediately to the south and east of Lake Maracaibo, respectively.

The 2nd Infantry Division (HQ San Cristóbal) covers the 1st Military Area and is made up of the Ist Infantry Brigade (HQ San Cristóbal) comprising the 11th *Coronel Antonio Ricaurte* Mechanised and 13th *Justo Briceño* Infantry Battalions and the 12th *Cedeño* Mountain Rifle Battalion, the 1st *Leonardo Infante* Motorised Cavalry Squadron, the 11th *Coronel Miguel Antonio Vázquez* Field Artillery Group, a heavy mortar battery, the 1st Air Defence Battery, an engineer company and a logistic support company. Additional infantry brigades will ultimately be formed at Mérida and Barinas, the motorised cavalry squadron is scheduled to be expanded to a group and an electronic warfare unit is expected to be established in the near future.

The 4th Infantry Division (HQ Maracay) covers the 3rd and 4th Military Areas and consists of the IIIrd Infantry Brigade (HQ Barquisimeto) comprising the 31st *Girardot-Prolong*, 32nd *Rivas-Dávila* and 41st *Carabobo* Infantry Battalions, the 73rd *Cruz Carillo* Field Artillery Group and a battery of heavy mortars, together with the IVth Infantry Brigade (HQ Caracas), made up of the 2nd *Caracas* and 3rd *Bolívar* Infantry Battalions, the 4th *Negro Primero* Motorised Cavalry Squadron, the 41st *General Salom* Field Artillery Group, the 1st *Francisco Avendaño* Combat Engineer Battalion and a signals company. The activation of the third brigade of this division is expected in the near future although its headquarters has not been announced.

The 1st Mechanised Cavalry Division (HQ San Juan de los Morros) covers the southern portion of the 4th Military Area, its major element being the IX Mechanised Cavalry Brigade (HQ San Juan de los Morros) comprising the 1st *Coronel Ambrosio Plaza* Armoured and the 3rd *Coronel Julián Mellado* Motorised Cavalry Groups, the 72nd *General de Divisón Laurencio Silva* Motorised Rifle Battalion, the 33rd *Coronel José Cornelio Muñoz* Field Artillery Group, a signals company and a support and maintenance company. This division will also ultimately include a second and third brigade, each to consist of two groups of motorised cavalry, a heavy mortar battery, an engineer company, a signals company and logistic support units.

Bolívar) covers the 6th Military Area and comprises the Vth Jungle Brigade (HQ Upata) which consists of the 61st *Urdaneta,* 62nd *Juan José Rondón* and 63rd *Coronel Vicente Campo Elías* Jungle Infantry Battalions, plus a battery of heavy mortars and a combat engineer battalion, and the incomplete VIth Jungle Brigade (HQ Caicará del Orinoco) consisting of the 51st *Sucre,* 58th *Tomás de Heres* and 64th *Montilla* Jungle Infantry Battalions, a heavy mortar battery and a combat engineer battalion. A third brigade is scheduled for activation, with its headquarters at Puerto Ayacucho.

The new 3rd Infantry Division, which is scheduled for activation in the medium term, will cover the 5th Military Area, with its headquarters at Barcelona and will be built around the existing 9th *Nariño* Infantry Battalion, plus combat and logistic support units and will also ultimately consist of three brigades.

Each division also includes a signals company and a military police company, attached to divisional headquarters.

The most important element of the Immediate Intervention Force is the Armoured Brigade (HQ Valencia) consisting of the 1st *Bermúdez,* 2nd *General Pedro León Torres* and 4th *Bravos de Apure* Armoured Battalions, the 46th *General José Anzoátegui* Mechanised Infantry Battalion, the 9th *General Jacinto Lara* SP Artillery Group, the 9th SP Air Defence Battery, a signals platoon and a logistic support company. For its part, the *Aragua* Airborne Regiment (HQ Maracay) consists of the 1st *José Leonardo Chirinos* Paratroop Battalion and the 42nd *Antonio Nicolás Briceño* Airborne Rifle Battalion, plus a unit of Commandos and is scheduled for expansion to a brigade.

The Ranger Brigade (HQ Maturín) is an administrative rather than a tactical or operational formation, controlling six ranger battalions distributed throughout the country on an ad hoc basis and comprises the 43rd *Genaro Vázquez,* 44th *General de División Diego Ibarra,* 45th *Coronel Montilla,* 53rd *Francisco Carvajal,* 71st *Páez* and 54th *Chaguaramal* Ranger Battalions, a signals company and a supply and maintenance company. The 1st *Ayacucho* Group of Medium Towed Artillery is also an army level unit, based at Caracas.

The independent anti-aircraft elements consist of the 1st *General José Félix Ribas* and 3rd *General de División Ascensión Barreras* Air Defence Artillery Groups at Caracas and the hydro-electric complex of El Gury respectively, plus the 2nd and 4th Groups forming at the important oil port of Maracaibo and at the military-industrial complex at Maracay.

Army troops comprise the Army HQ Battalion, the *Agustín Codazzi* Construction Engineer Regiment (comprising the *J. Uslar* and *Coronel Thomas Ilderton Ferrier* Construction Engineer Battalions), the Combat Communications Regiment (with the *General P. B. Méndez* and *Agroz* Communications Battalions), the *José de San Martín* Military Police Regiment (consisting of the 1st *José Miguel Lanza* and 2nd *Capitán Abdón Calderon* Military Police Battalions), the Logistic Support Regiment, composed of an ordnance battalion, an administrative battalion, a supply battalion and a transport battalion, and the *General de División León Febres Cordero* Army Air Regiment which comprises the *General de Brigada Florencio Gómez* Air Support and Assault Group, the 1st *José María Carreño* Support Battalion and the Army Air Training Centre.

The main infantry weapon is the FN FAL in 7.62 mm calibre, which is assembled locally under licence and is scheduled for replacement by the Matacán rifle, a locally developed version of the FNC in 5.56 mm. The Uzi and Beretta M12 submachine guns, both in 9 mm calibre, have largely supplanted the Madsen Model 46 and 53 as the main light automatic weapons and will soon be joined by the locally developed Orinoco. The FN MAG, in 7.62 mm calibre, is the standard general-purpose machine gun although US M1919 0.30 calibre and M2HB 0.50 calibre weapons remain in service, mainly with armoured and cavalry units. Thompson-Brandt mortars, in 60 mm,

81 mm and 120 m, have superseded the US Second World War vintage mortars previously in use. The US M40 106 mm RCL, usually jeep-mounted, now supplemented by the French SS-11 ATGW, are the main anti-armour weapons.

The 2nd and 4th Armoured Battalions are equipped with the AMX-30, of which 108 are on inventory, while the 1st Armoured Cavalry Group has 40 AMX-13s. The 1st Armoured Battalion is equipped with 35 reconditioned US M18 Hellcat tank destroyers while AMX VCIs equip the two mechanised infantry battalions, the motorised cavalry units being equipped with some 120 V-150 Commando AFVs. An indeterminate number of Dragoon 300 AFVs, some equipped with the 90 mm Cockerill Mk III gun in an Arrowpointe turret, are on order.

The six towed artillery groups are equipped with a dozen US M114 155 mm, 30 US M101 and 60 Oto Melara Model 56 105 mm towed howitzers while the SP artillery group has 20 French Mk F.3 155 mm tracked SP howitzers. The so-called "Missile Artillery Group" is equipped with 36 Israeli LAR 160 mm multiple rocket launchers mounted on AMX-13 chassis. The anti-aircraft artillery has 20 US M42 twin 40 mm SP and 36 Breda-Bofors 40 mm/L70 towed AA guns, plus about a dozen Bofors 40 mm L/60 pieces, the anti-aircraft battery of the Armoured Brigade operating 12 Panhard AML S.530 twin 20 mm SP guns. A number of Roland surface-to-air missile systems have also been recently acquired.

The Army aviation service operates a total of approximately 40 aircraft including six IAI Aravas, two Aeritalia G222s, a single Pilatus-Britten-Norman Islander, a Beech Super King Air 200, a King Air E90 and a Queen Air, plus four Cessna Stationair and three Skylane light fixed-wing aircraft and two Bell 47, seven UH-1H, one Bell 206, six Agusta A109 and four Agusta-Sikorsky AS-61N helicopters.

The Military Academy at El Valle, which was established in 1910, offers a four-year course for officer cadets who may pursue a degree course at one of the civilian universities or at the *Universidad Politécnica de las Fuerzas Armadas* after commissioning in the rank of 2nd lieutenant. The *Escuela Superior de Guerra* is at Chorrillos and aspirants to promotion beyond the rank of lieutenant colonel must successfully complete either its command and staff course or a course at a recognised foreign military establishment of equivalent category. Most officers also pursue post-graduate studies abroad, usually in the United States. The NCO school and the infantry, armoured forces, artillery, engineering, signals and transport schools are all located at Maracay which is the principal military centre in the country. Conscripts receive their non-specialist training in the units to which they are assigned on induction.

Navy

Manpower:	10,000 (including Naval aviation and Marines)
Major units:	6 missile frigates 2 destroyer escorts 3 submarines 6 fast attack craft 5 LSTs 3 transports
Marines:	4 infantry battalion groups 1 amphibious assault group 1 mixed artillery battalion 1 special forces group 1 signals company 1 engineer company 1 transport battalion 1 military police regiment 1 river command (battalion)
Heavy equipment:	LVTP-7 amphibious APCs EE-9 Cascavel armoured cars EE-3 Jararacá scout cars EE-11 Urutú APCs Oto Melara M.56 105 mm howitzers M42 40 mm SP AA guns Seacat SAMS
Naval aviation:	1 maritime patrol squadron 1 ASW squadron 1 transport squadron
Aircraft:	Grumman Tracker S-2E CASA-212 PM and 212-200 DHC-7 Rockwell Turbo Commander Beech Super King Air 200

***Venezuelan "Lupo" class frigate* General Urdaneta (Dr R. Scheina)**

Aircraft (cont)

Beech King Air 90
Cessna 310 and 402
Agusta-Bell AB.212

Like the Army, the modern Venezuelan Navy dates from the 1880s. The Navy however benefitted little from the patronage of the succession of dictators who relied upon the armed forces as the main prop of their power, receiving significant quantities of modern equipment only during the Péréz Jimenez regime of the 1950s. Since that period it has remained a well-equipped and trained force.

The main strength of the 10,000-man Venezuelan Navy currently lies in its six Italian-built "Lupo" class missile frigates, the two German-built Type 209 submarines so far completed out of a proposed group of four and the six British-built "Constitución" class fast attack craft, two of which are armed with Otomat missiles, the remainder having only a gun armament. Two old ex-US destroyers were recently scrapped and the two surviving "Almirante Clemente" class destroyer escorts (of a class of six built in Italy during the 1950s) appear to have gained a new lease of life with their recent refit as did the old "Guppy" class submarine *Picúa*.

The main base is at Puerto Cabello, with minor bases at La Guaira and Falcón. The river bases at San Fernando de Atabapo and San Carlos de Rio Negro on the Orinoco and at Puerto Páez on the Meta and Punta Brava at the mouth of the Amacuro are being upgraded.

As part of the Naval Reorganisation Programme, complimentary to the Army's *Plan Carabobo*, the Venezuelan Navy has recently completed a reorganisation of its fleet units which broadly involves grouping its major combat, amphibious and auxiliary units under the existing Fleet Command and the transfer of its patrol, hydrographic and support units to the Coastal Guard, which was formed in 1982 as an integral part of the Navy with primary responsibility for the surveillance of the 200-mile Exclusive Economic Zone.

The Venezuelan Fleet now consists of a frigate squadron comprising the 2200-ton "Lupo" class missile frigates *Mariscal Sucre*, *Almirante Brión*, *General Urdaneta*, *General Soublette*, *General Salom* and *Almirante José de García*, a submarine squadron with the 1300-ton Type 209 *Sabalo* and *Caribe* and the 1900-ton reconditioned "Guppy II" class *Picúa*, a patrol craft squadron with the 170-ton fast attack craft *Constitución*, *Federación*, *Independencia*, *Libertad*, *Patria* and *Victoria*, an amphibious vessel squadron with the 2600-ton ex-US LST *Amazonas* and the 2000-ton South Korean-built *Capana, Esequibo, La Guajira* and *Los Llanos* and a service craft squadron, comprising the transports *Puerto Cabello, Valencia* and *Margarita* and the sail training ship *Simón Bolivar*.

The Coast Guard Squadron comprises the 1300-ton former destroyer escorts *Almirante Clemente* and *General Morán*, now rated as ocean-going patrol vessels, the 1200-ton ex-US "Cherokee" class armed tugs *Felipe Larrazábal* and *Miguel Rodríguez*, the 560-ton surveying vessel *Puerto Santo*, the 90-ton hydrographic launches *LH-11* and *LH-12* and the harbour tug *Fernando Gómez*.

Some minor craft, including the tug *Cardones*, four "Apure" class patrol launches, two LCUs and 12 LCVPs are subordinate to the River Command, which is a responsibility of the Marine Corps.

With a strength of over 4500, representing approximately 45% of its total manpower, the Venezuelan Marines are an important element of the Navy and now consist of the 1st *Libertador Simón Bolívar* Battalion Group at Maiquetía, the 2nd *General Rafael Urdaneta* Battalion Group at Puerto Cabello, the 3rd *Mariscal José Antonio de Sucre* Battalion Group at Carúpano and the 4th *General Francisco de Miranda* Battalion Group at Punto Fijo, supported by the *Capitán de Corbeta Miguel Ponce Lugo* Amphibious Tractor Unit, the Special Operations unit, a mixed artillery group, an engineer company, a signals company, a trans-

port unit, an ordnance unit and a regiment of Naval Police. Also forming part of the Marines is the *General Frank Rísquez Irribarén* Marine River Command, a battalion-sized unit which patrols inland waterways and performs general security functions on the country's navigable rivers, a paracommando unit and a unit of frogmen commandos.

The personal and support weapons of the Marines are essentially the same as those of the infantry units of the Army. The *Unidad de Tanques Anfíbios* is equipped with 11 LVTP-7 amphibious assault vehicles, six EE-9 Cascavel armoured cars, eight EE-3 Jararacá scout cars, and 30 EE-11 Urutú APCs while the artillery group is equipped with two batteries of Oto Melara Model 56 105 mm howitzers, two of Thompson-Brandt 120 mm mortars and one each of M-42A1 SP AA guns and of Seacat SAMs, the latter used for base defence at Puerto Cabello.

The *Aviación Naval* consists of approximately 30 aircraft, organised in Squadron AS-01 with six Grumman S-2E Trackers and four CASA 212 PM Aviocars, Squadron TR-02 with four CASA 212-200 Aviocars, one Beech Super King Air 200, one King Air 90, one Rockwell Turbo Commander, one DHC Dash 7-200, two Cessna 310s and a Cessna 402 and Squadron MP-03 with six Agusta Bell 212 helicopters, deployed aboard the "Lupo" class frigates. Most aircraft are based at Puerto Cabello, but there are minor naval air stations at La Carlota Airport, Caracas, Maiquetía, La Orchila, La Blanquilla, Punto Fijo and Güiria. Training is undertaken by the Air Force.

The Naval Academy at Mamón, La Guaira, offers a five-year course for officer cadets which leads to a commission in the rank of ensign. As with the Army, post-graduate training may be pursued at any of the country's universities or abroad. The Navy's specialist schools are located at Puerto Cabello naval base.

***Venezuelan submarines* Sabalo *and* Picúa (Dr R. Scheina)**

***Agusta 212 ASW helicopter of Venezuela's* Aviación Naval *aboard frigate* Almirante Brion (Dr R. Scheina)**

Air Force

Manpower: 9000

Units: 10 groups comprising:-
5 fighter squadrons
3 bomber squadrons
1 special operations squadron
1 helicopter squadron
2 transport squadrons
1 executive transport squadron

Fighters: General Dynamics F-16
Canadair CF-5A/D
Dassault Mirage III and 5

Bombers: English Electric Canberra
Rockwell OV-10E

Transports: Beech Queen Air
Boeing 737
DC-9
Cessna Citation
Dassault-Breguet Falcon 20
Aeritalia G222
Grumman Gulfstream
Lockheed C-130

Helicopters: Bell UH-1, 47 and 206
Aérospatiale Alouette III

Trainers: Beech T-34
Rockwell T-2D
EMB-312 Tucano

Canberra Mk 82 bomber of the 39th Squadron of the Venezuelan Air Force **(British Aerospace)**

C-130 transport of the Venezuelan Air Force's 1st Transport Squadron
(Lockheed Aircraft Corpn.)

Military aviation in Venezuela dates from 1920, the Air Force having become independent of both the Army and Navy in 1949. During the Pérez Jiménez dictatorship it became the best equipped air force in Latin America and it has remained

one of the leading military air arms of the region.

The *Fuerza Aérea Venezolana* currently has a personnel strength of about 9000 manning approximately 200 aircraft of all kinds and is organised in three commands, controlling ten groups and a total of 14 squadrons.

Air Combat Command controls Fighter Group No 11 (HQ *Base Aérea El Libertador*, Palo Negro), which consists only of Fighter Squadron No 36 with nine Dassault Mirage IIIs and seven Mirage 5s; Fighter Group No 12 (HQ *Base Aérea Teniente Vicente Landaeta*, Barquisimeto), comprising Fighter Squadron No 34 with ten Canadair CF-5s at Barquisimeto and Fighter Squadron No 35, also with ten Canadair CF-5s, at *Base Aérea Luís del Valle García*, Barcelona; Fighter Group No 16 (HQ Palo Negro) consisting of Fighter Squadron No 37 with 12 General Dynamics F-16s and Fighter Squadron No 38 with similar equipment. This Command also includes Bomber Group No 13 (HQ Barcelona) comprising Bomber Squadron No 38 with 13 Canberra B. Mk 82s at Barcelona and Bomber Squadron No 39 with seven Canberra B(1) Mk 88, PR. Mk 83 and T. Mk 84s at Barquisimeto: Special Operations Group No 10 (HQ Palo Negro) consisting of Helicopter Squadron No 42 with 16 Bell UH-1s, two 212s and ten Alouette IIIs and Special Operations Group No 15 (HQ Maracaibo) which consists of Bomber Squadron No 40 with 12 Rockwell Broncos and Special Operations Squadron No 41 with nine Cessna Skylanes.

Air Logistics Command controls Transport Group No 4 (HQ *Base Aérea Francisco de Miranda*, Caracas) consisting of the Presidential Squadron with single examples of the Boeing 737, Cessna Citation, Douglas DC-9, Grumman Gulfstream and the Bell UH-1N helicopter, Transport Group No 5 (HQ Caracas) comprising the un-numbered Mixed Liaison and Reconnaissance Squadron with two Dassault-Breguet Falcons, four Cessna Citations, six Beech Super King Air 200s and six Beech Queen Airs and Transport Group No 6 (HQ Palo Negro) comprising Transport Squadron No 1 with five Lockheed C-130s at Palo Negro and Transport Squadron No 2 with six Aeritalia G222s at *Base Aérea Mariscal Sucre*, Maracay.

Air Training Command controls Air Training

Bell 412 helicopter of the 42nd Squadron of the Venezuelan Air Force
(Defence Helicopter World)

Group No 14 (HQ Maracay) with no squadron organisation and comprising the *Esquela de Aviación Militar* with about 20 Beech T-34s, which are being supplemented by 30 EMB-312 Tucanos at Maracay and 20 Rockwell T-2Ds at Palo Negro.

There is also an aerobatic flight equipped with five Pitts S-2A and B Specials.

Base Aérea Mayor Buenaventura Vivas at Santa Domingo, Tachira, is being upgraded as is *Base Aérea Capitán Miguel Ríos* at Carrizales, Guárico, the former being designated as the future base of Bomber Squadron No 40 while the latter is expected to accommodate elements of Fighter Group No 16, Transport Group No 6 and Special Operations Group No 10.

For base defence the Venezuelan Air Force has mixed batteries of Short Tigercat SAMs and twin-mounted IAI TCM-20 20 mm guns. For mobile defence there are also a number of IAI RAM V-1 scout cars and jeep-mounted M40A1 106 mm RCLs. The former paratroop units of the Air Force were transferred to the control of the Army in 1978.

Aspiring officers must complete the four year course of the *Escuela de Aviación Militar* at Maracay before commissioning in the rank of *subteniente*. After commissioning, the young officer may proceed to complete a degree course at either one of the civilian universities or at the Armed Forces Polytechnical University. The Air Force also operates various specialist schools, the courses of which must be successfully completed for promotion to specific ranks and a Command and Staff School for the training of general staff and higher grade officer ranks. The Venezuelan Air Force also trains officers for several of the smaller countries in the region, by arrangement with their respective governments.

Paramilitary forces

Manpower:	22,000 (National Guard)
Major equipment:	UR-416 and Shorland APCs 46 coastal patrol craft 25 fixed-wing aircraft 15 helicopters

The 22,000-man National Guard, established in 1937, serves primarily as a federal police force and also polices the country's land and sea frontiers. It includes a maritime element and a growing air detachment for coastal patrol tasks.

There are three regional commands, with headquarters at San Antonio de Táchira, Maracaibo and Caracas. The basic operational unit is the detachment which corresponds to an army battalion. In addition to local detachments, there are eight mobile detachments under the direct command of general headquarters, which serve as an intervention force in support of the former. The National Guard also provides guards for public buildings, penal institutions and major economic targets, such as oil wells.

The National Guard is equipped with a complete range of light infantry personal and support weapons, up to and including 60 mm mortars. The Guard also has 25 UR-416 and 15 Shorland APCs, 46 coastal patrol craft of up to 70 tons displacement and an air section operating three IAI Arava light transports, three Beech Queen Air 80s, a Pilatus-Britten-Norman Islander, a Beech King Air 90 and 17 assorted Cessna light aircraft, plus three Agusta A109s and six examples apiece of the Bell 47 and Bell 206 helicopters.

The headquarters of the Air Support Command of the *Guardia Nacional* is located at *Base Aérea General Francisco de Miranda* at Caracas and the Guard maintains three Air Support Detachments: No 3 at Maracaibo, No 5 at Caracas and No 7 at Margarita. There are also three Special Air Support Units: No 2 at Valencia, No 6 at San Fernando de Apure and No 8 at Tucupita, in the Delta Amacuro Territory. The Guard maintains an air training unit, the *Centro de Adiestramiento Aéreo Mayor Pedro José Lanz Rodríguez* on the island of Margarita.

The National Guard is a completely volunteer force although a citizen may pre-empt compulsory military service by enlisting in it for a minimum of two years. Recruitment standards are however extremely high, less than 50% of applicants being accepted. Recruits spend a year in training at the Ramo Verde School, Los Teques. Less than one sixth of the applicants for commissions in the Guard are accepted and these spend four years at the Officers' Training School at Caracas, before commissioning with the rank of *subteniente* and a bachelor's degree. The courses of the Advanced

Officers' School at Caricuao, near Caracas, must be successfully completed before promotion to senior rank.

Sources of defence material supply and current requirements

Prior to the Second World War, Germany, France and Belgium were the principal suppliers of defence material to the Venezuelan government although the United States was already making inroads into this market in the late 1930s. During the Second World War and for the remainder of the 1940s the United States became almost the sole supplier of armaments and other war materials to Venezuela. From the early 1950s onwards, Venezuela shopped widely abroad, purchasing combat aircraft and naval vessels in Britain, small arms from Belgium, armoured vehicles and aircraft from France and naval vessels and artillery pieces from Italy. More recently Israel Spain and Brazil, together with the German Federal Republic, have become significant suppliers of defence equipment. No country may however be said to have a monopoly of the supply of any type of material to Venezuela.

Despite recent acquisitions, current requirements continue to fall mainly in the areas of armoured personnel carriers, air defence weapons, fast attack craft and combat aircraft.

Until recently Venezuela had no significant domestic defence industry and although the Venezuelan shipbuilding industry is the fifth most developed in Latin America, construction for the Navy has so far been limited to small craft. Venezuela does however now manufacture its own small arms, together with ammunition of up to 40 mm calibre. Under an agreement reached between the Spanish firm of Empresa Nacional Santa Bárbara and the Venezuelan government in 1983, the former is to set up a major armoured vehicle repair and maintenance facility in Venezuela and this development will represent a quantum leap for the Venezuelan defence industry. The manufacture of armoured vehicles in Venezuela is also projected. Long-term plans envisage total self-sufficiency in defence production. Their realisation however remains remote.

Summary and prospects

The Venezuelan armed forces were the last in mainland South America to succumb to professionalisation, but have an honourable record of a quarter of a century of faithful service to a series of democratically elected governments. Venezuelan democracy itself, after a late start, appears to be firmly rooted and has survived the threat of active armed subversion during the 1960s.

Although Venezuela has never fought a foreign war since independence, its Army appears to be among the most efficient and best equipped in Latin America.

The Venezuelan Navy is currently at a level of efficiency and operational potential unsurpassed at any previous stage of its relatively short history and expansion plans envisage the construction of a light aircraft carrier, three corvettes, two additional submarines, four to six minesweeper/hunters, two LSMs, a replenishment tanker and a surveying vessel, the establishment of two additional battalion groups and two more river units in the Marines and the acquisition of combat aircraft and transport helicopters by the *Aviación Naval*.

The Air Force remains one of the most efficient and best equipped in Latin America. The Canberras of Bomber Group No 13 are scheduled for deactivation in July 1989, their probable replacement being multi-role aircraft such as the Brazilian AMX. Expansion plans include the increase in the total number of Mirages to 24, the acquisition of 24 jet trainer/light strike aircraft, a sixth C-130 transport and one or two KC-130s, together with airborne early warning aircraft and the replacement of the existing fleet of helicopters with a similar number of Aérospatiale AS.332 Super Pumas and Bell 412s.

Six medium helicopters of unspecified type are also on order in the United States for the National Guard which remains one of the most respected national police forces in Latin America.

Having successfully dealt with the guerrilla insurgency of the previous two decades, the Venezuelan armed forces of the late 1980s appear adequate in strength, organisation, equipment and training to deal with any probable external threat. The heavy concentration of troops in the western part of the country is notable while the strengthening of the Jungle Division on the border with Brazil reflects the suspicion of Brazilian expansionism felt to varying degrees by all of Brazil's neighbours. Although Venezuela claims most of the territory of Guyana, the relatively low concentration of military units in the eastern part of the country indicates the correspondingly low priority given to this latter frontier dispute.

The main long-term problem which the country faces is the diversification of its economy when eventually oil ceases to be its main earner of foreign exchange, the current recession in oil prices being reflected in a minor economic crisis which is nevertheless not of the proportions experienced by other countries of the region. A progressive imbalance between the urban and rural sectors of the population and high unemployment has a potential for socio-political instability.

Despite its problems, Venezuela is developing as one of the major democratic powers in Latin America and as such, its international influence is also certain to increase.

THE WEST INDIES

Introduction

The small island states of the Eastern Caribbean form the outer defensive perimeter of the Caribbean and the Gulf of Mexico and are thus of major strategic importance, particularly to the United States, 45% of the external trade of which and 55% of its oil imports pass through the region. Any immediate direct external military threat to these small states seems minimal, despite the presence of a militant Communist regime in Cuba and a Marxist-dominated one in Nicaragua. However, Britain's disengagement from its former colonies has left them in something of a military vacuum and the recent experience of Grenada also demonstrates not merely their vulnerability to political subversion but that there are other powers willing and able to fill such a vacuum once it is permitted to arise.

Although both Britain and France still have military commitments in the Caribbean region, the former no longer retains either the political will or the military means to discharge its obligations to its clients, despite the token military presence maintained in Belize. The limited commitments of France require little more than the token military presence which it is willing and able to provide. Nominal though the French military presence in the Caribbean may be, it is noteworthy that in manpower it nevertheless exceeds both that of Britain and the combined strengths of the defence forces of the independent states of the Eastern Caribbean. The only exceptions are those of the Dominican Republic, the only independent state in the region, which, apart from Cuba, maintains anything approaching a realistic defence establishment. The Netherlands also maintains a

***Patrol vessel* Marlin *of the Bahamas Coast Guard* (Vosper-Thorneycroft)**

limited military presence in its remaining American possessions, the Netherlands Antilles, while the United States has important base facilities in Puerto Rico which constitute the major defence potential of the Eastern Caribbean region.

Among the former British possessions in the Caribbean only Belize, Jamaica and Trinidad-Tobago maintain defence forces worthy of individual treatment in this book and an analysis of the existing military capabilities of the remaining states of the Eastern Caribbean is far from reassuring in the context of their strategic importance.

THE BAHAMAS

The northernmost state of the island chain is the Commonwealth of the Bahamas. Comprising an archipelago of over 700 islands, with a total land area of 5353 sq miles (13,864 sq km) and a largely black population of approximately 240,000. Despite being one of the wealthier countries of the region, with an annual GNP of US$1.648bn, the Bahamas maintains no armed forces although it does house a US naval experimental station and its 1200-man police force is a paramilitary organisation, equipped with modern small arms. The Bahamas also maintains a Coast Guard which comprises one large and five small patrol craft, four very small inshore patrol craft and some minor vessels, with a personnel strength of 500, but its security forces have no air element.

TURKS AND CAICOS

To the south-west of the Bahamas and north of the Dominican Republic and Puerto Rico, the Turks and Caicos Islands, with a total land area of 192 sq miles (430 sq km) and a largely black population of between 7000 and 8000, are direct dependencies of Britain which however shows no perceptible interest in their defence. They have no defence forces of their own nor the economic or human resources to provide them.

***Patrol craft* Inagua *of the Bahamas Coast Guard* (Vosper Thorneycroft)**

PUERTO RICO

To the east of the Dominican Republic lies the Commonwealth of Puerto Rico, with an area of 3435 sq miles (8891 sq km) and an economy which is heavily subsidised by the United States to produce an artificially inflated nominal annual GNP of approximately US$7bn. The 3,200,000 Puerto Ricans, who exhibit an ethnic mix comparable to that of Cuba, with a predominance of persons of mixed Spanish and black racial origins, appear to have achieved the near ideal situation of being independent in all but name while enjoying an ambiguous relationship with the United States of which their country is technically neither a state, a federal territory nor a colonial possession.

The armed forces of the Commonwealth consist of the Puerto Rican National Guard, a part-time organisation which is nevertheless equipped on the scale of the regular US armed forces and which furnishes the 92nd Infantry Brigade of the US Army and the 198th Tactical Fighter Squadron of the US Air Force on mobilisation. Of key importance in the defence of the outer perimeter of the Caribbean Basin, the United States maintains large army, naval and Coast Guard bases in Puerto Rico but does not normally deploy major units of its armed forces within the Commonwealth.

ANGUILLA, ST. KITTS-NEVIS, BARBUDA, ANTIGUA AND MONTSERRAT

To the east of Puerto Rico and the minor US possessions of the Virgin Islands and St Croix lie the small British Associated Territories of Anguilla, Saint Kitts-Nevis, Barbuda, Antigua and the British colony of Montserrat, for all of which Britain retains a responsibility for external defence which has become purely nominal.

With the exception of Antigua, with an area of 108 sq miles (280 sq km) and a largely black population of approximately 80,000, the population of none of these statelets exceeds 20,000, their individual military potential being correspondingly slight. Antigua and Saint Kitts-Nevis each has a small part-time military force of about 100 men; none of the others maintain even nominal ground forces. Antigua and Montserrat each operates a small coastal patrol boat, as do Saint Kitts-Nevis and Anguilla although none of them operates any fixed or rotary winged aircraft.

DOMINICA, GUADELOUPE AND MARTINIQUE, SAINT LUCIA, SAINT VINCENT AND THE GRENADINES

Flanking Dominica, an independent republic within the British Commonwealth with an area of 305 sq miles (790 sq km) and a population of about 90,000, in which once again blacks predominate, to the north and south lie the French Overseas Departments of Guadeloupe and Martinique, with respective areas of 686 sq miles (1756 sq km) and 431 sq miles (1103 sq km) and largely black populations of 324,000 and 319,000. Further to the south lie the independent island states of Saint Lucia and Saint Vincent and the Grenadines, both members of the British Commonwealth with respective areas of 238 sq miles (618 sq km) and 150 sq miles (389 sq km) and predominantly black populations of about 120,000 in each case.

France still maintains a nominal military presence amounting to some 3000 army naval and air force personnel in its American territories, which also include Guiane, the last remaining colonial enclave on the South American mainland, with an area of 35,100 sq miles (90,900 sq km) and a largely black population of 55,000. This presence comprises three Marine and Foreign Legion infantry battalions, two frigates, a maritime reconnaissance unit equipped with Breguet Atlantique aircraft and a transport unit with C-160 Transall fixed-wing aircraft and some Puma and Alouette II helicopters.

Dominica has a part-time defence force of about 100 men and operates a medium-sized coastal patrol craft. Saint Lucia also has a small defence force of about 100 members and operates three very small inshore patrol craft while Saint Vincent and the Grenadines operates one large and one small patrol craft although it has no ground defence element. None of these states operates any military aircraft.

BARBADOS

To the east of Saint Vincent lies Barbados, an independent state within the British Commonwealth, with an area of 166 sq miles (430 sq km) and again a largely black population of approximately 280,000. Relatively wealthy by regional standards, with an annual GNP of approximately US$440m, Barbados has a single-battalion part-time Army expanding to 3000 on mobilisation and a Coast Guard with one sea-going, three-coastal and two inshore patrol craft. There is no air force although some small civilian aircraft are sometimes operated in support of the surface elements of the Barbados Defence Force.

GRENADA

To the south-west of Barbados lies Grenada, also an independent state within the British Commonwealth, with an area of 133 sq miles (344 sq km) and a largely black population of about 120,000. Under the Marxist regime nipped in the bud by the United States invasion of October 1983, Grenada was training a relatively formidable army by local standards of 2200 men, equipped with light armoured vehicles, infantry support weapons and anti-aircraft guns, although it lacked either a navy or an air force. Currently Grenada maintains no armed force of its own and remains effectively under US occupation.

THE NETHERLANDS ANTILLES

The other remaining colonial enclave in the region is the Netherlands Antilles, an autonomous territory within the Kingdom of the Netherlands, lying off the coast of Venezuela. It comprises Aruba, Bonaire, Curaçao and the Windward Islands (St Martin, Saba and St Eustatius) with a total land area of 394 sq miles (1020 sq km) and a predominantly black population of approximately 250,000 and an annual GNP of US$652m. The Netherlands maintains a detachment of Marines, a frigate and a maritime reconnaissance element of two Fokker F.27MPA aircraft in the territory.

Summary and prospects

Although an apparently logical attempt at federation of the smaller former British states following their achievement of independence rapidly collapsed in disorder, the viability of many of these as individual independent entities and thus their continued survival, is problematic. With fragile economies, based for the greater part on the export of tropical produce and tourism and exploding and in many cases racially heterogeneous populations, with an in-built potential for extreme internal instability, none of them can afford to maintain adequate defence or even internal security forces.

While apparently content with its present peculiar relationship with the United States, Puerto Rico also suffers from chronic poverty exacerbated by population pressures and still experiences occasional stirrings of militant nationalism manifested in isolated acts of terrorism which have included attacks on the installations of the Puerto Rican National Guard. Although its present Constitution permits Puerto Rico to opt for complete independence at any time, the United States, particularly under its present administration, is unlikely to look with favour or even sympathy on any aspirations towards complete independence on the part of the only major territory in the eastern perimeter of the Caribbean over which it enjoys any measure of direct control. The ability of an independent Puerto Rico to maintain adequate defence forces of its own would also be highly problematic.

Largely neglected by the United States until the recent events in Grenada focussed attention upon it, the Grenadan experience underlines the fact that the Eastern Caribbean potentially poses as great a strategic problem to the US as that which it currently faces in Central America.

Table 1

THE LATIN AMERICAN MILITARY ESTABLISHMENT AS A PERCENTAGE OF POPULATION

Country	Population	Active military personnel	Force level as % of population
Argentina	31,320,000	102,000	0.33%
Belize	163,000	600	0.37%
Bolivia	6,524,000	28,000	0.43%
Brazil	140,000,000	285,900	0.20%
Chile	12,300,000	99,000	0.80%
Colombia	20,540,000	69,000	0.34%
Costa Rica	2,600,000	6000	0.23%
Cuba	10,200,000	162,000	1.59%
Dominican Republic	6,275,000	22,500	0.36%
Ecuador	10,400,000	45,100	0.43%
Guatemala	7,260,000	32,000	0.44%
Guyana	850,000	5500	0.65%
Haiti	5,540,000	7000	0.13%
Honduras	4,500,000	19,000	0.42%
Jamaica	2,350,000	2150	0.09%
Mexico	81,160,000	139,500	0.17%
Nicaragua	3,310,000	53,000	1.60%
Panama	2,140,000	4500	0.21%
Paraguay	3,480,000	26,200	0.75%
Peru	20,340,000	127,000	0.62%
El Salvador	5,620,000	42,600	0.75%
Suriname	380,000	2500	0.66%
Trinidad & Tobago	1,190,000	2100	0.18%
Uruguay	2,920,000	31,600	1.08%
Venezuela	18,900,000	66,000	0.35%

Figures are those obtaining at the end of 1986. In the case of Central America in particular, these have increased quite dramatically. The figures for Costa Rica and Panama include forces performing predominantly civilian police functions.

Table 2

LATIN AMERICAN DEFENCE EXPENDITURE AS PERCENTAGE OF GNP

Country	GNP in millions of US$	Annual defence expenditure in US$	Defence expenditure as %age of GNP
Argentina	$68,290.0m	$1,335.0m	1.95%
Belize	$192.0m	$3.6m	1.88%
Bolivia	$8,220.0m	$216.1m	2.63%
Brazil	$214,705.0m	$1,055.0m	0.50%
Chile	$15,996.0m	$1,242.0m	7.76%
Colombia	$32,686.0m	$274.1m	0.83%
Cuba	$17,150.0m	$1,612.0m	9.39%
Dominican Republic	$4,656.0m	$68,89.0m	1.48%
Ecuador	$12,884.0m	$223.9m	1.74%
Guatemala	$9,397.0m	$179.8m	1.91%
Guyana	$461.9m	$44.9m	9.71%
Haiti	$2,130.0m	$90.0m	4.23%
Honduras	$3,360.0m	$90.0m	2.68%
Jamaica	$2,132.0m	$25.6m	1.20%
Mexico	$175,410.0m	$659.6m	0.38%
Nicaragua	$5,340.0m	$598.0m	10.52%
Panama	$4,677.0m	$96.5m	2.01%
Paraguay	$5,808.0m	$76.4m	1.31%
Peru	$16,979.0m	$640.6m	3.78%
El Salvador	$5,606.0m	$177.8m	3.17%
Trinidad & Tobago	$8,792.0m	$75.0m	0.85%
Uruguay	$5,050.0m	$124.4m	2.46%
Venezuela	$49,654.0m	$954.0m	1.92%

Table 3

FOREIGN MILITARY ASSISTANCE TO LATIN AMERICAN COUNTRIES

Country	Military aid in millions of US $ (1950–1977)	Military students trained (1950–77)	Value of military aid received in US $ (1986–87)
Argentina	$46.9m	4023	nil
Bolivia	$38.6m	4437	6.0m
Brazil	$223.58m	8657	nil
Chile	$97.4m	6883	nil
Colombia	$96.84	7392	20.0m
Costa Rica	$1.83m	696	3.7m
Dominican Republic	$30.8m	4021	4.0m
Ecuador	$43.4m	5123	3.8m
Guatemala	$23.6m	3339	4.8m
Haiti	$3.4m	610	0.5m
Honduras	$12.8m	3004	87.0m
Mexico	$2.4m	868	nil
Nicaragua	$18.2m	5401	nil
Panama	$7.96m	4623	14.4m
Paraguay	$14.9m	1874	nil
Peru	$93.1m	7865	8.16m*
El Salvador	$10.3m	1972	125.4m
Uruguay	$46.8m	2807	2.5m
Venezuela	$13.9m	5511	nil

These figures refer to US financial and training aid only, a large proportion of the former figure being made up by the transfer of surplus material to the indicated value.

US military aid to El Salvador and Honduras has been at a massive level since 1981, the former country receiving military assistance to the value of $5.95m in 1980, $35.49m in 1981 and $82m in 1982, rising to $126m in 1983 and peaking at $197m in 1984. For its part, Honduras received aid valued at $3.98m in 1980, $8.94m in 1981 and $31.28m in 1982, continuing to rise to $48.3m in 1983, $76,5m in 1984 and 61.3m in 1985.

Cuba and Nicaragua receive military aid to an undisclosed value from the Soviet Union which also trains military personnel from both of these countries and from Peru. Cuba, although itself largely dependent on Soviet military assistance, also furnishes surplus military equipment and training aid to Nicaragua and possibly also to Guyana.

The financial value of Eastern bloc military aid to its American clients is impossible to assess with any degree of accuracy. Between 1970 and 1984 the Eastern bloc countries are believed to have transferred a total of 469,100 tonnes of defence equipment to Cuba, the peak year being 1982 during which 68,300 tonnes were transferred. Nicaragua is estimated to have received 40,450 tonnes of military equipment between 1980 and 1984 of which 18,000 tonnes were received during the latter year. More recent figures are not available.

* Peru received a loan of $20.0m from Argentina in 1986 for the construction of a new military air base at Collique.

APPENDIX 1

REGIONAL ALLIANCES IN LATIN AMERICA

The Organization of American States

The OAS derives from the first International Conference of American States held in 1889–90. This led to the establishment of the Pan American Union which was instrumental in defuzing the confrontation between Bolivia and Paraguay in December 1928 although it was unable to prevent the outbreak of the Chaco War four years later. The Chaco Peace Conference of 1935–38, which led to the Treaty of Buenos Aires between Bolivia and Paraguay, was however held under the auspices of the Pan American Union. The Pan American Union also supervised the ceasefire between Peru and Ecuador after the brief war of July 1941 and was instrumental in drafting the Protocol of Rio de Janeiro, which attempted unsuccessfully to solve the territorial dispute between these two countries.

In 1948, a Conference of American States held at Bogotá established the Organisation of American States, consisting basically of the signatories of the Rio Treaty of 1947. Cuba remains a member of the OAS, although its membership was suspended by a resolution of a meeting of the Organisation held at Punta del Este in Uruguay in 1962. The OAS provided an umbrella for US sanctions against Cuba and the subsequent naval blockade of the island in which naval units of several members joined with the United States following the Cuban missile crisis.

In 1965, following the Dominican civil war and US intervention in that country, an Inter-American Peace Force, drawing contingents from Brazil, Costa Rica, Honduras, Nicaragua, Paraguay and the United States, was active in the Dominican Republic for a period of 15 months. The OAS arranged a ceasefire during the war between Honduras and El Salvador in 1969 and more recently defused the potentially explosive situation between Ecuador and Peru in January/February 1981.

The original states have now been joined by Barbados, Dominica, Grenada, Jamaica, Saint Lucia and Trinidad & Tobago.

United States support for Britain, a non-member, against Argentina, a founder member, in the Anglo-Argentine War of 1982, greatly strained the cohesion of the Organization.

The Rio Treaty of 1947

In 1942, an Inter-American Defence Board was set up and in 1945, at a Conference held in Mexico City, the Act of Chapúltepec confirmed the agreement of the 20 Latin American Republics to the principle of regional security. In 1947 all the existing Latin American republics, together with the United States, signed the Inter-American Treaty of Reciprocal Assistance at Rio de Janeiro. The Rio Treaty reaffirmed the will of the American states to remain united in an Inter-American system consistent with the Charter of the United Nations, at the same time reiterating their adherence to the principle of Inter-American solidarity and co-operation. Under Articles 1 and 2 of the Treaty, the parties pledge themselves not to resort to war and to submit any controversies arising between them to methods of peaceful settlement before referring them to the General Assembly or the Security Council of the United Nations. The Treaty also affirms the resolve of its signatories to unite in defence against any extra-hemispheric aggression against any one of them. The attitude adopted by the United States during the Falklands War has rendered the functioning of the Treaty highly questionable.

UNITAS

This is an organisation, set up by the United States in 1961 under the overall umbrella of the Rio Treaty of 1947 to foster naval co-operation between the Latin American Republics and the USA. It has regularly conducted joint naval manoeuvres during August and September every year since its inception. Since 1983, as a protest to US support for Britain in the Anglo-Argentine War the previous year, Argentina has declined to participate in the exercises.

The Central American Defence Council–CONDECA

This was set up following a meeting in Guatemala City of representatives of the five original Central American republics in 1963 and functions, under the aegis of the Organisation of American States as a co-ordinating body for regional defence planning between the general staffs of the participating countries and the Inter-American Defence Board, in Washington, CONDECA achieved considerable success in co-ordinating the defence effort of the five member states but became something of a dead letter after the 1969 war between Honduras and El Salvador. It has been revived recently by Guatemala, Honduras and El Salvador in face of the perceived politico-military threat from Nicaragua.

Appendix 2

PRINCIPAL TREATIES AND INTERNATIONAL AGREEMENTS BETWEEN LATIN AMERICAN STATES DURING THE 20TH CENTURY

The General Arbitration Treaty of 1902

Ratified under the auspicies of King Edward VII of Great Britain, this Treaty defused the long-standing frontier dispute between Argentina and Chile which had led to an arms race between the two countries around the turn of the century. Under its terms all future territorial disputes between the two countries were to be referred to the arbitration of the British Crown. The Treaty also led to the Latin America's only naval disarmament treaty to date whereby both countries undertook not to complete or dispose of various warships under construction.

The Treaty of Tacna Arica 1929

Under the terms of this Treaty the province of Tacna, occupied by Chile after the end of the Pacific War of 1879–83, was returned to Peru. The province of Tarapacá, which included Arica and Antofagasta, had originally belonged to Bolivia, but had been retained by Chile. While it temporarily reduced tensions between Chile and Peru, the Treaty did nothing towards satisfying the aspirations of Bolivia towards regaining an outlet to the sea and was thus an indirect cause of the Chaco War of 1932–35, by which Bolivia sought an outlet to the sea via the Paraguay river.

The Chaco Peace Treaty 1938

Following negotiations which lasted longer than the Chaco War itself, this Treaty awarded 80% of the territory in dispute between Bolivia and Paraguay to the latter country, setting the boundaries between the two countries which remain in existence. As the Paraguayans had actually conquered more than the entire territory in dispute the Treaty failed equally to satisfy both Paraguayan and Bolivian extremists. It also provided for the granting of customs-free port facilities to Bolivia on the Upper Paraguay river, a provision with which Paraguay has still not complied almost 50 years later.

The Latin American Nuclear Non-Proliferation Treaty

This Treaty, also known as the Treaty of Tlatelolco, was ratified by 22 Latin American states in 1967, the signatories agreeing not to manufacture, receive, store or test nuclear weapons or nuclear launching devices. Significantly, it was not signed by either Argentina, Brazil or the United States, the only countries in the region which were either actual or potential nuclear powers nor by Cuba, the Dominican Republic, Nicaragua or Paraguay.

The Panama Canal Treaty 1979

Under this Treaty the United States ceded sovereignty over the Panama Canal Zone, which it had exercised under the previous Panama Treaty of 1903, to Panama which was to assume the full responsibility for its defence by 1999. In return Panama recognised the right of the United States to retain military bases in the former Canal Zone although the number of these was to be reduced from 14 to three by 1999. In addition, the School of the Americas at Fort Gulick, which had been the main centre for the training of Latin American military personnel in counter-insurgency techniques under the Rio Treaty of 1947, was to be closed in 1984. The United States retains the right of military intervention if the neutrality and freedom to shipping of the Canal is threatened.

The Beagle Channel Treaty 1984

This Treaty defuzed the danger of war between Argentina and Chile over the ownership of the islands of Picton, Lennox and Nueva in the Beagle Channel to the south of Tierra del Fuego and was enacted under the auspicies of the Vatican, Argentina having refused in 1977 to recognise the recommendations of British arbitration under the General Arbitration Treaty of 1902. Under the terms of the Treaty, the three islands in dispute were recognised as Chilean, with a territorial limit of three miles to seaward, the meridian of Cape Horn (67 degrees west of Greenwich) being recognised as the dividing line between the Argentine and Chilean Exclusive Economic Zones, each country thus being confined respectively to the Atlantic and Pacific Oceans with regard to the sovereignty of their territorial seas. Provision was also made for the freedom of navigation in the Magellan Straight and the Beagle Channel and for economic co-operation between the two countries.

INDEX

Aircraft

Anti-aircraft weapons

Tanks

Armoured cars

Tracked and wheeled APCs and other armoured vehicles

Anti-tank weapons

Artillery

Infantry weapons

(a) Handguns

(b) Machine guns

(c) Mortars, grenade launchers

Various missiles and their launchers

Warships (classes)

Abbreviations used:
CM = corvette
CMG = missile corvette
DD = destroyer
DDG = missile destroyer
DE = destroyer escort
FAC = fast attack craft
FF = frigate
LSM = landing ship, medium
LST = landing ship, tank
ML = mine layer
MS = mine sweeper
SSK = submarine

Personalities